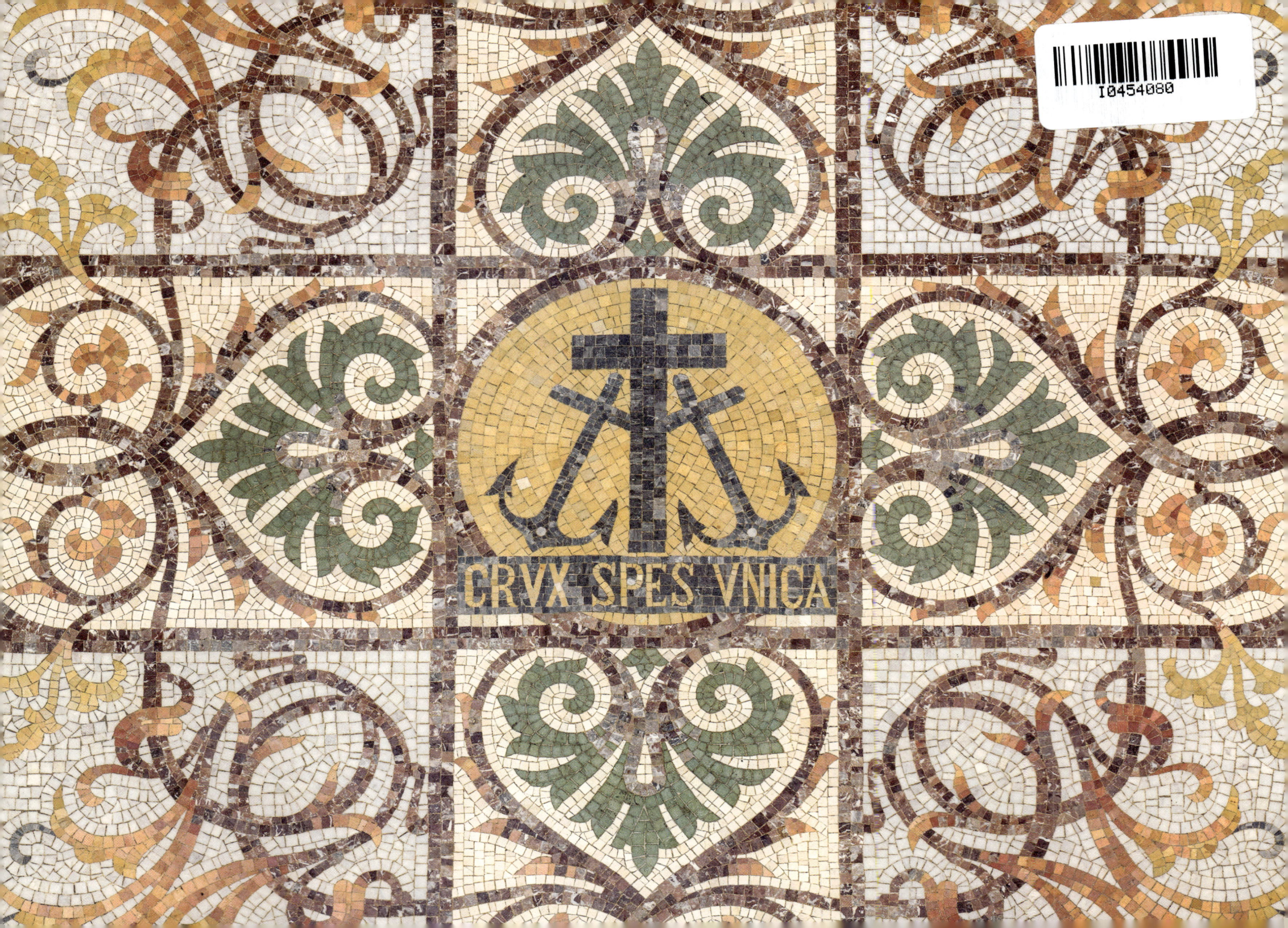

CRVX SPES VNICA

THIS PLACE CALLED NOTRE DAME

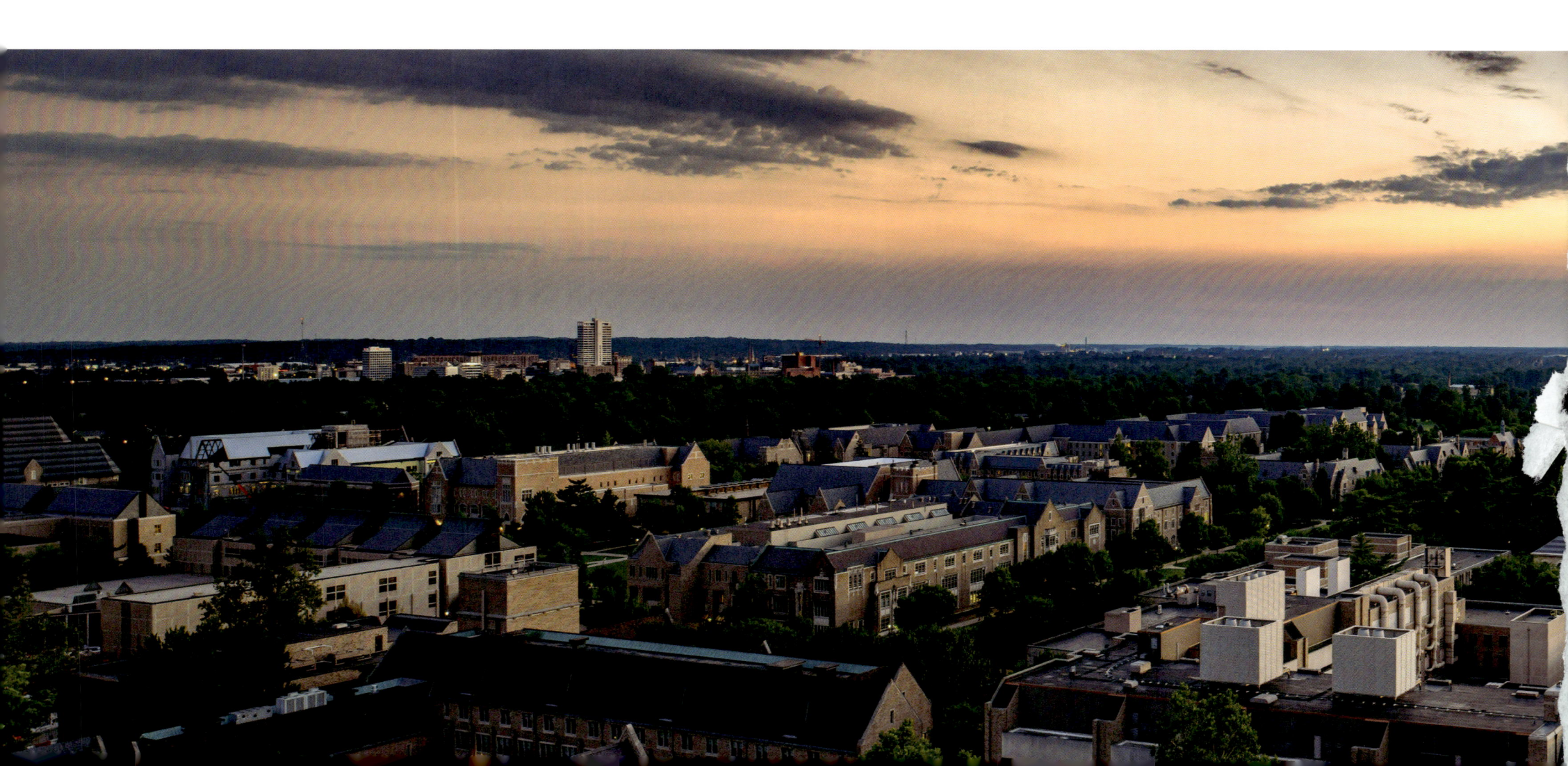

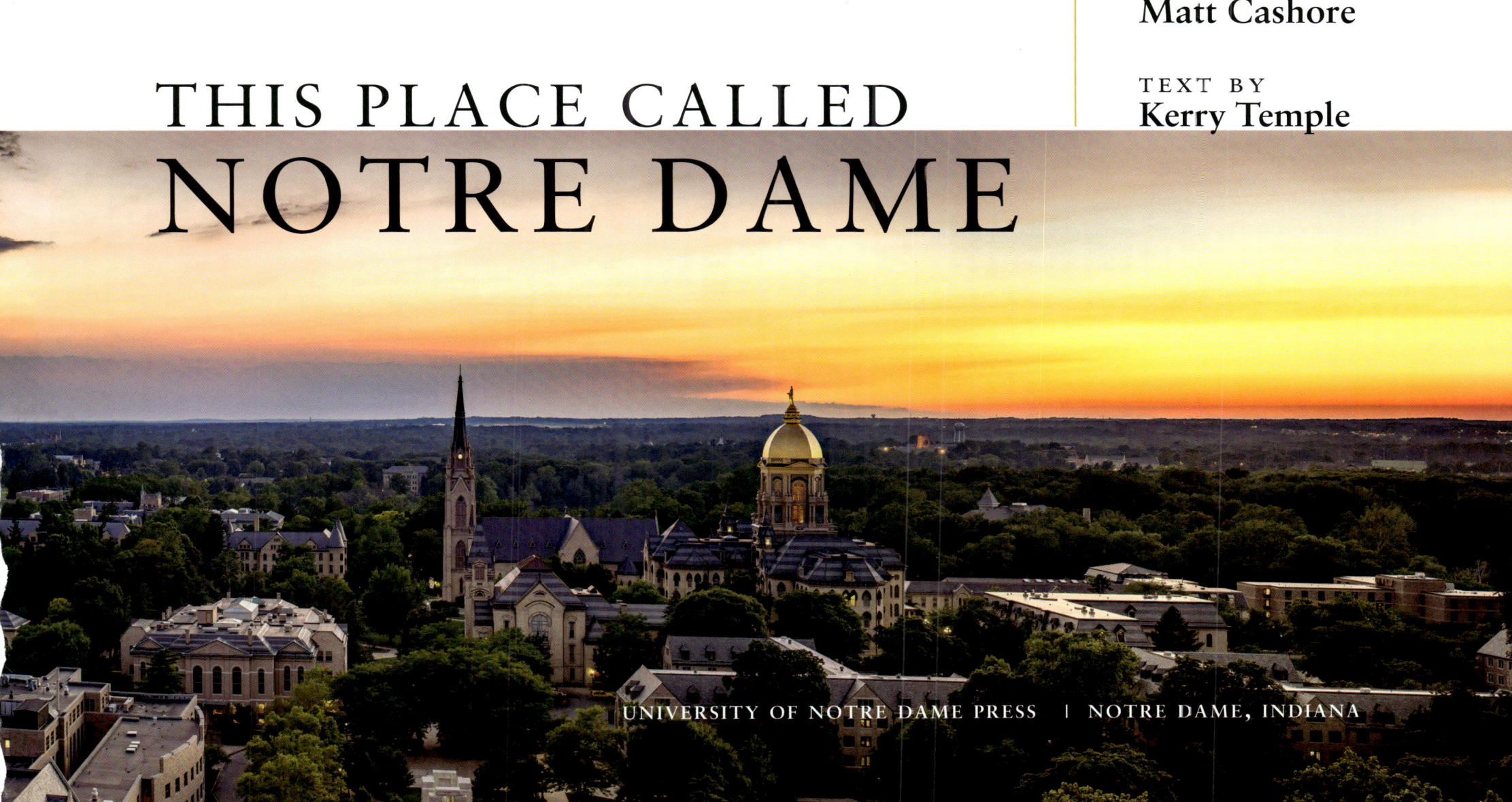

THIS PLACE CALLED
NOTRE DAME

PHOTOS BY
Matt Cashore

TEXT BY
Kerry Temple

UNIVERSITY OF NOTRE DAME PRESS | NOTRE DAME, INDIANA

Printed in Canada by Friesens Corporation
Reprinted in 2021, 2022

All photos in this book are available as prints at: photos.nd.edu

Library of Congress Cataloging-in-Publication Data

Names: Cashore, Matt, photographer. | Temple, Kerry, author.
Title: This place called Notre Dame / photos by Matt Cashore ; text by Kerry
   Temple.
Description: Notre Dame, Indiana : University of Notre Dame Press, [2018] |
   Identifiers: LCCN 2018021931 (print) | LCCN 2018030713 (ebook) | ISBN
   9780268104832 (pdf) | ISBN 9780268104818 (cloth : alk. paper) | ISBN
   0268104816 (cloth : alk. paper)
Subjects: LCSH: University of Notre Dame—Pictorial works. | University of
   Notre Dame—History.
Classification: LCC LD4113 (ebook) | LCC LD4113 .C37 2018 (print) | DDC
   378.772/89—dc23
LC record available at https://lccn.loc.gov/2018021931

∞ *This paper meets the requirements of ANSI/NISO Z39.48-1992 (Permanence of Paper).*

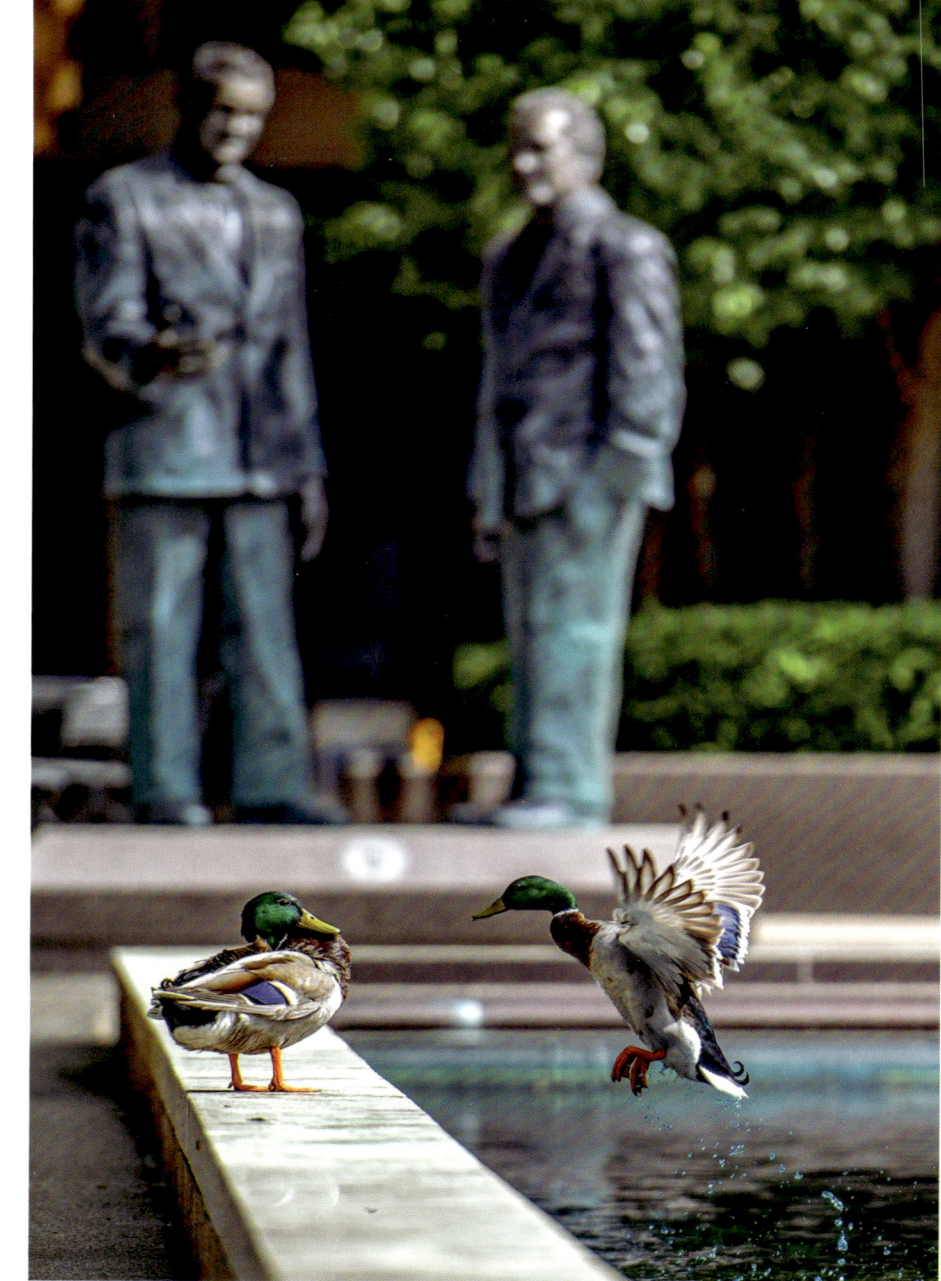

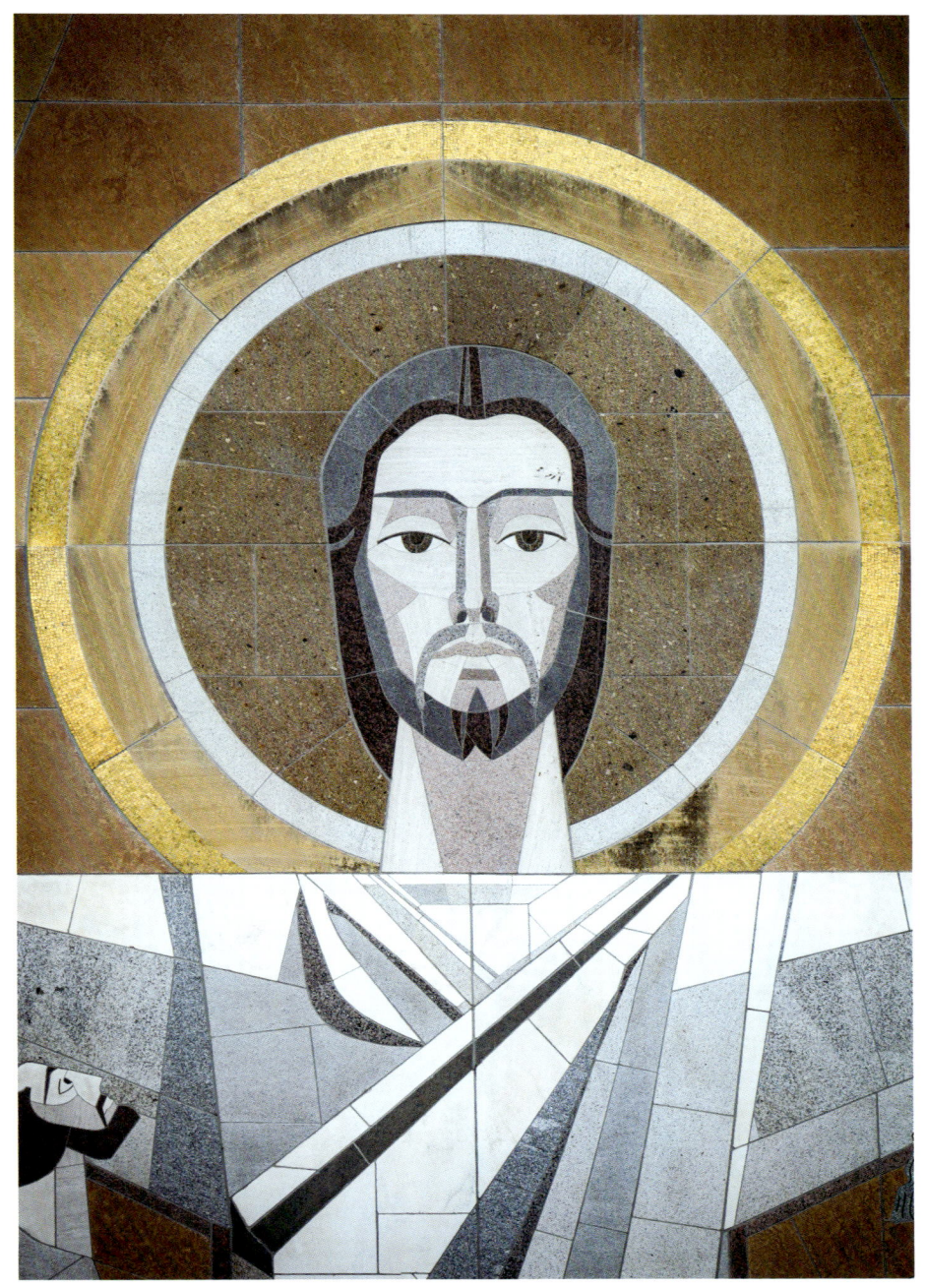

To Maria and Madeline
—MC

To Jessica
—KT

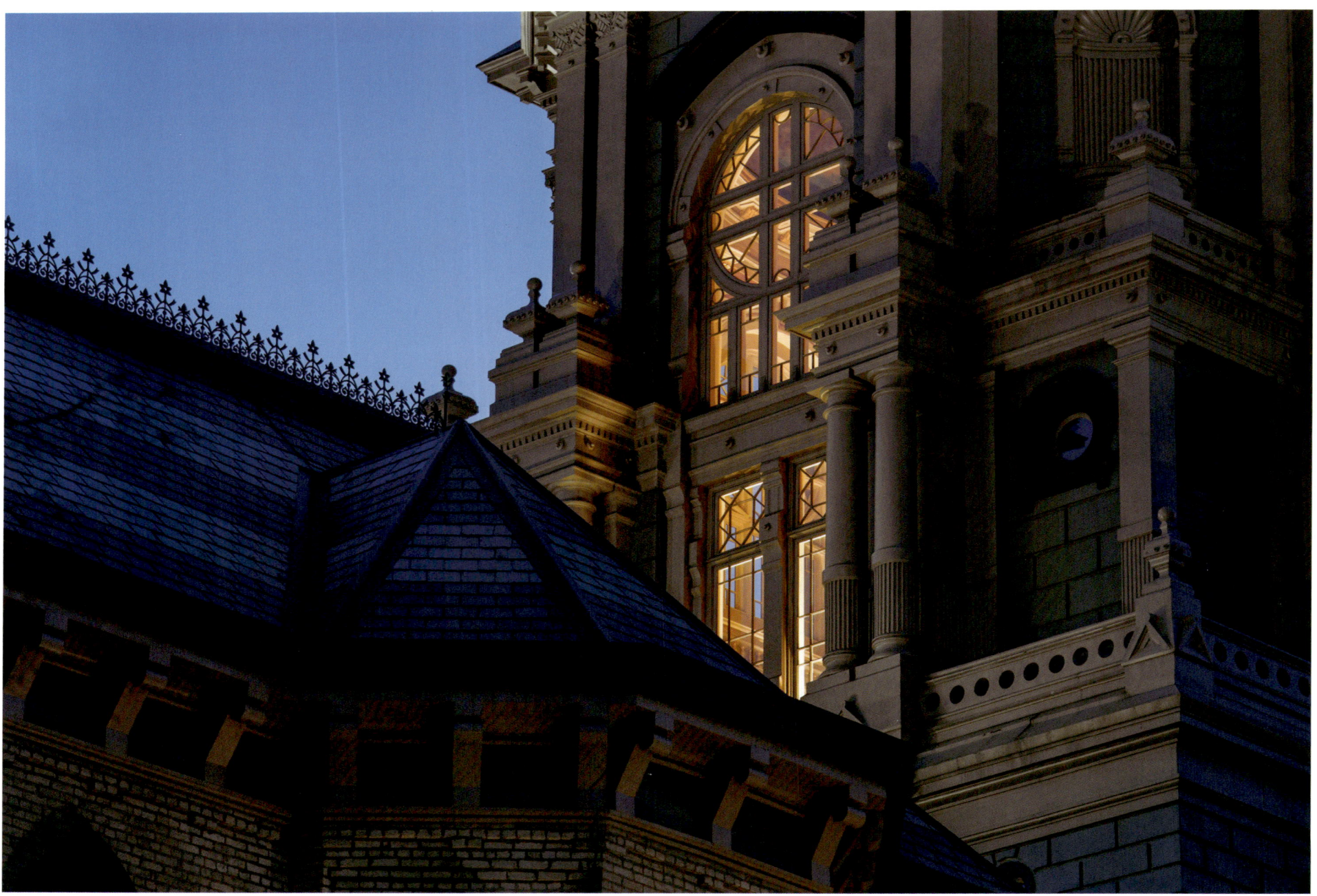

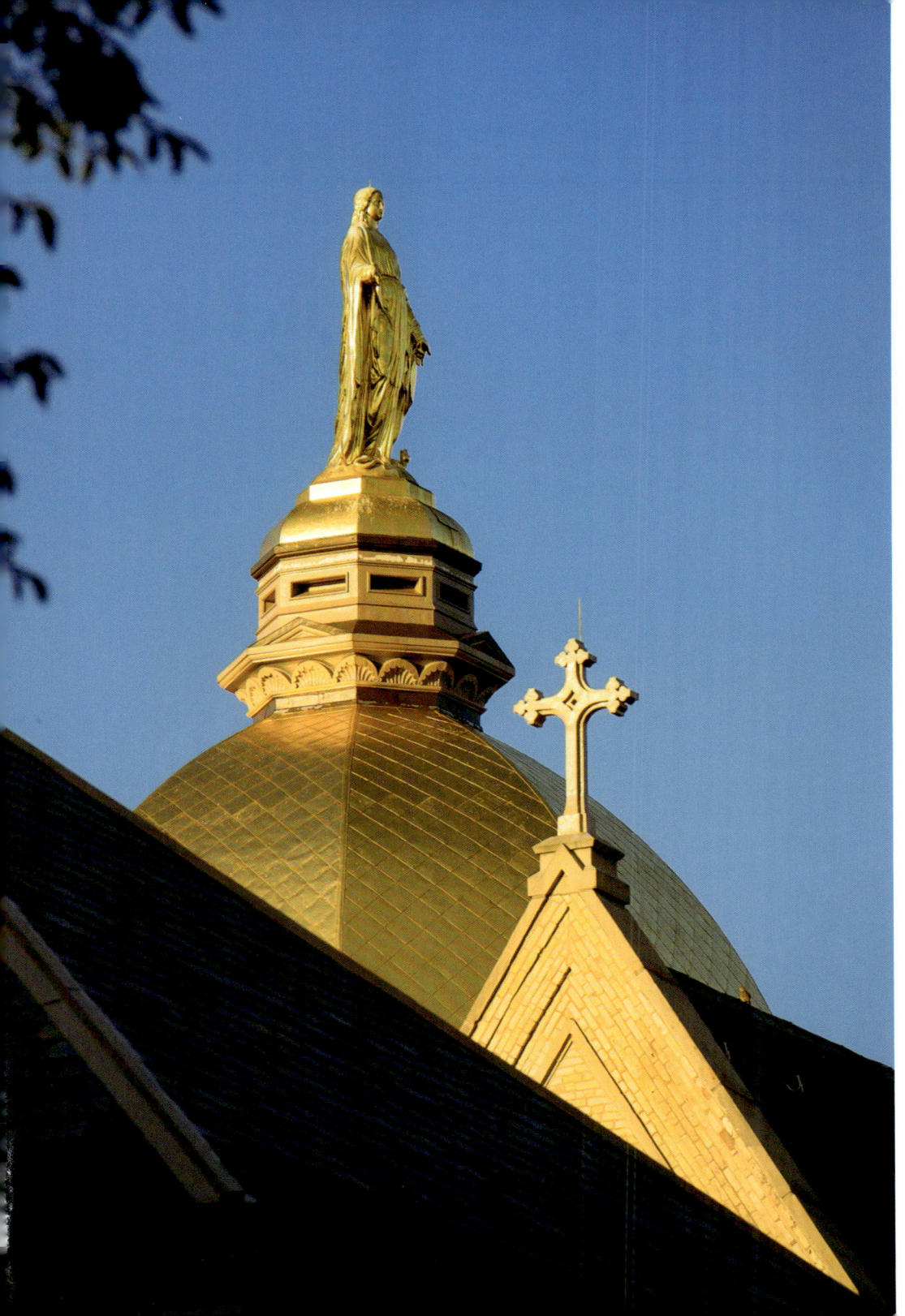

CONTENTS

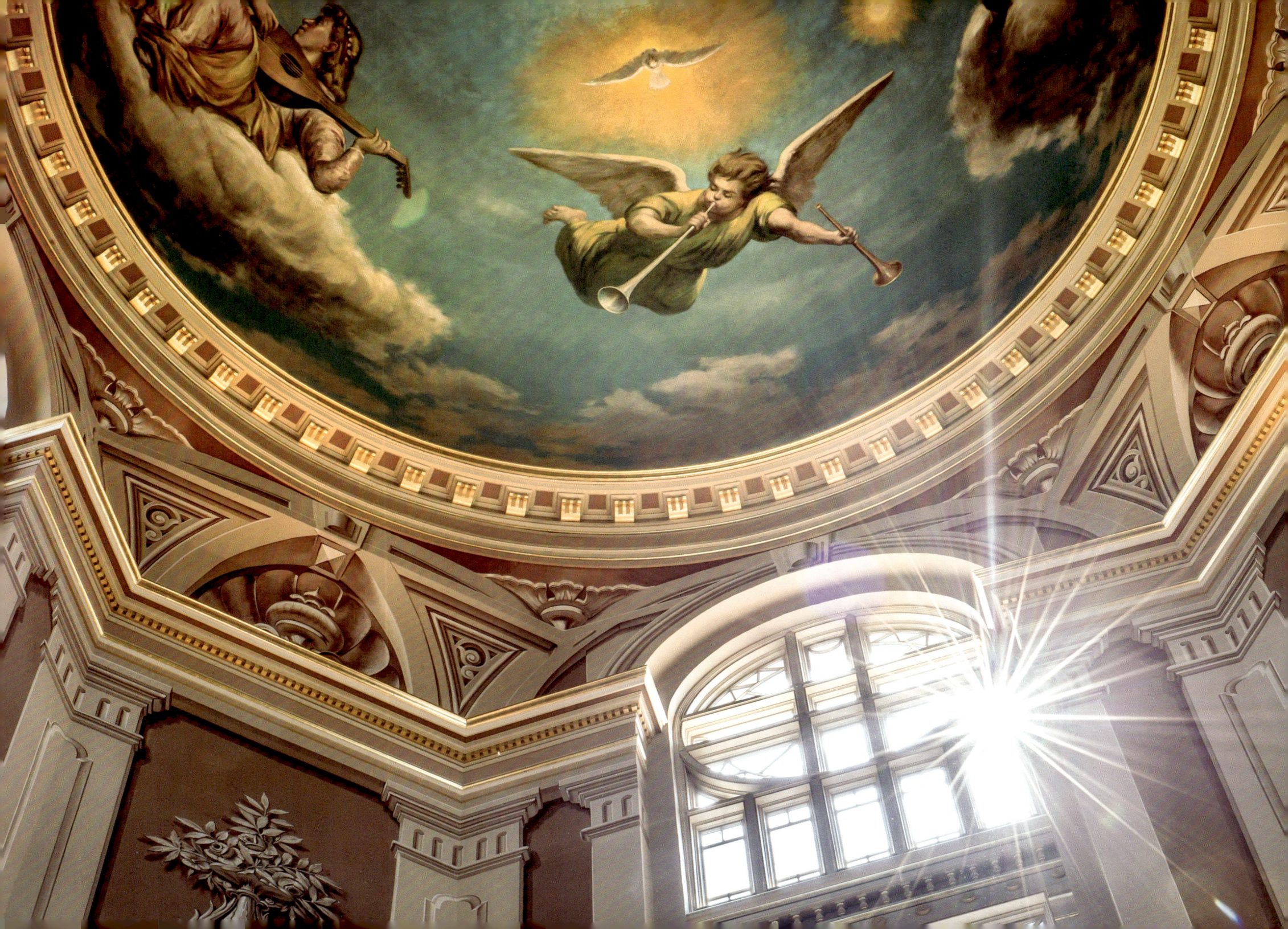

My days in Farley brought me some of my deepest living experiences I have known in a lifetime. A generation ahead of the first Farley women, I simply moved into their midst and opened my door. They came in, questioned me incessantly on endless topics, picked my brain, and searched my heart, asking me to share my wisdom. They let me confront them with strong words and congratulate them with deep joy.

We laughed and cried and discussed and danced and argued and ate and cheered together. We prayed together and forgave one another. They let me worry about them. Best of all, they let me believe in them.

—Sister Jean Lenz, O.F.M.,

Loyal Sons and Daughers: A Notre Dame Memoir

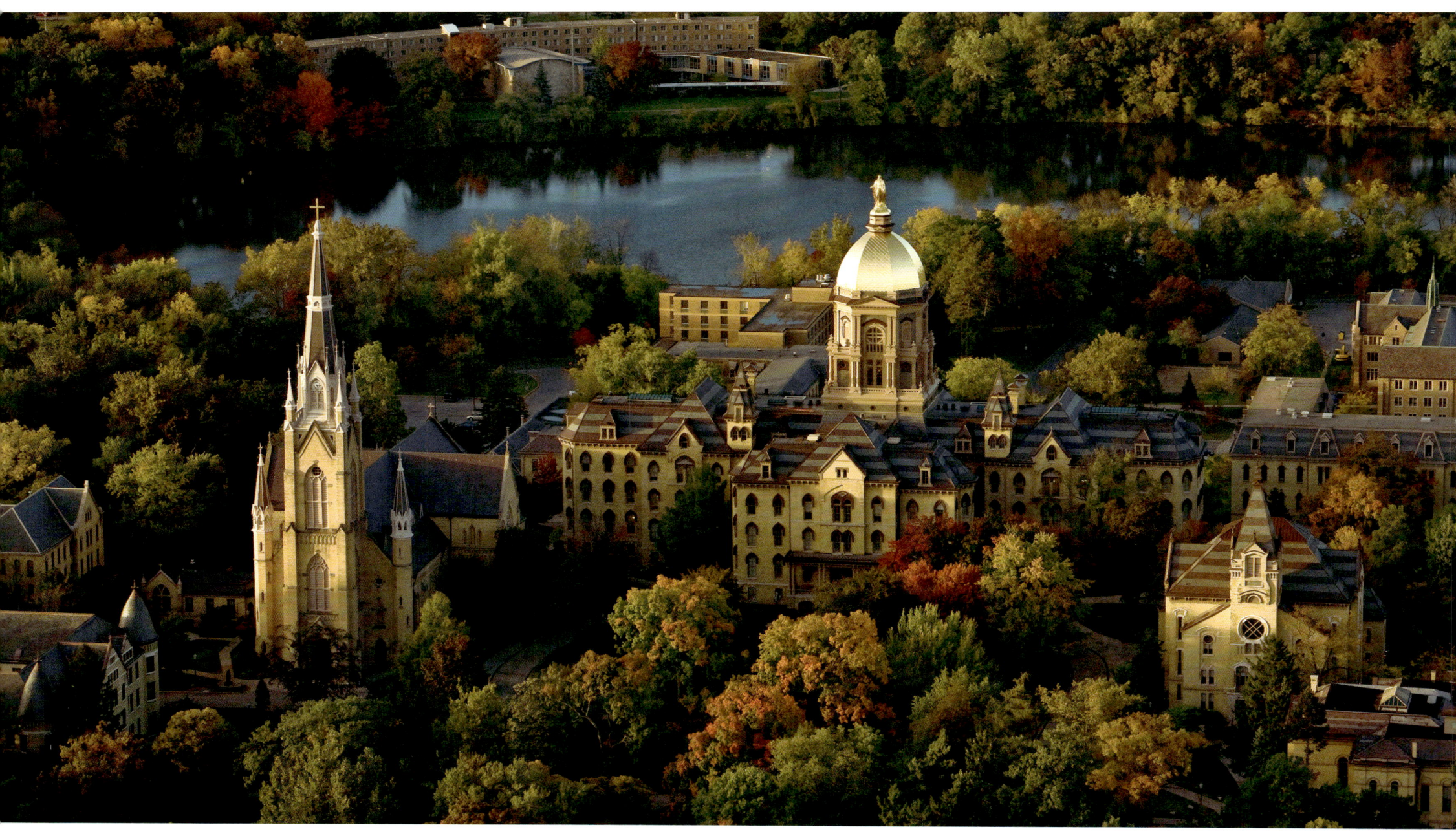

I always return to the lakes. Whatever excursions, detours, or distractions have carried me away, however campus has changed or grown, I always find my way back to the lakes. Those pathways are as right as rock. They are familiar, like the foot-worn trail leading home in childhood's twilight. I know the land's rise and fall, subtle as it is, and the tree roots roping out of the earth. I know the winding contours, curves, and mud-wet puddles that never dry. The staunch and leafy sycamores. The wispy willow, draping lakeside. Glimmering petals of sunlight flashing off the wind-rippled water.

I remember when Holy Cross Hall was there and students played hockey on the lakes in winter. Despite the taming, tending, and gentrification, the rutted path, unkempt grass, and shaggy woods persist. My favorite views of the Dome come from across the lakes at night. And the trail still takes me around and back and through time, a walk that begs reflection.

I came to the lakes as an eager but lonesome freshman, feeling out of place and over my head, far from my Southern home. The trees, trails, and natural order provided refuge, a welcoming place apart from the onerous enterprises, from roommates not yet friends, from classrooms where the intellectual sparring exceeded me. I can remember sitting alone

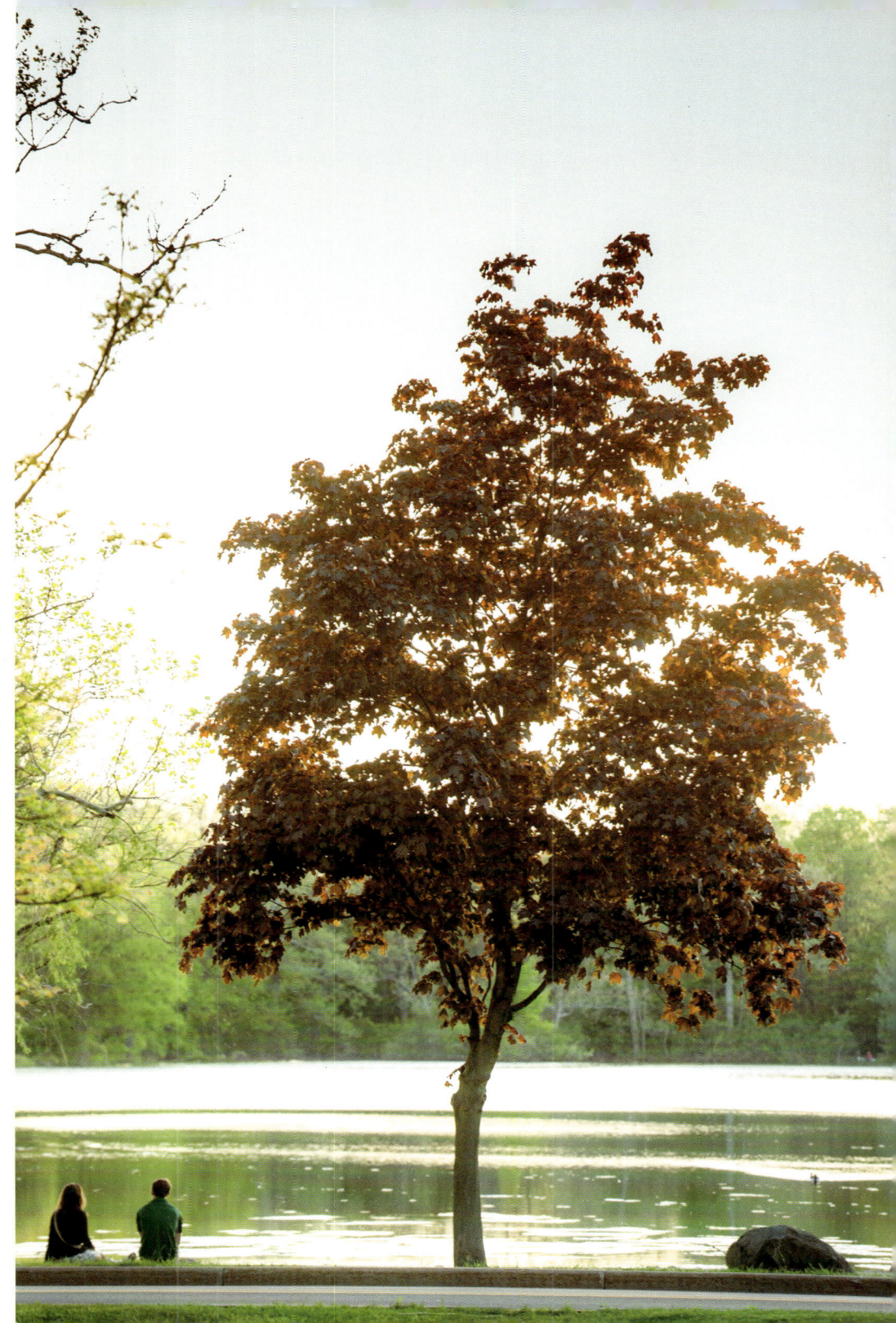

on Sunday afternoons that first fall—trying to read but mostly thinking. I remember walking late at night in winter, consoling and encouraging myself that I was here not to achieve but to learn—and to spend my time here trying to figure out who I was, what the world was all about, and how I might fit into it. Questions that never go away.

Often those nighttime walks and interior examinations—whether as a senior perplexed by an uncertain future or as a man in his middle years rerouting charted courses—have really been prayers spoken to starry skies, amid the trees and rustling winds and lapping water and candles flickering warmly at the Grotto nearby.

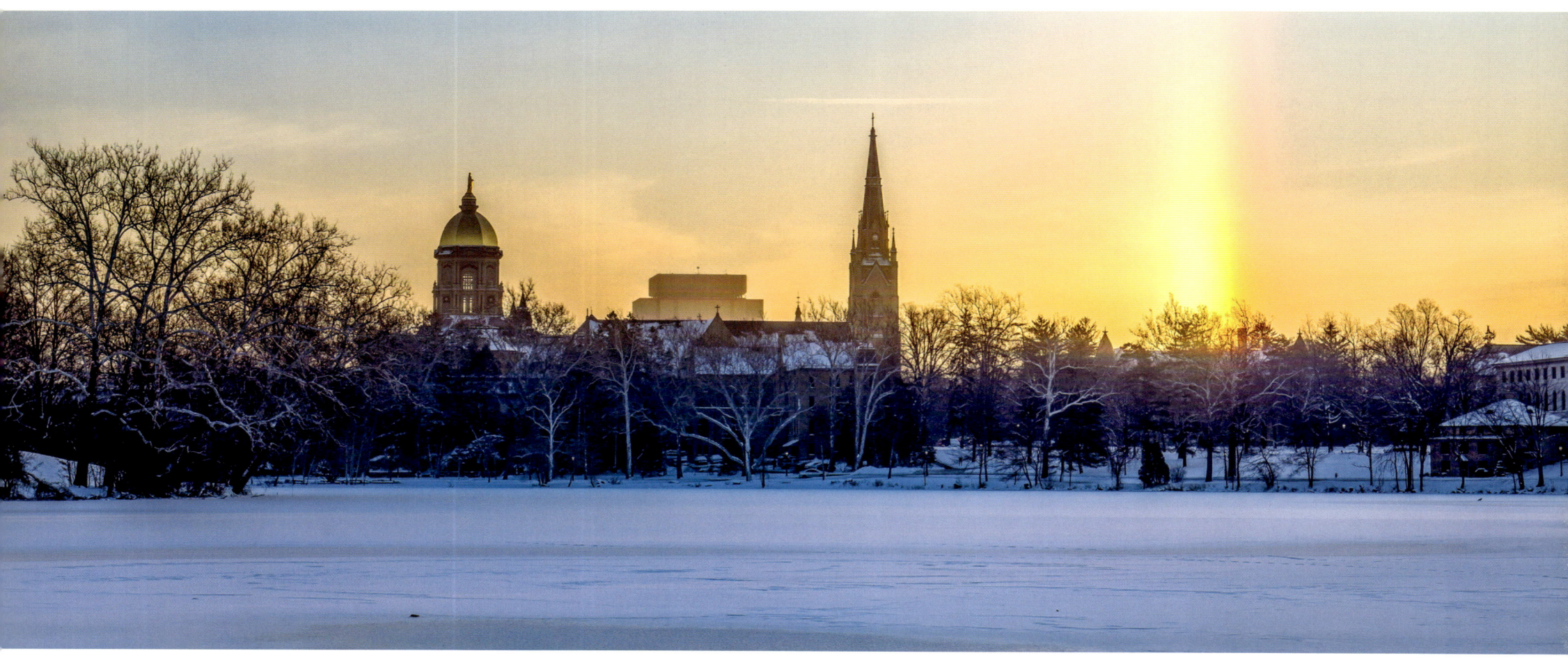

When I was a student, I ran around these lakes, ice skated over them, swam the length of both, and once tumbled drunkenly onto their grassy edges, singing "Wild Thing" with roommates who had become dear friends. One night with windows open in Lyons Hall a friend said, "Shut your eyes and listen to the ducks quacking. It sounds like they're all laughing at dirty jokes." It did; still does. Sometimes I'd stow away on that thickety little island in St. Joseph's Lake, before the concrete walkway got blocked with wrought iron fencing, and once watched a guy snag fish by cupping his submerged hand so steady and still that fish would drift into his palm and he'd snatch 'em up quicksilver quick. Briny fish flapping in his grasp. Fisher of fish.

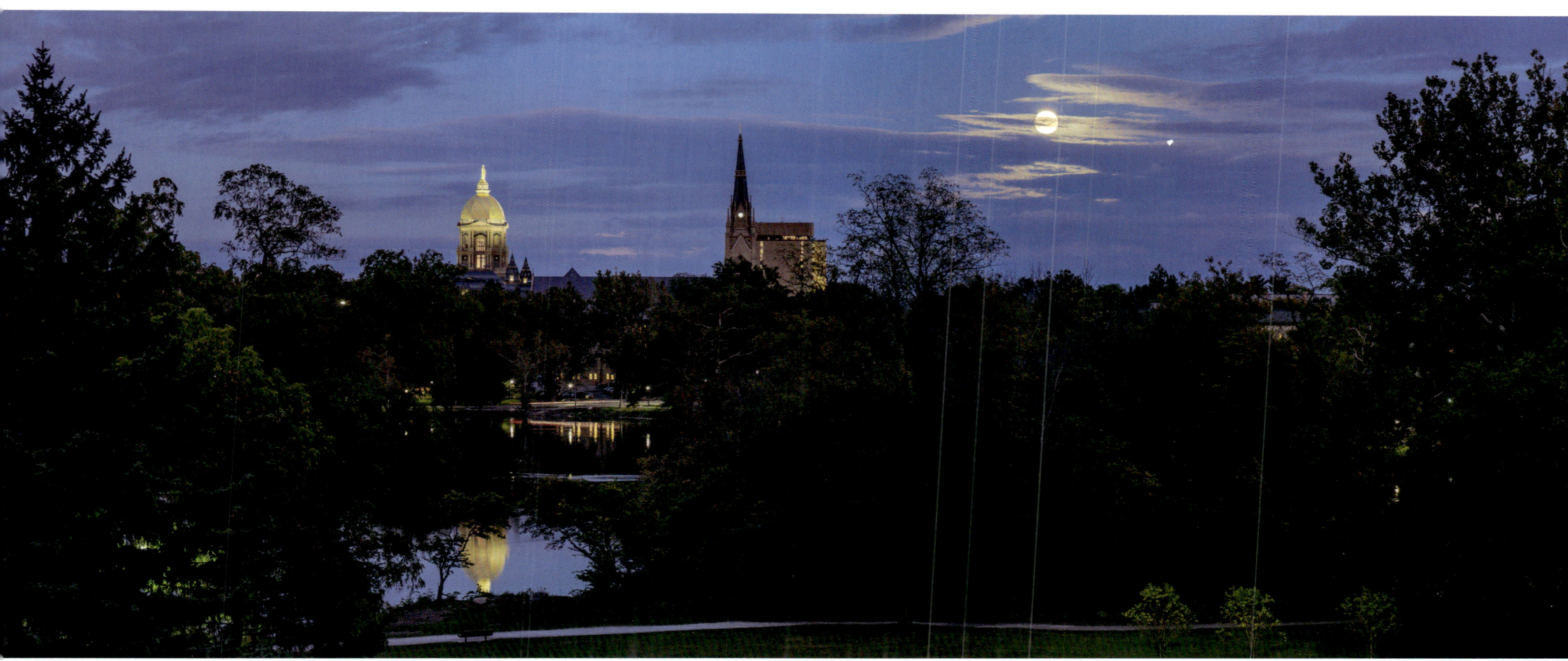

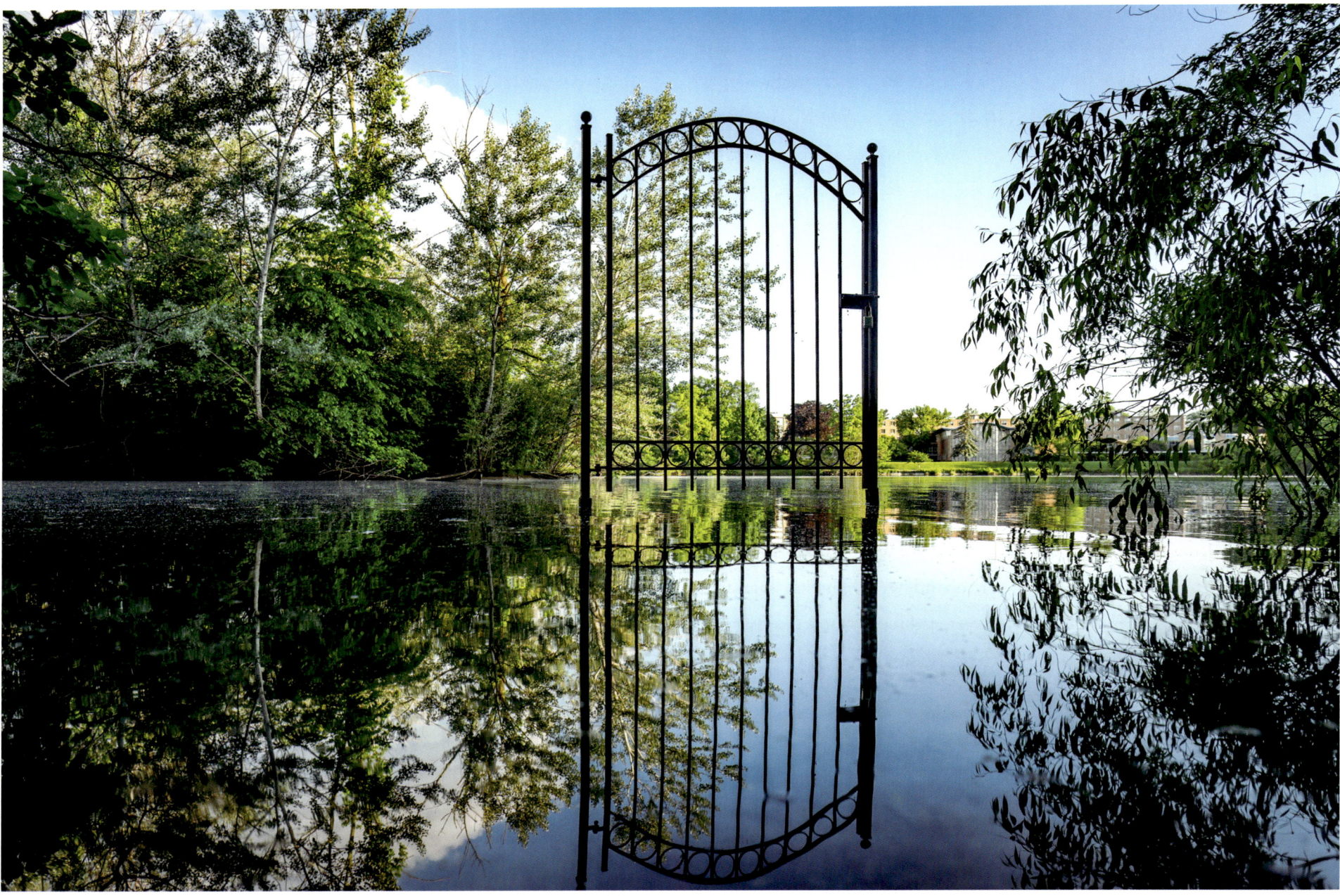

Then, with those undergrad years suddenly past, one spring dawn in 1974, I came to the lakes, having been awake all night. It was Senior Week with friends, and we had concluded our celebrations with a trip to Fat Shirley's and—by now carless—walked back to campus from that distant greasy spoon. We arrived on the shores of Saint Mary's Lake just as light peered into the day, greeted by a regatta of paddleboat ducklings in the fresh morning sun. I remember thinking then of the cycles of time and seasons and renewal, and how new and future generations—human and fowl—take their turns here.

I have since ambled these foot trails with toddlers, fed the ducks and geese with children, bicycled here with kids when they were able, and used the time circling the lakes on foot at sunset to talk with them about the things that matter. I have played hoops under the lights at night on the outdoor court near Carroll Hall, circled the lakes with a priest friend talking of God and his mischievous ways, and climbed trees on the far side of Saint Joseph's Lake to hang out over the water there. The boathouse. The beach and dock. Blue heron and wood ducks, mallards, Canada geese, and swans. Girls on blankets, old men fishing. A heart full of memories and images, the same yearning person inside, my legs having aged from youthful to well-worn still carrying me around the lakes.

I was in high school when I first encountered the lakes. I had come for a campus visit and was having second thoughts about this place I had long dreamed of attending. I was tired of working so hard and knew Notre Dame would be harder still. The university was seen then as a kind of Catholic service academy. There were no girls, no social life, no cars,

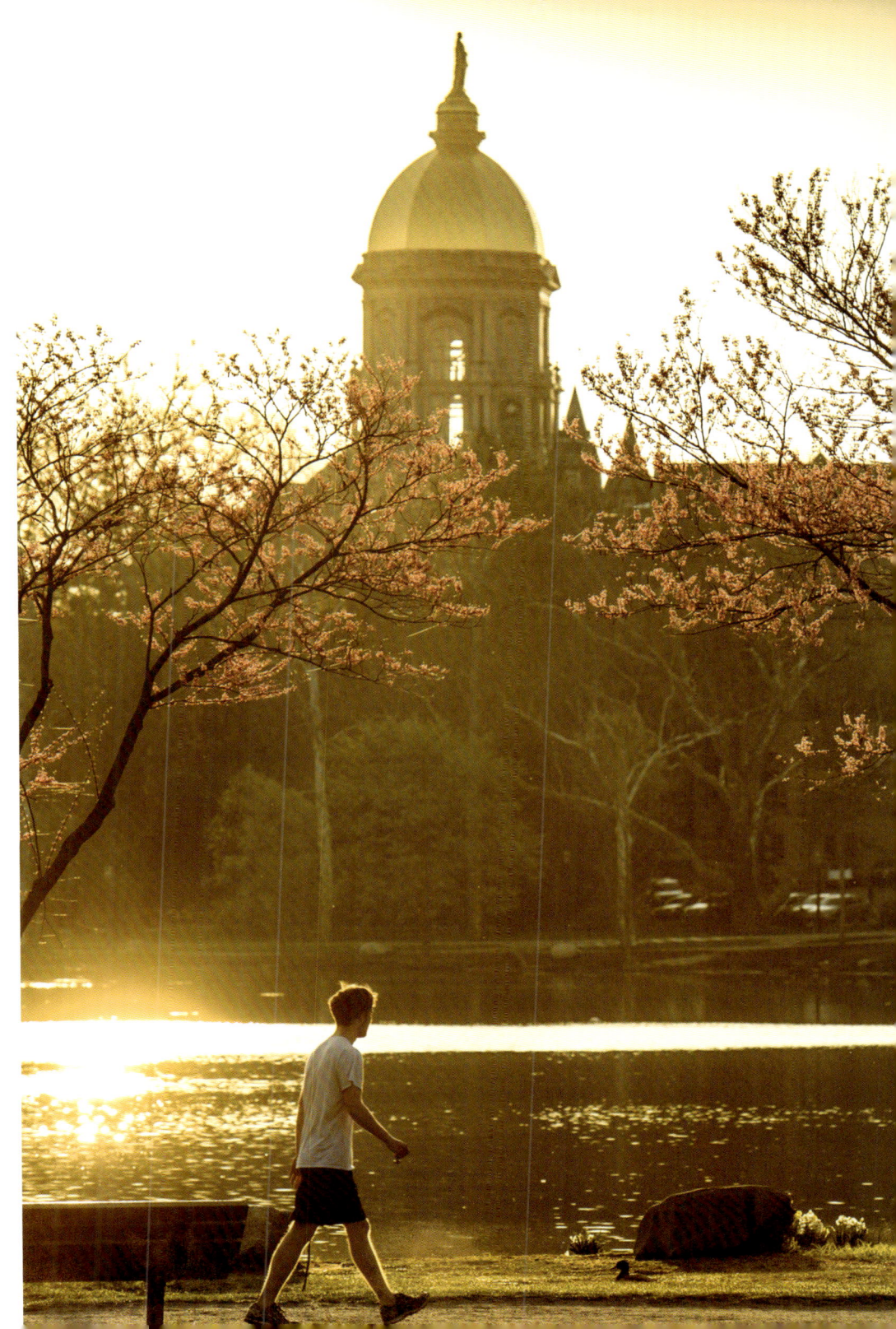

the only fun a pickup game of basketball at the Rock and a room full of guys. It was colder and greyer and windier than I imagined Siberia to be. I was thinking a warm-climate state university was the place for me as our family drove slowly between the Rockne Memorial and Saint Mary's Lake. The lake was frozen solid, and I had never seen such a thing. My sister, a Saint Mary's student, was talking about all the ducks on the lake, and my mother asked, "But where do the ducks go in the wintertime?"

Few people would understand the poignancy of this question, but I—a keen reader of J. D. Salinger's *The Catcher in the Rye*—knew its significance, for during Holden Caulfield's flight to New York City he is concerned about the ducks in Central Park in winter. On several occasions he asks just that: "Where do the ducks go in the wintertime?" So my mother's question carried an eerie echo, and I looked to the lake and saw, dotting its frozen surface, whole flocks of ducks—looking miserable perhaps, but holding their own on the Siberian landscape. Then, as the

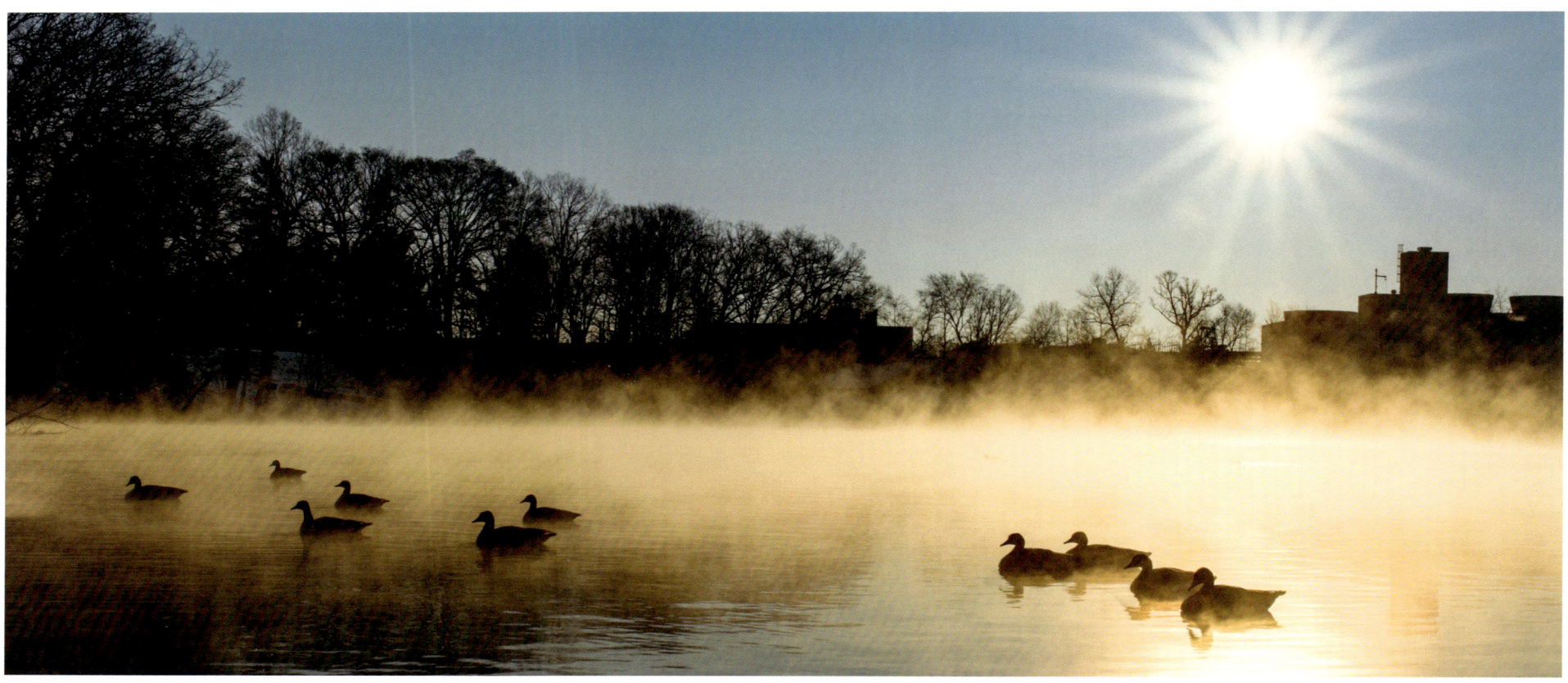

car turned past the Grotto, my sister said, "They stay here I guess," and just then I looked up and saw the Dome. It was shining brilliantly through the trees. I took it as a sign.

I have returned to this notion—Notre Dame as a kind of beacon, a place that defied harsh or profane elements—often over the years. When the ways of the world have gotten me down, when the course of human affairs felt misguided or wrong, I'd take solace in Notre Dame as a place of hope and virtue, or at least good intentions and a diligent conscience.

In some ways, the university is countercultural in its heritage and values, its singular commitment to doing what's right, acting on principle rather than pursuing temporal temptations and seeking worldly rewards. When discouraged—by the institution or life—I'd hold fast to the many good people who are here, and be buoyed by their example. "Their blood is in the bricks," the legendary teacher Frank O'Malley used to say of those who had given their lives to Notre Dame. Their gifts and memories reside in me.

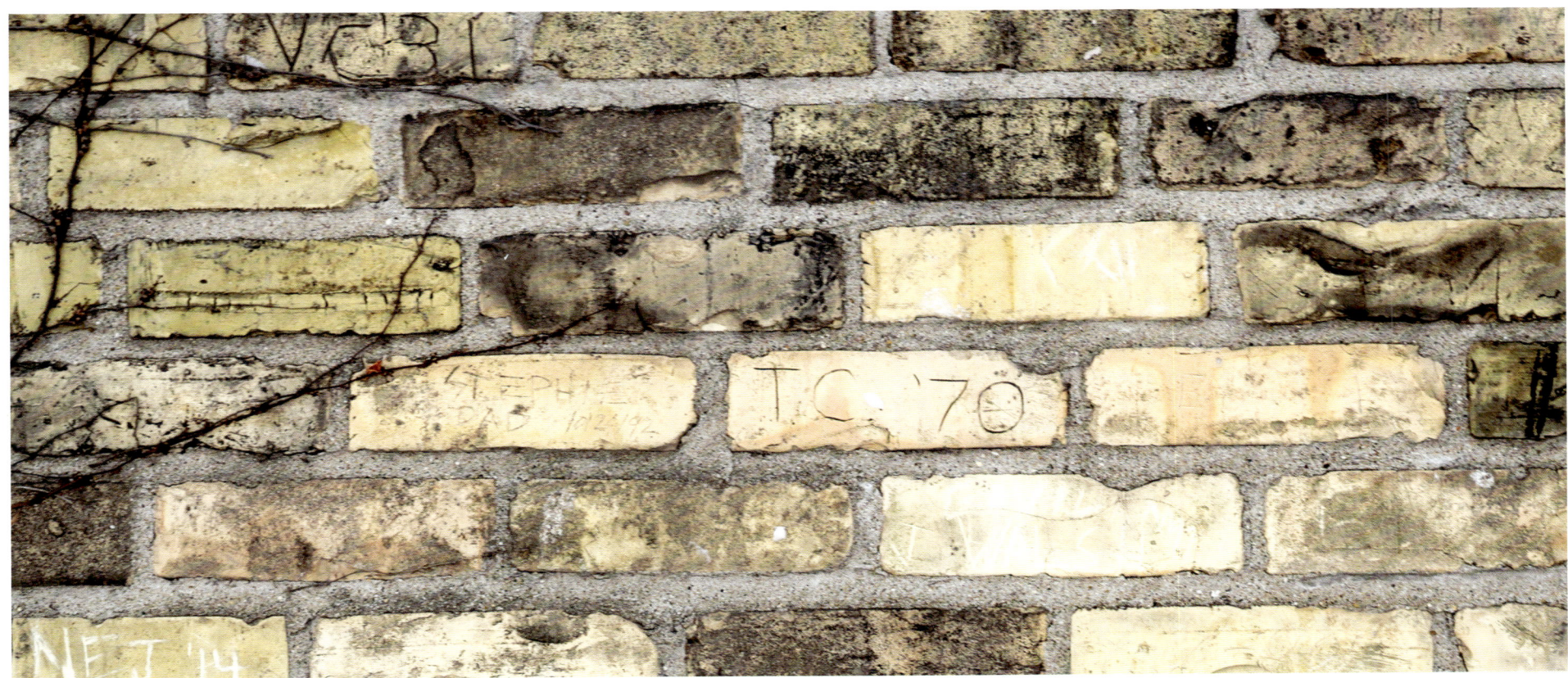

Notre Dame is indeed a place apart, a refuge, and yet a community—whose neighborhood is the wider world, not so much in need of enlightenment or redemption as it deserves care and service. Notre Dame is a place where you may speak of God or the soul without ridicule or derision. A place to welcome the good-hearted, where idealism isn't silly, where sentiment is respected and expressed without embarrassment.

There is to me—I sensed it when I first walked onto campus—a defining but undefinable spirit here, an abiding presence. Invisible but real, ineffable but palpable, it permeates the physical, tangible reality of campus. A touch of the divine dwells here. And we feel it, I think, because that quiet, mysterious presence resonates with something deep inside us— some other ineffable presence, spirit, or soul that responds to this sacred and very special place.

There was a time when people here spoke of "the Notre Dame mystique," and the meaning was known, without need for explanation. Some years later, when discussing a commercial venture he thought risked turning that spirit into a commodity, being traded or parlayed into profit or public relations, an older colleague warned, "Let us not squander the mystique." Change, of course, is inherent in the place; a university is dedicated to advancement, to growth, to superseding the boundaries of previous generations. But it's good to stay rooted. And to honor that presence that lives beyond words.

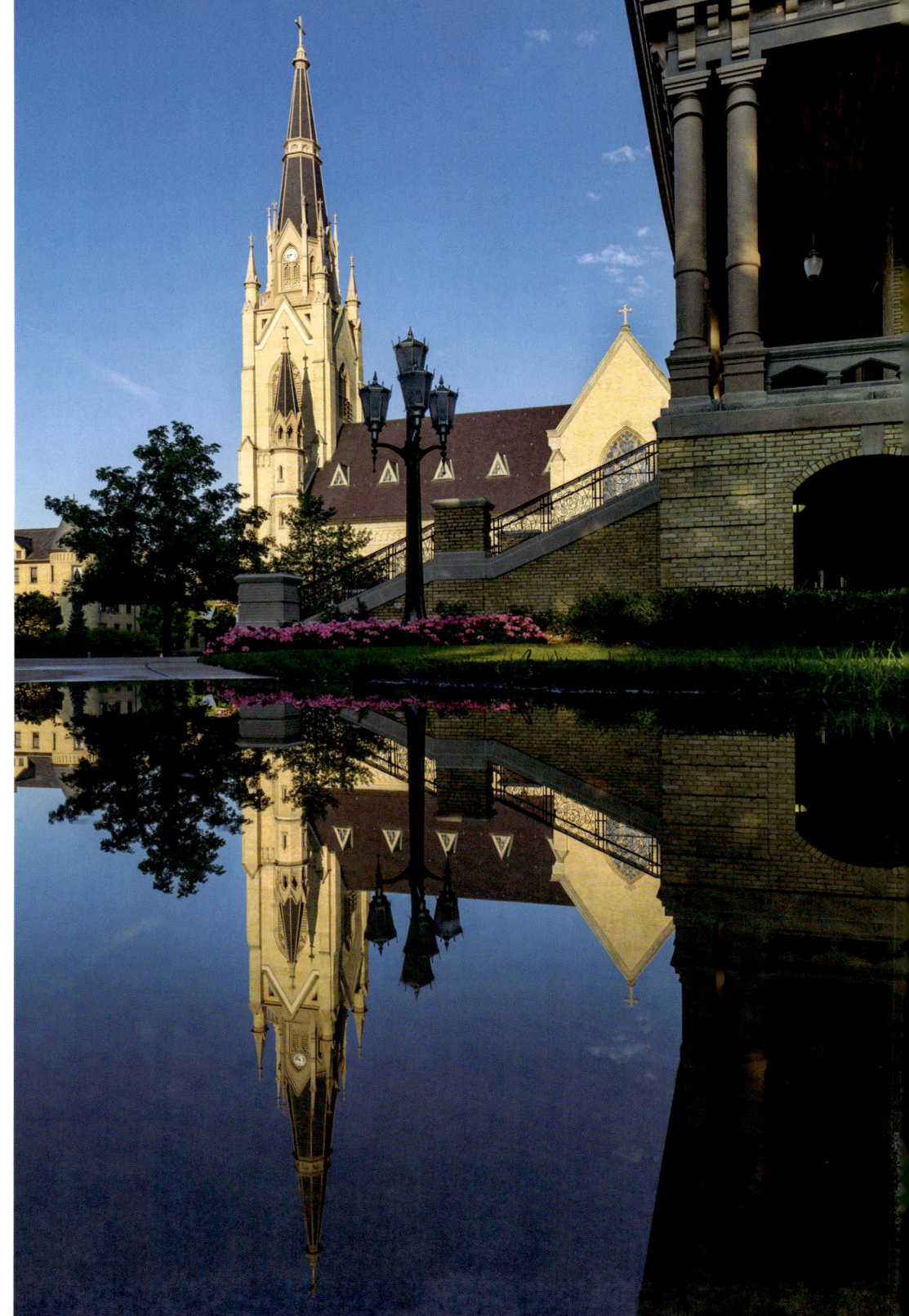

So the lakes remain my favorite patch of campus, the sanctuary I still return to for grounding when other pathways have carried me away. Others may find their niche at the Grotto, a residence hall chapel, or the Basilica of the Sacred Heart. Or even a bench on God Quad, still the university's heart and core. But I prefer the lakes—with Old College and the Log Chapel quietly standing by.

I also favor the lakes because that's where it all began—and because in those beginnings, in the naked beauty and clarity of the lakes, I can still feel Notre Dame's earthy, essential nature. For me, who has walked these lakes for almost half a century now, those footpaths lead to the purest spirit of the place.

The Notre Dame story—now more than 175 years old—starts at the lakes, in an origin story both fun and now familiar. Edward Frederick Sorin, a priest of the Congregation of Holy Cross, had come from France to the woolly reaches of the American frontier. He wanted to build a school, a university, he proclaimed, that would "be one of the most powerful means of doing good in this country." Sorin was twenty-eight years old then, bold, brash, visionary, defiant of authority. A bishop in the fledgling state of Indiana offered the tenacious priest a parcel of land far to the north—a mission station, a shambly log building on the banks of a smallish lake not far from the St. Joseph River. It had served Father Stephen Badin, the first priest ordained in America, in ministering to the Potawatomi who were native to the lushly wooded area.

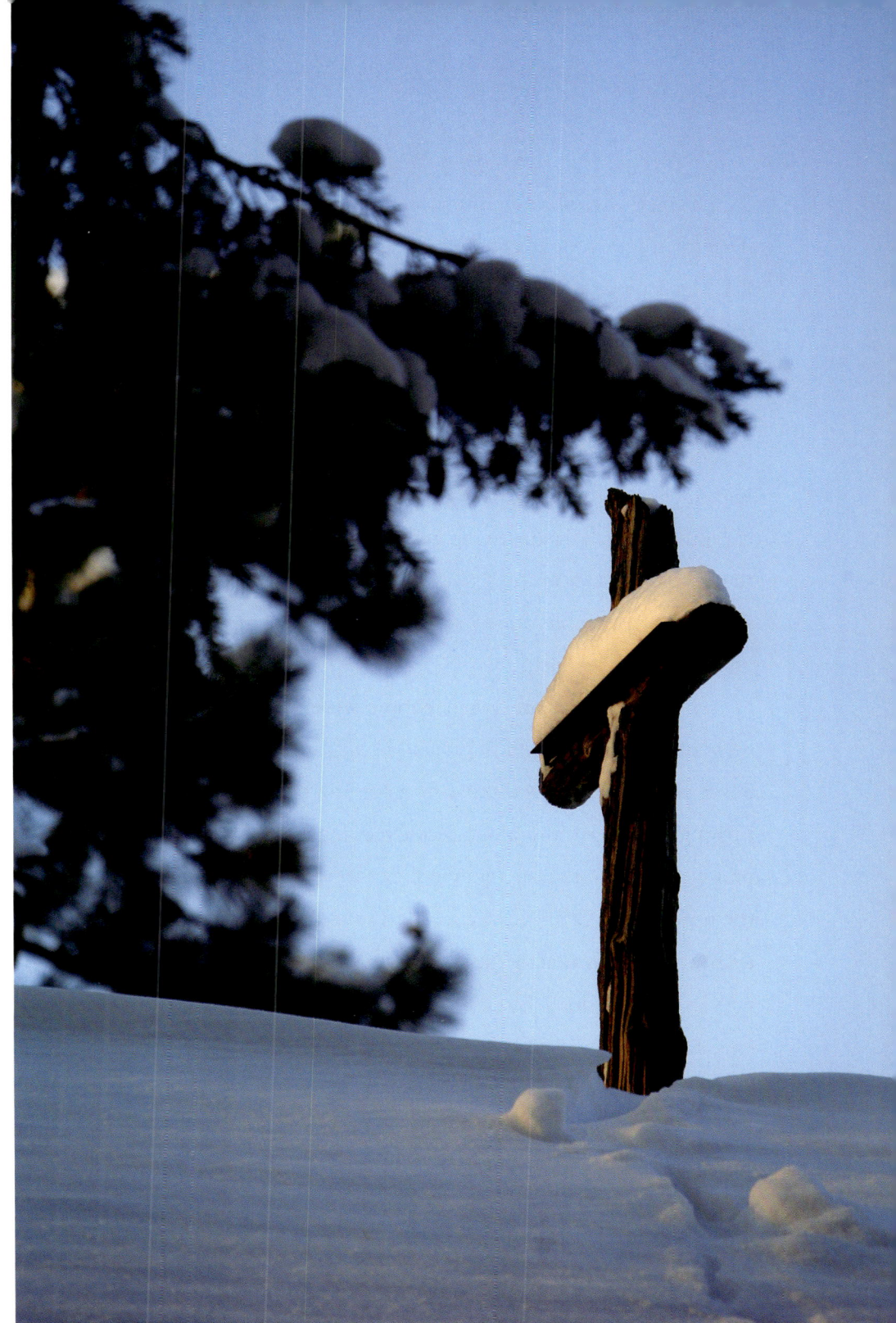

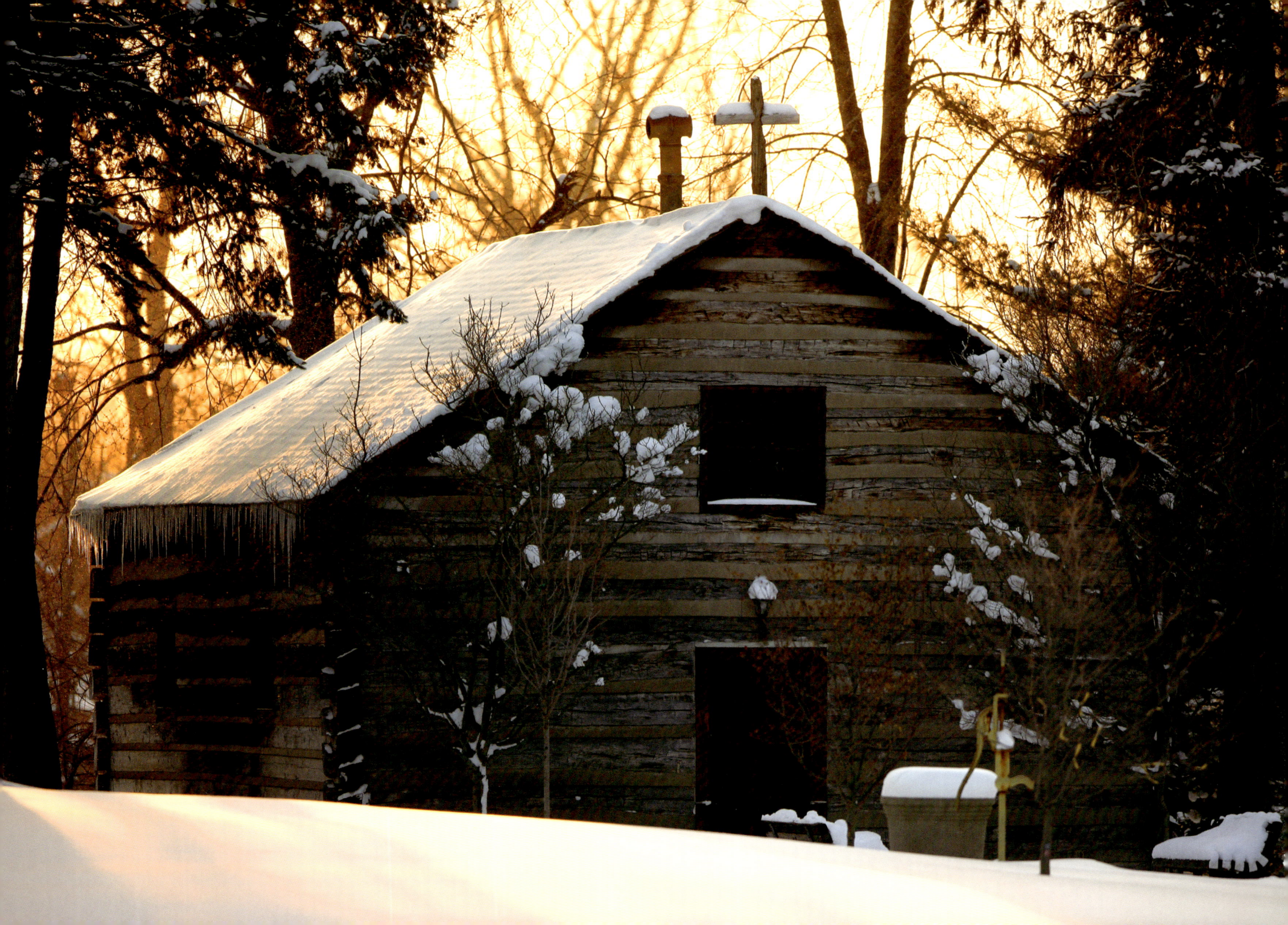

It is here that Sorin's dream took root and clung resiliently. He and his companions arrived on a cold, late November day in 1842. "Everything was frozen," he wrote in a letter to his religious superior two weeks later, "and yet it all appeared so beautiful. The lake, particularly, with its mantle of snow, resplendent in its whiteness, was to us a symbol of the stainless purity of Our August Lady." He named his school *l'Université de Notre Dame au Lac*.

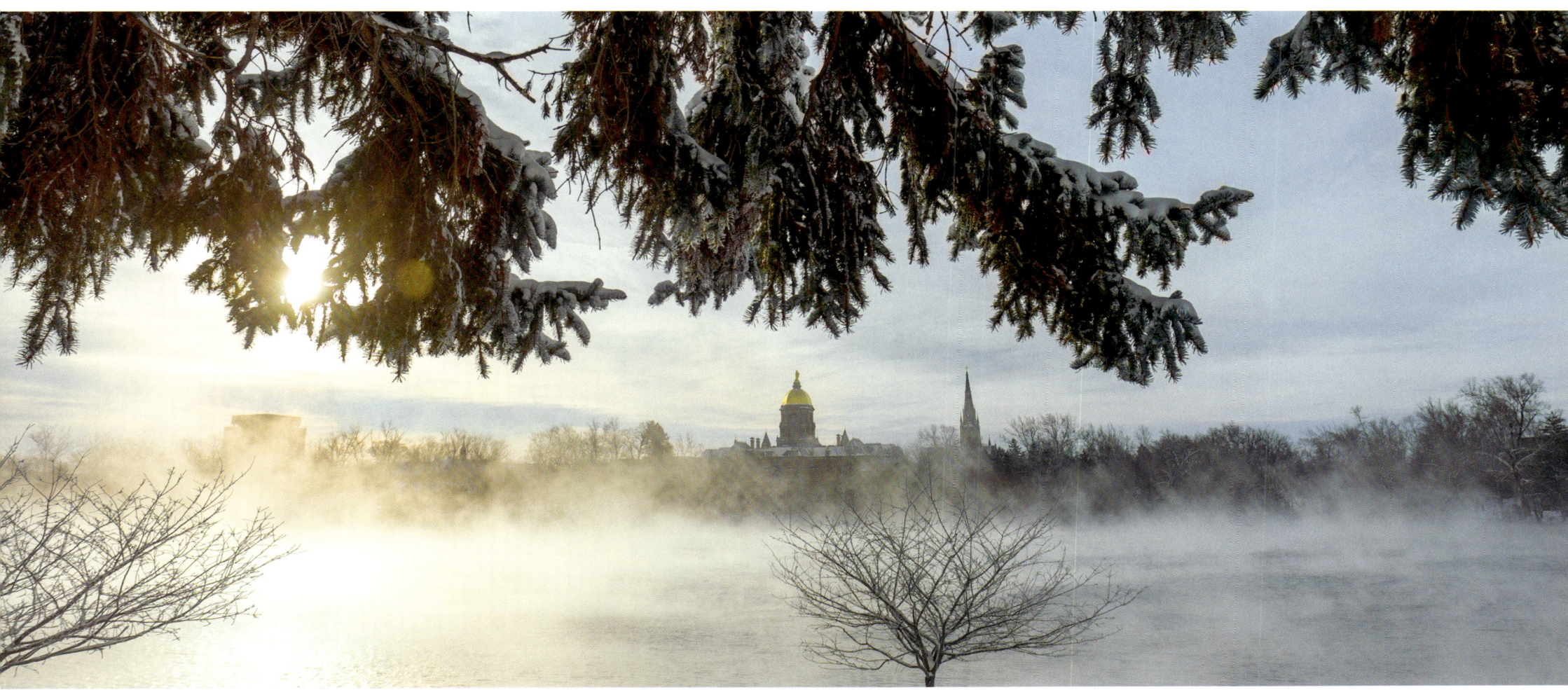

But here is my favorite line: "Like little children, in spite of the cold, we went from one extremity to the other, perfectly enchanted with the marvelous beauties of our new abode."

Still today, I cannot walk the lakes without imagining the joyous exuberance of their discovery, their happy arrival, of coming home to this teeming outpost. I love the image of those religious frontiersmen—rugged, ardent, unyielding—galloping lakeside like kids turned loose, darting among the trees, encircling the lakes, giddy with what they had found. I like to think that the same sense of faithful adventure still pervades all we do here—cheerful exploration, the delight of learning, eager investigations into the universe outside our doors.

To be sure, Notre Dame has grown far beyond its frontier origins. The lakes are no longer the site of weekly communal bathing; the lake ice is no longer harvested in winter to be used for storing and preserving perishables. The university farms—barns full of prizewinning cows and hogs, acres of barley, wheat, corn, beans, and rye—have been supplanted by dignified academic buildings and residence halls. An institution that once ran a brickmaking operation to stay afloat financially has now underwritten an array of entrepreneurial ventures to translate innovative thinking and intellectual property into resource-generating enterprises.

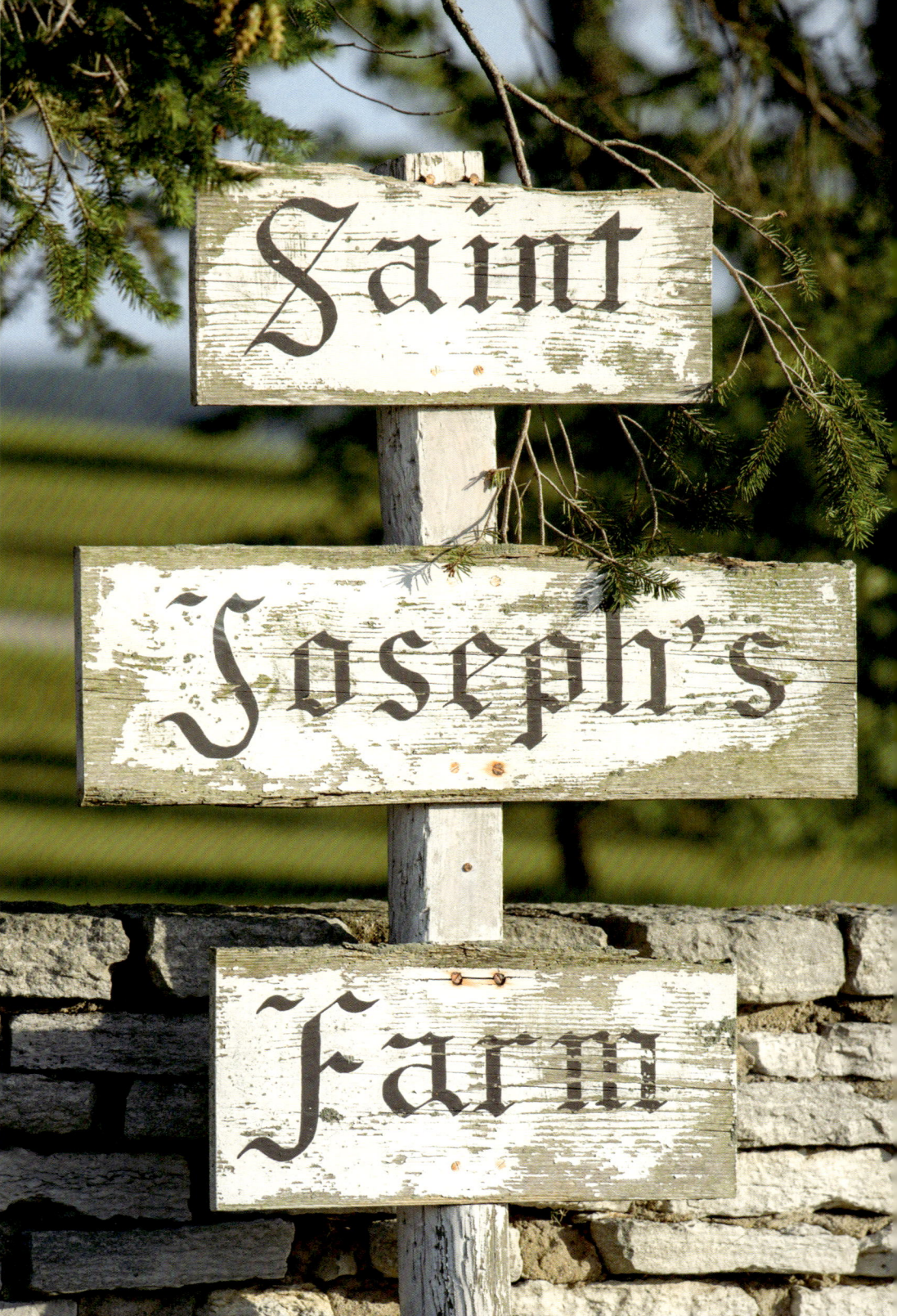

The elementary, manual labor, and prep schools are long gone; today nationally elite graduate and professional schools push forward the front lines of scholarly investigation to foster learning for its own sake as well as learning that advances the prospects for the human race in the twenty-first century. A teaching faculty once valued primarily for offering undergrads "a Notre Dame education" has evolved into a teaching and research faculty expected to provide its students an unparalleled undergraduate experience while performing innovative research.

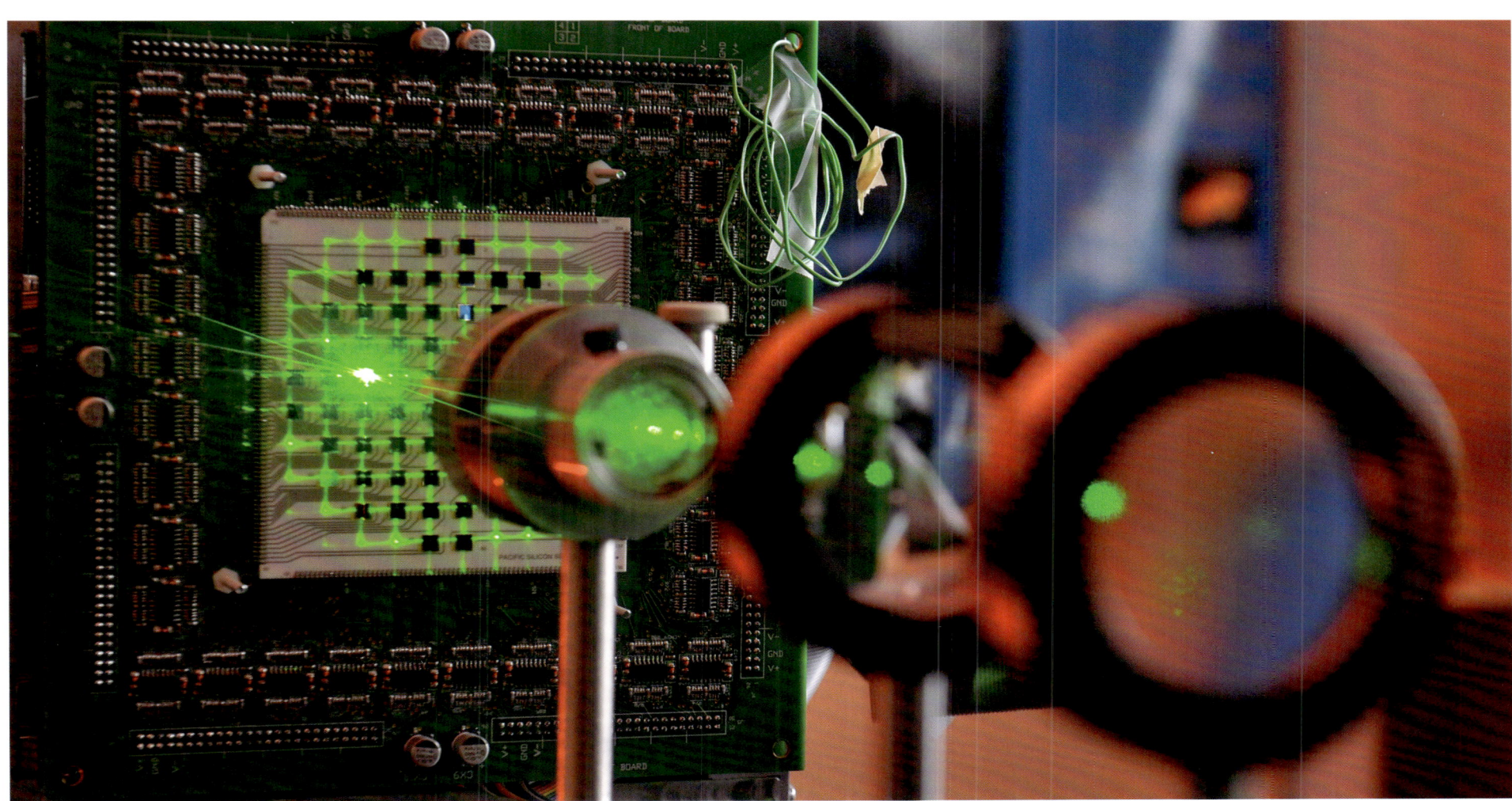

Researchers who once pioneered flight, transmitted the first wireless message, and installed electric lights throughout campus have been succeeded by scholars, scientists, and engineers who smash atoms, explore the heavens, cure pernicious rare diseases, combat mosquito-borne illnesses, and apply leading-edge technology to remedy some of humanity's most ominous challenges. From nanotechnology to neutrinos, from "dark matter" to the God particle, their expeditions extend the limits of human knowledge and bring their students along on their quests.

I came to Notre Dame to work in 1977 largely because of the vision outlined by Father Theodore M. Hesburgh, C.S.C., during his presidency from 1952 to 1987. He talked of Notre Dame being a crossroads where all the intellectual currents of the time could engage in conversation, where both believers and nonbelievers could grapple with society's most vexing questions, where research and scholarship could foster humanity's enrichment. That was the Notre Dame I knew and loved—a place for fervent dialogue and learning, the exchange of ideas, and the pursuit of truth wherever those interrogations might lead.

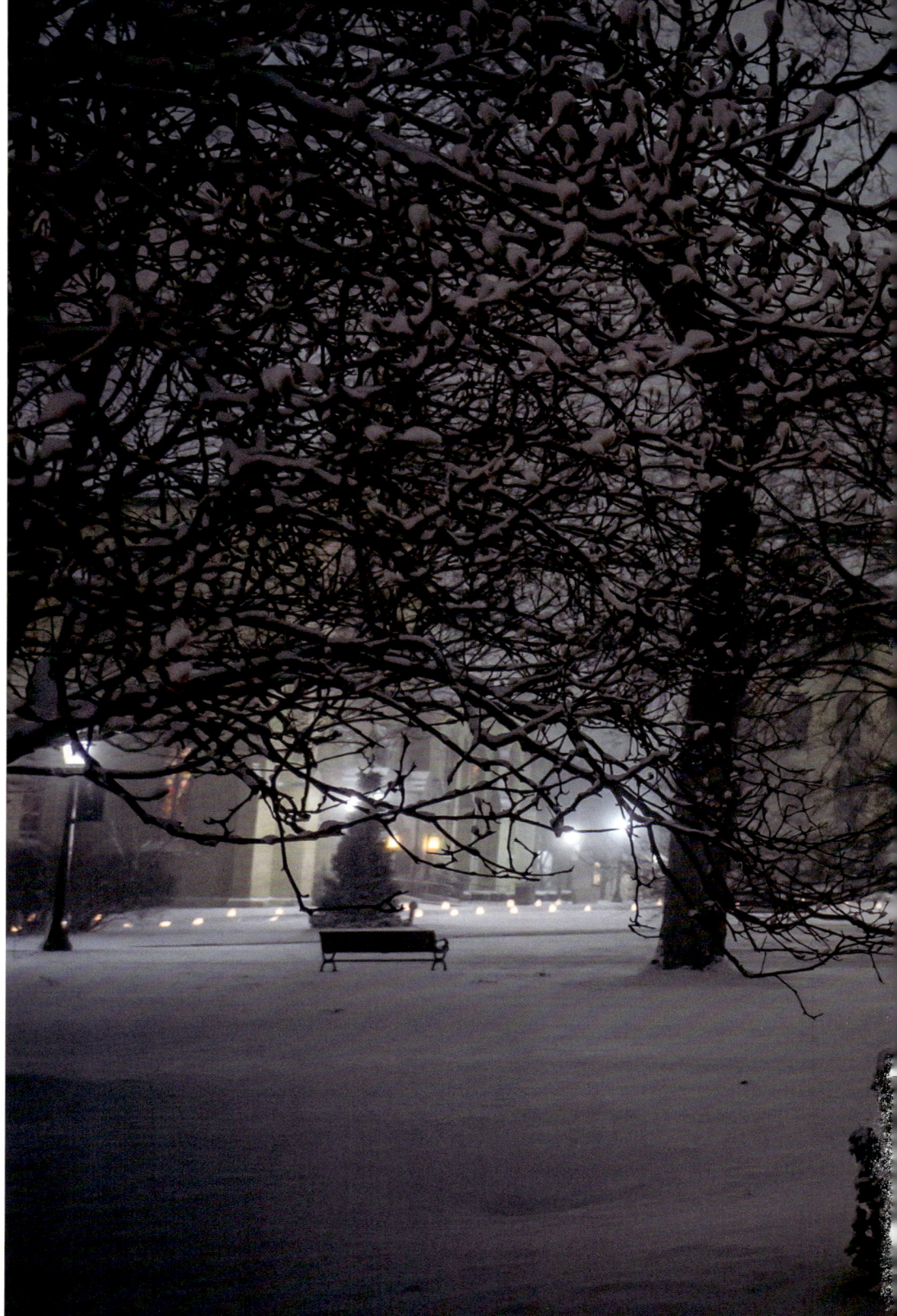

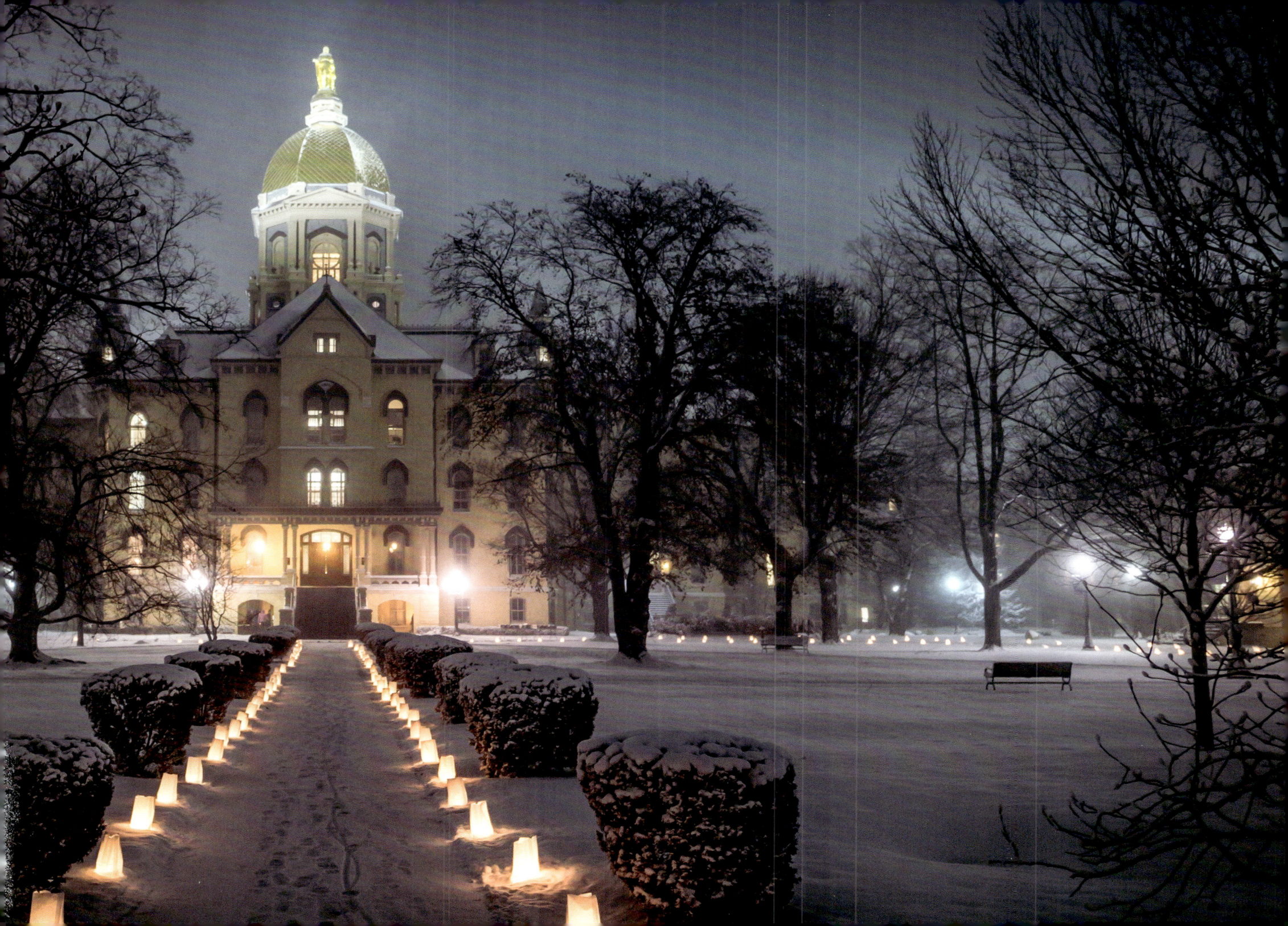

I had come of age during the civil rights movement, Vatican II, the Vietnam War, and all the societal upheaval associated with the Woodstock generation. It was an exciting yet perilous time: cultural norms were in flux, societal order was in jeopardy, the world in disarray. But it was also a period of exciting, idealistic re-imagining. I took to heart Father Hesburgh's words that "this changing world will confront humankind with enormous new moral problems of unprecedented proportion and consequences," as well as these words that called out to me:

Universities, the font of most human knowledge and knowledgeable people, will be at the heart of generating the people who, in turn, will generate the change. And secondly, it will take a special kind of university to direct change in such a way that humans do not destroy themselves and their world.

All this is meant to indicate that the future, uncertain though it is, will not be all that frightening if we have some institutions that undertake the dual task of transmitting and expanding knowledge, but at the same time, the more difficult role of educating persons with that sense of moral responsibility and judgment required to manage change and to use knowledge for mankind's betterment and progress, instead of for its destruction. It is this kind of institution that Notre Dame aspires to be.

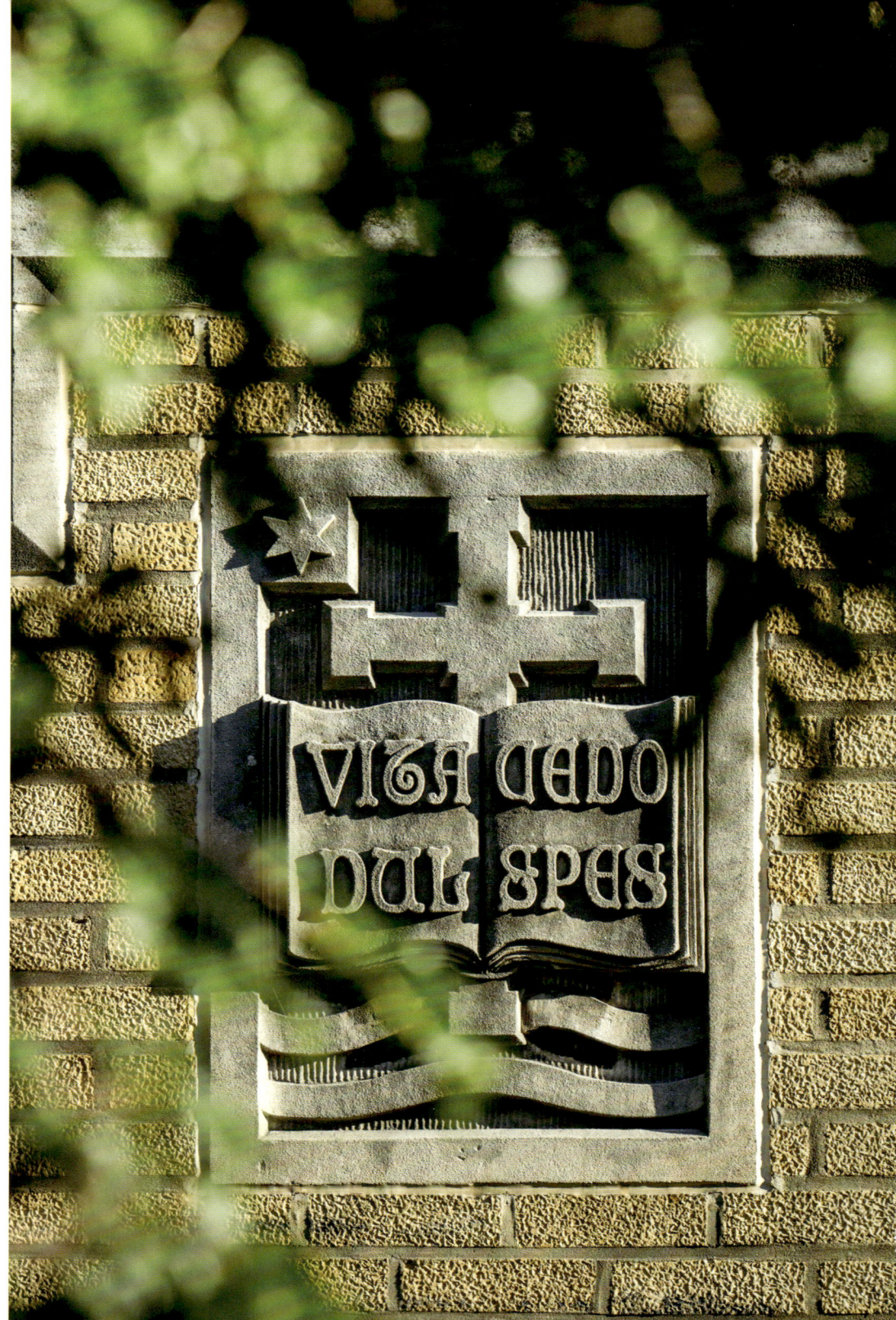

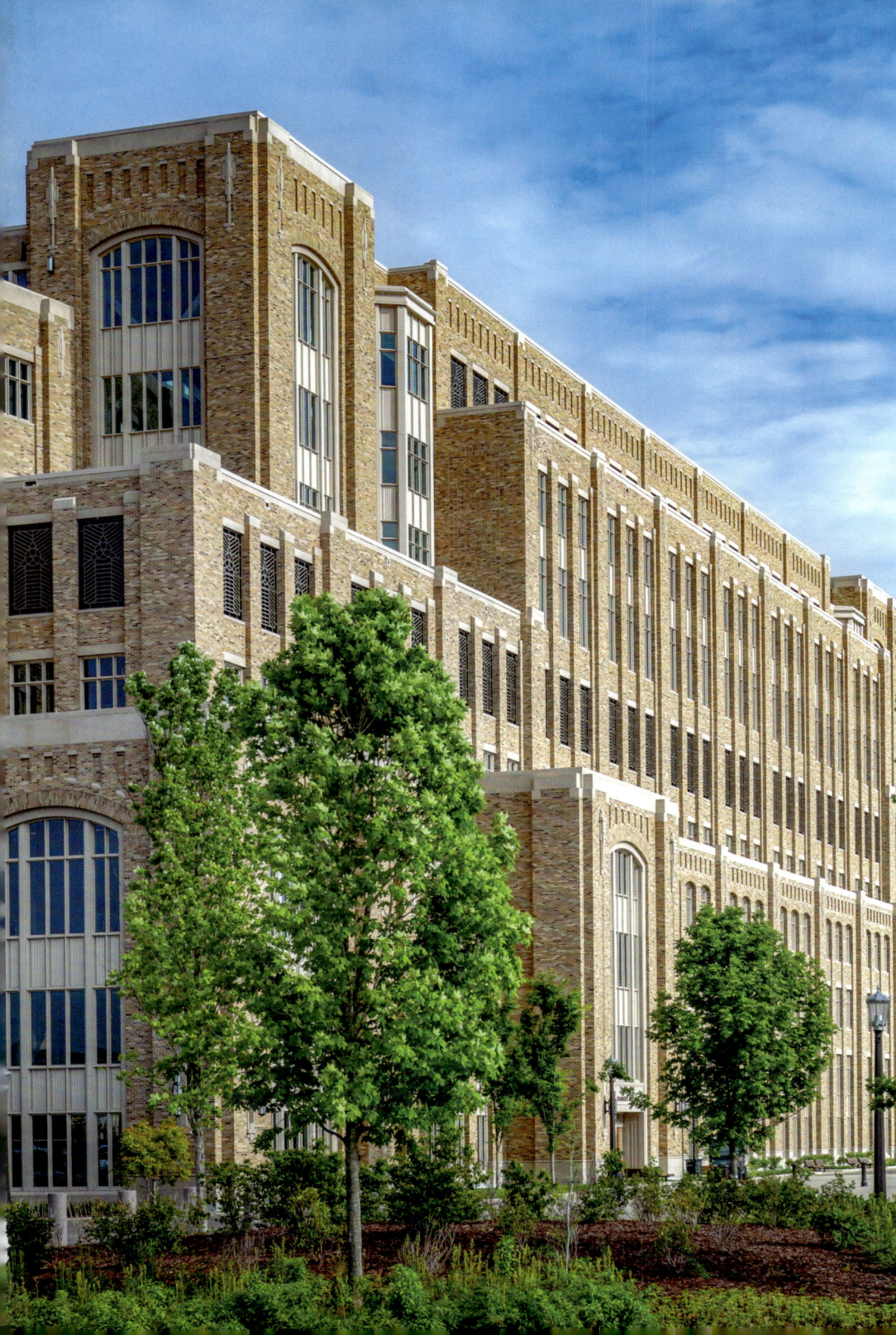

That's why I came to work at Notre Dame—to be part of that. I came to help tell the Notre Dame story and to bring Notre Dame's voice into vital but sometimes contentious national conversations, to bring the moral, ethical, and spiritual dimensions into dialogue with a more secular world. I could see how university research and scholarship sought solutions to some of humanity's greatest challenges, and I understood what Hesburgh meant when he said just causes were not well served by tepid convictions or intellectual mediocrity. Hesburgh maintained that Notre Dame would stay firmly true to its Catholic character, but find its niche among the world's elite universities.

That's been the aim ever since.

In the ensuing years—under the leadership of presidents Edward "Monk" Malloy, C.S.C., and John I. Jenkins, C.S.C.—the university has taken impressively long strides in fulfilling that promise. The faculty is superb, the student body among the best undergraduate populations in America, the graduate school thriving, the endowment robust, and university research and scholarly pursuits attracting unprecedented financial support and contributing cutting-edge advances in expanding human knowledge. And the place, consistently ranked among the top 20 universities in America, is genuinely, devotedly Catholic—while welcoming into its community earnest scholars and students of diverse perspectives.

Although physical facilities are but one measure of institutional advancement, the transformation of Notre Dame's landscape over the past decade has been stunning. New residence halls extend the school's treasured residential tradition. Shining, state-of-the-art facilities nurture engineering and scientific research and education. A new architecture building gives room to a school that ranks among the nation's top programs in classical design while offering a welcoming face to the new-born Eddy Street Commons at the southern end of campus. Innovation Park, not far away, and the University Idea Center support university ingenuity and initiatives to translate laboratory breakthroughs into commercial ventures.

The crown jewel of recent campus development may well be the crossroads project that affixed several major facilities—Corbett and O'Neill halls along with the Duncan Student Center—to the football stadium, housing a half-dozen academic units, student center, and myriad spaces to enhance campus social, athletic, and cultural experiences. The grand edifice is steel, brick, and mortar evidence of Notre Dame's approach to a holistic education—and an indication of its confidence in its mission.

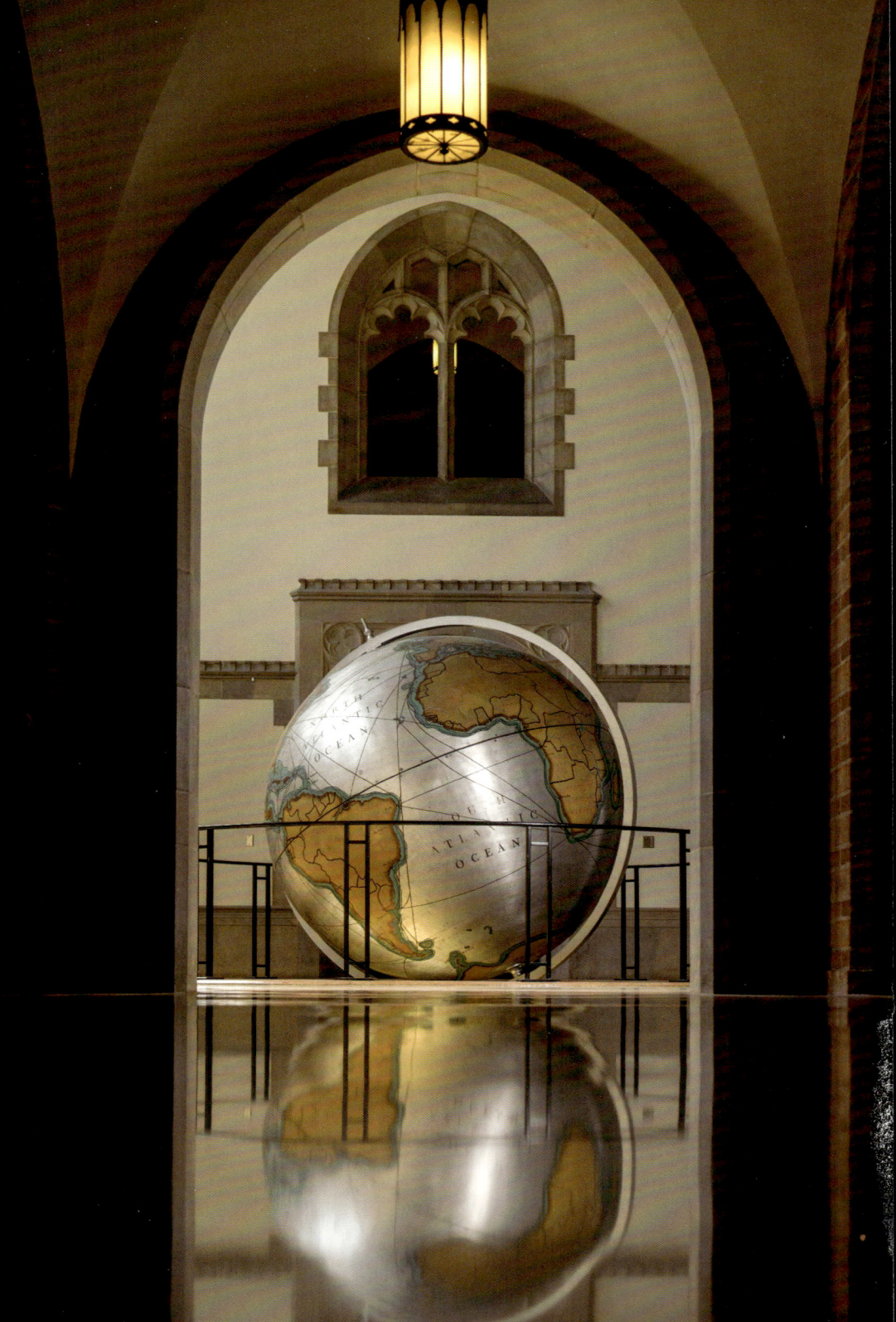

Additionally, the Keough School of Global Affairs was established in 2014, bringing an array of international programs and institutes under a single umbrella organization to better direct the university's efforts to address the human predicament on a global scale. That enterprise, too, inhabits a handsome new facility reflecting the institution's aspirations to bring about positive change throughout the world.

Of course, globalization is in Notre Dame's blood. After all, the school was established by a French priest from a religious order whose founder, Blessed Basil Moreau, deployed priests and brothers on missionary expeditions not just to America but to distant corners of the world.

Early in its history the school drew a significant number of students from South and Central America, from Cuba and the Philippines. Father John O'Hara, C.S.C., one of Notre Dame's most influential presidents—and the son of the American consul to Uruguay early in the twentieth century—expanded the university's Latin American network and presciently established Notre Dame's business school with an emphasis on international trade and commerce. Notre Dame's academic environment was further enriched in the 1930s when it welcomed notable refugee scholars fleeing the spread of Nazism in Europe.

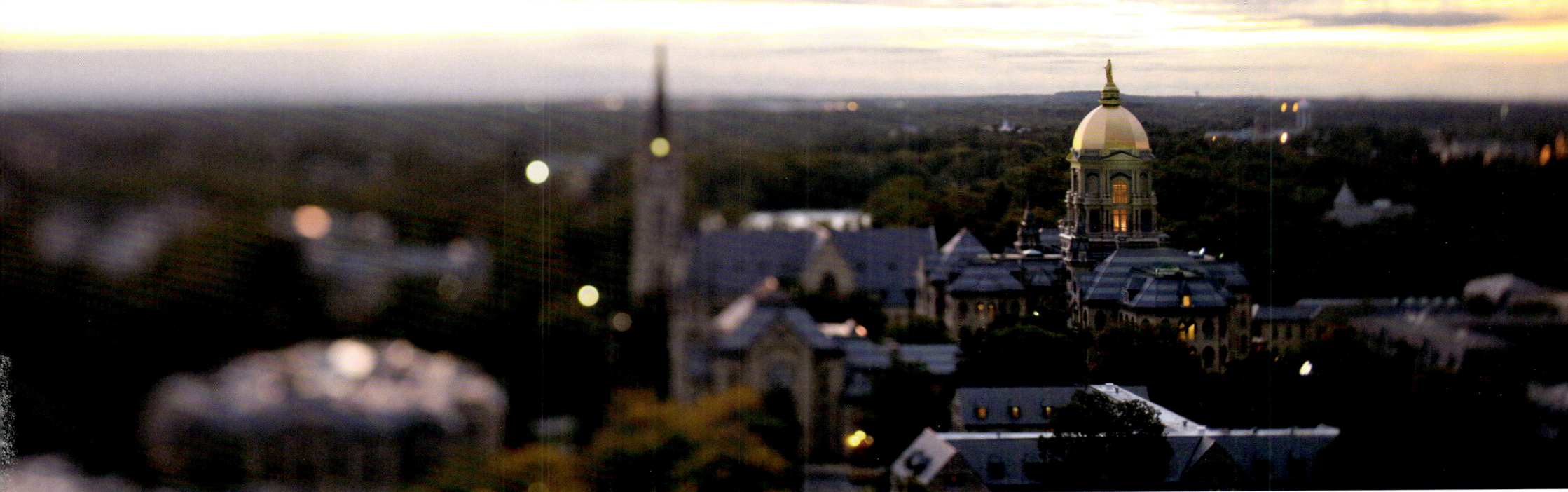

The university has a long tradition of providing undergraduates study-abroad opportunities and has perennially been among the leaders in the number of students living and studying overseas—as well as an early leader in the Peace Corps effort, typically sending more alumni to serve in foreign lands than other colleges or universities. So the place—a product of Catholicism's international dimension—has always looked beyond national borders, and its legacy is education, scholarship, and service with a global reach. In addition to the Keough School, Notre Dame International now operates a gateway network with centers and programs in about a dozen countries around the world.

It is eminently clear to most any observer that the university is flourishing, that the Jenkins administration has overseen significant advances, and that decades of promise and preparation, growing pains and devotion to mission are finding fulfillment today in a burgeoning global enterprise. The school launched with meager resources has overcome devastating fires, a cholera epidemic, damaging and debilitating wars, anti-Catholic prejudices, and societal turbulence; it is today one of the most respected institutions of higher learning in the world, a multinational corporation.

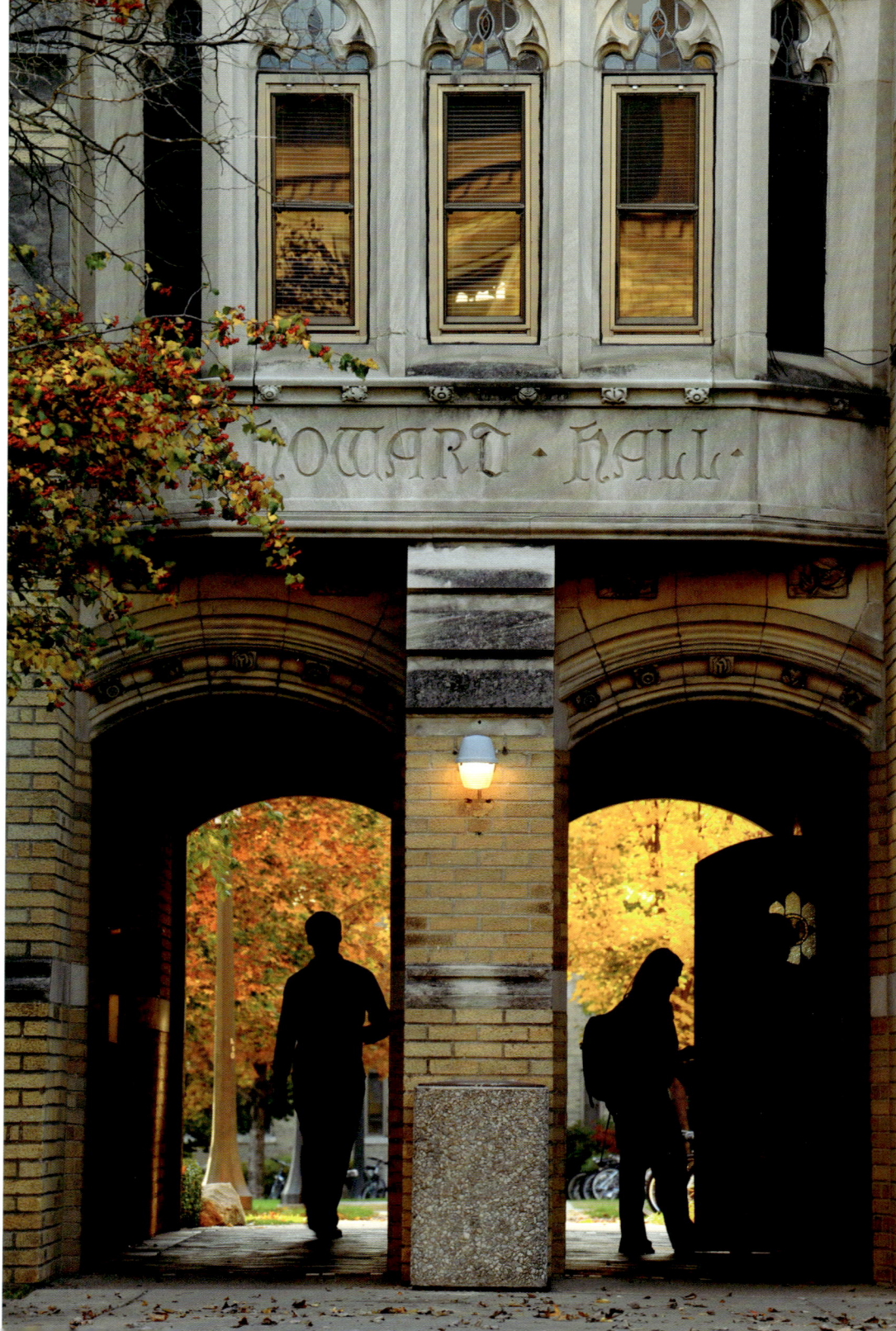

Notre Dame is a thriving, bustling, dynamic, purposeful enterprise. Yet it is communal, familial even, with residence-hall traditions that spawn lifelong friendships. The academics are rigorous, demanding, exhausting; but the student-teacher relationships are both stimulating and nurturing. Standards are high, expectations often daunting—and not just in the classroom or laboratory, in Jordan and McCourtney halls, but in broader contexts: in friendships and service, as students, colleagues, and human beings. But Notre Dame is populated with people who care, and that—probably more than anything else—is the hallmark of life here. Good people. Good people committed to the place and each other.

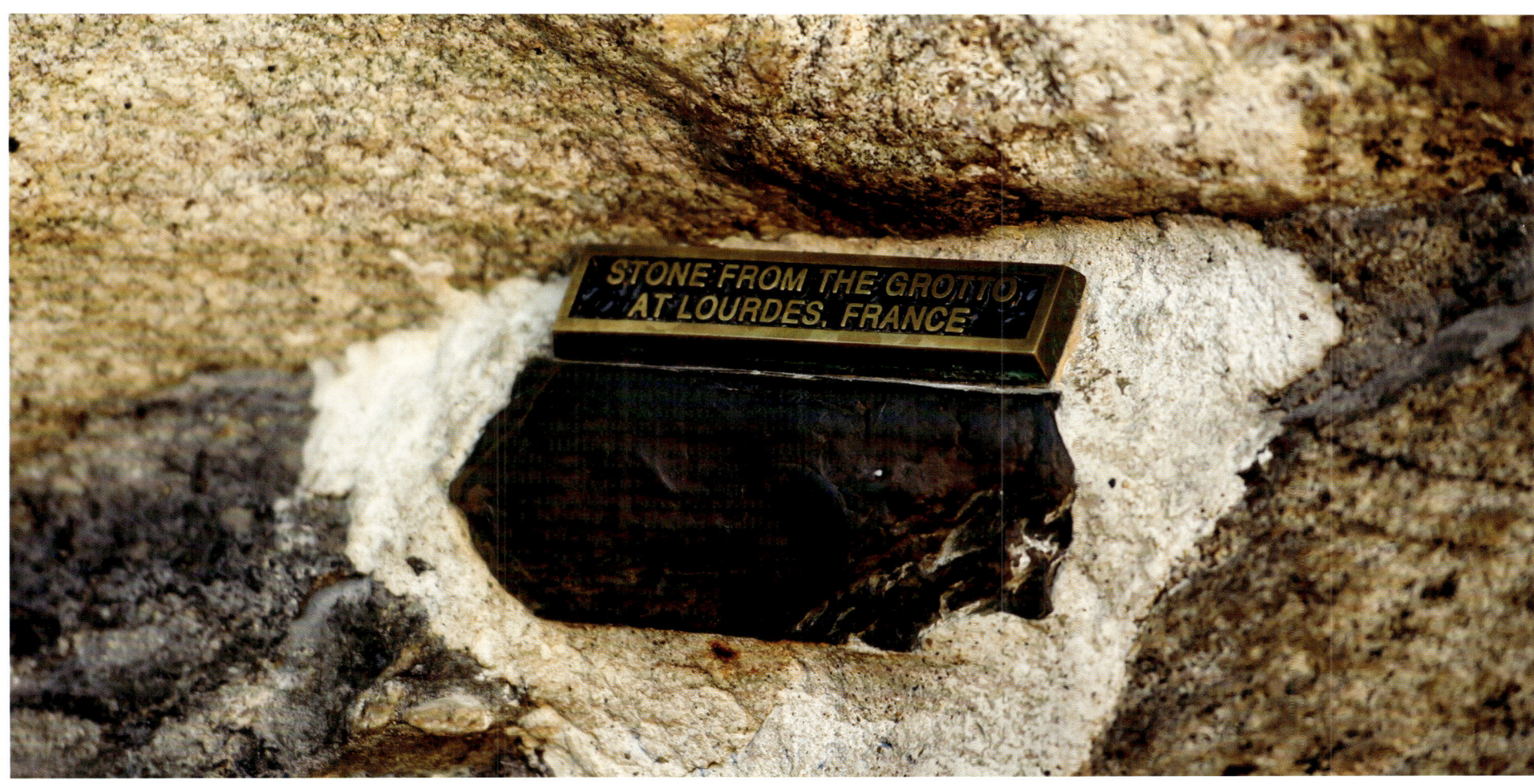

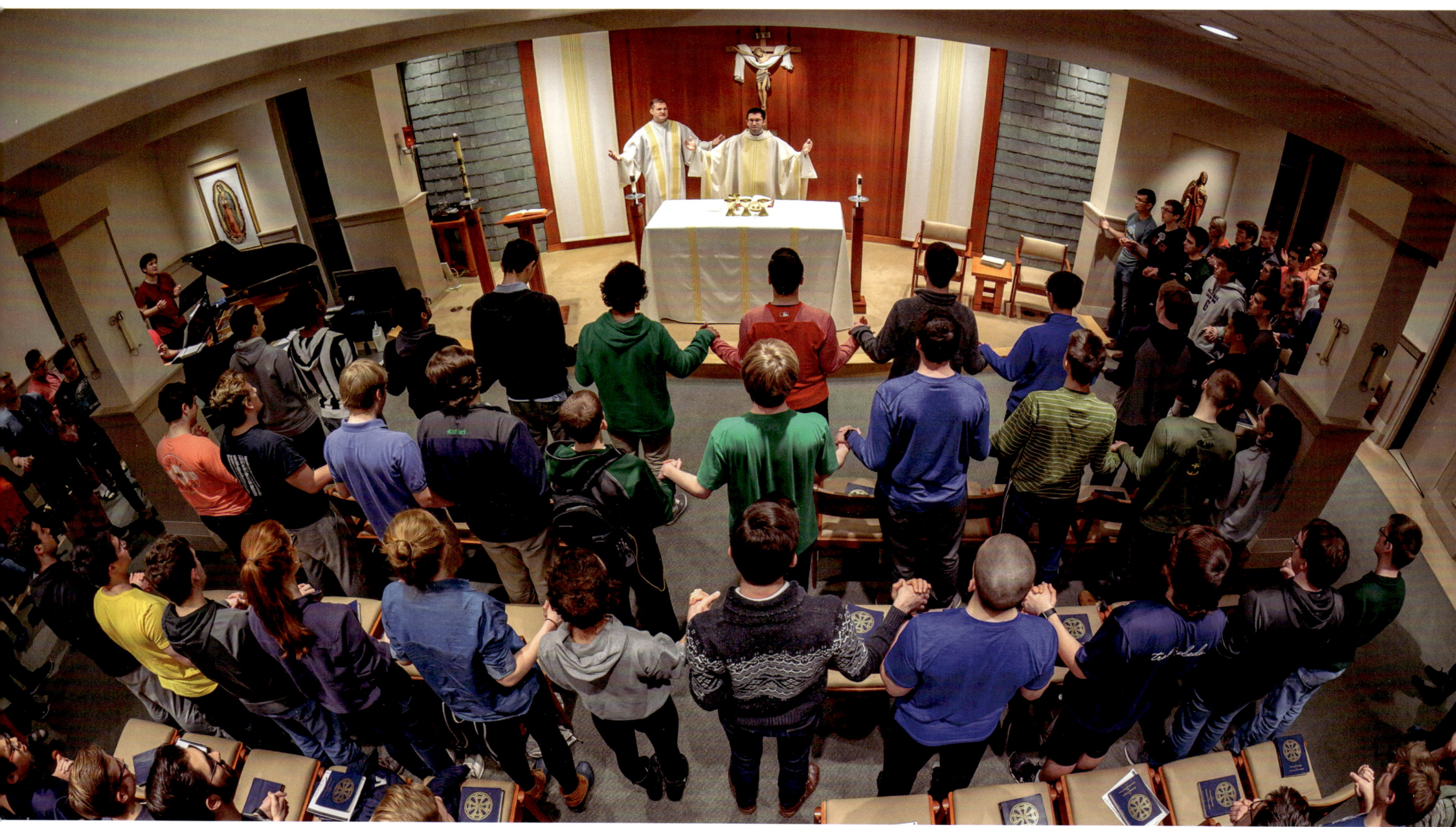

"Never have I found a greater concentration of goodness than on this campus," the longtime professor Ed Fischer once noted, having recalled his service in the military, years as a journalist, and international travel as a writer. "The 'helpfulness quotient' at Notre Dame is indeed high." This legacy is passed to succeeding generations. It's a responsibility and a gift to be part of it, to be animated by the collective industry.

But in the midst of the energy and achievements, the acceleration and expeditiously expanding universe, Notre Dame offers a quiet center. The university fosters an appreciation of contemplation and reflection, of prayer. It understands the need—both personally and institutionally—to occasionally retreat, to stand back and reassess, to rediscover those foundational beliefs that inform all we do here.

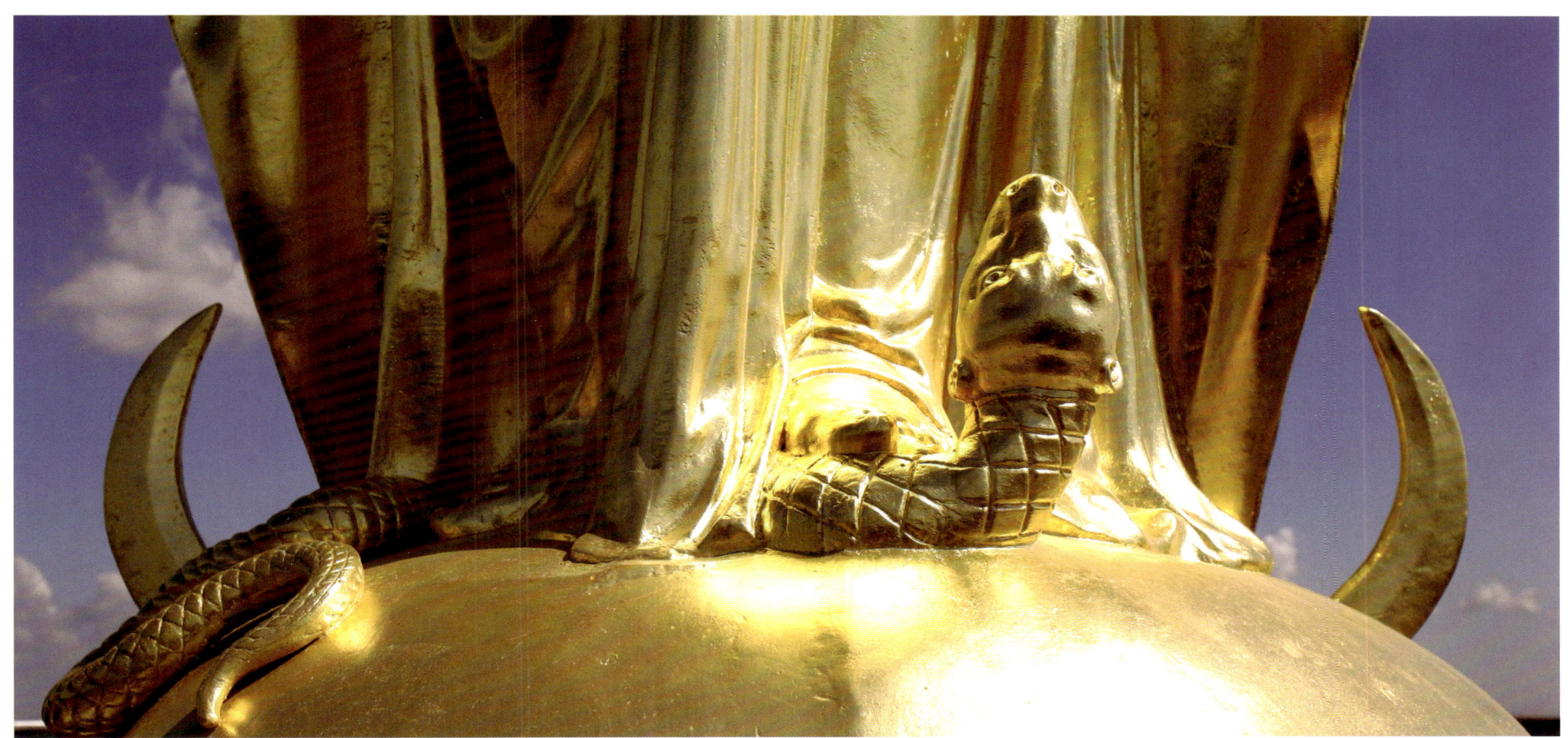

Blessed Basil Moreau, the founder of the Congregation of Holy Cross and the cleric who dispatched Sorin and his confreres to America, was a product of the French Revolution, a convulsion that left two-thirds of the Catholic priests there dead or disappeared. As an antidote to the anti-Catholic fervor, Moreau established a religious congregation of men and women to serve as educators focusing on the mind and heart, supporting family and serving God, the poor, and the afflicted. These themes are woven inextricably into the Notre Dame fabric. The heart and soul and intellect. The life of the mind. Care, compassion, service. Family and God.

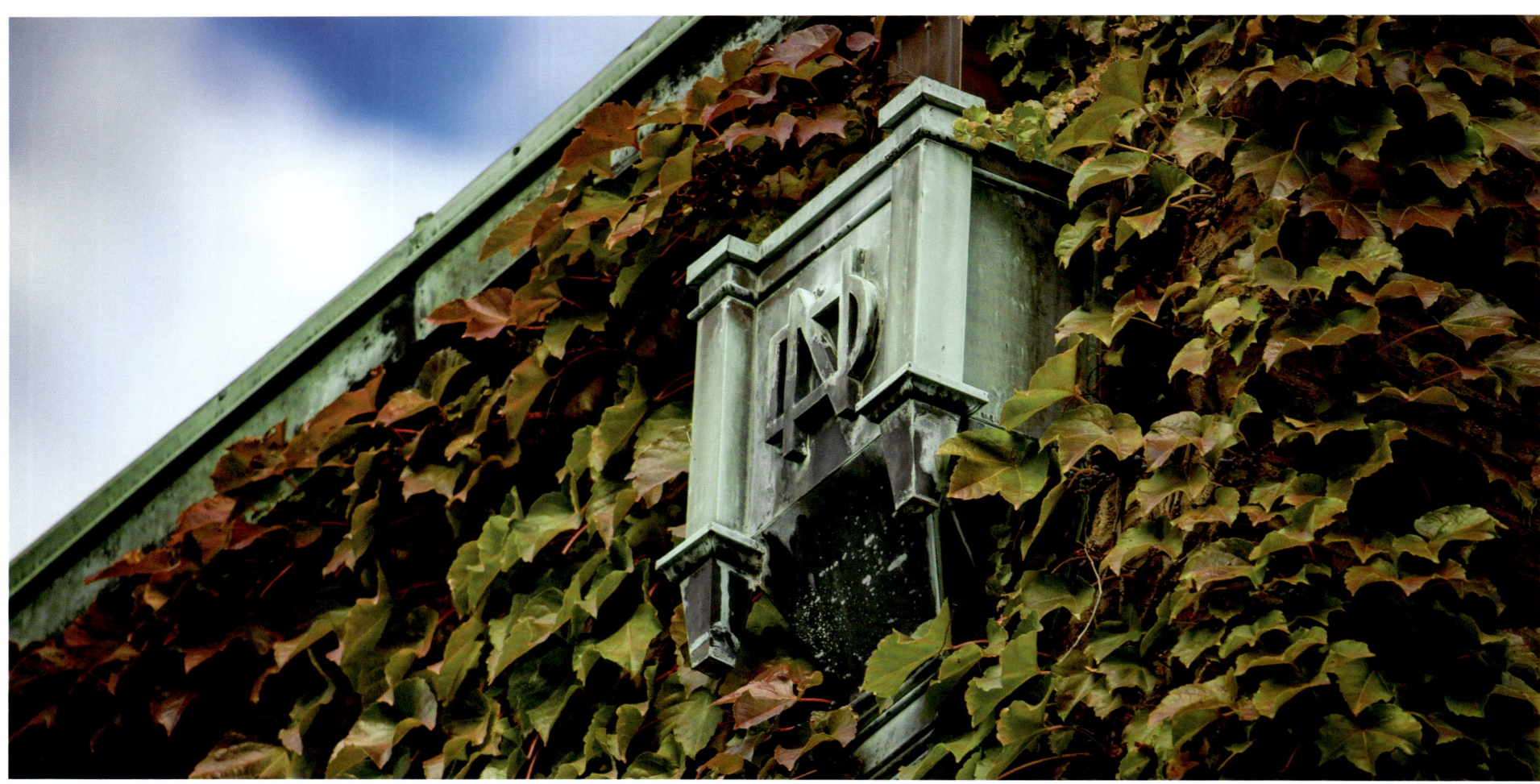

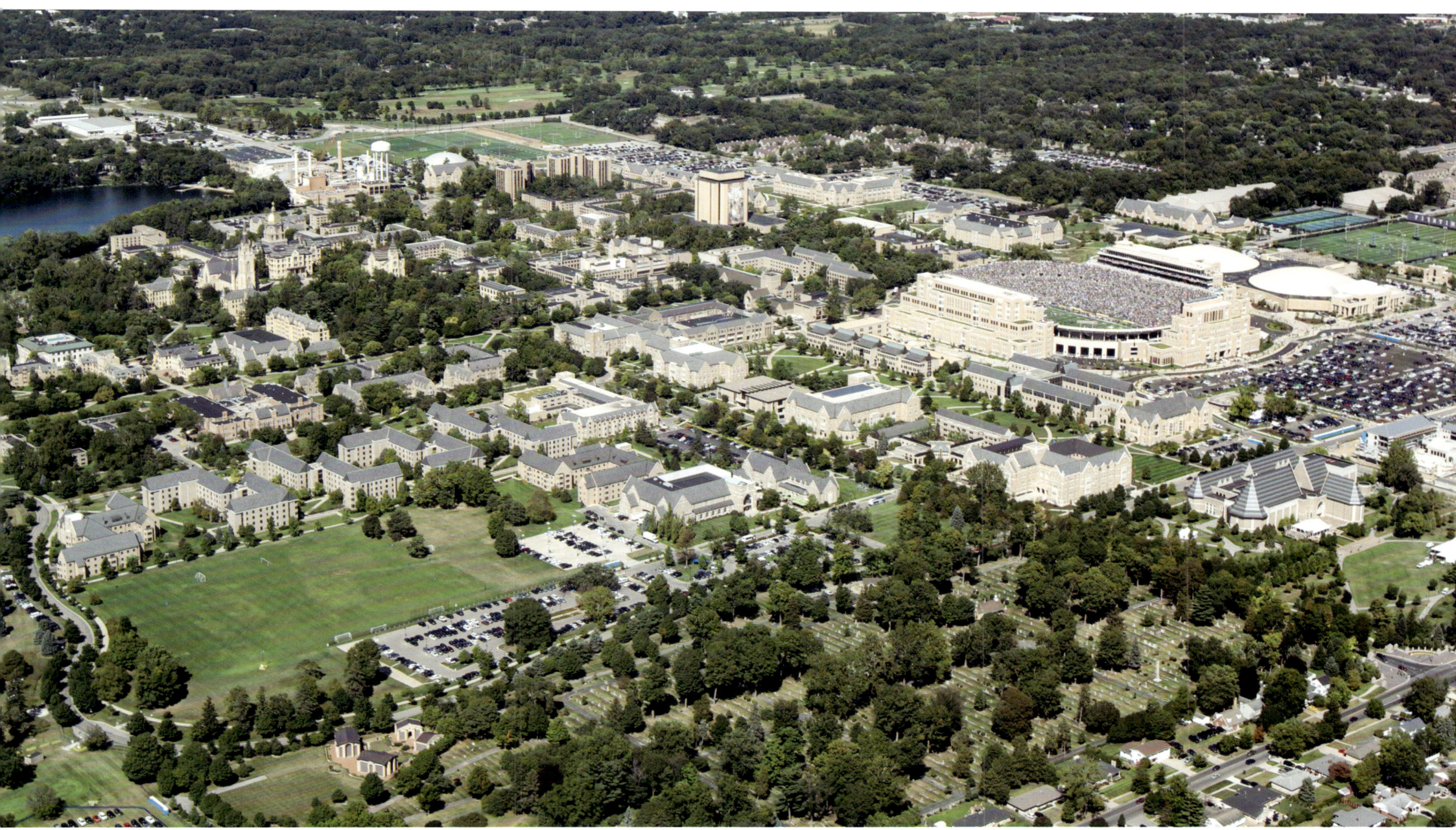

These are the deep-water currents I think about while circling the lakes. There is another layer, too, for me personally, in which these institutional resonances are enduring and clear. Here's what I mean: When I walk the lakes, bending my steps north, east, south, and west, I am mindful of the four directions and what they meant in the prayer life of those native to this land.

When I face or consider the north, I think of winter. Cold and cleansing winds come from the north, laying bare the earth, clearing the landscape; it is a force of purification, those frigid winds sailing the length of Lakes Superior and Michigan down from Canada. The siege of arctic winter drives people indoors, makes for long nights and studious intro-spection. The human world seems to go away; what remains is solitude and an examination of self. It is a time of discernment, of seeing through the things of this world, to find one's place among eternally sustaining truths.

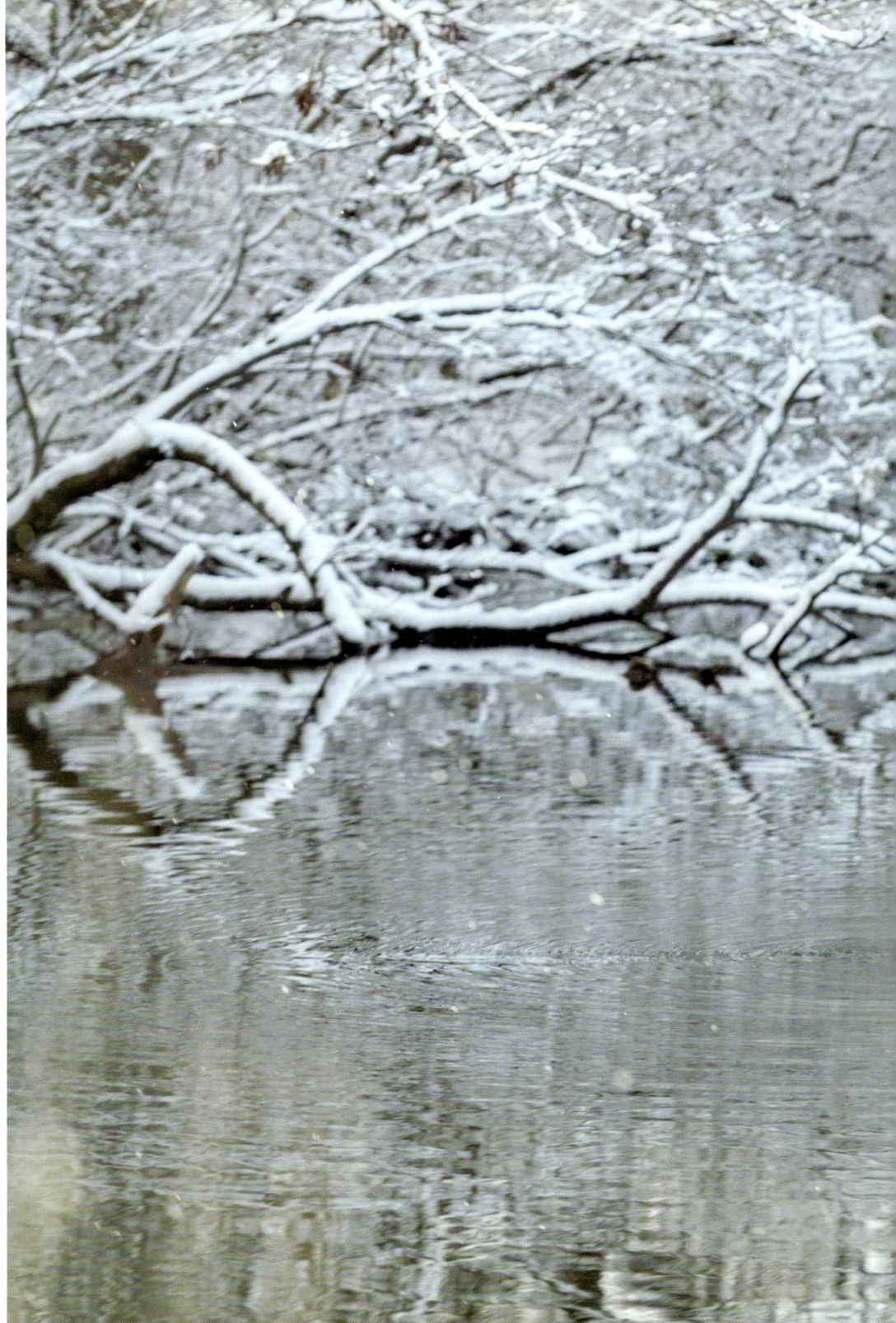

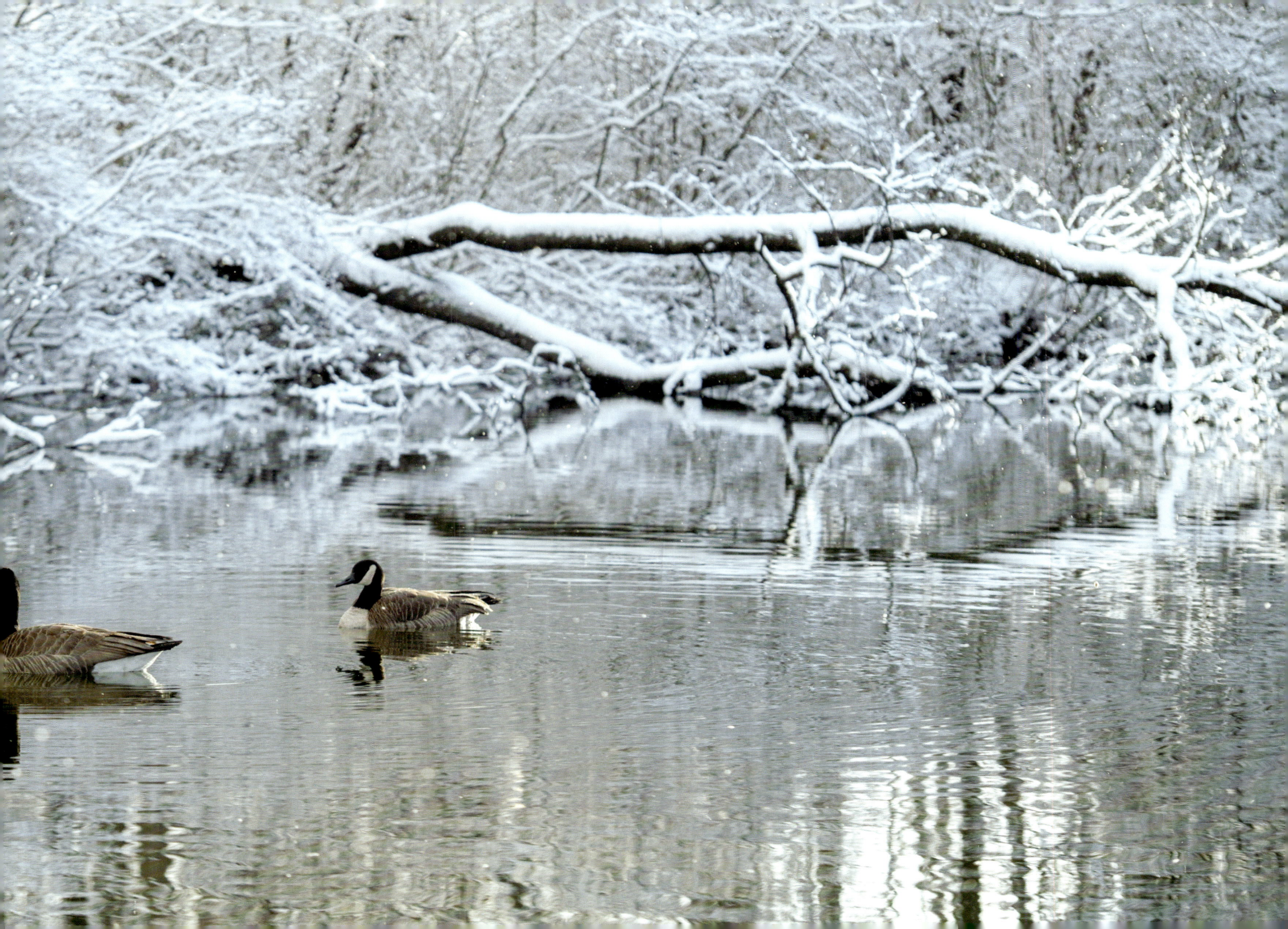

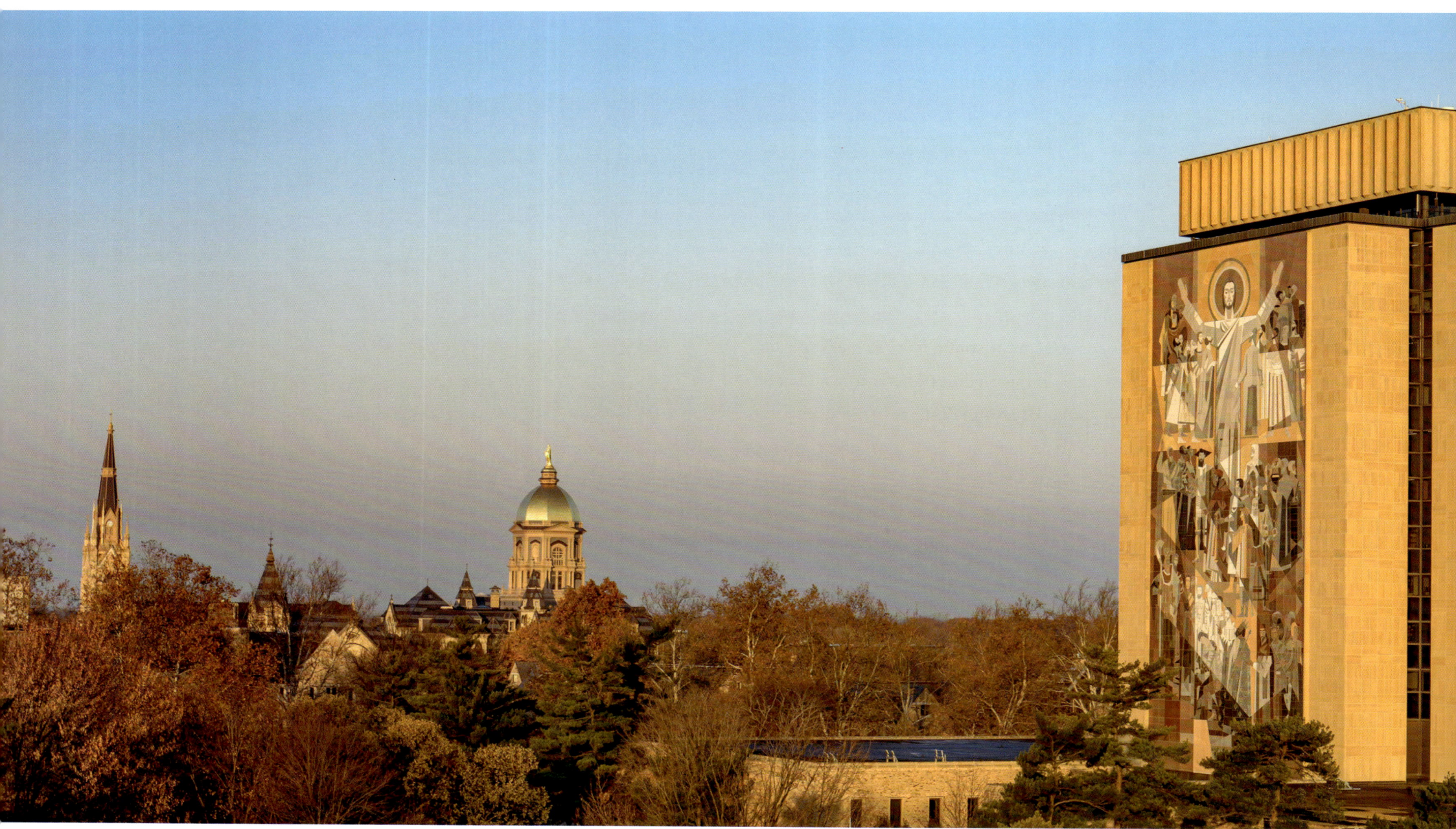

Notre Dame as an institution has a long tradition of being *in* the world but not *of* the world. I often start my walk with such meditations, and to associate the seclusion of winter with the need to periodically sequester oneself, to ensure that all things still sit right, stay true to course.

Of course, the sun comes up in the east, a signal of enlightenment, awareness, newness, and discovery. The spring awakening, the Easter of life. When I face or walk toward the east, I think of these bursts of illumination. I think of knowledge and wisdom, learning and the life of the mind. Classrooms and laboratories, corridors and lunch tables where ideas fly and brains engage, intellects on fire.

Similarly, warm breezes come from the south; it is summer's terrain. And the warmth of summer suggests the qualities of comfort and care, compassion and generosity of spirit. The realm of the heart. The place of community, service, fellowship. The pastoral nature of life together, seeing neighbors in strangers. The Notre Dame family.

Finally the west. Thunderstorms come out of the west, and the strong and turbulent winds that shake the trees and propel dark clouds. Spiritual uprisings. If the north promises the path of purification and the pilgrim's journey through the world, if the east speaks of the mind and the south to the heart, then the west calls out the spirit, the mysterious forces that work in our lives, the radical journey of faith, the Gospel's disruptive call. And just as the other compass points align with the seasons, the west evokes autumn, the approaching winter, that sense of mortality that begs a consideration of one's life with God.

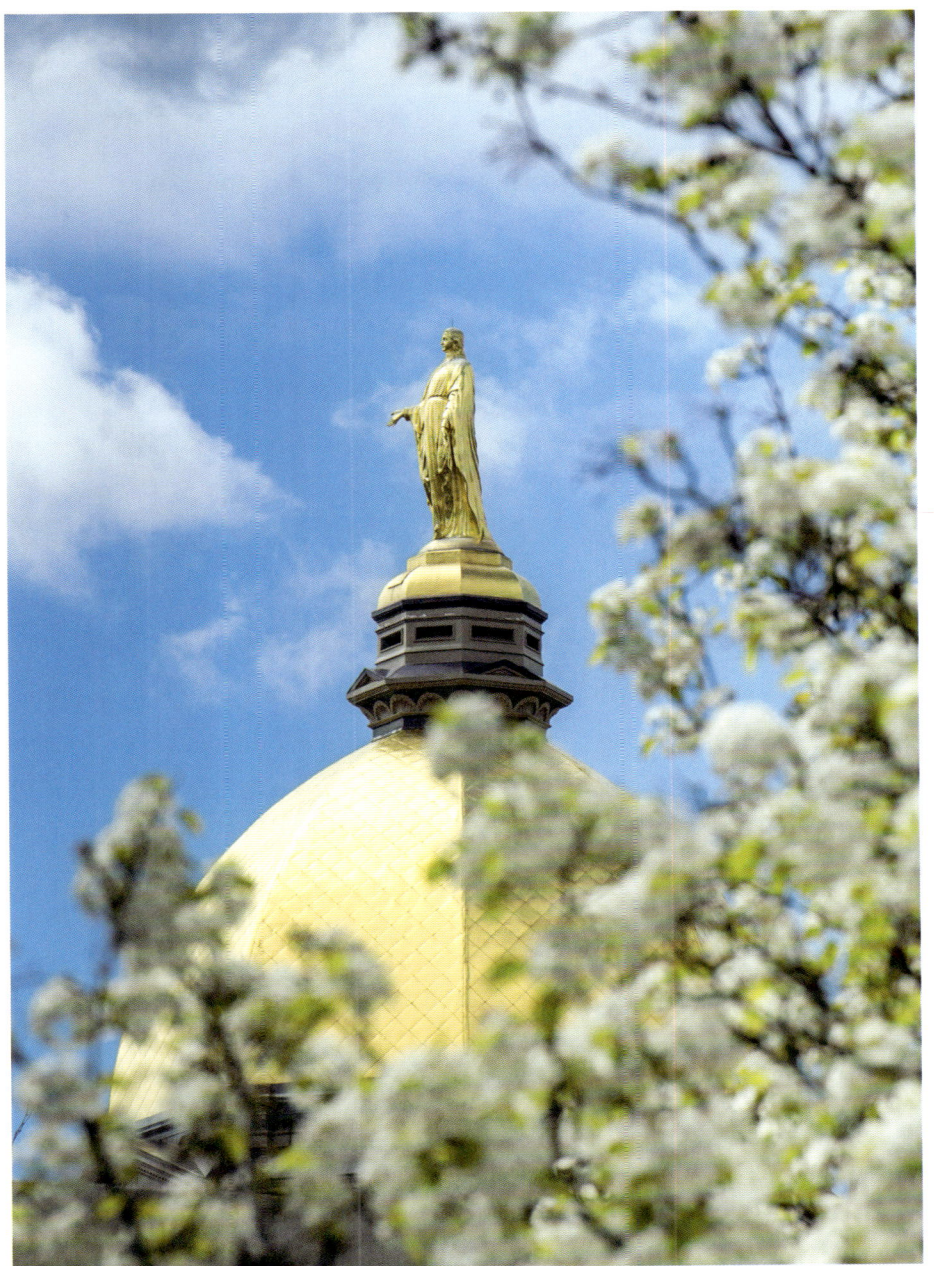

So I carry these thoughts as I walk the lakes, along with a lifetime of memories and my affection for this place called Notre Dame. Notions of Sorin and Moreau and all the good men and women here, those whose blood is in the bricks and those who passed through, leaving gifts. Hesburgh, Griffin, Dunne, O'Malley, Pitz, Werge, Lenz, Conklin, Emil T., Sedlack, Suddes—we all have our lists.

I have been around long enough to have seen a good many changes here. There are women in Farley, an office building where I once played Bookstore Basketball, a residence hall on the intramural football field, sumptuous feasts where once was served rainbow meat. Flanner and Grace are office buildings, Senior Bar long gone, cell phones an invasive species that has overrun the quads, classrooms, and choice eateries, while also giving everyone immediate access to people, knowledge, and news events throughout the world. Alumni returning to campus say they don't recognize the place; students enrolling these days are brilliant, exceptional, committed earth-shakers. The world is better because of all of them.

Notre Dame has been transformed in many ways—the abundance of research, the scholarly reach, the expanding infrastructure, the vitality and quality of the faculty, the commodious resources. Some are nostalgic for a hallowed past, a simpler time. Some see in this transformation not a deviation from a longstanding institutional mission but the result of decades-long advancement, lofty aspirations, abounding generosity, and the bold realization of dreams first conceived by a visionary priest who happily landed at this parcel of earth surrounding lakes with faith, hope, and fire in his heart.

So I go back to the lakes. Others may rightly point to all that has happened here, the impressive growth and world-changing accomplishments, the graduates produced, the ambitions fulfilled. And there is great sustenance and pride in that robust enterprise. But there is, too, in those trails around the lakes—and in the air and light and hidden campus corners—a presence, a peace, and the meanings from which the adventure is born. The place has a quiet soul that deserves careful tending.

Kerry Temple '74

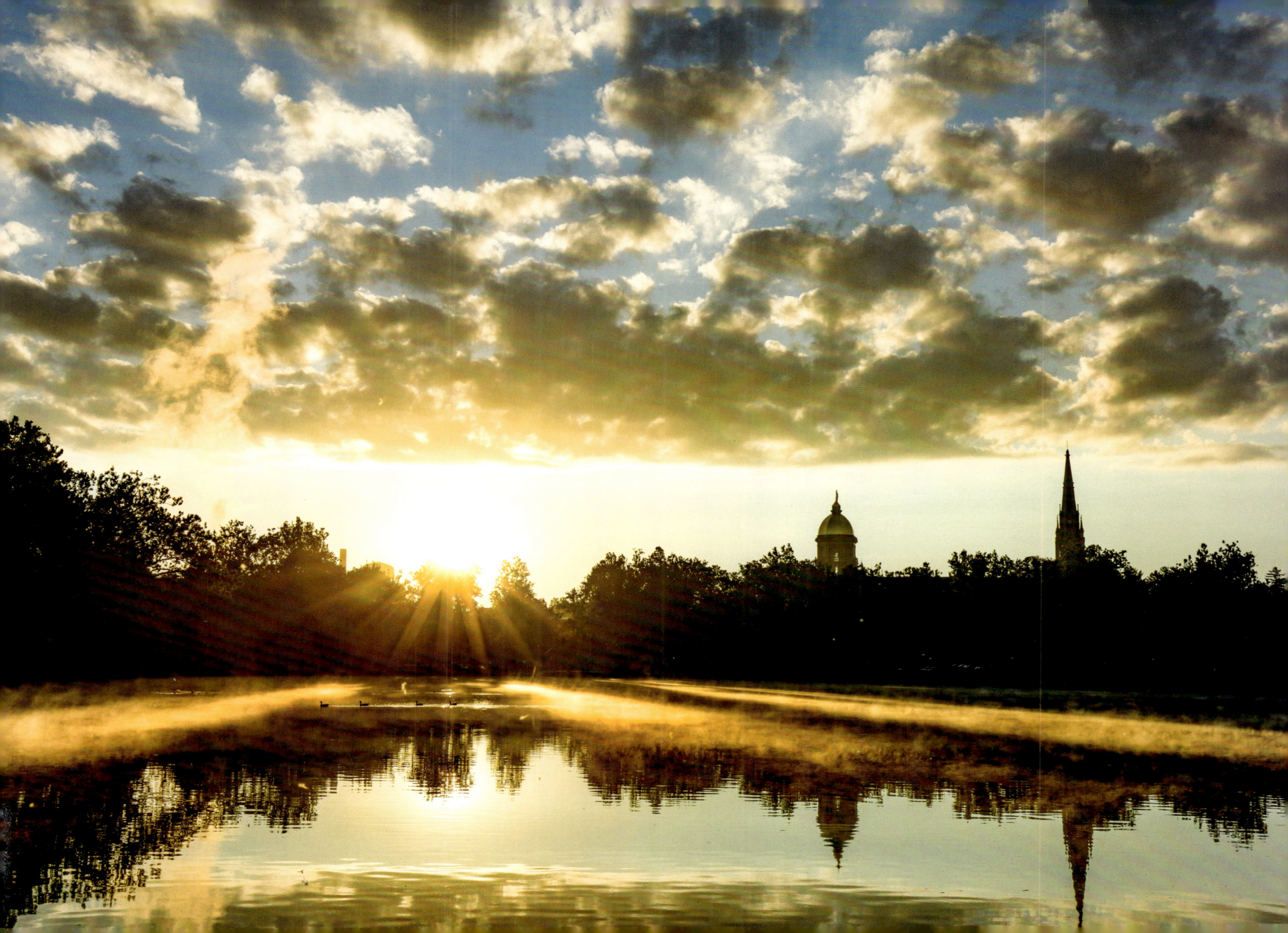

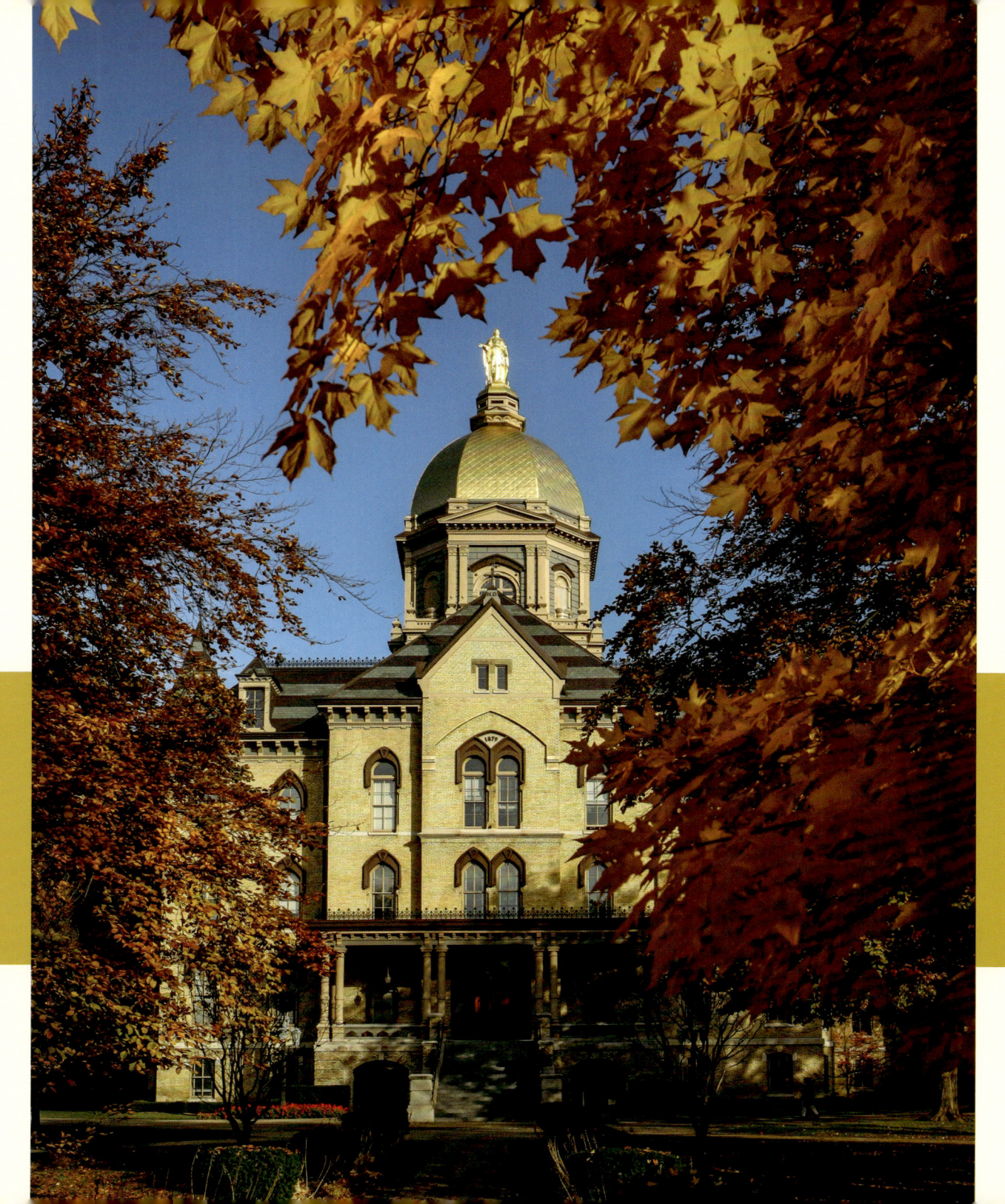

Outlined against a blue-gray October sky, the Four Horsemen rode again. In dramatic lore they are known as Famine, Pestilence, Destruction and Death. These are only aliases. Their real names are Stuhldreher, Miller, Crowley and Layden. They formed the crest of the South Bend cyclone before which another fighting Army football team was swept over the precipice at the Polo Grounds yesterday afternoon as 55,000 spectators peered down on the bewildering panorama spread on the green plain below.

—Grantland Rice, writing in the
New York Herald Tribune,
October 18, 1924

AUTUMN

At Notre Dame summer turns to fall in a weekend. The campus surges into motion as 10,000 students arrive from points all over the globe. There's an infusion of energy, an insurgency of youth, a whirling carnival of collegiate commotion. Lines of SUVs and minivans navigate narrow passageways (it's a walker's campus), and grins and hugs rekindle spirited friendships. Homemade signs and yellow-jacket ushers direct newcomers to thirty residence halls. Parents of first-year students stand by, watch, carry boxes, lift, embrace, bid farewell—with pride and tears welling simultaneously. Their sons and daughters are on the ledge of tomorrow, hardly looking back. But I watch. And I see the letting go, and understand the eighteen years of worry, love, and labor to move these young people toward their dreams. For many that dream was admission here, to an elite institution of higher learning, one that educates and cares for, guides and launches. It is a poignant threshold, and I cannot observe these little dramas of growing up and turning loose without sensing that familial accomplishment, that sinking loss, and that perennial prayer for hopeful horizons.

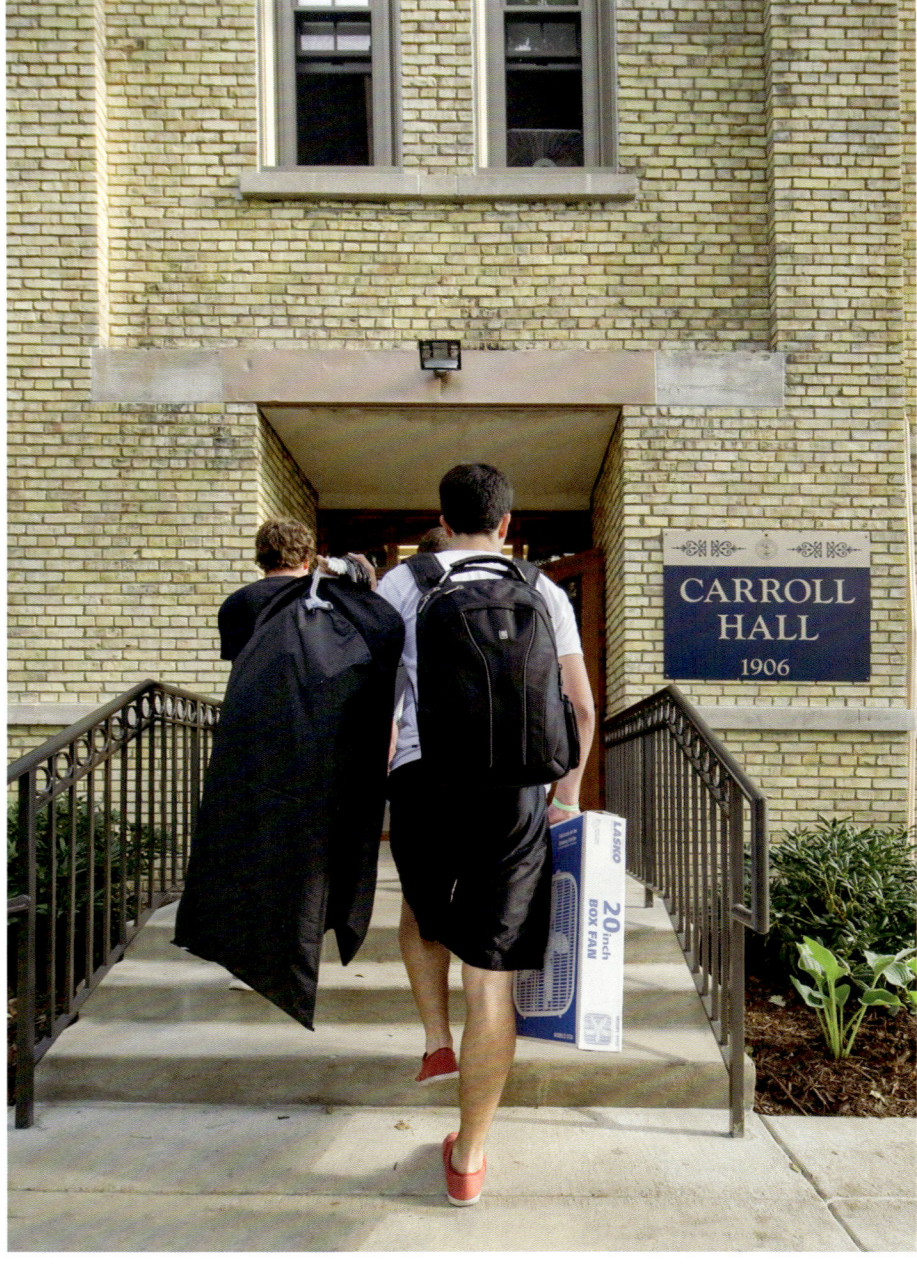

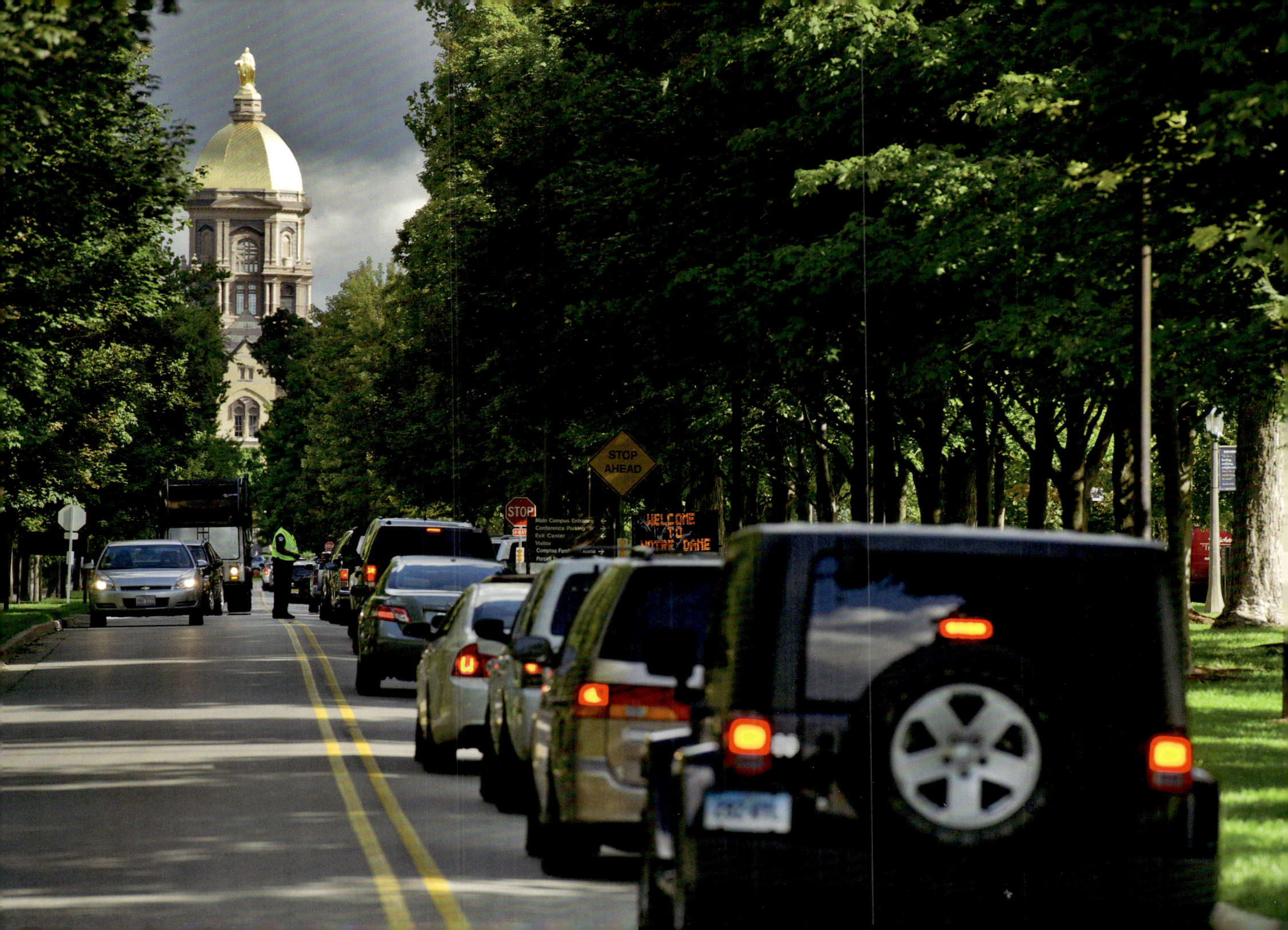

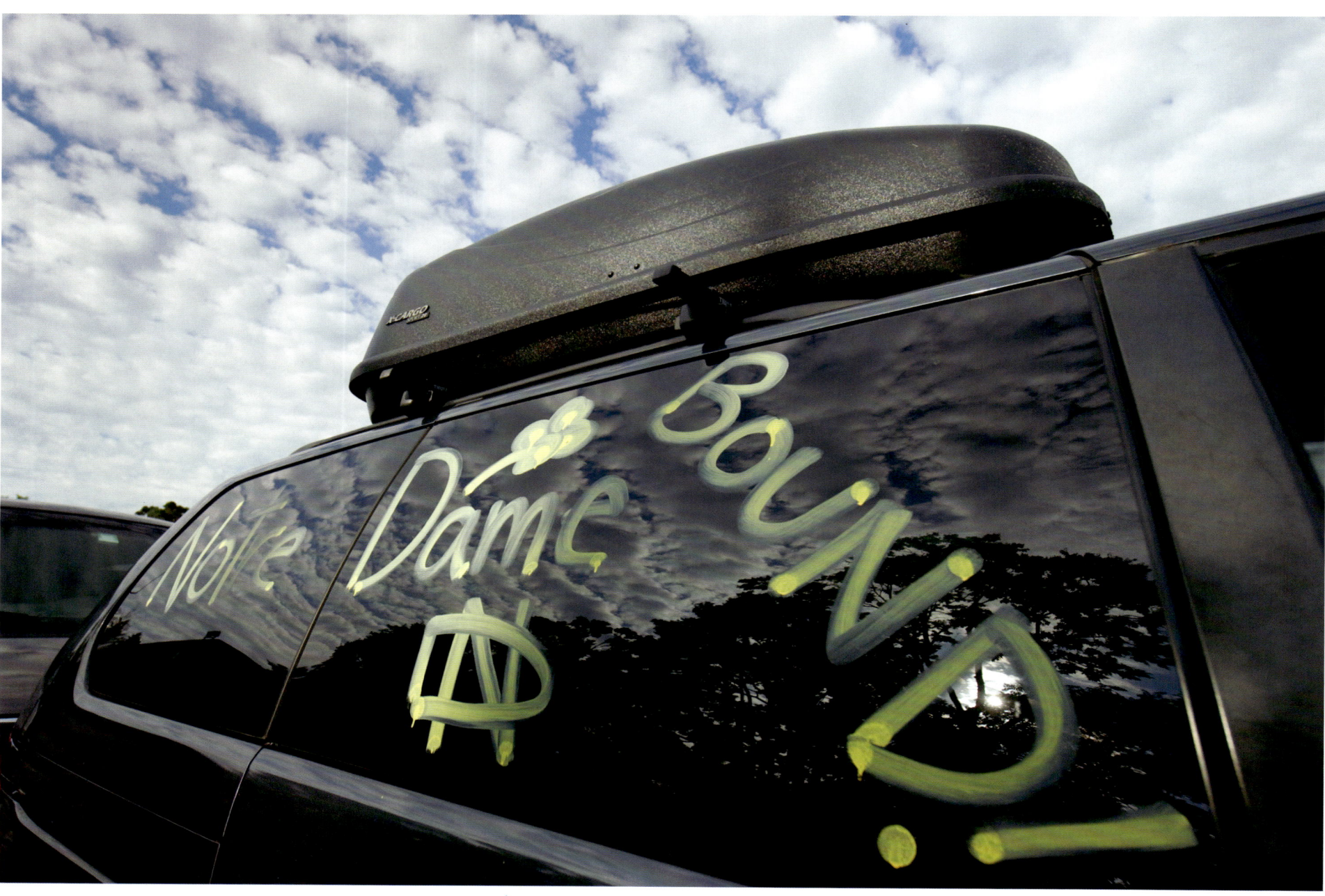

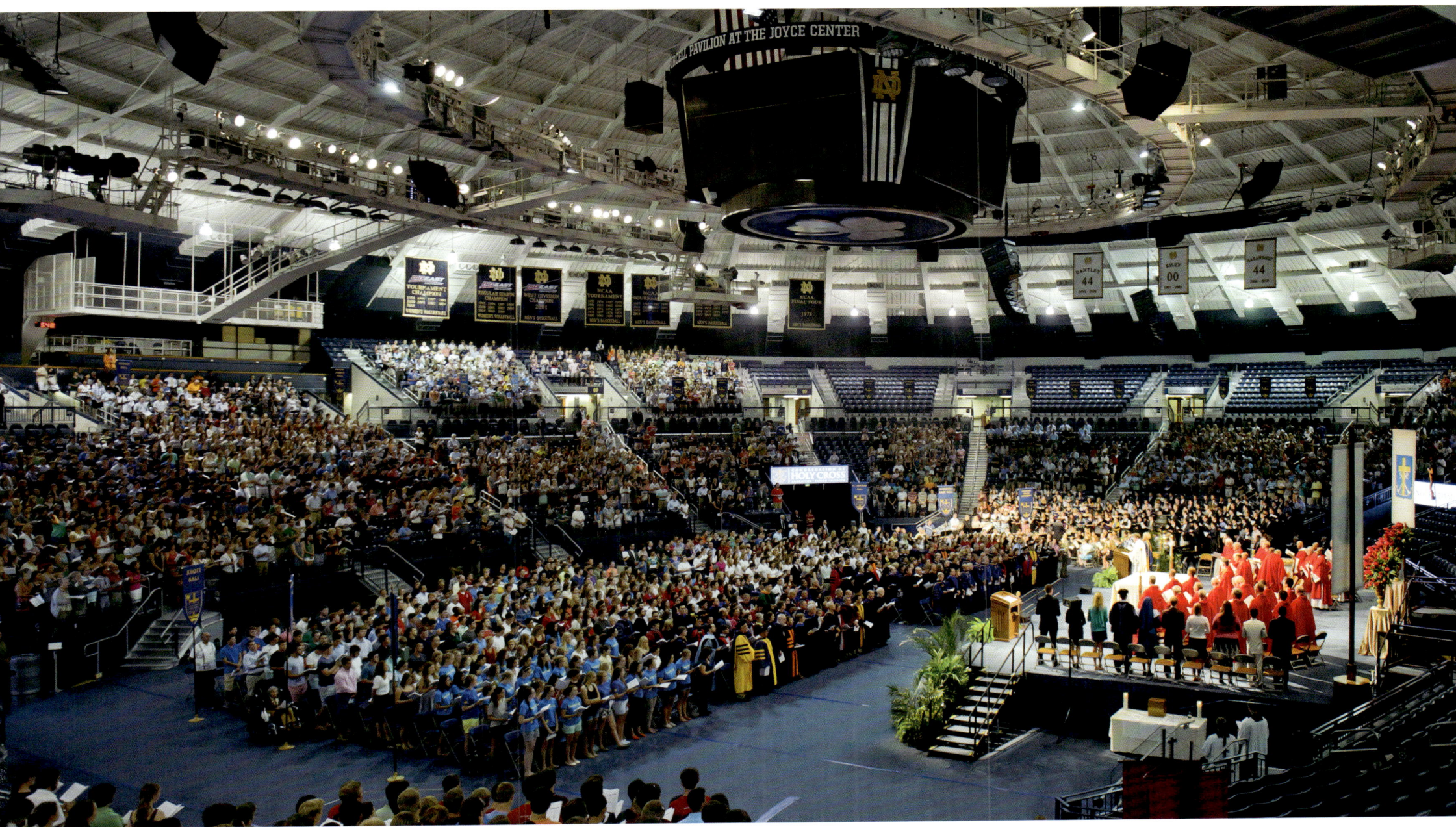

Notre Dame is all about beginnings. It is where young people—idealistic, earnest, talented, intent—come to launch their dreams, their careers, their entrance into the wider world. From here they embark upon their expeditions into various fields of study, professional opportunities, global issues, the complicated give-and-take of human relationships. Faculty, with an infectious passion for research and scholarship, become the mentors, scouts, and visionaries, the role models for the academic enterprise and its sense of exploration, examination, experimentation. Each class, each book, each day is new . . . and each holds promise for what tomorrow might bring. The excitement is nearly palpable, the energy obvious and abundant.

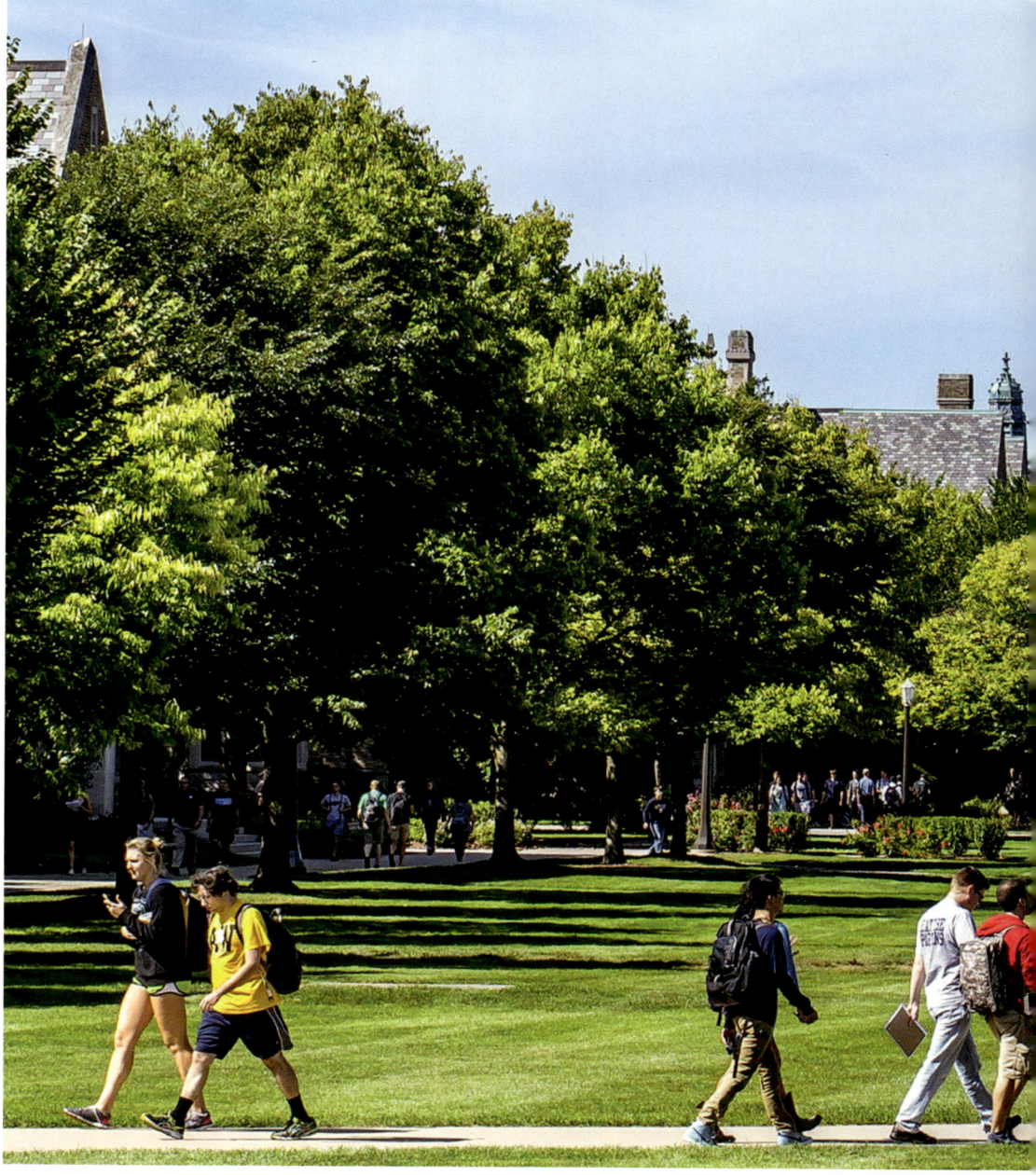

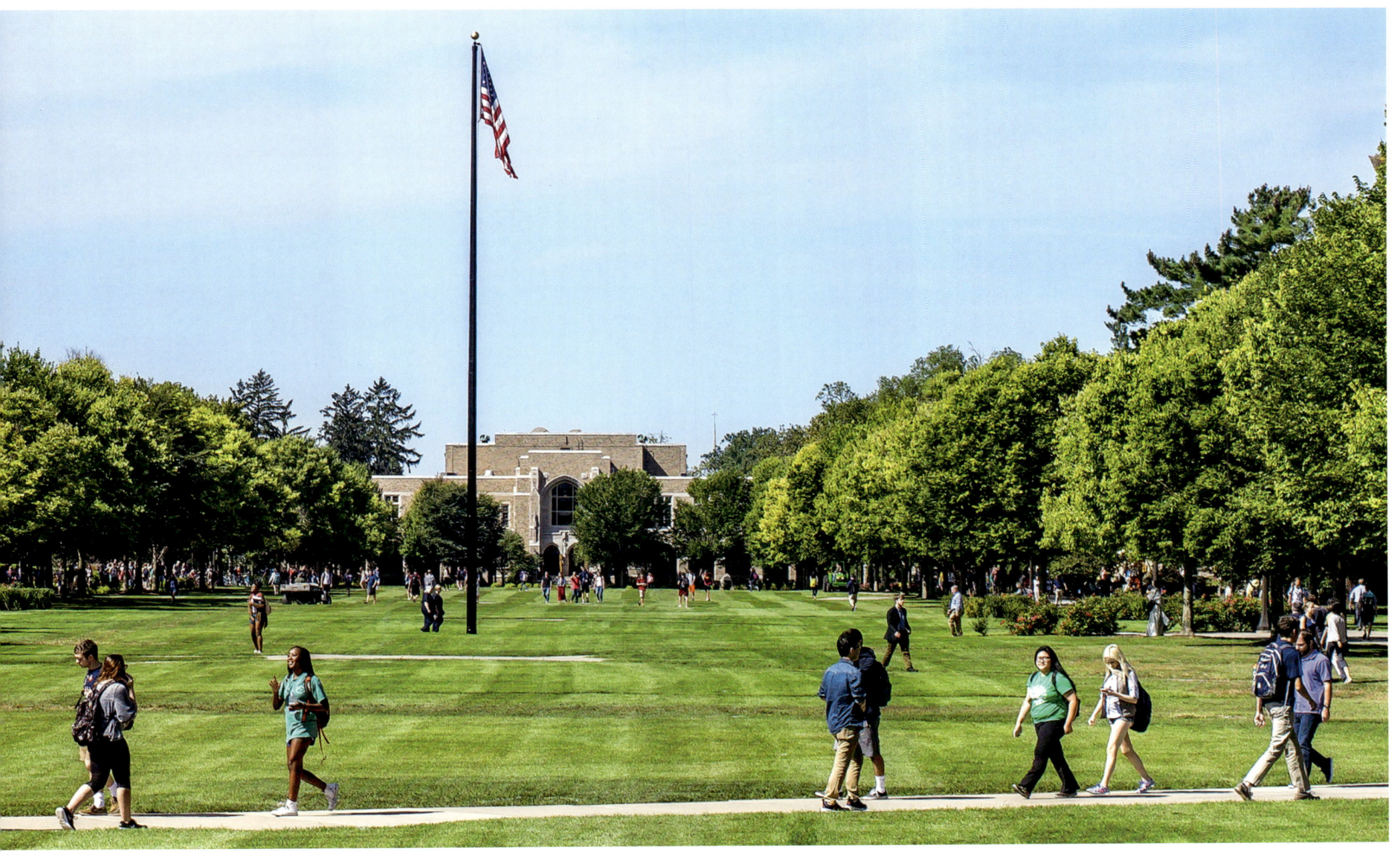

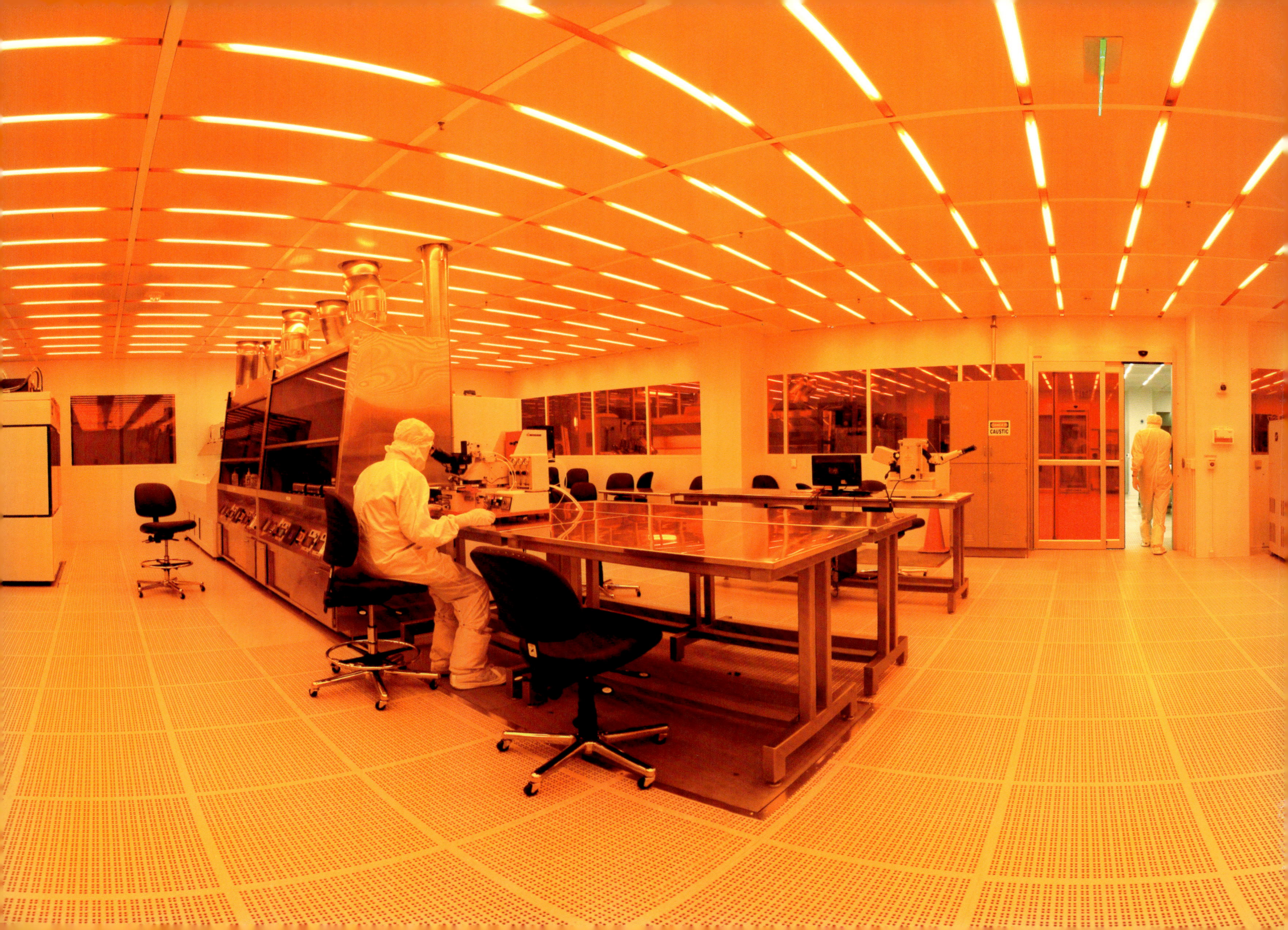

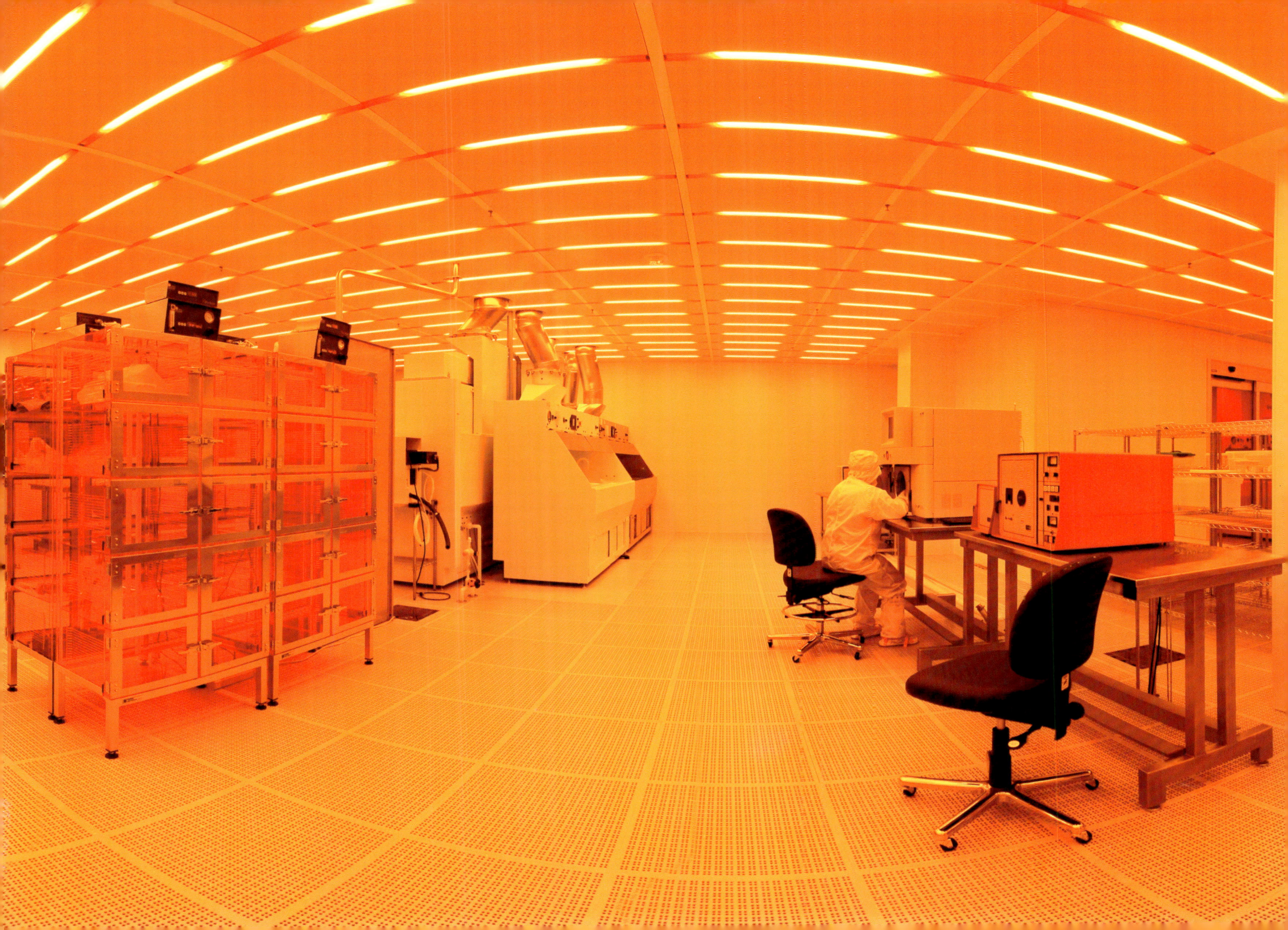

"Parents send us their young," the longtime art professor Bob Leader once explained, "because they still believe that this is a special place, a place with an intimate chemistry between student and teacher, and between those two and God Almighty. While concerned that their offspring acquire employable skills, the parents trust that their children will also be marked by encounters with passionate souls who love learning and beauty for themselves, and who love the faith of their fathers."

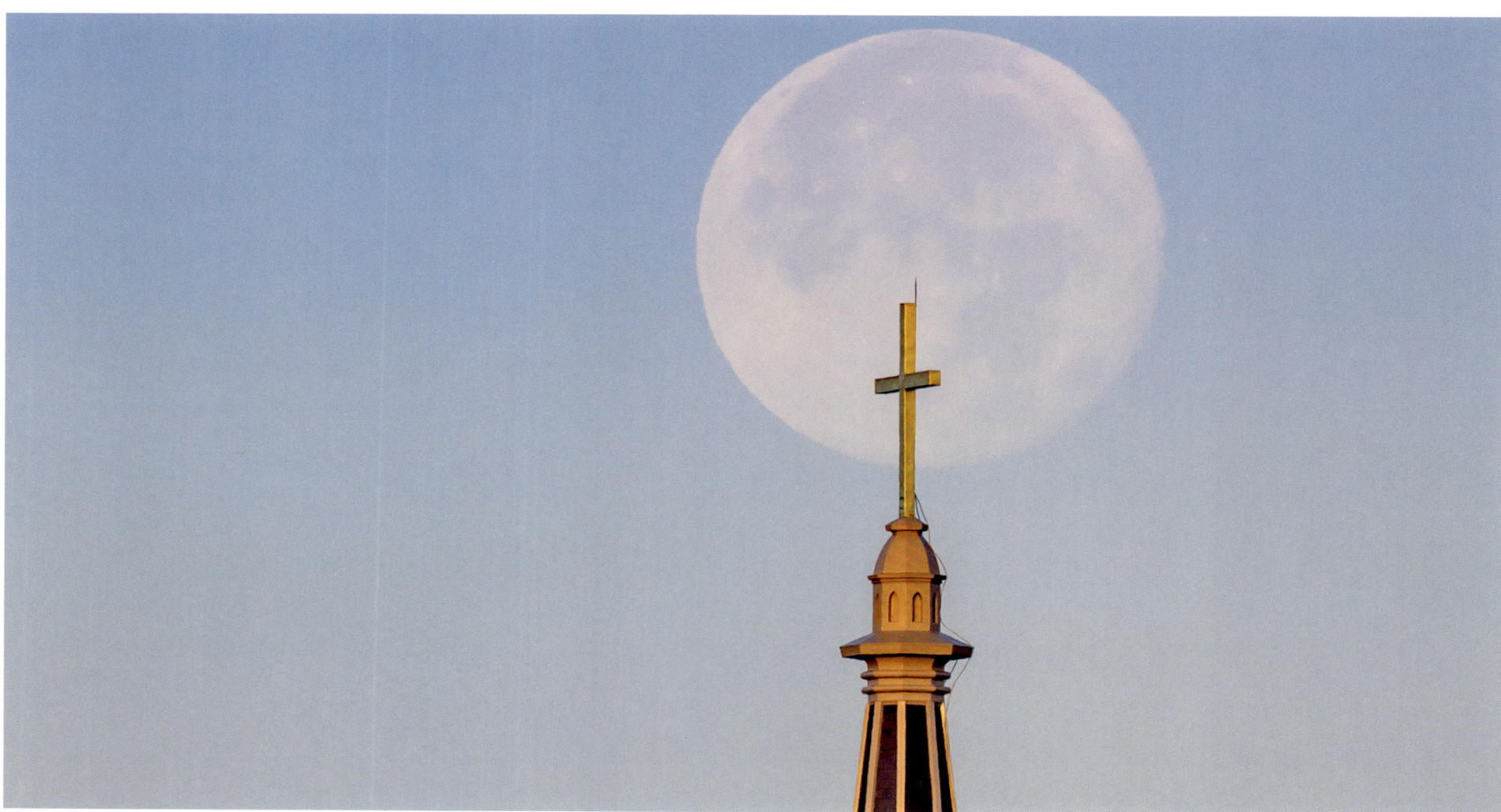

It does not take long for the giddy school-year lift-off to settle into the quotidian routines of academic life, the cycles of classes, papers, tests, and readings. Lab work in Jordan or Fitzpatrick, group presentations in Mendoza, late nights in the studios of Reilly where, a century ago, a young chemistry student named Knute Rockne assisted Father Julius Nieuwland, the discoverer of synthetic rubber. But there are shining October days when the sky is radiantly blue and the trees are aflame in yellows and golds, burnt orange and crimson. It's a dazzling display of nature's turning, the fireworks transition from emerald green to autumn harvest, with whole piles of dry, crackling leaves to walk through, kicking. These are windblown, sun-bathed days—all susceptible to the intrusion of those surprising holy moments.

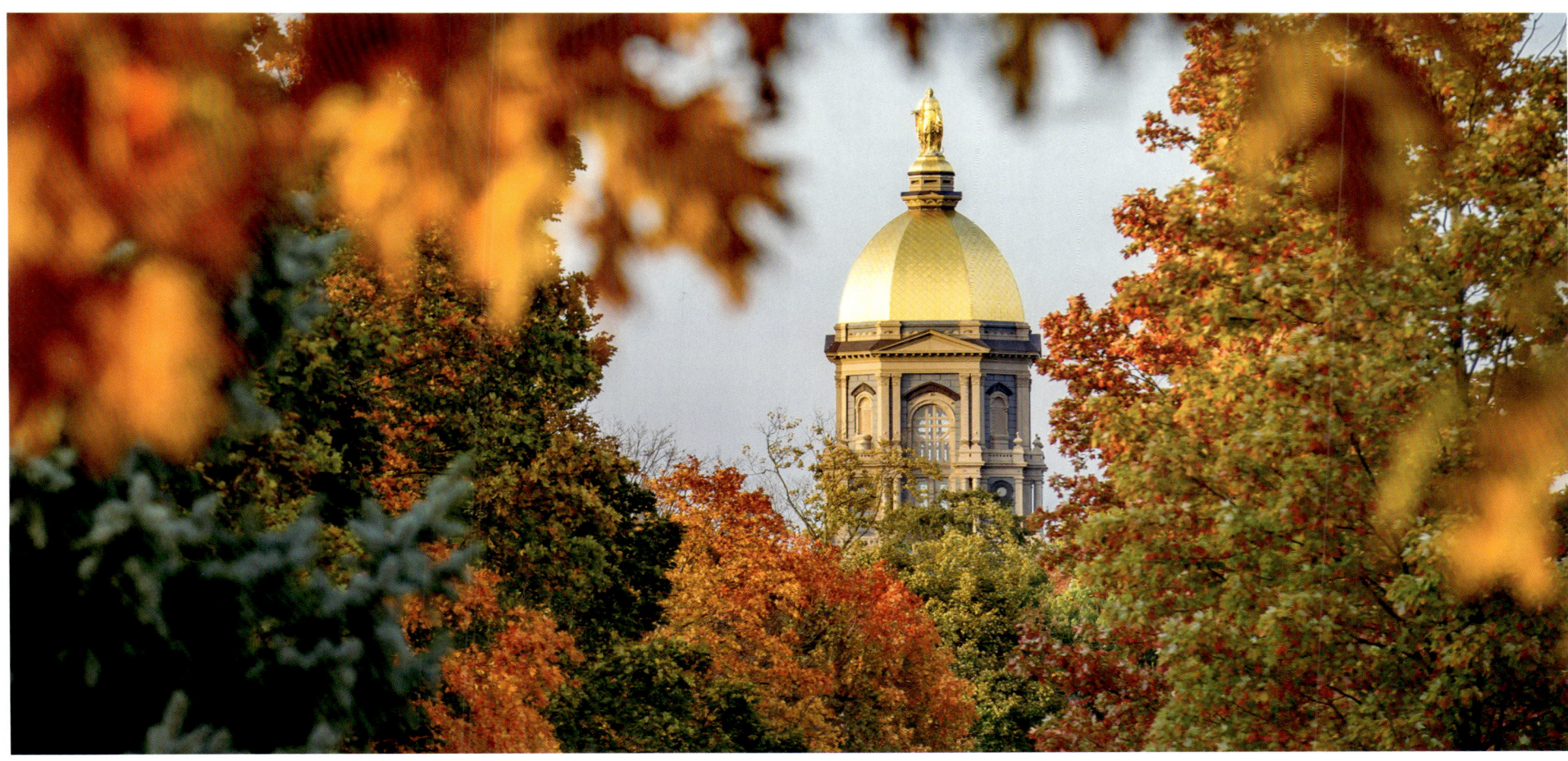

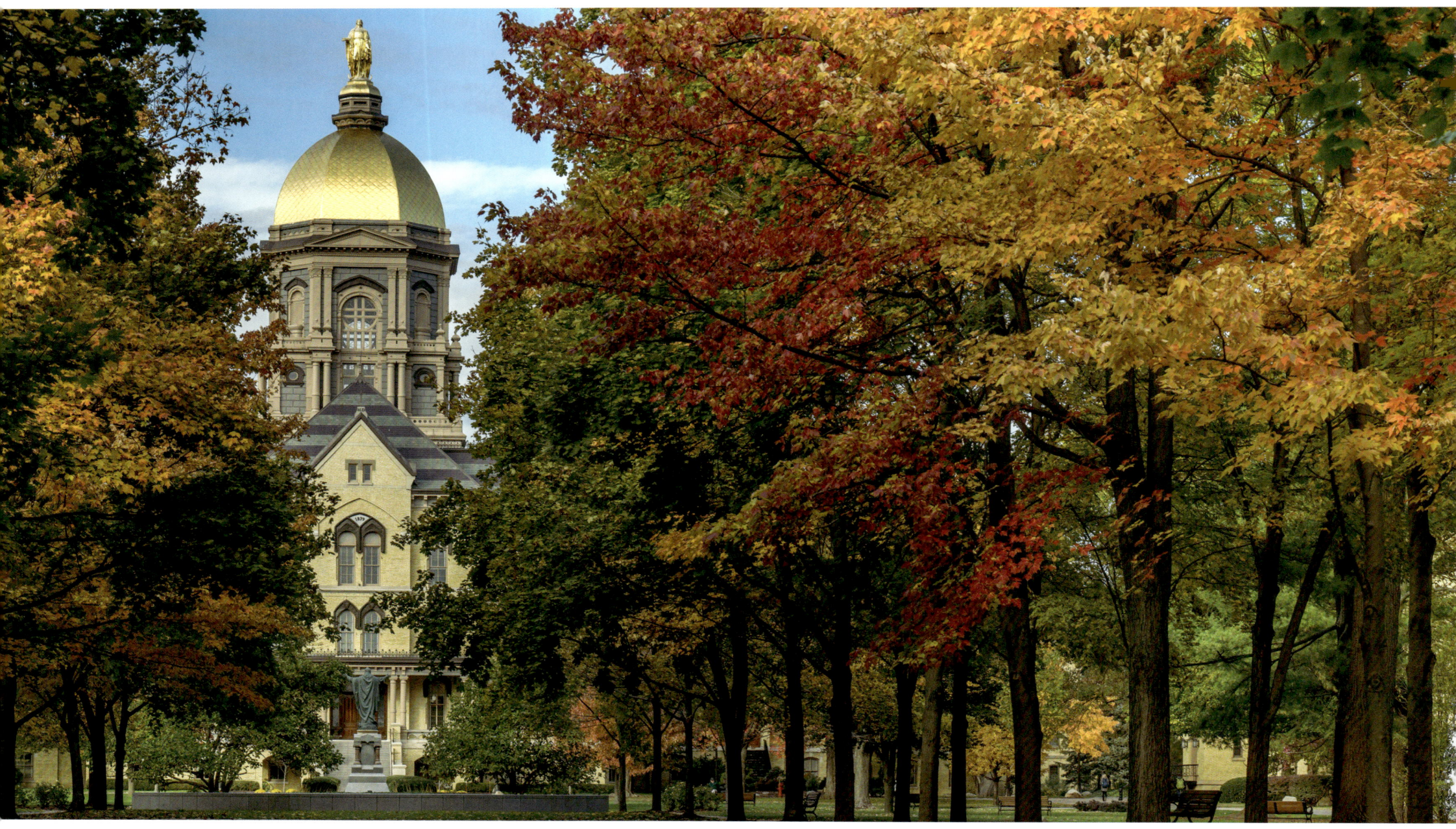

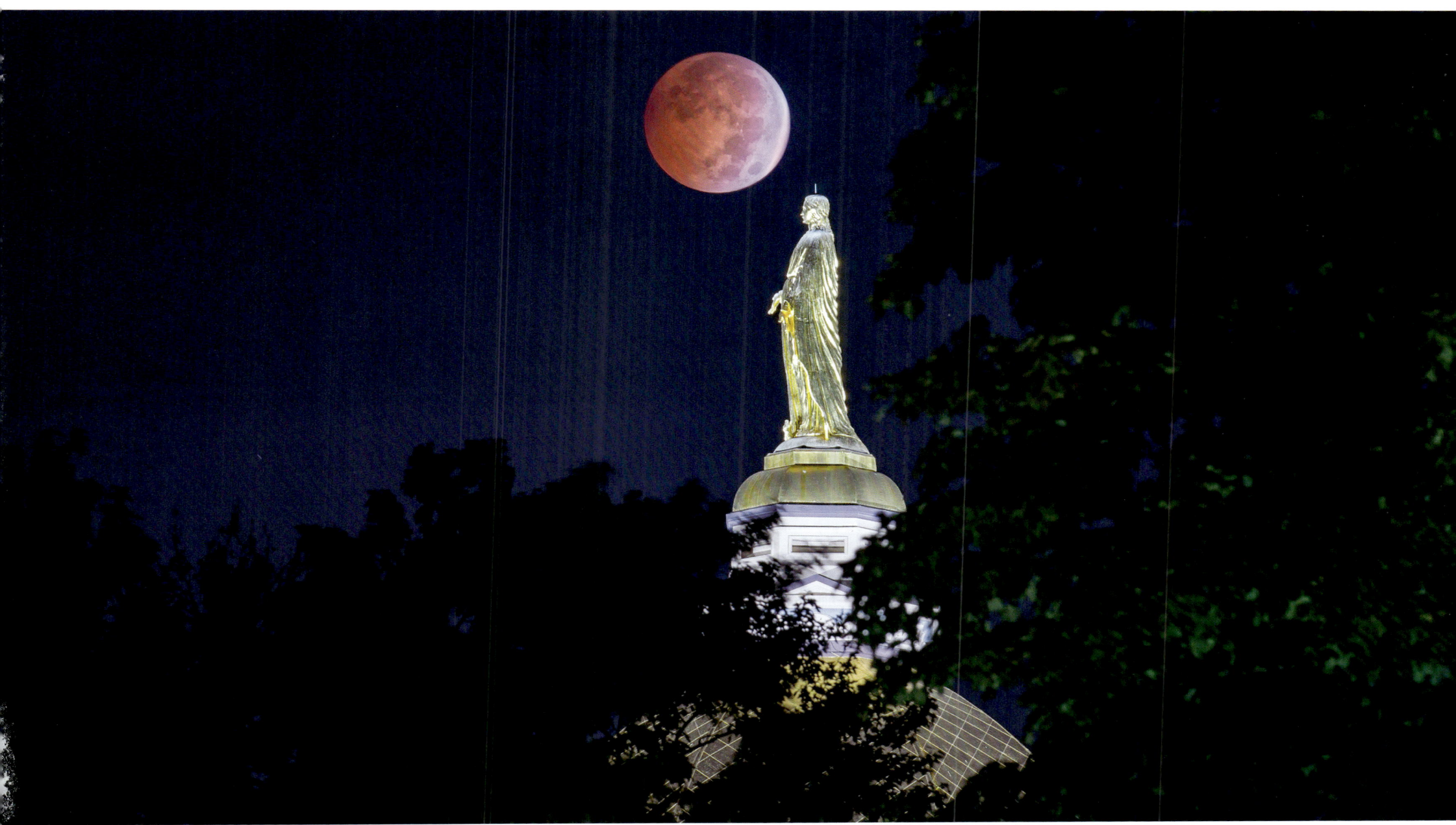

"When you walked," wrote Richard Sullivan in *Notre Dame: Reminiscences of an Era*, "you were surrounded by the place, by an atmosphere, by a whole embracing, exciting, confirming tradition. Down a flight of stairs, around a bend, in the hall chapel, there was God."

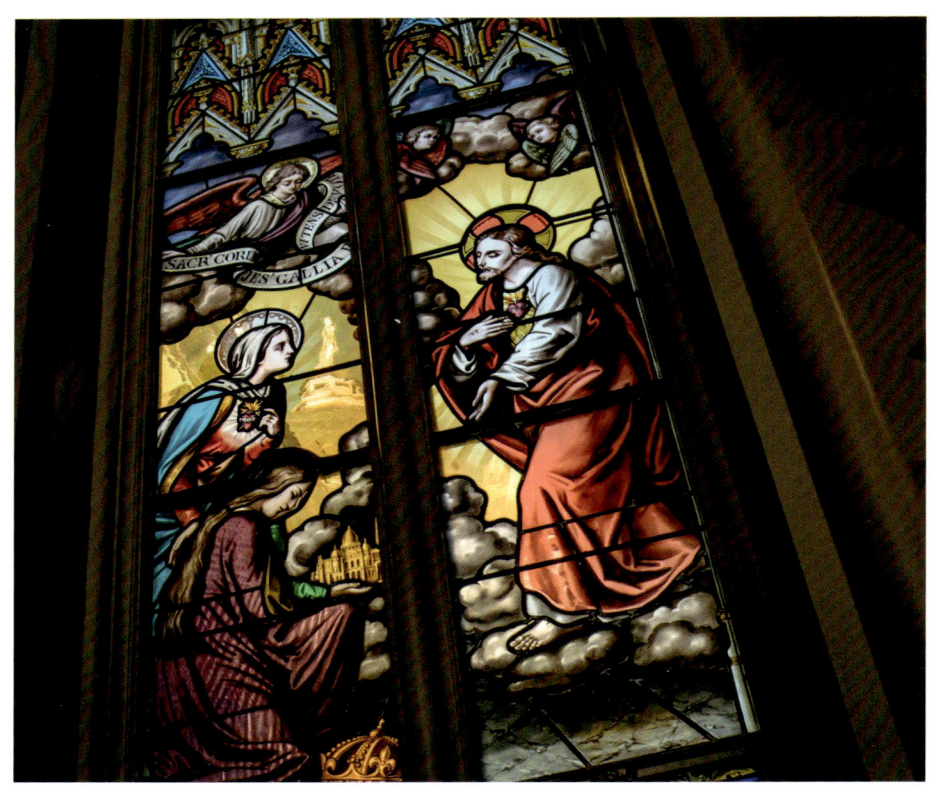

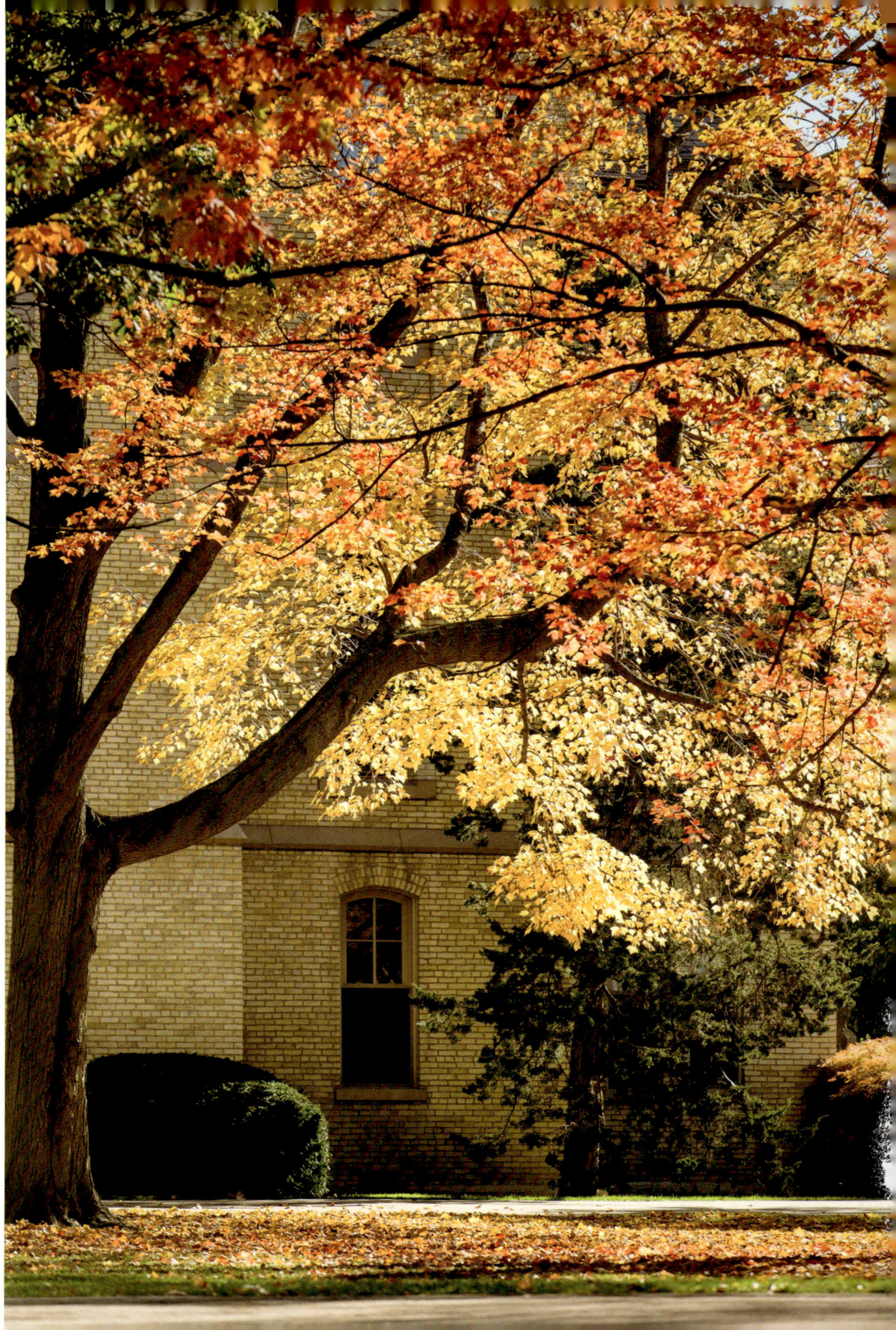

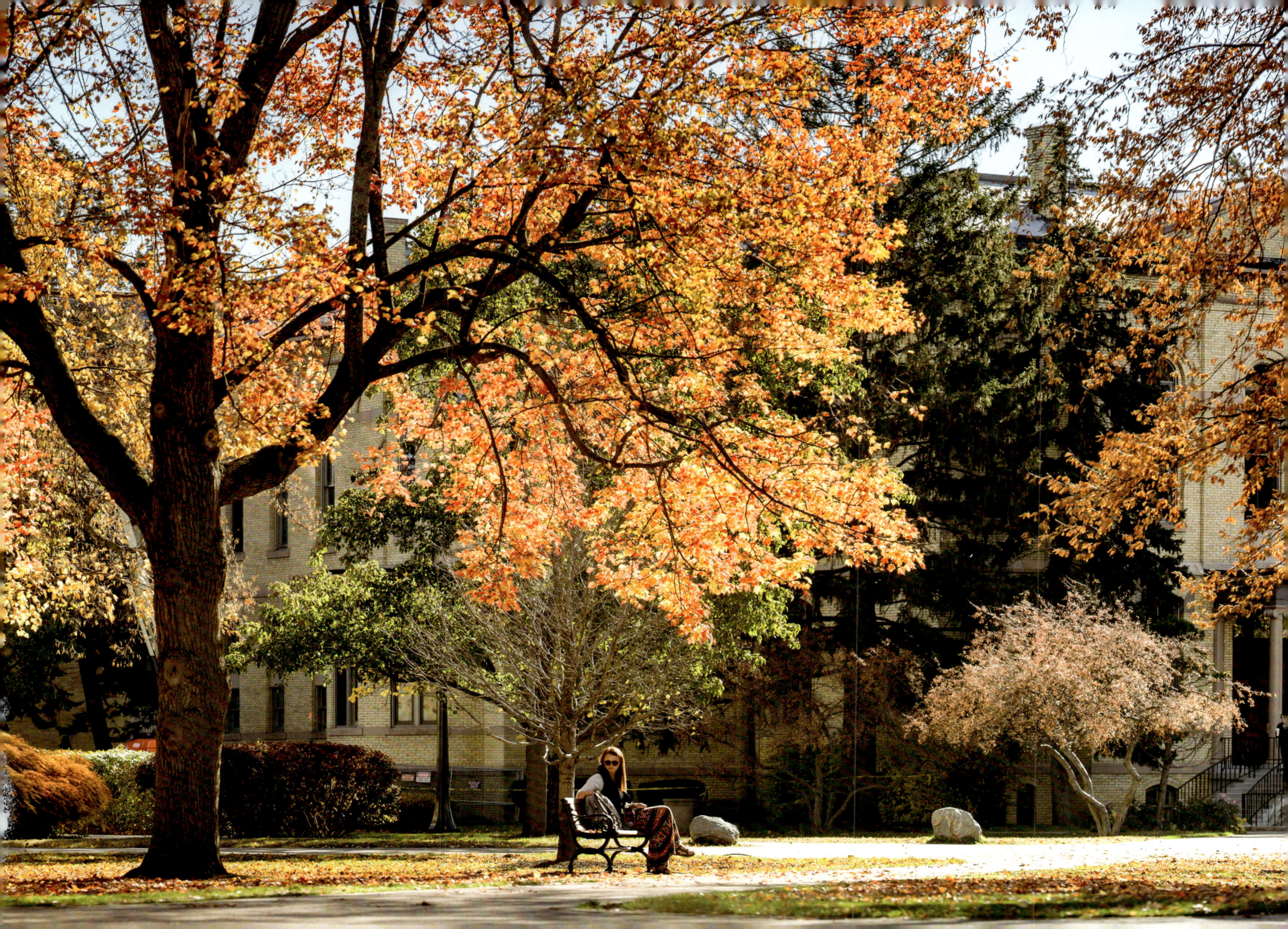

I felt the presence on those early autumn days myself. It wasn't just the Dome. It was the lakes, the Grotto, the Main Quad. It was the Log Chapel, perched on a hillside and tucked into brush, the creaky water pump, blocky Old College, the aged remnants of charming rusticity and simple beginnings. It was the campus architecture and yellowish bricks and the abundant beauty of trees. It was Tom Dooley's letter at the Grotto and the flickering candles nearby. The Huddle, the solemn serenity and stained-glass windows of Sacred Heart Church. The muted statues of Sorin, Christ, and Corby.

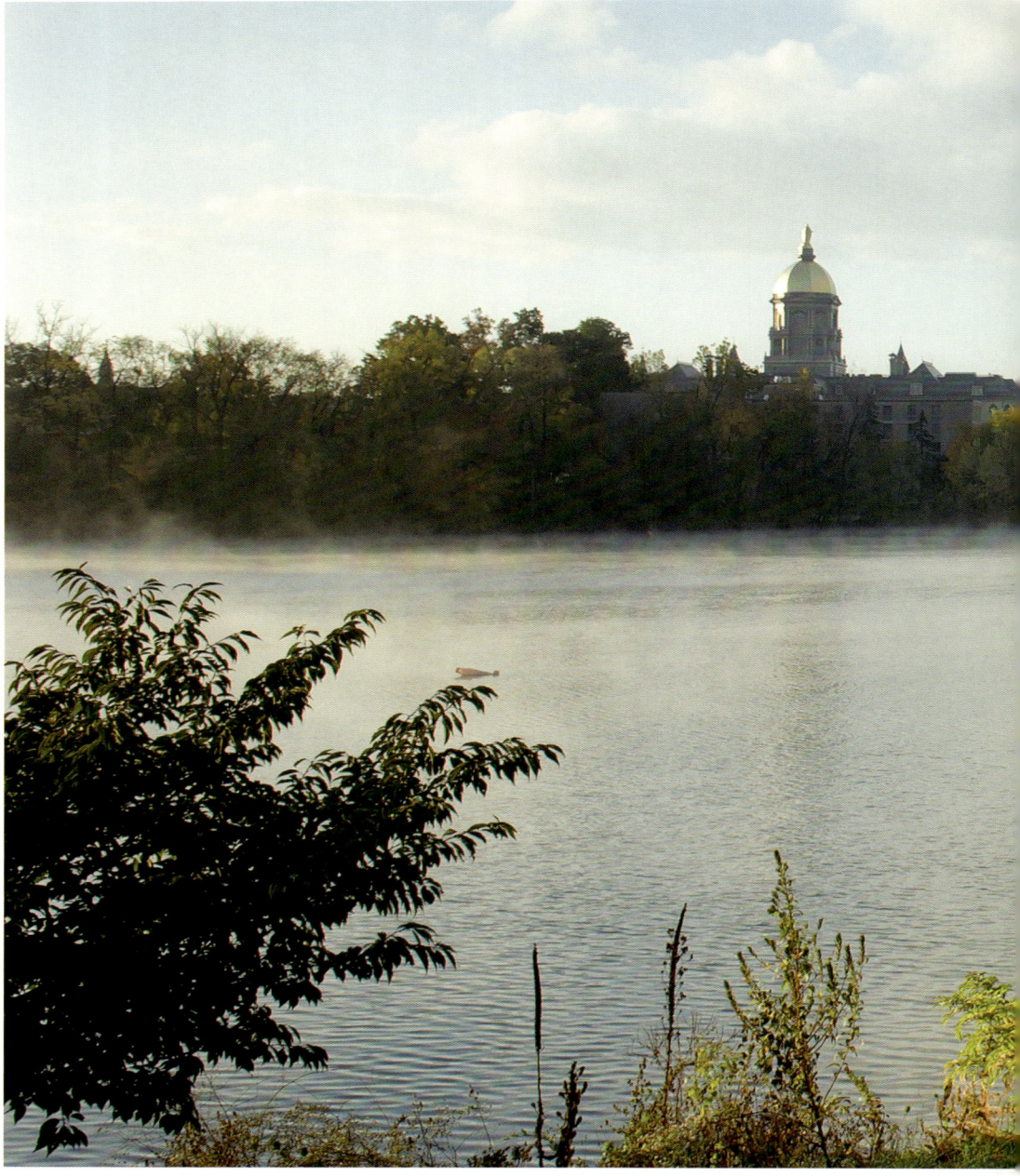

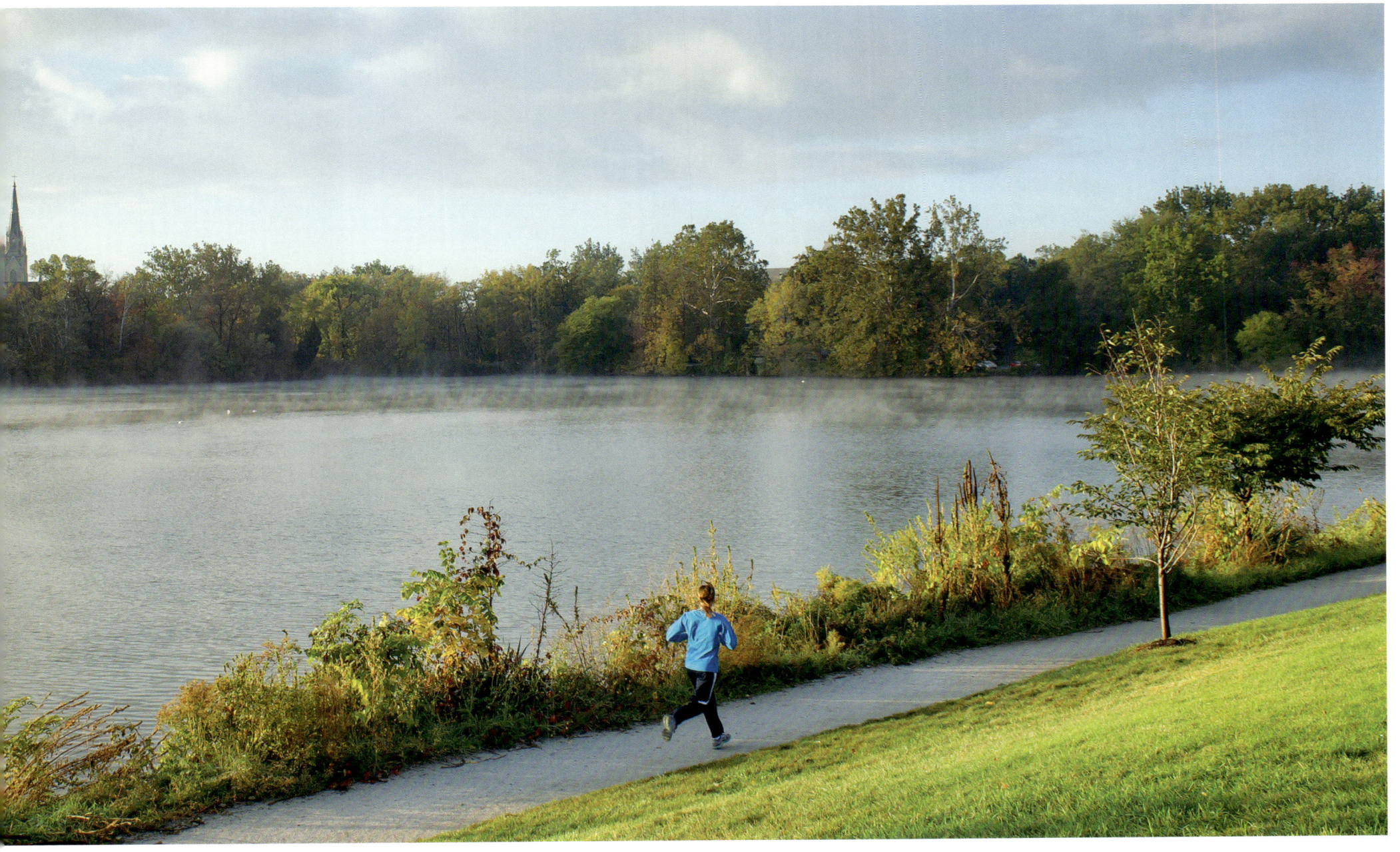

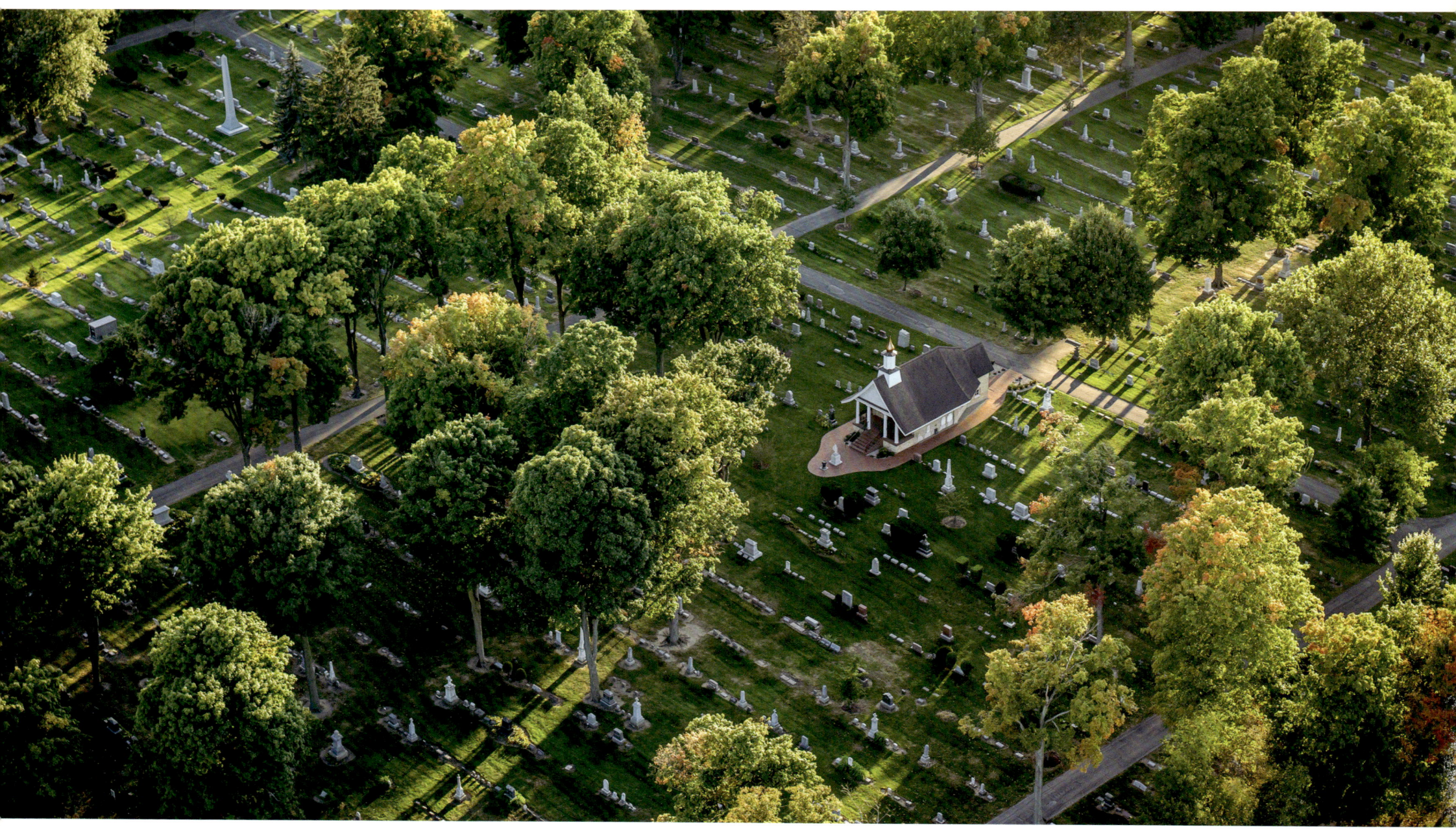

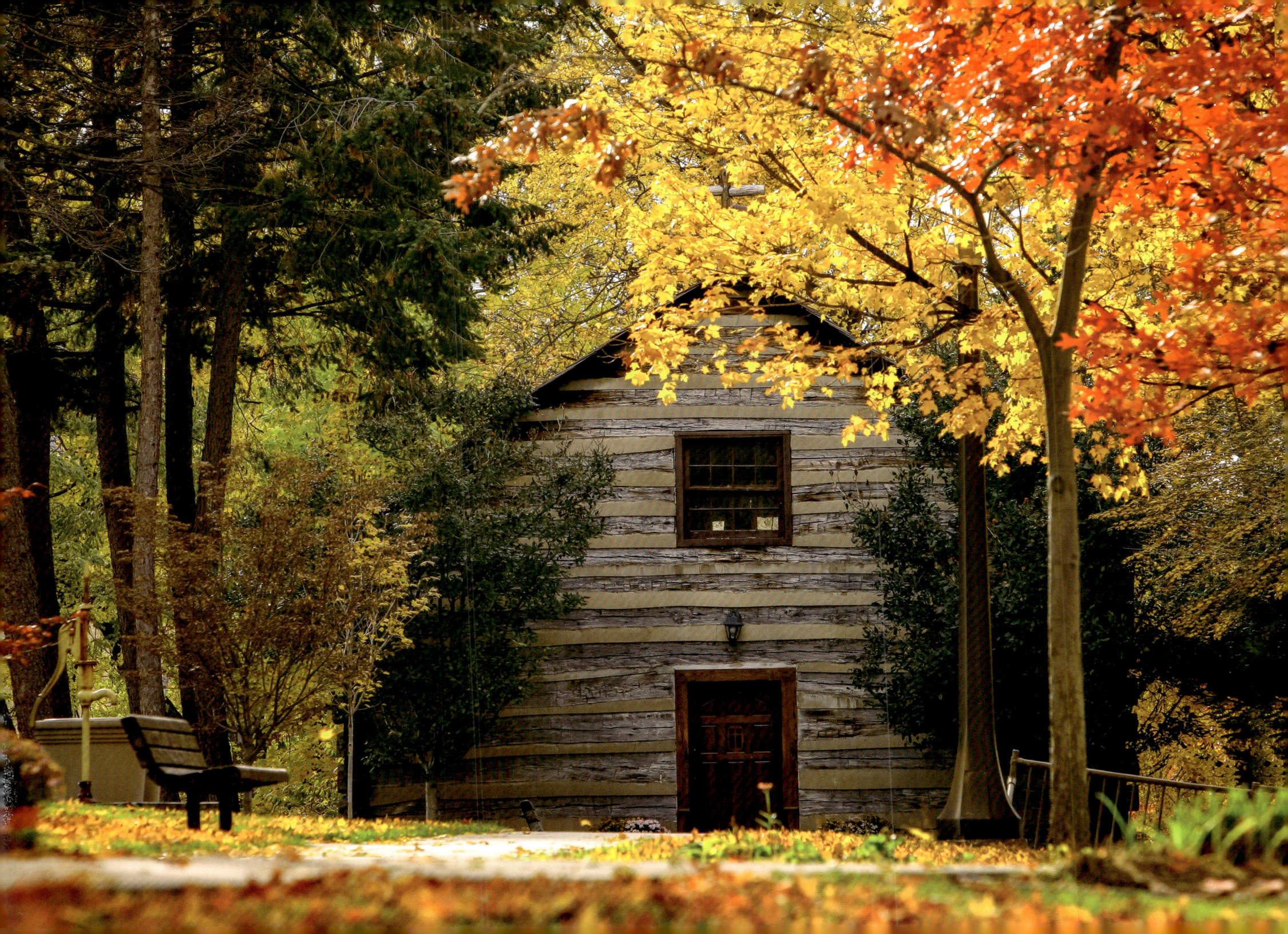

The autumn light and the burnished air still evoke a time in life, that sense of discovery, the colorful kaleidoscope that is Notre Dame. Freshman biology in the engineering auditorium, swim class at the Rock, Bob Kerby and the Civil War in the old Main Building. For others it's the Voice of Faith Gospel Choir or Glee Club, Frosh-O and career decisions, spring-break plans and internship applications. It's Fair Catch Corby, Touch-down Jesus, and No. 1 Moses. The Hesburgh Library and Rolfs, Reckers and the Rad Lab, Kellogg and Kroc, lectures and late-night conversations. It's performances in Washington Hall and DPAC, exams in O'Shaugh-nessy, Nieuwland, even Stepan Center, dinner at the dining hall, trips to the post office, Fatima Retreat Center, Club Fever, or Finnie's.

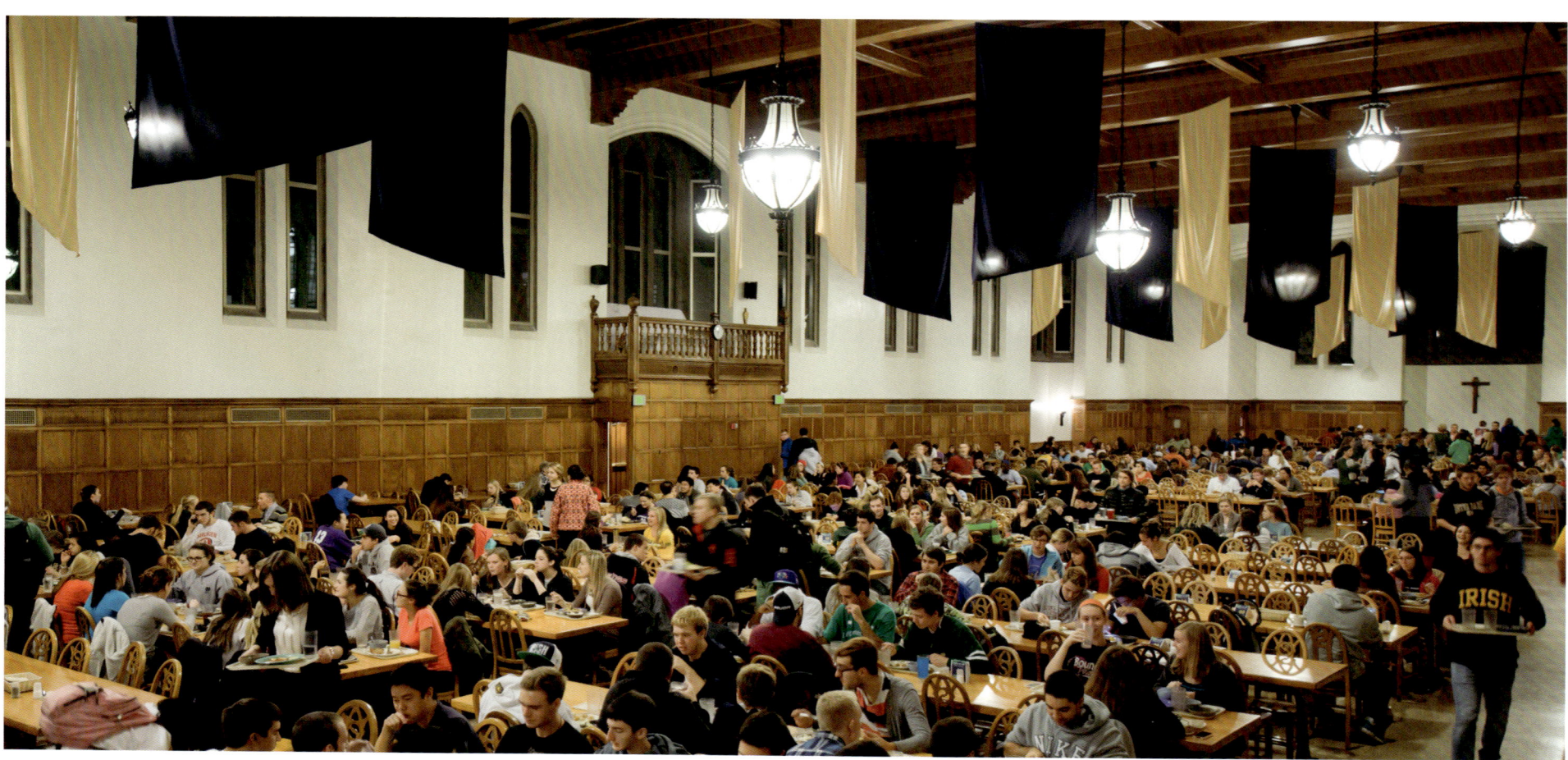

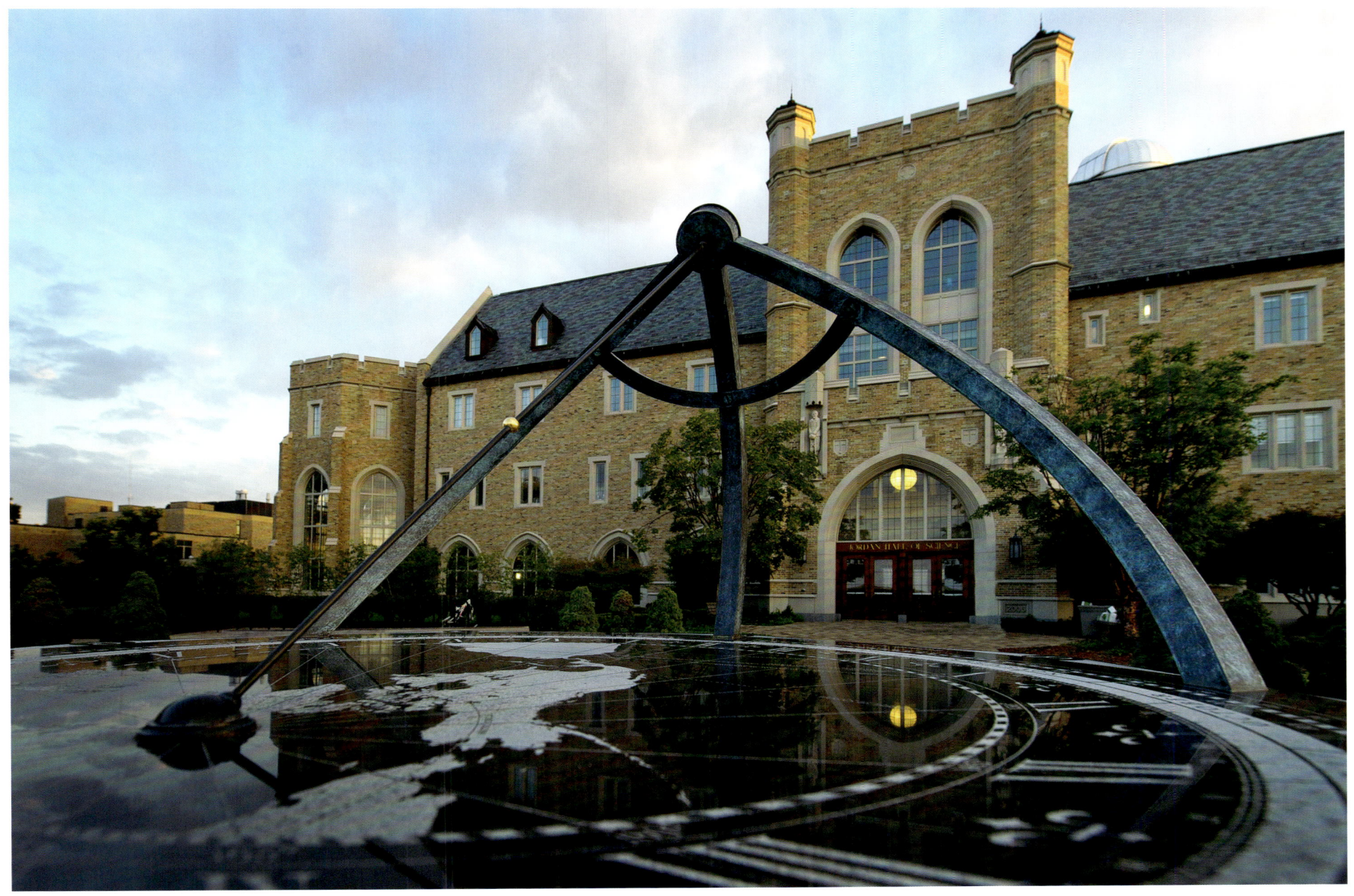

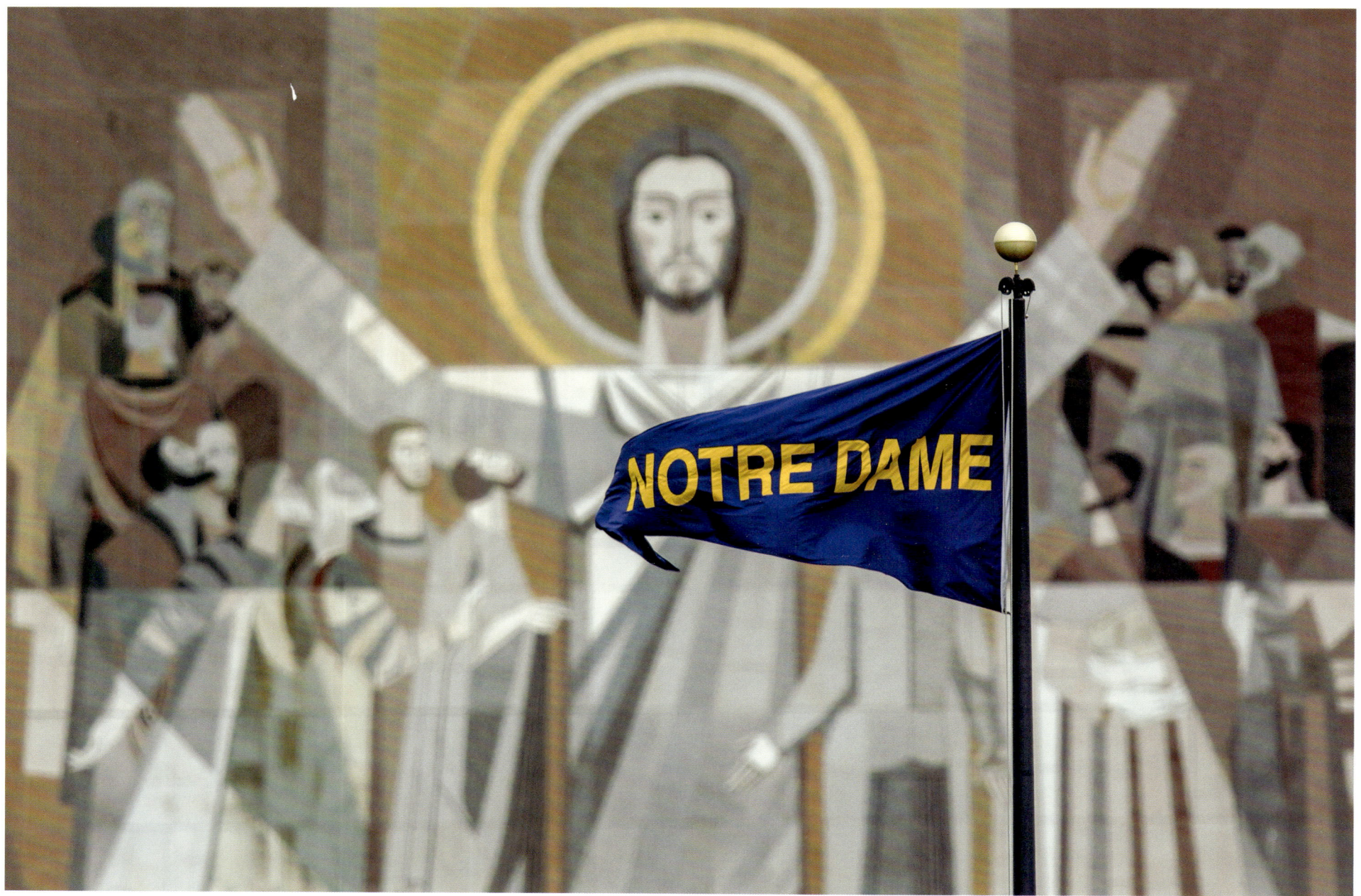

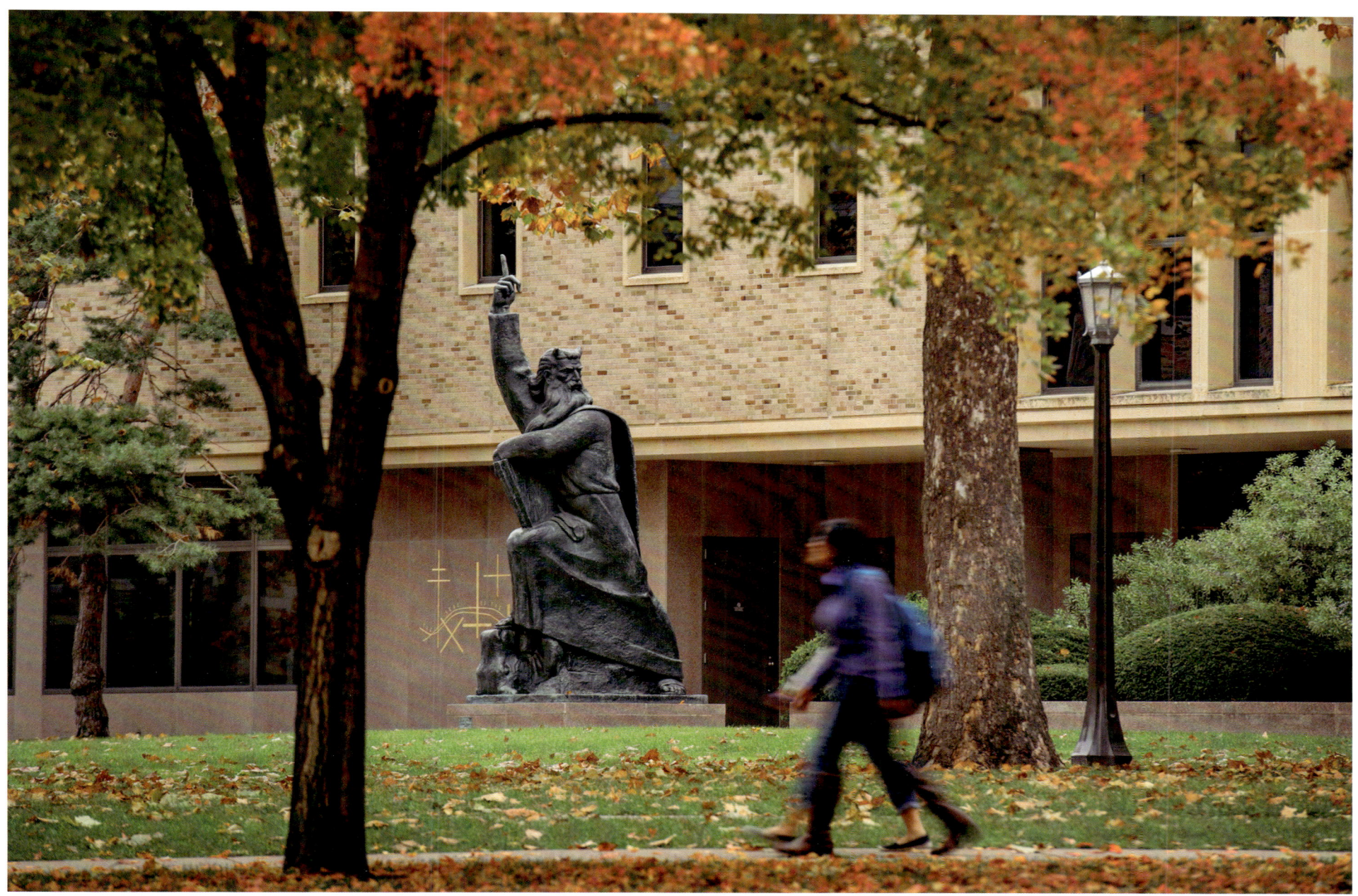

Notre Dame is the ceremony and ritual of a football weekend and the celebration of Mass at Sacred Heart Basilica. It's long and lonely nights of isolation in a dorm room and the crowded jubilation of a rock concert. It's roommates and classmates, professors, mentors and rectors, girlfriends, boyfriends, friends for life. It is memories and dreams, enervating stress and minor triumphs, instructive disappointments and life-changing ordeals.

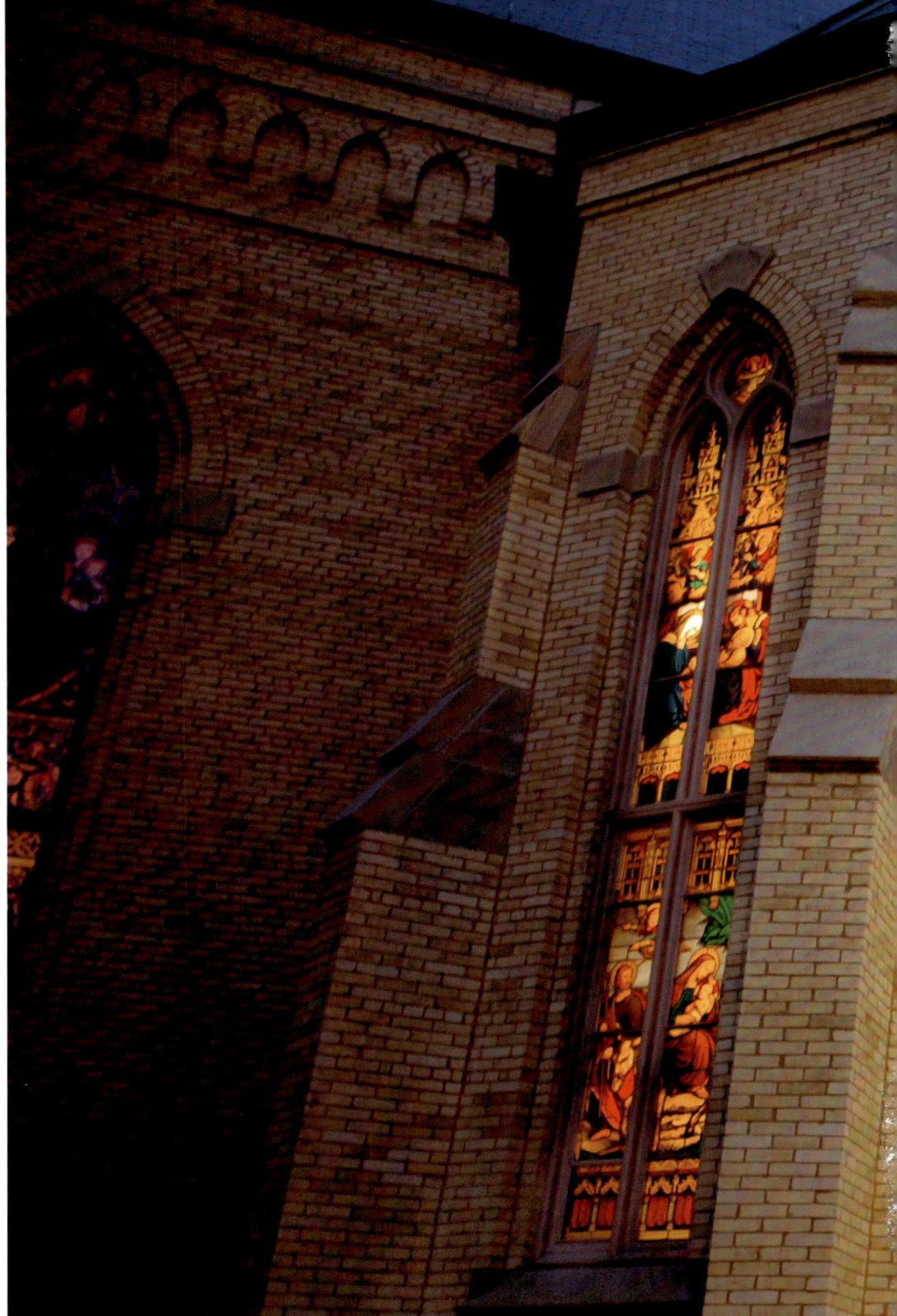

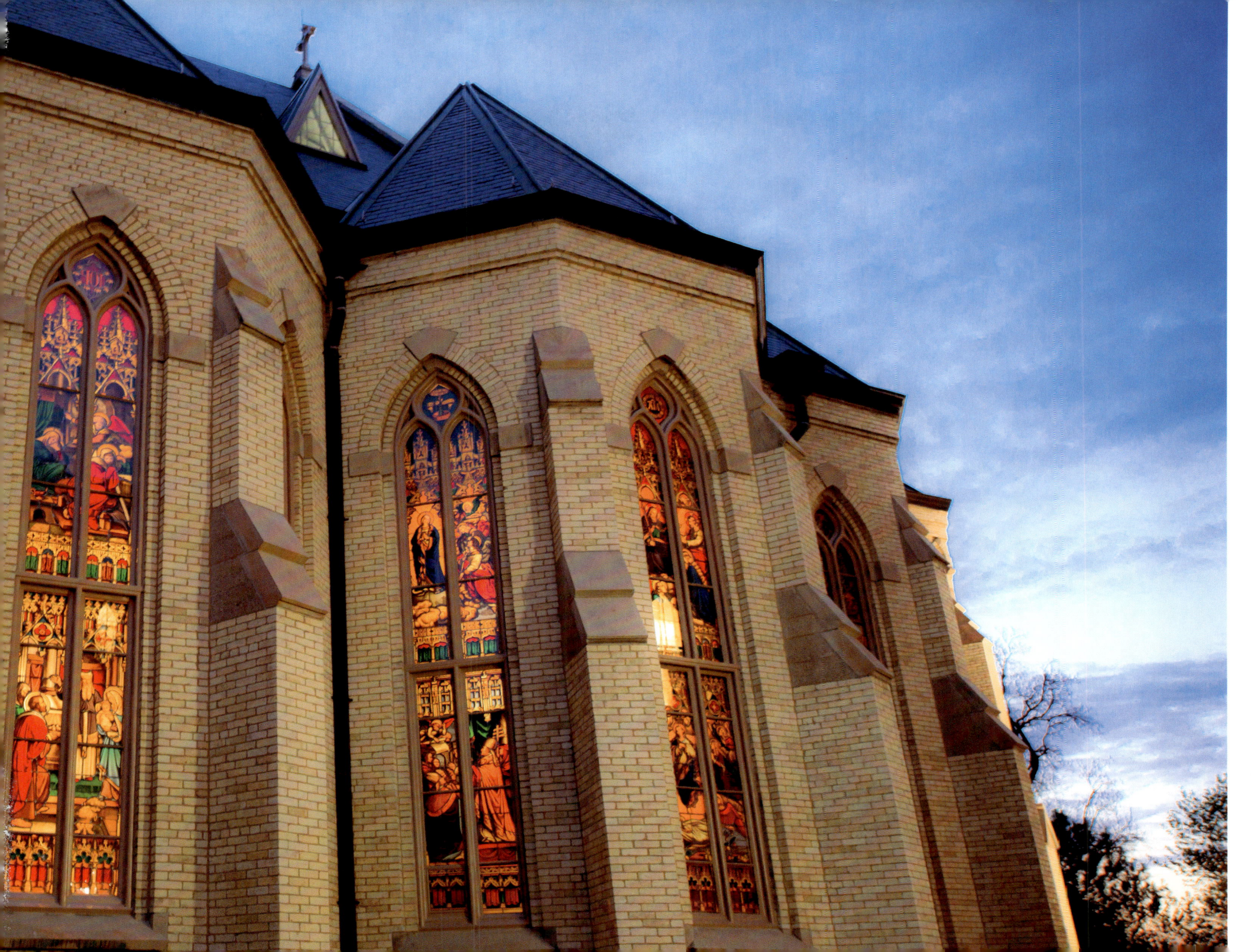

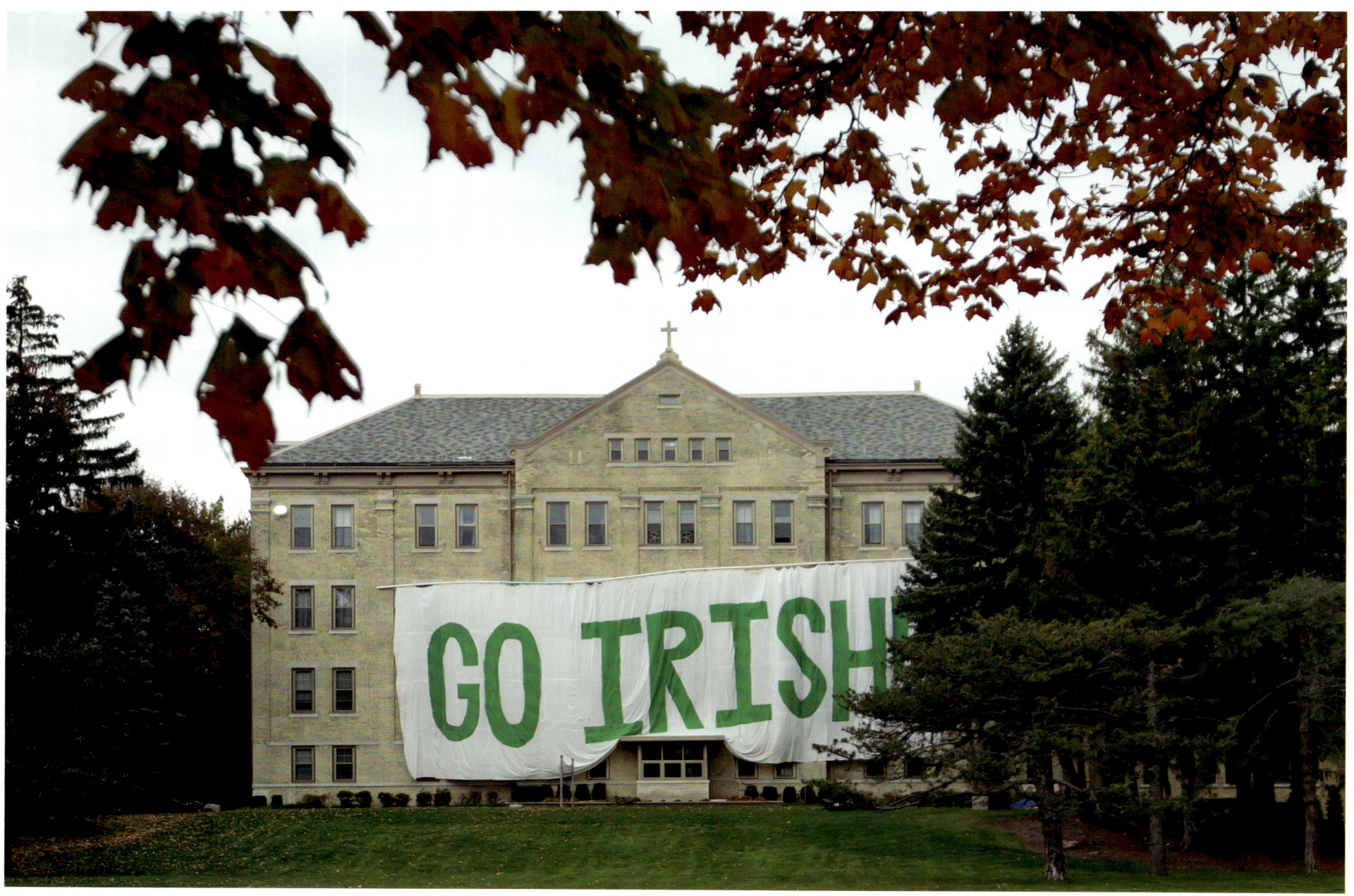

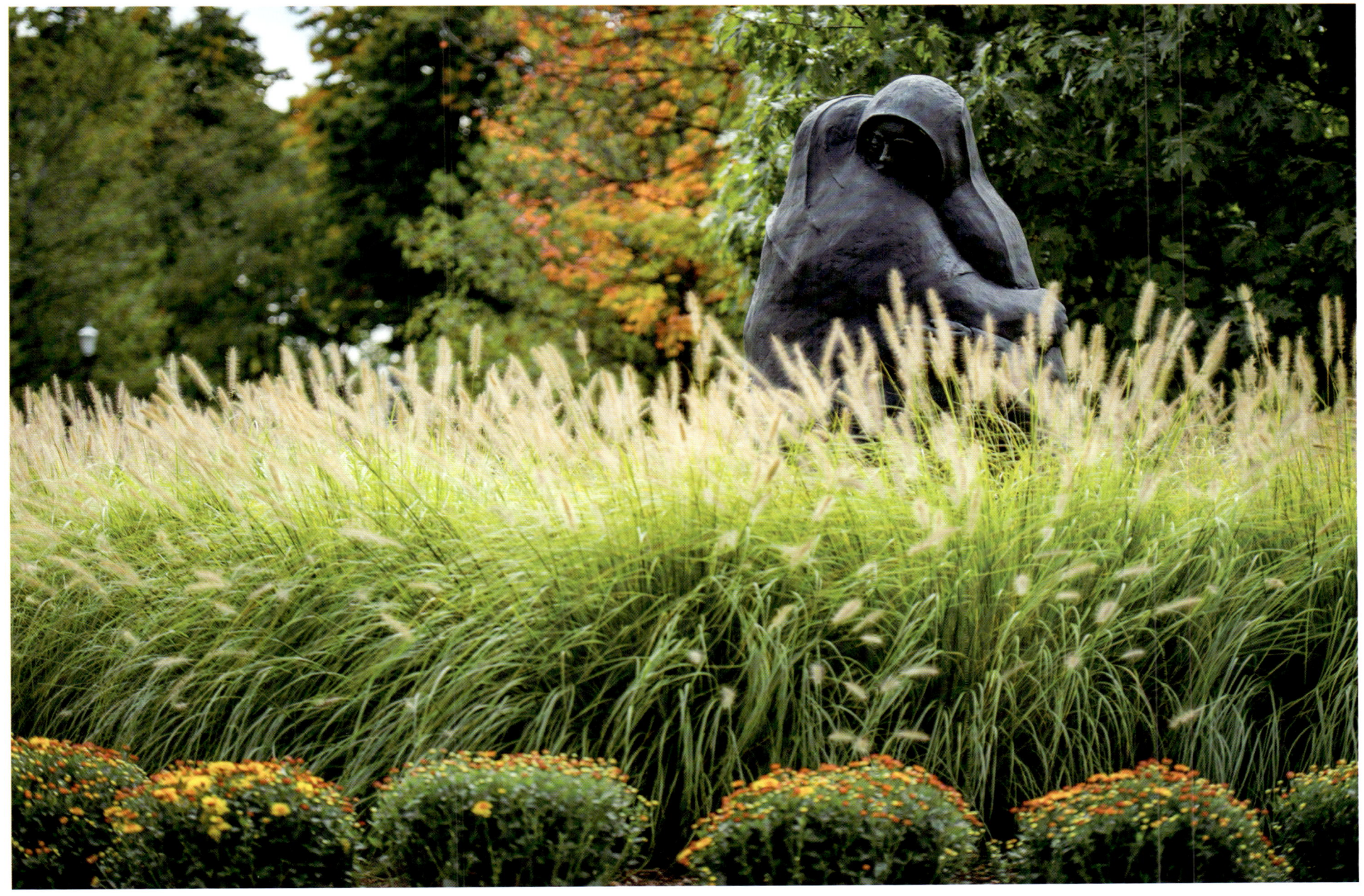

Then, too, you could start your Notre Dame story not with goodbyes, hellos, academic rigor, or walks around the lakes but with football. Many of us first learned of Notre Dame through its gridiron exploits and celebrations of Fighting Irish spirit broadcast on national television every Saturday in the fall. The games are fun, sure, and it's more fun during a winning season, when the Fighting Irish are victorious, but, win or lose, the team raises helmets to the student section in the corner of Notre Dame Stadium where thousands sway, arms draped over shoulders, and sing the Alma Mater in a communal playtime ritual.

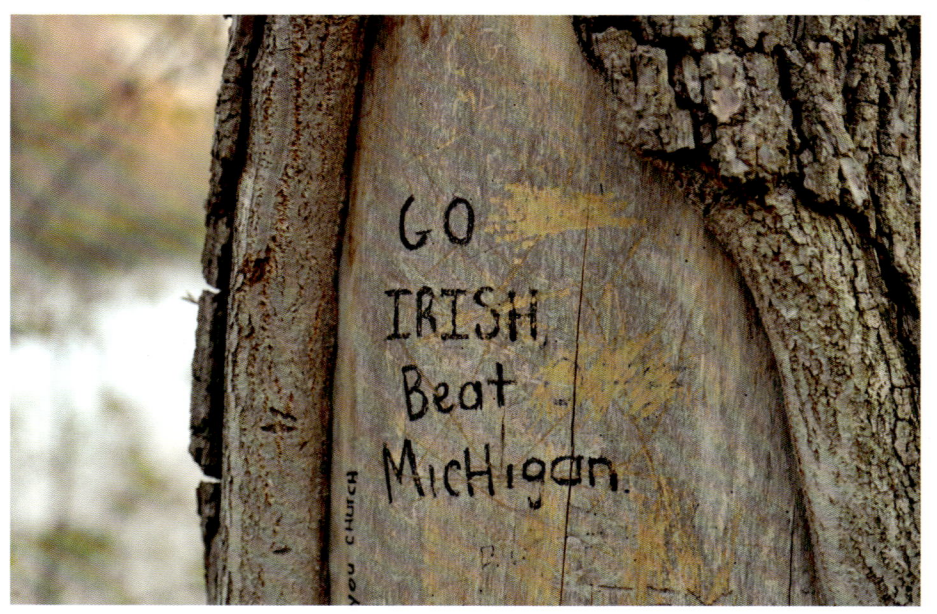

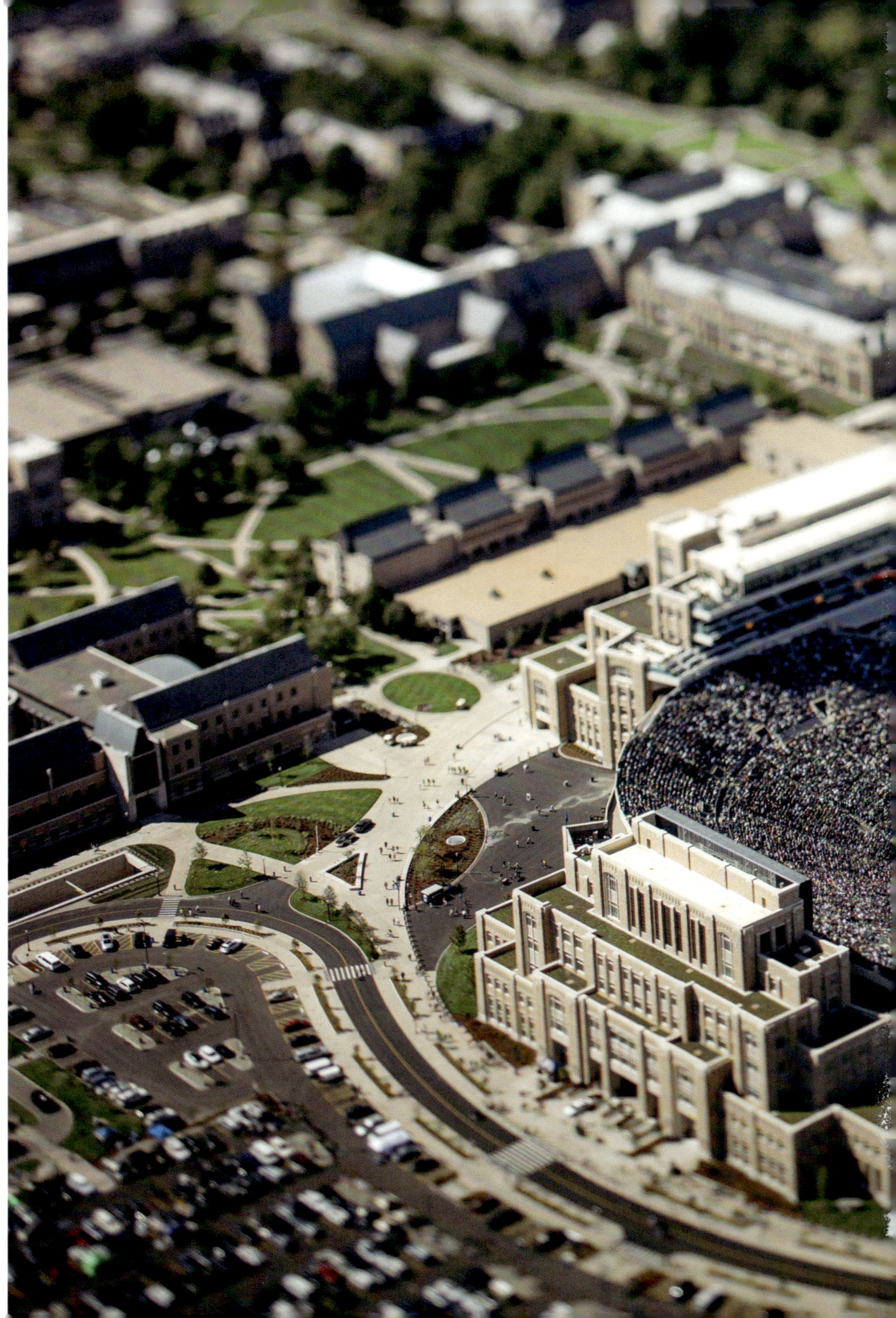

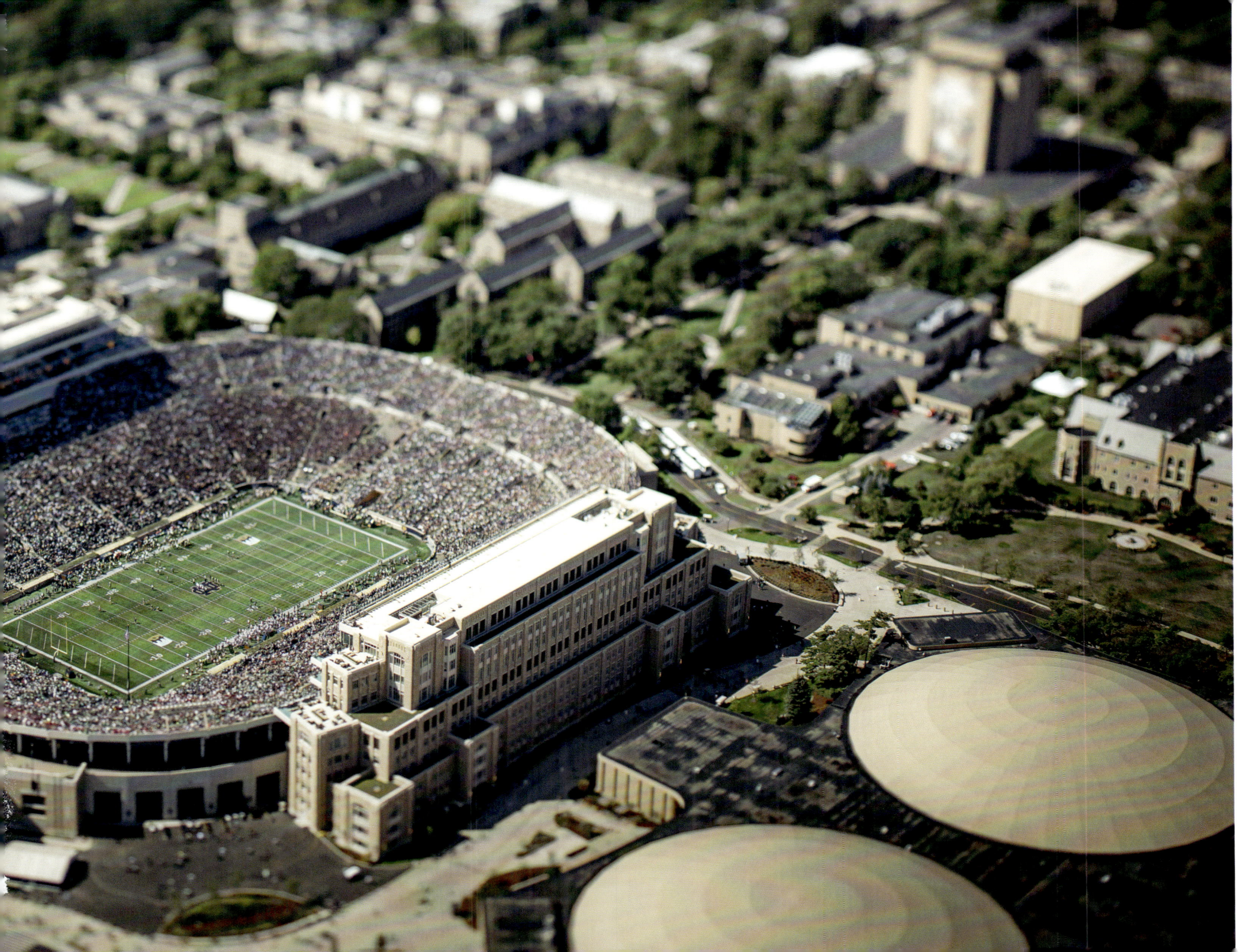

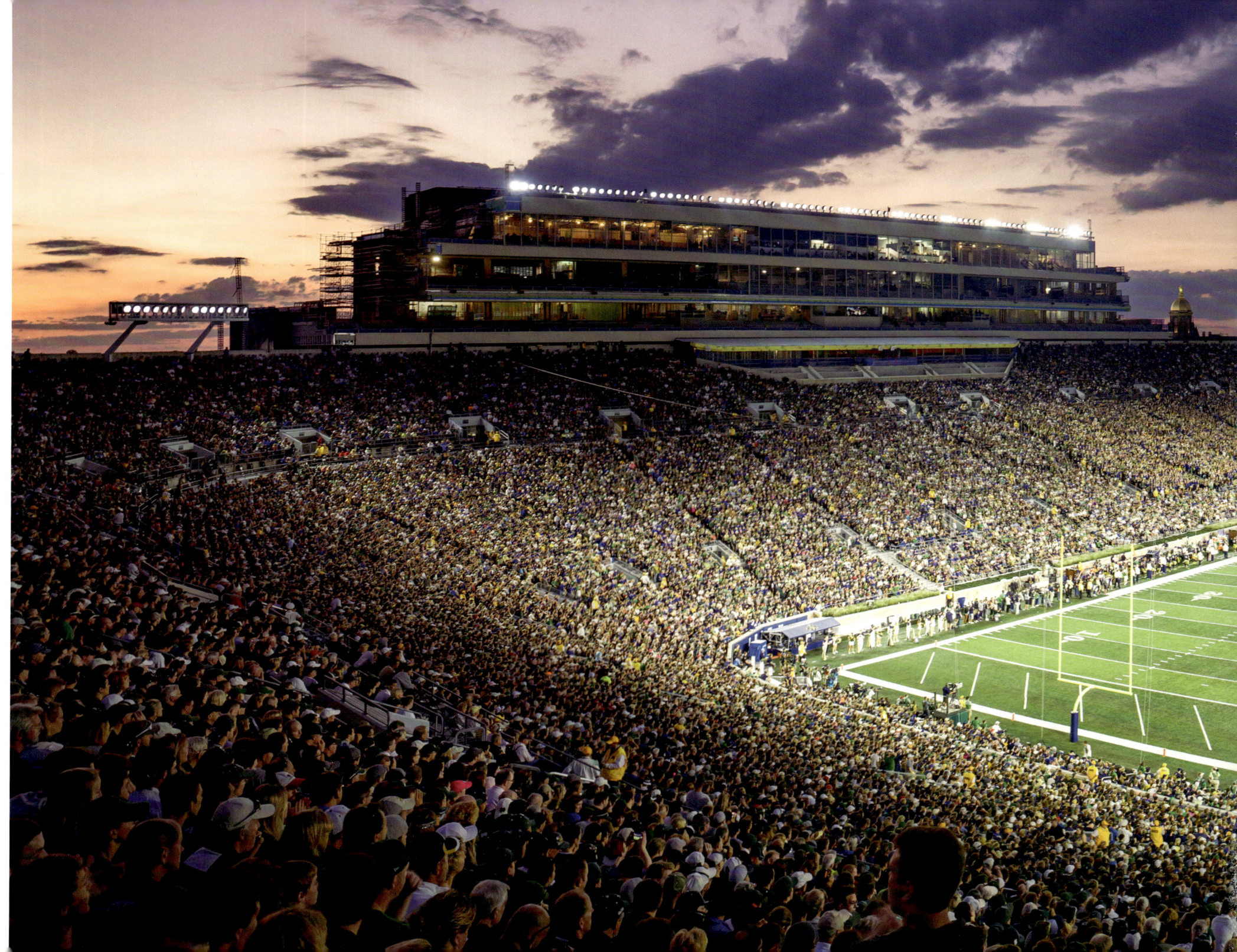

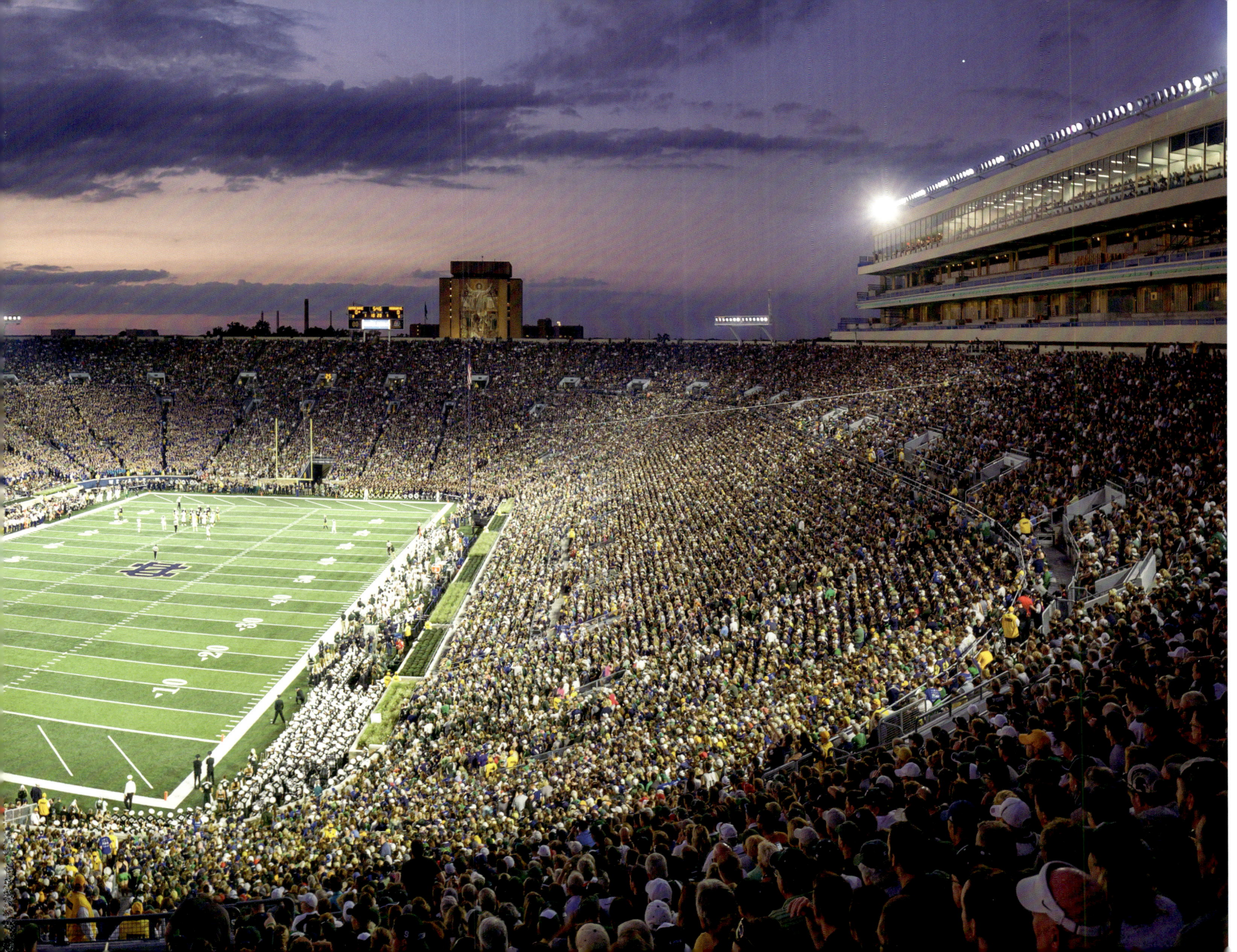

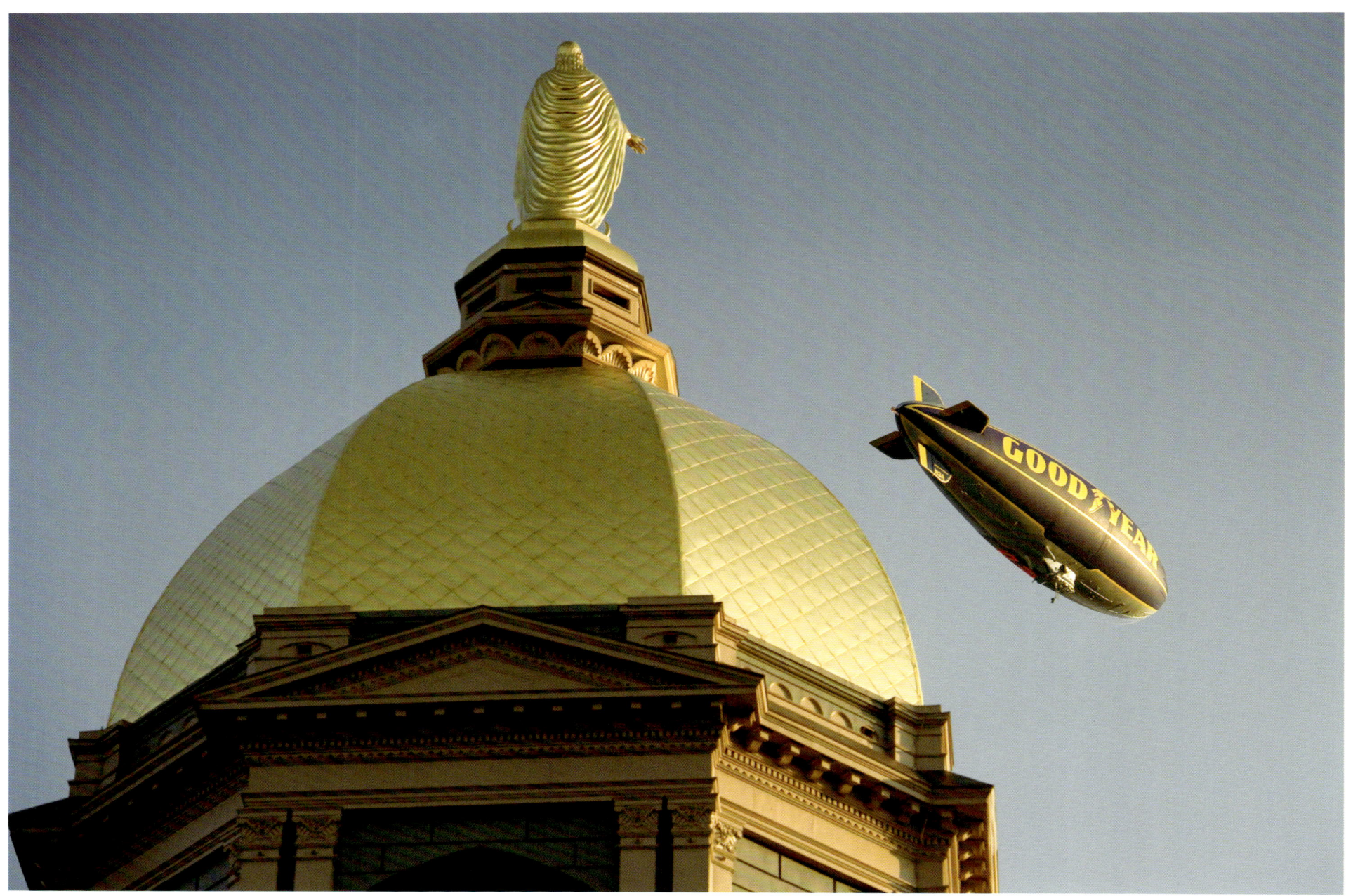

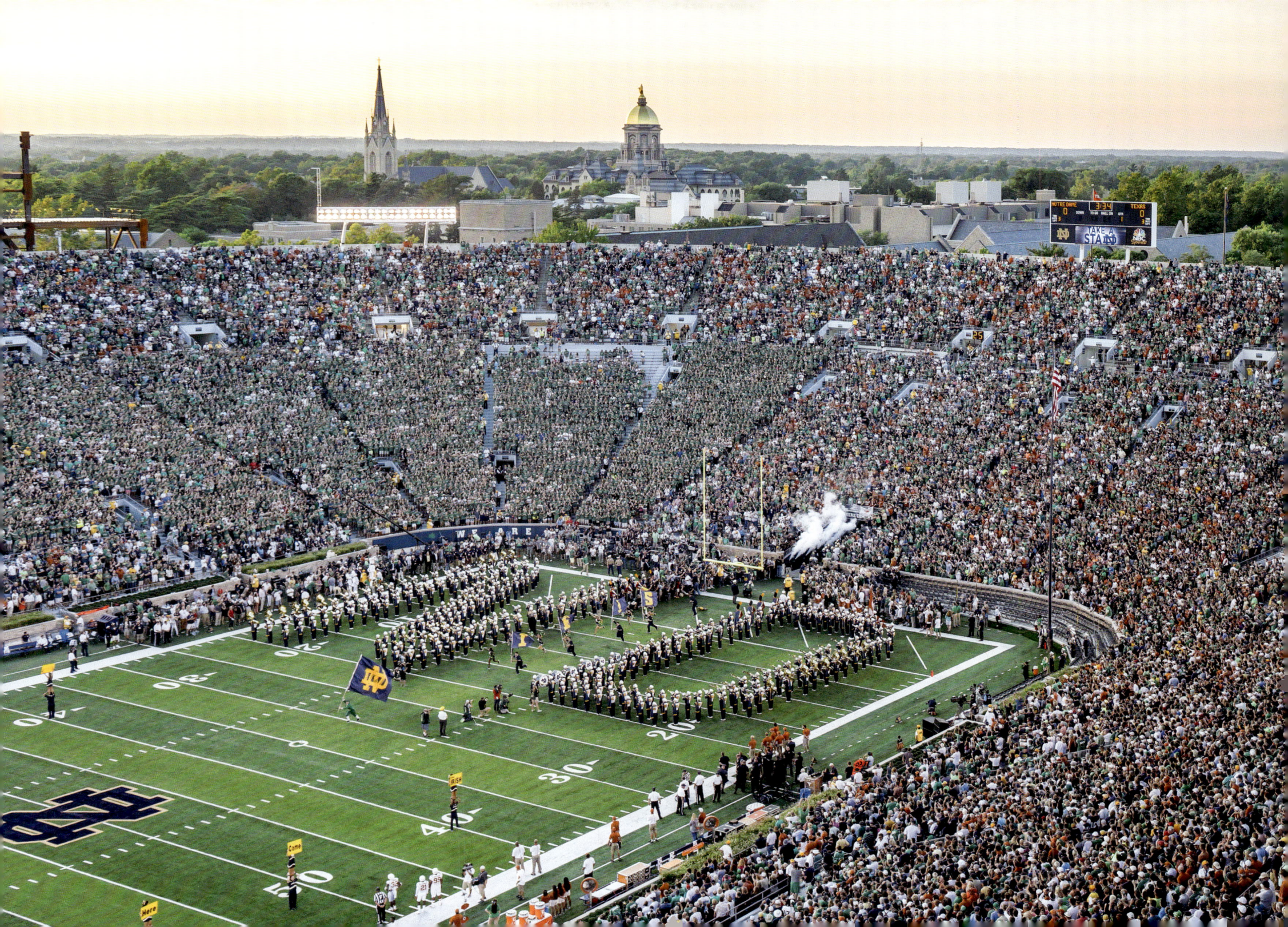

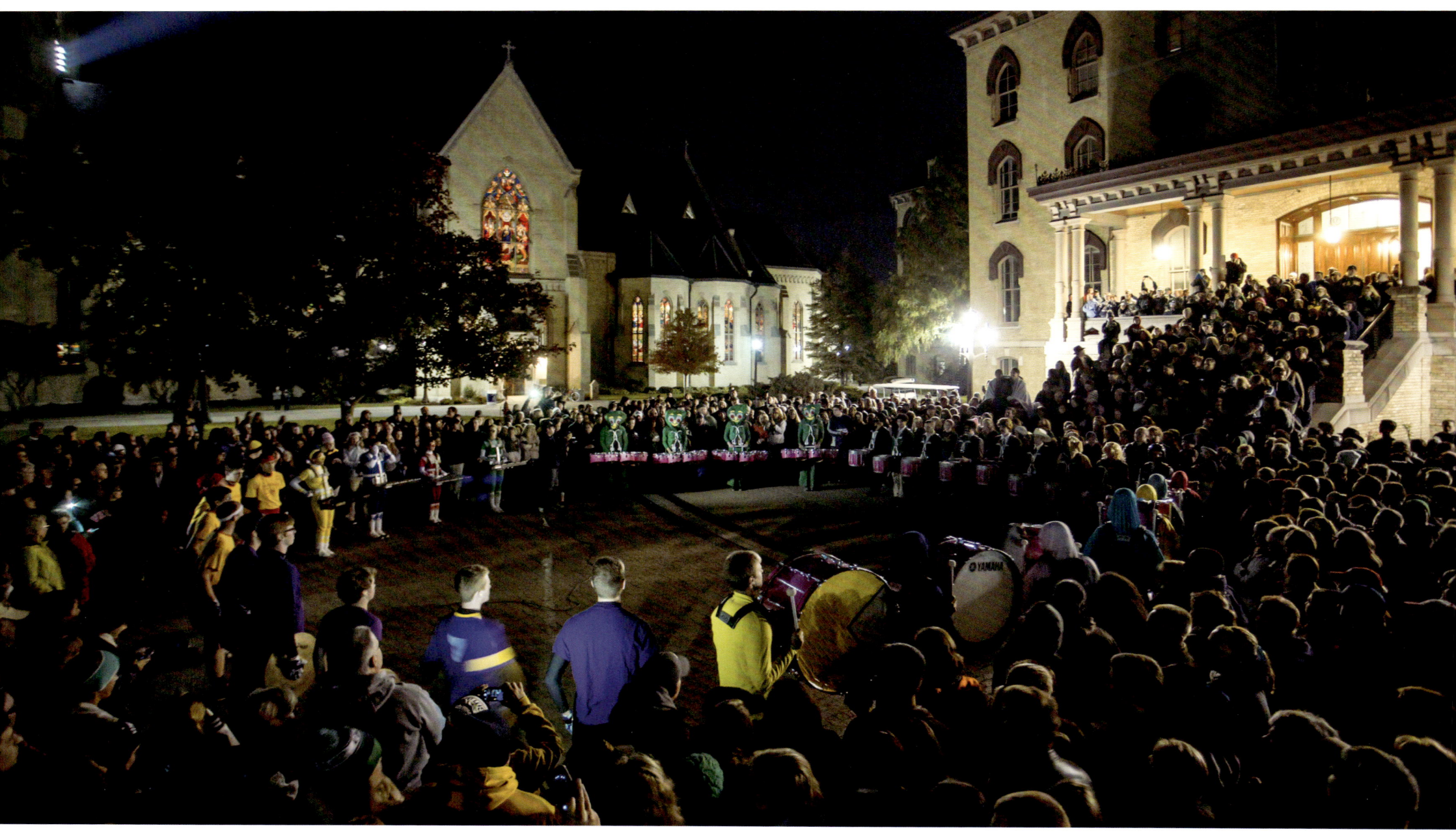

Notre Dame football isn't just about the games. A football weekend is a sprawling party, a fall festival, a family reunion. The marching band threads through campus on a Friday afternoon, entertains the gathered throngs on Saturday morning, then breaks into the drum circle or trumpets under the Dome before leading a parade to the game that attracts grinning alumni, with kids hoisted onto shoulders and shamrock-clad clans and old Domer friends remembering when.

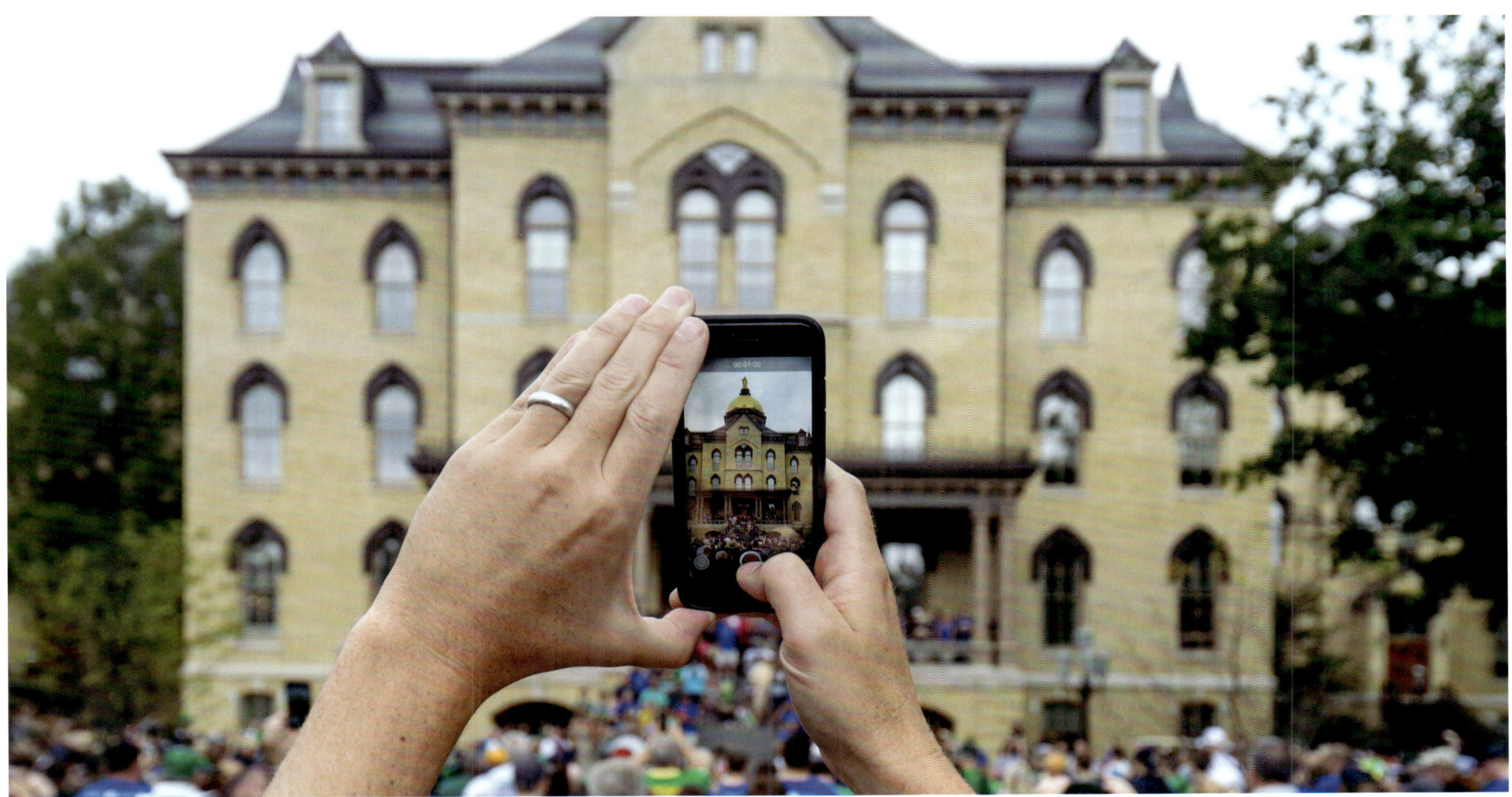

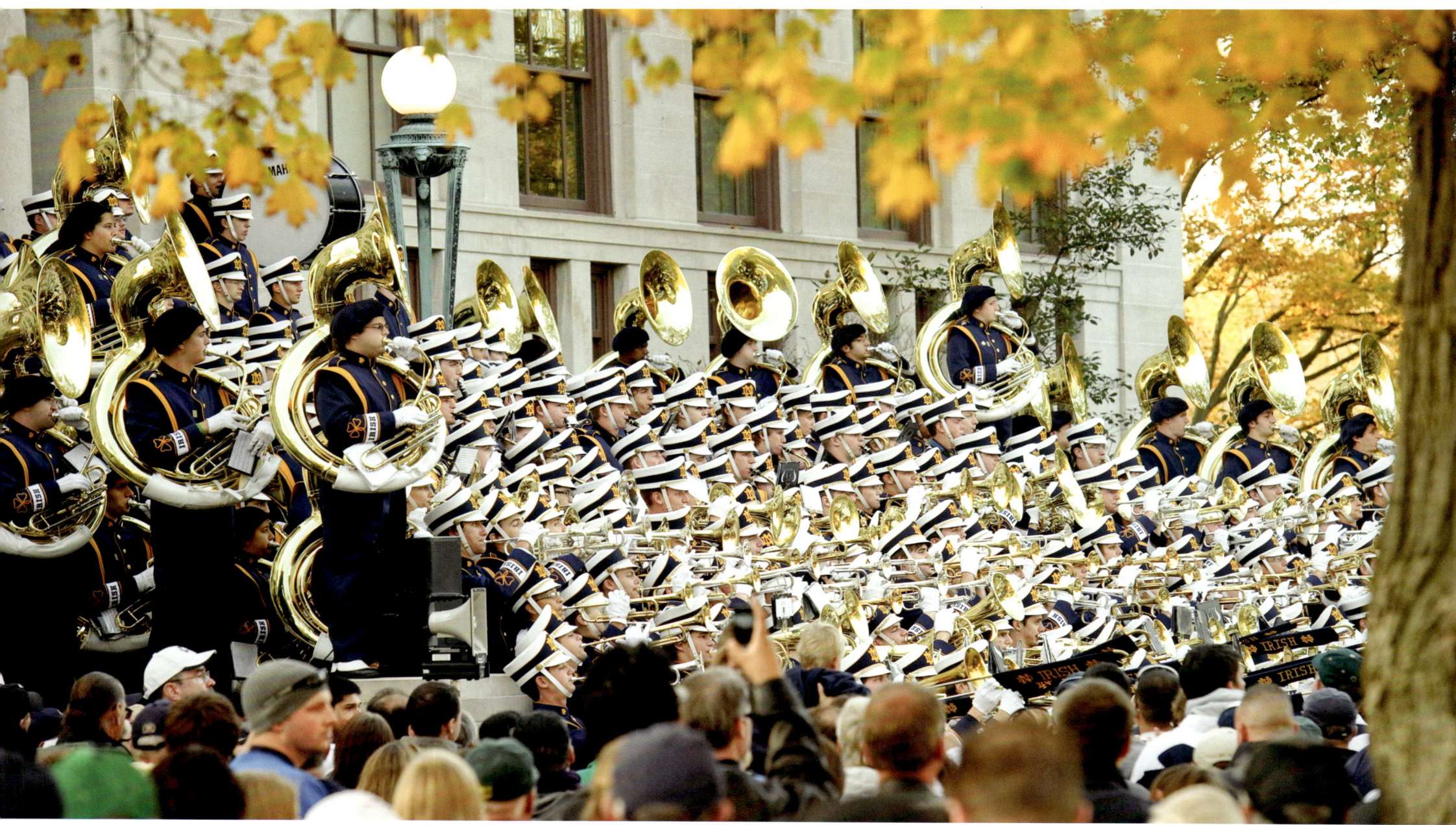

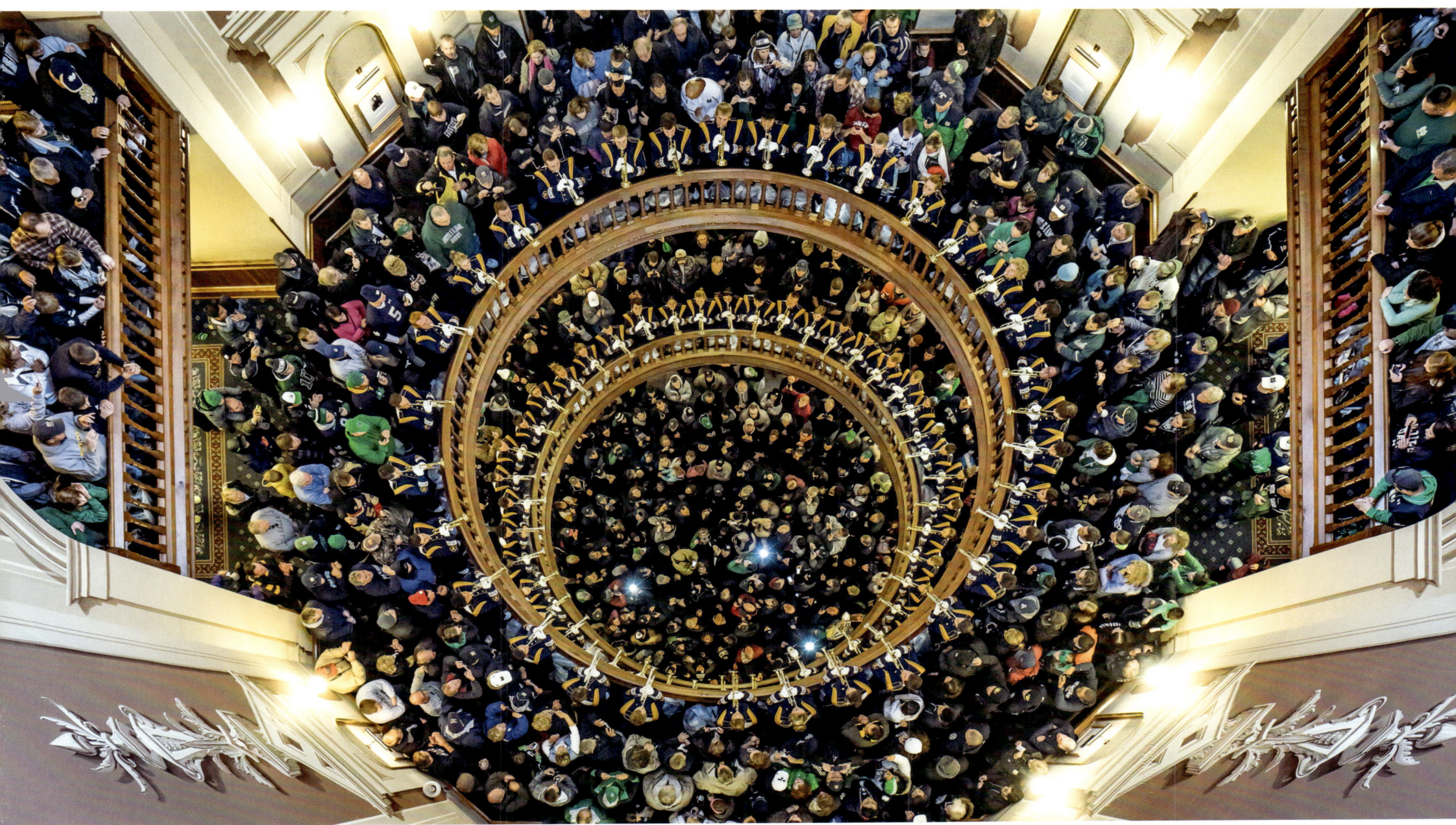

Students grill hot dogs, burgers, and brats. Kids toss footballs on the green-carpet quads. There's the Irish Guard and a sea of tailgaters flying flags and trafficking in food, drink, laughter, and yarns. We're all here because of football, but football is only the main event. It's the magnet and adhesive. It is our common ground, our *lingua franca*.

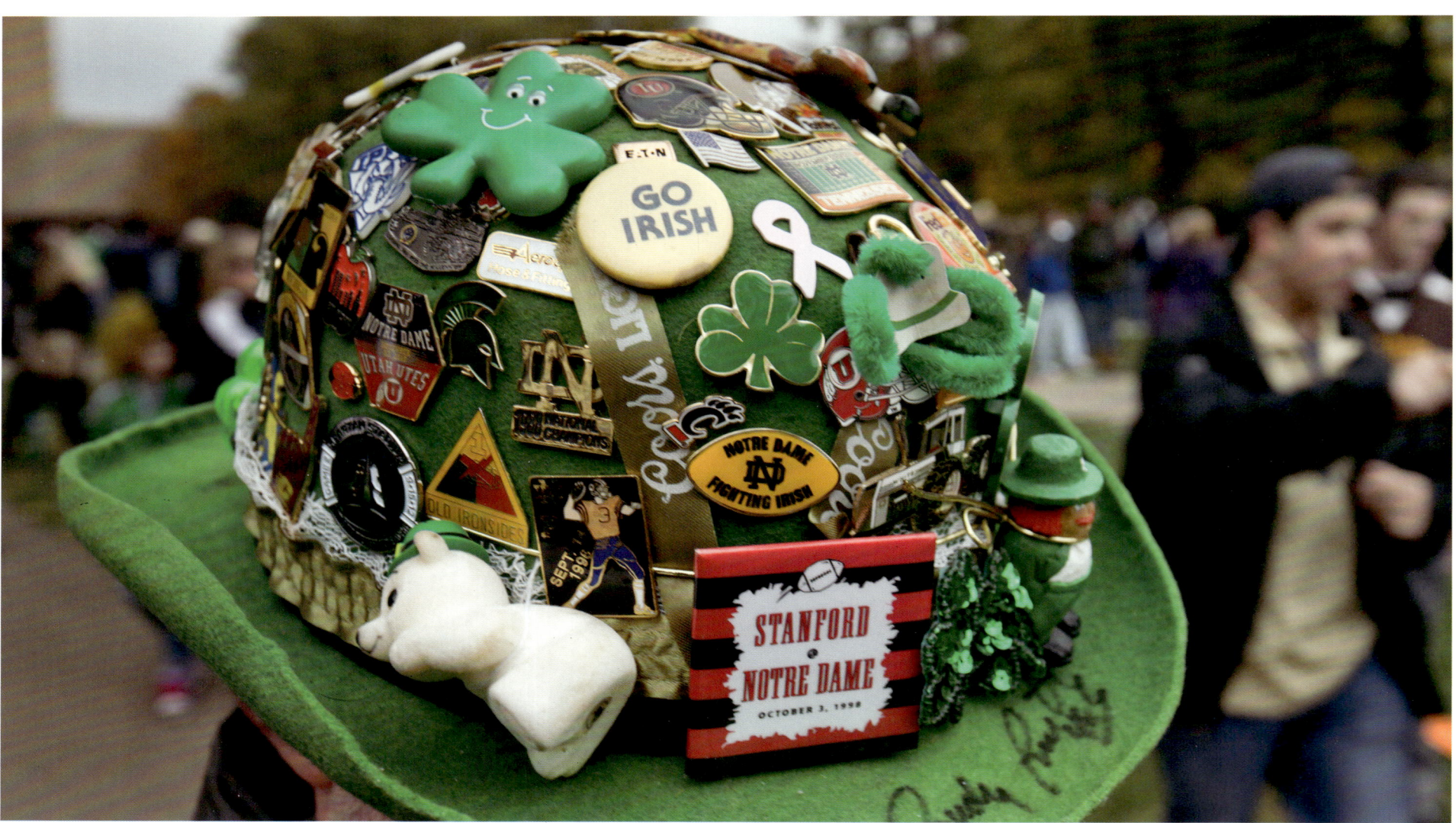

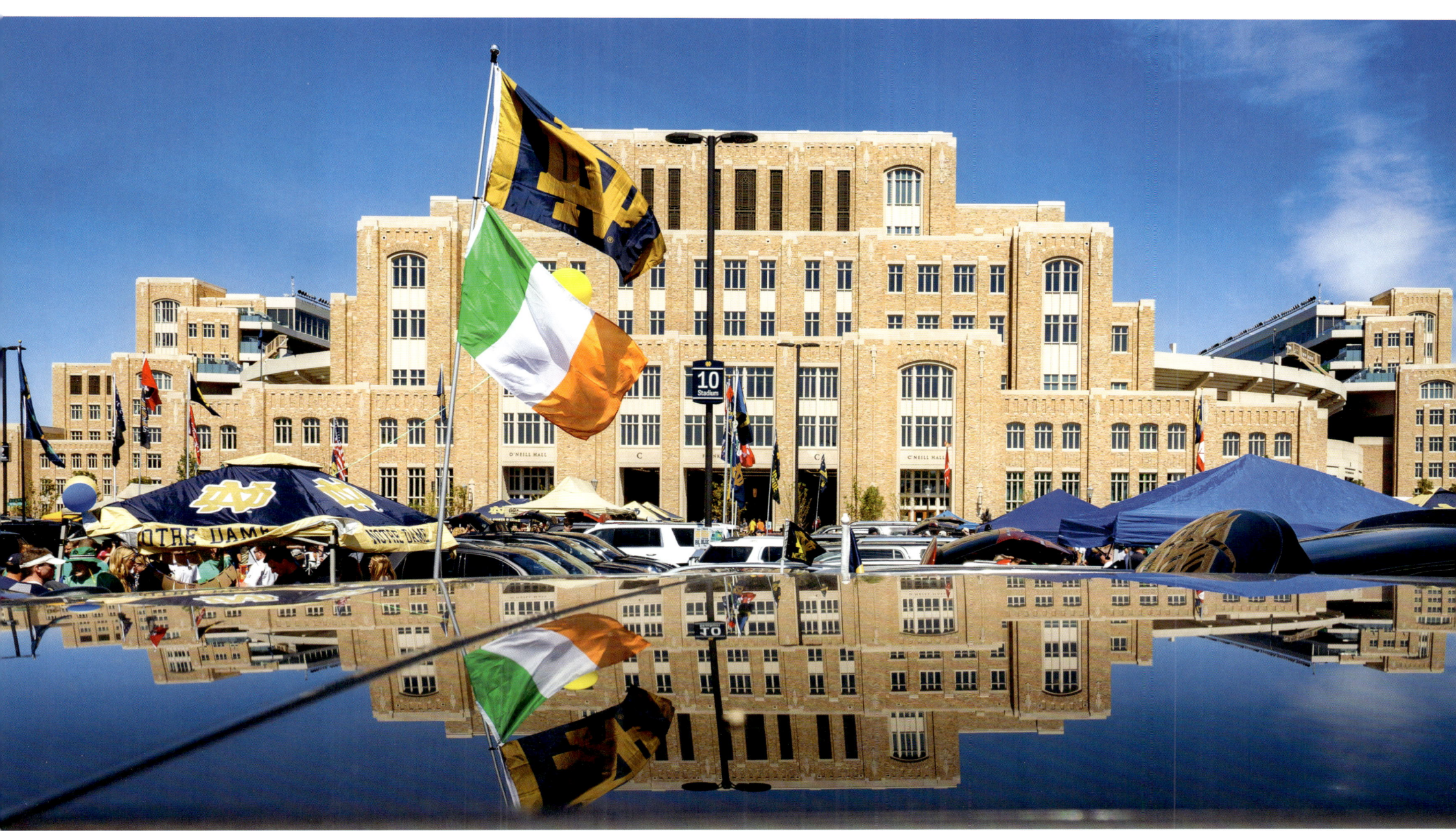

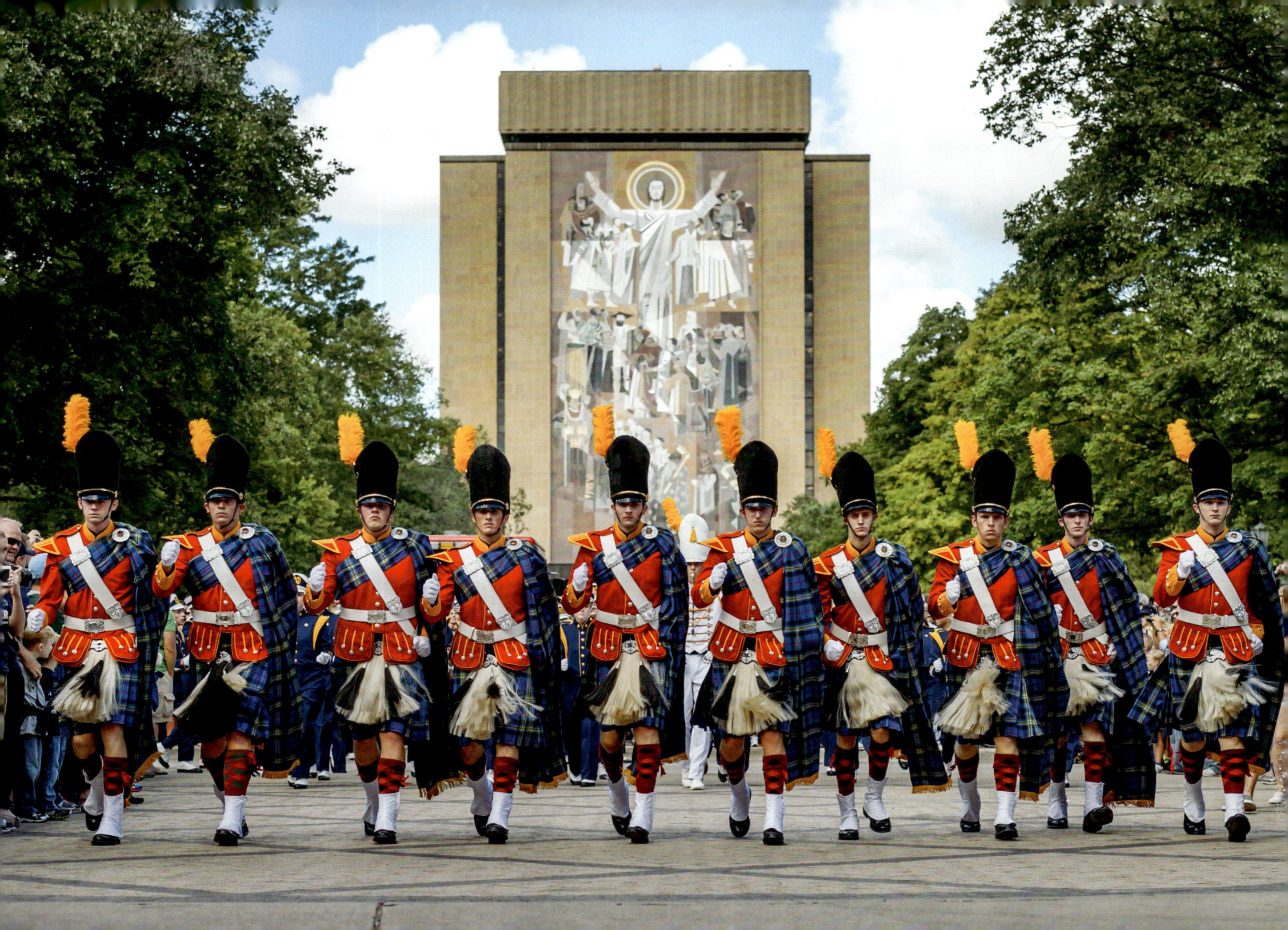

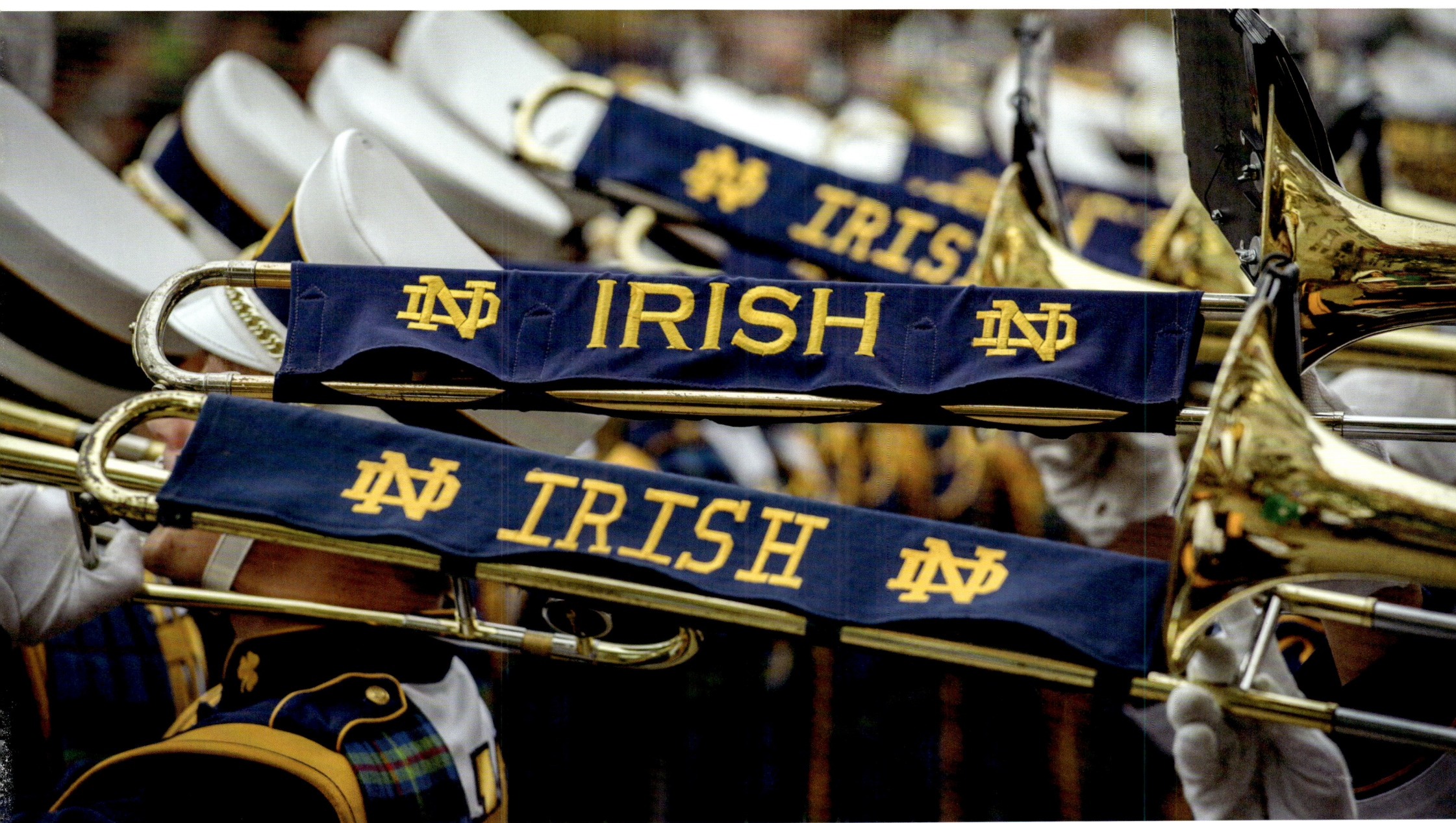

The Notre Dame football tradition goes back more than a century now, through high tides of national prominence and low ebbs when disgruntled alumni complained the sport was being de-emphasized. Critics complain of Notre Dame being perceived as "a football factory," of the disproportionate power it has over the institution and the corruption of big-time college athletics of which they see Notre Dame as being a part. But those scholars who grouse about the game overshadowing academics opine with authority on coach and quarterback. And most everyone acknowledges that it was the sport that propelled the university into the national consciousness and provided the institution with a proud sense of self.

For more than a century the Fighting Irish have been powerful emissaries for institutional values and societal achievements that have made the football field a stage upon which bigger games are won. And, even as the university settles into its place among the nation's foremost institutions of higher learning, autumn is still undeniably, incurably football season. The passion and fervor run deep. Football is in the bloodstream here; it's an elixir that helps keep the place happy and fun and its psyche secure and healthy.

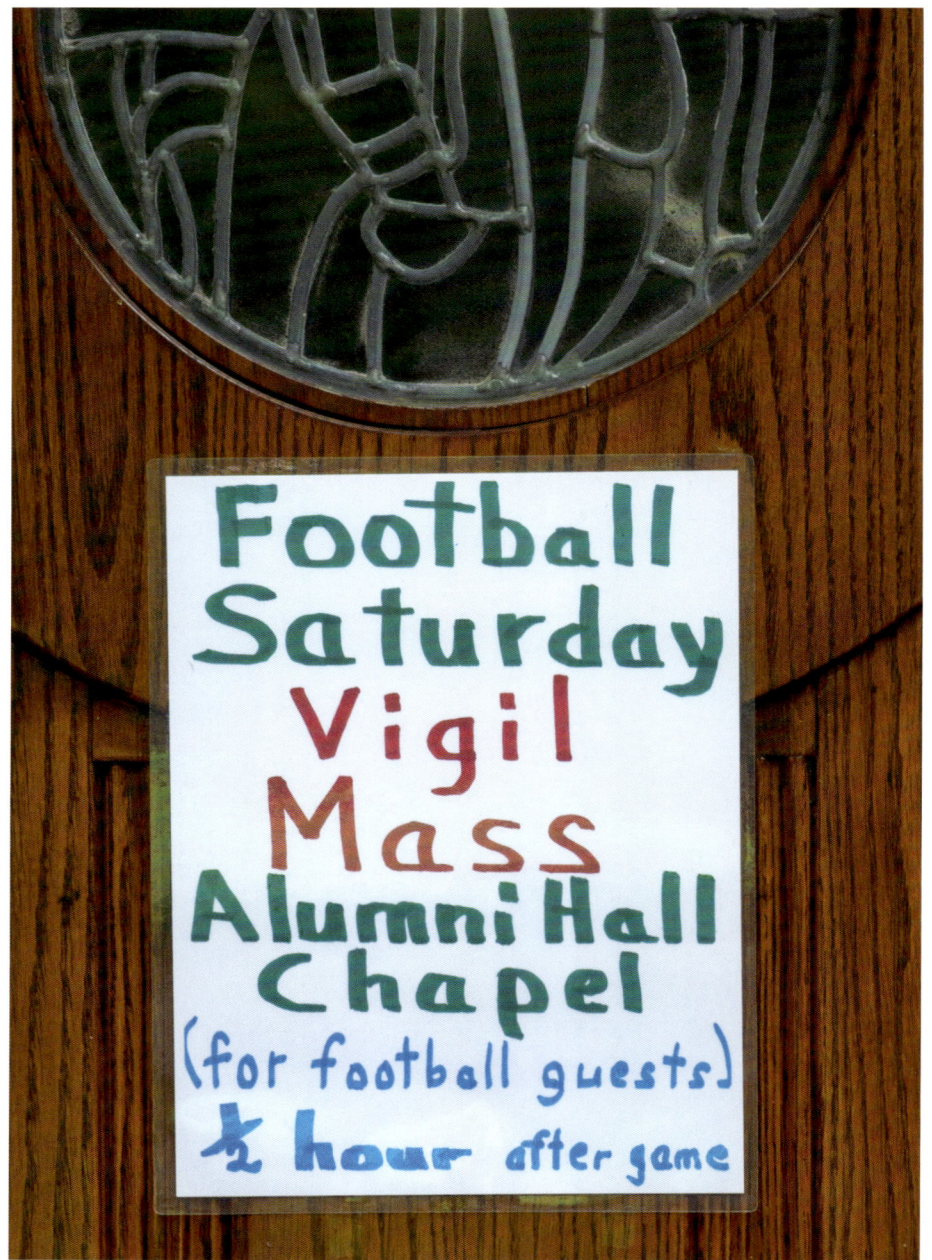

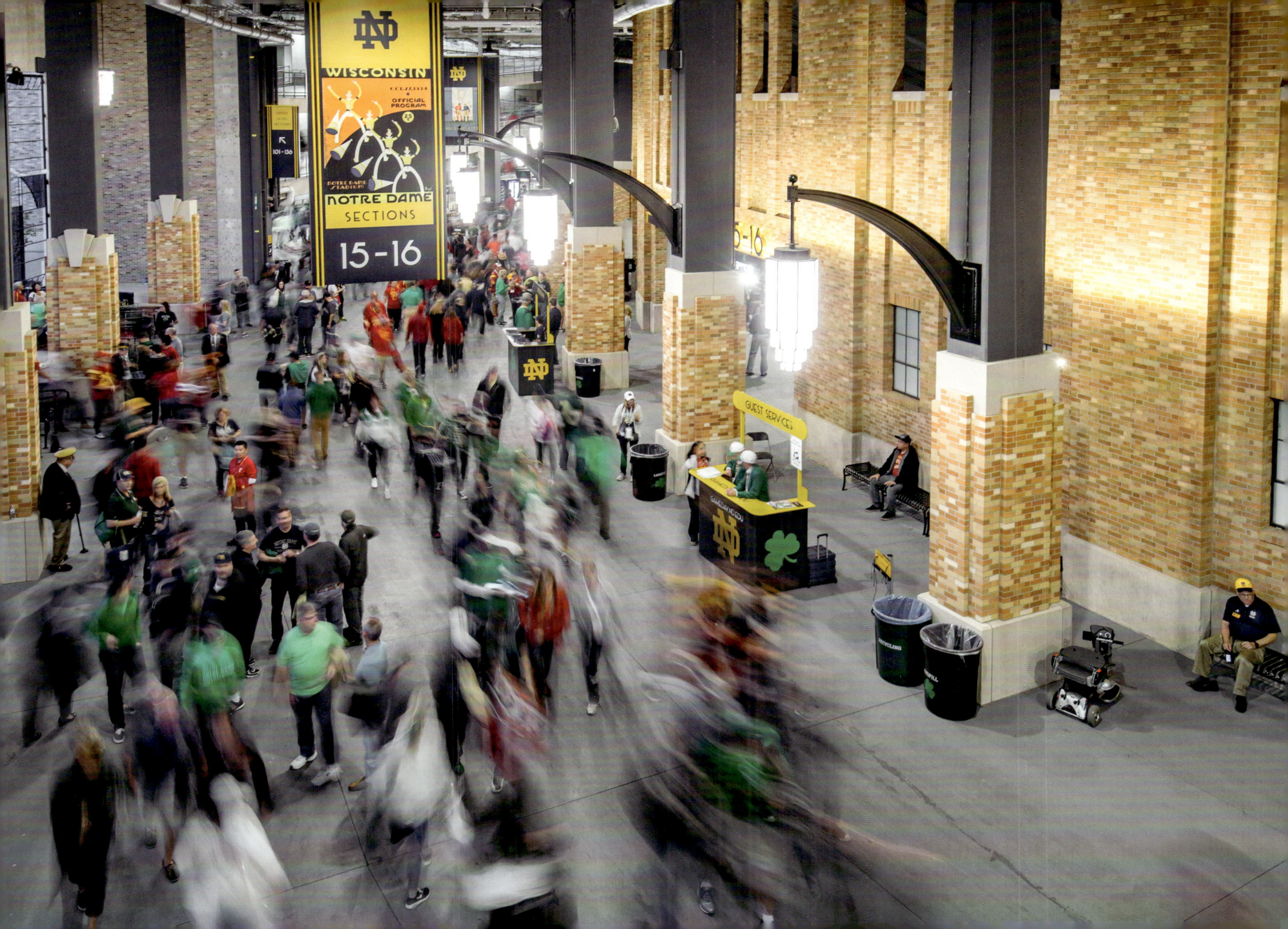

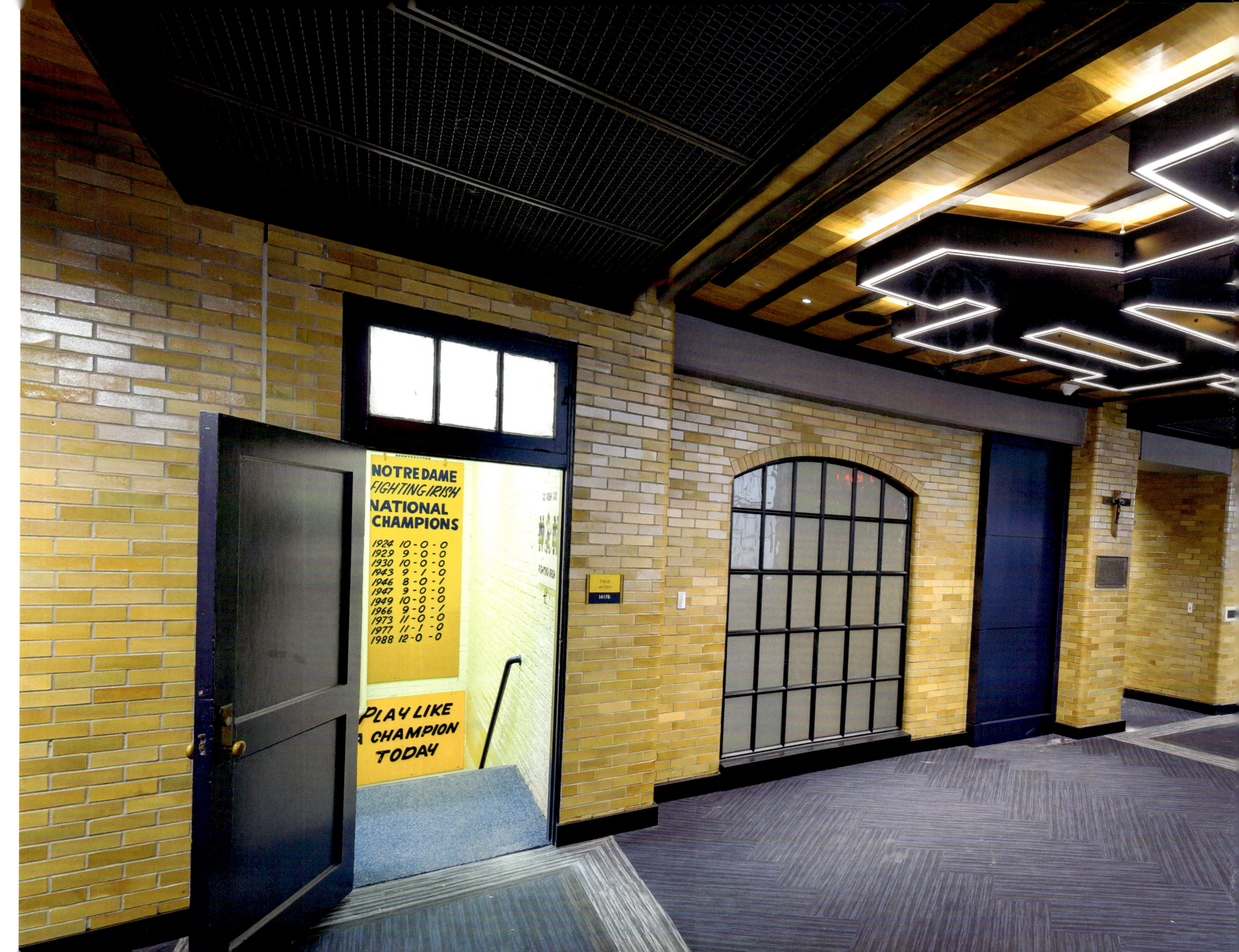

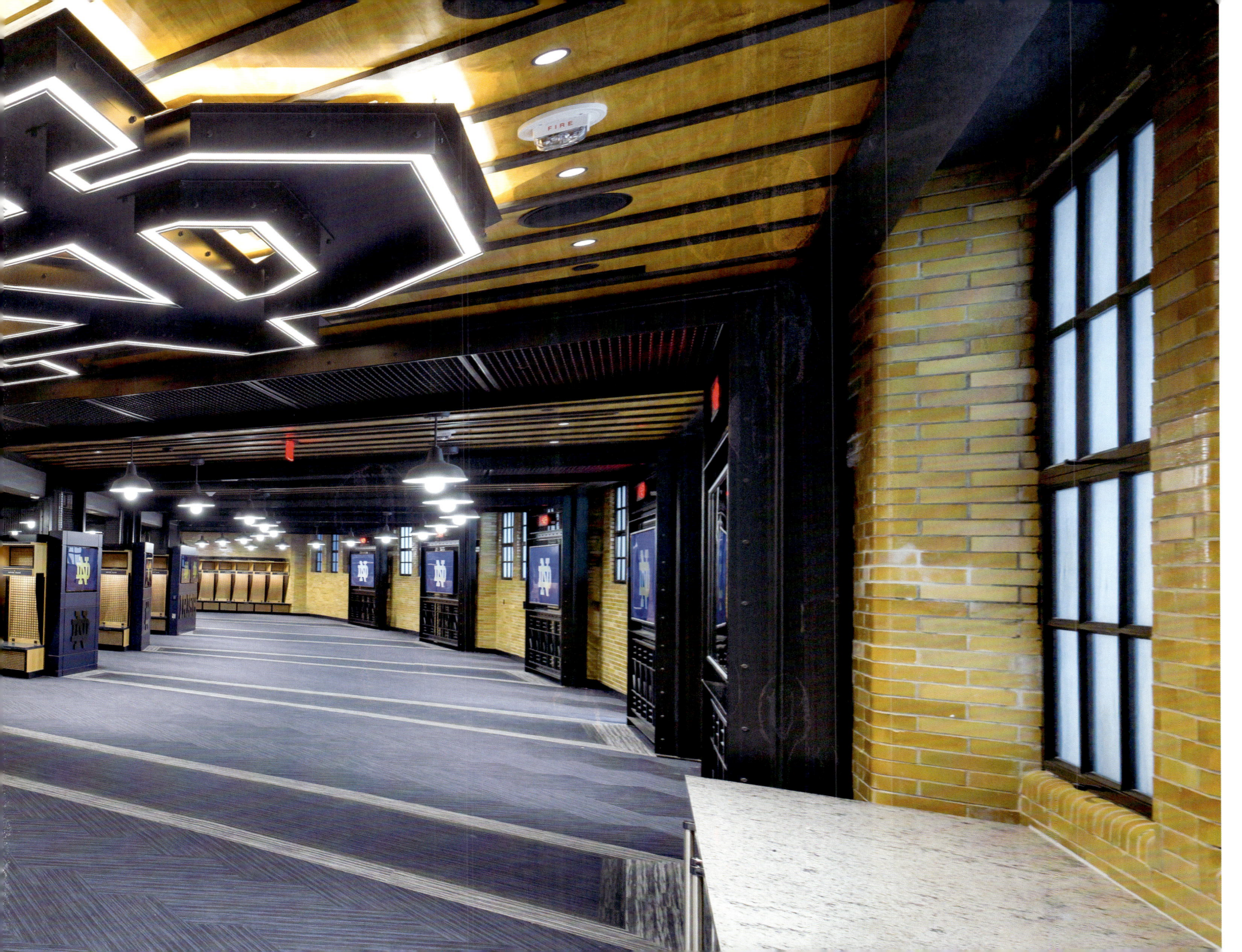

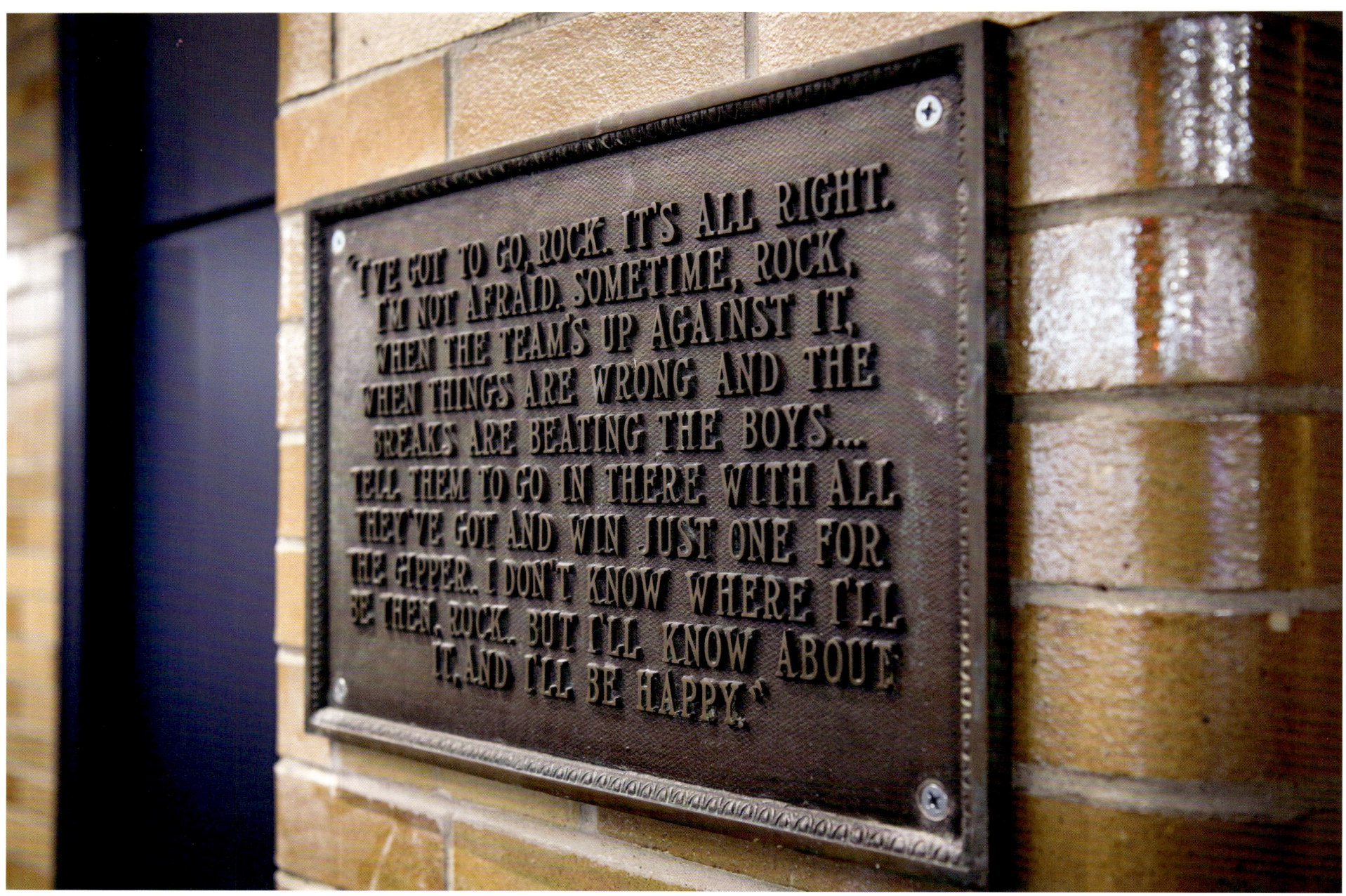

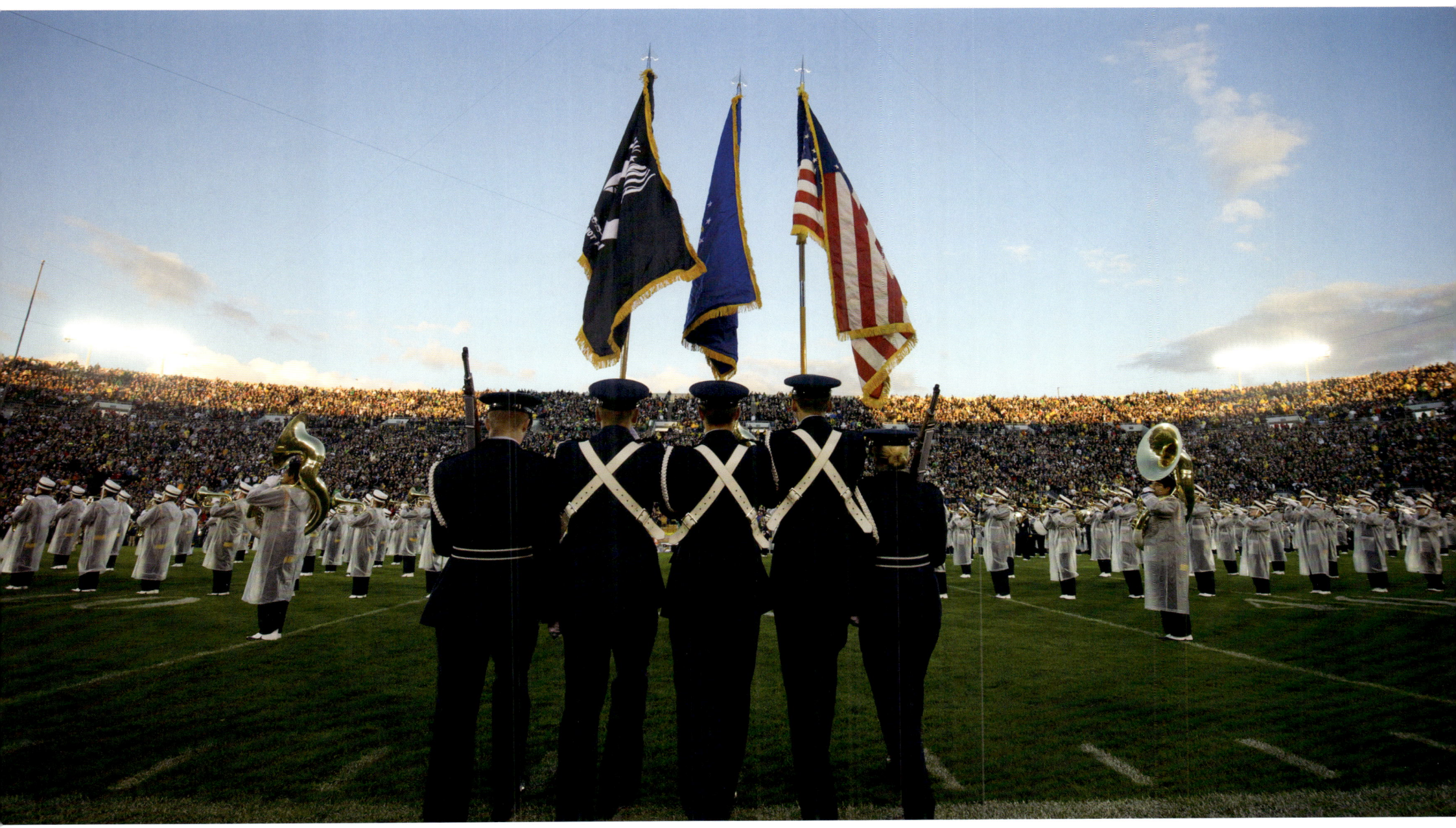

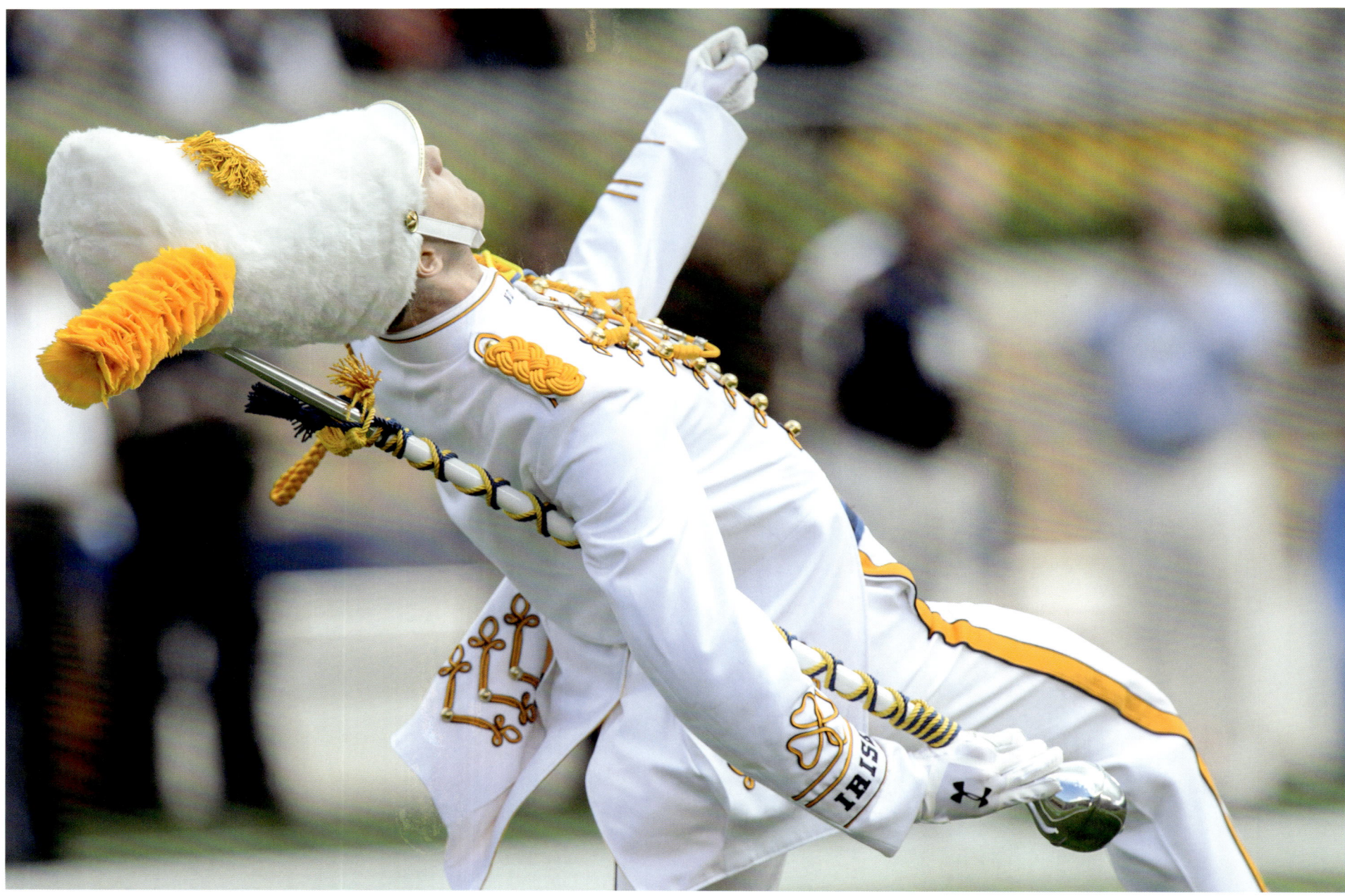

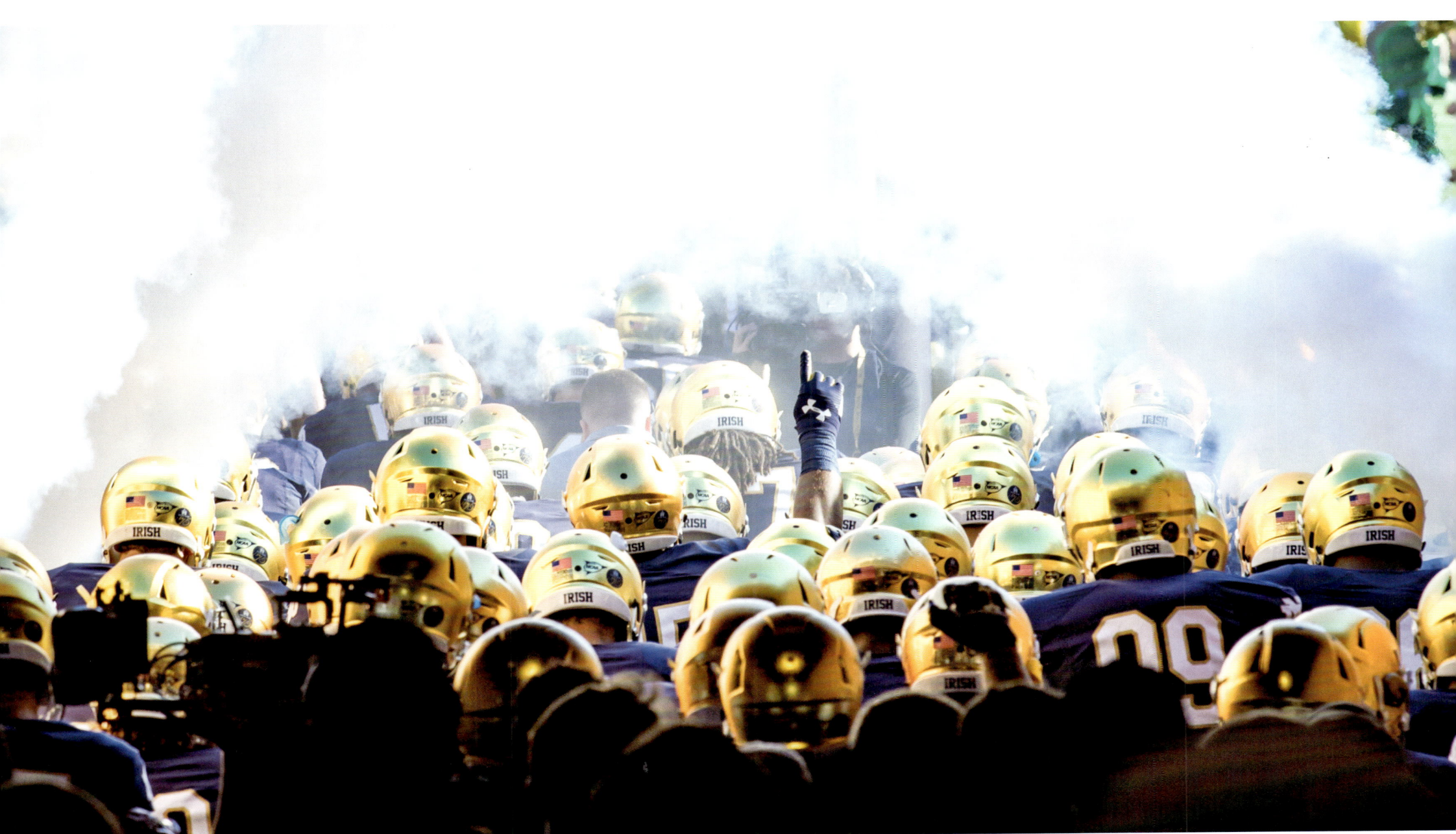

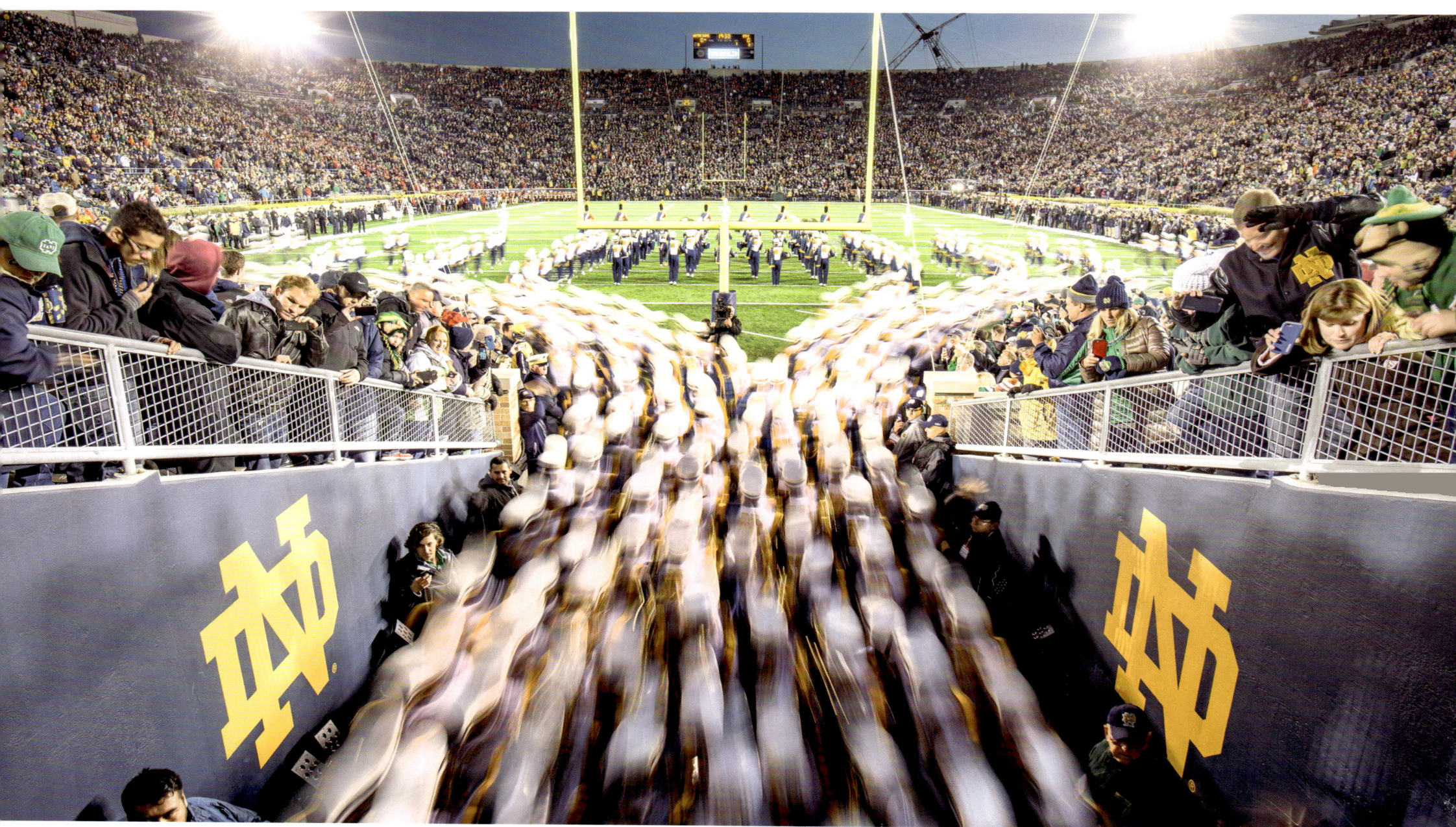

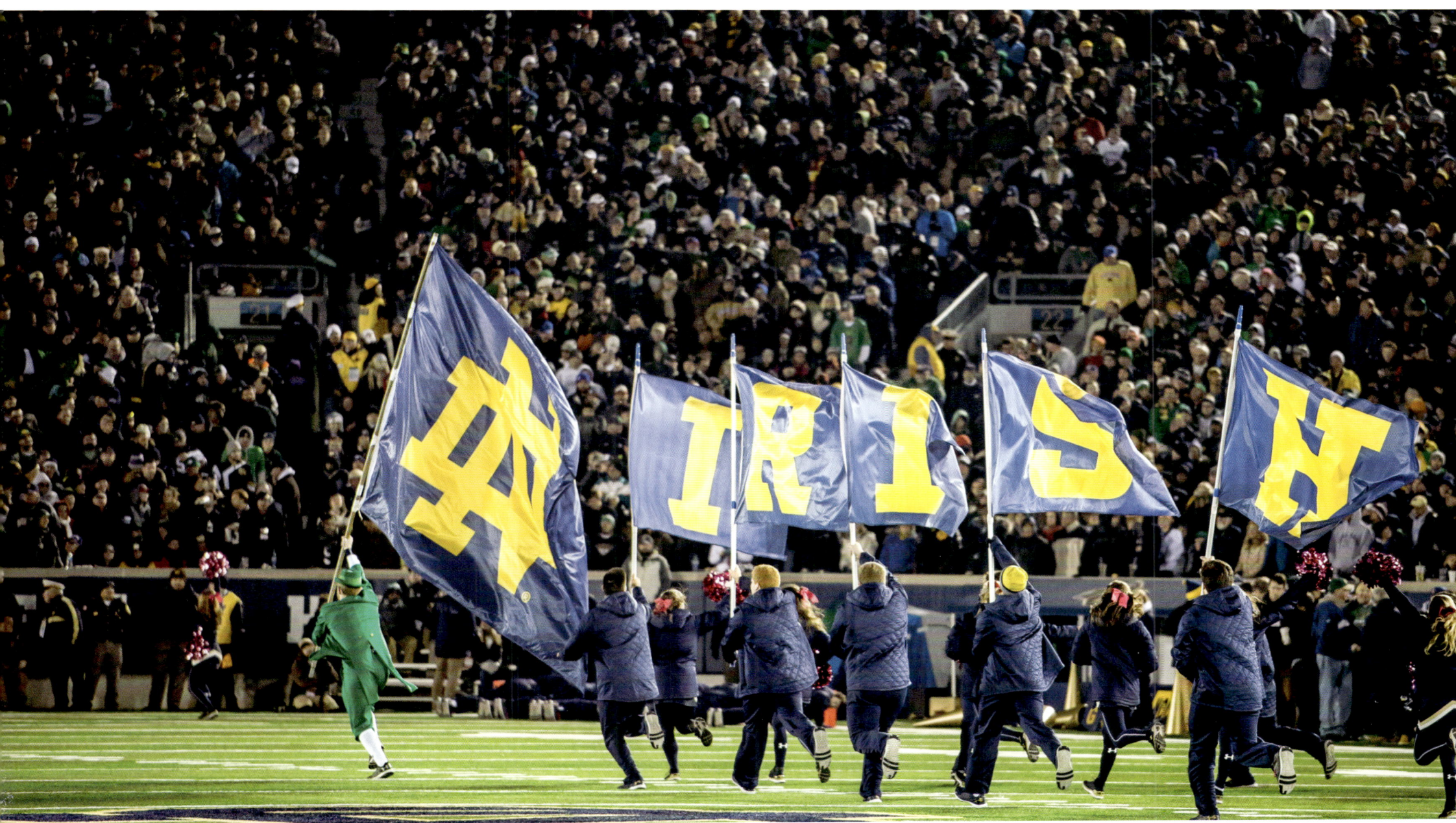

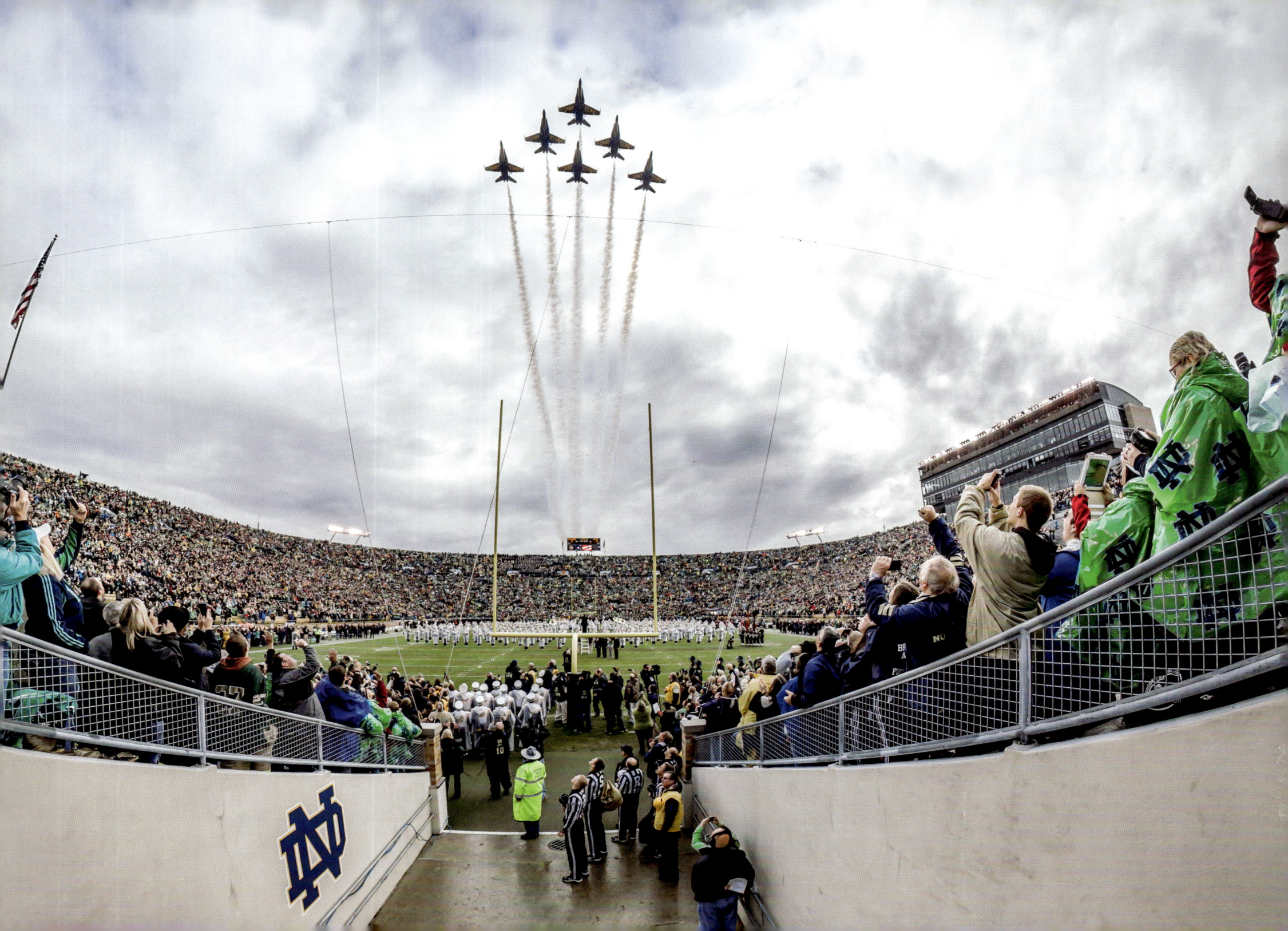

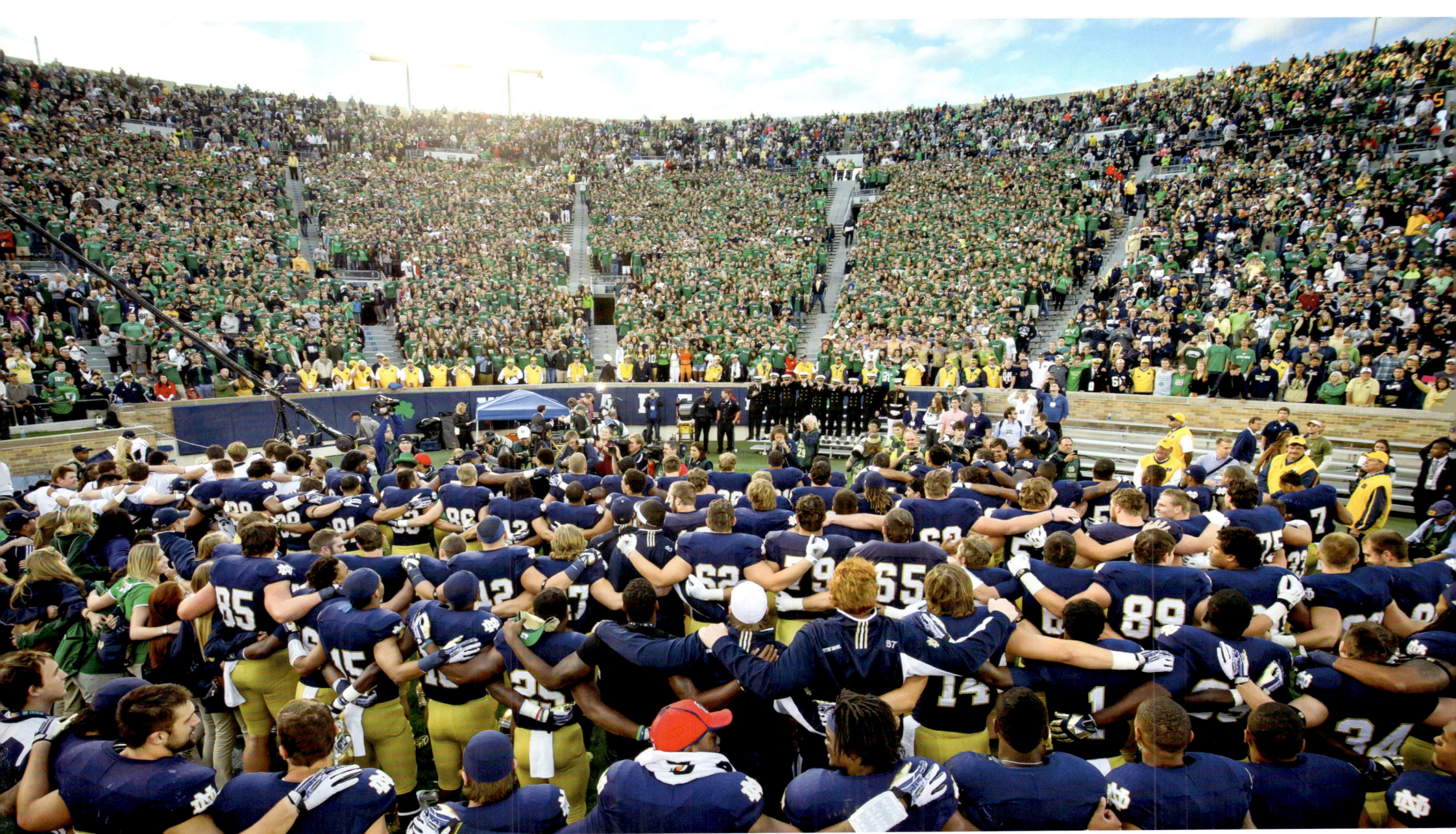

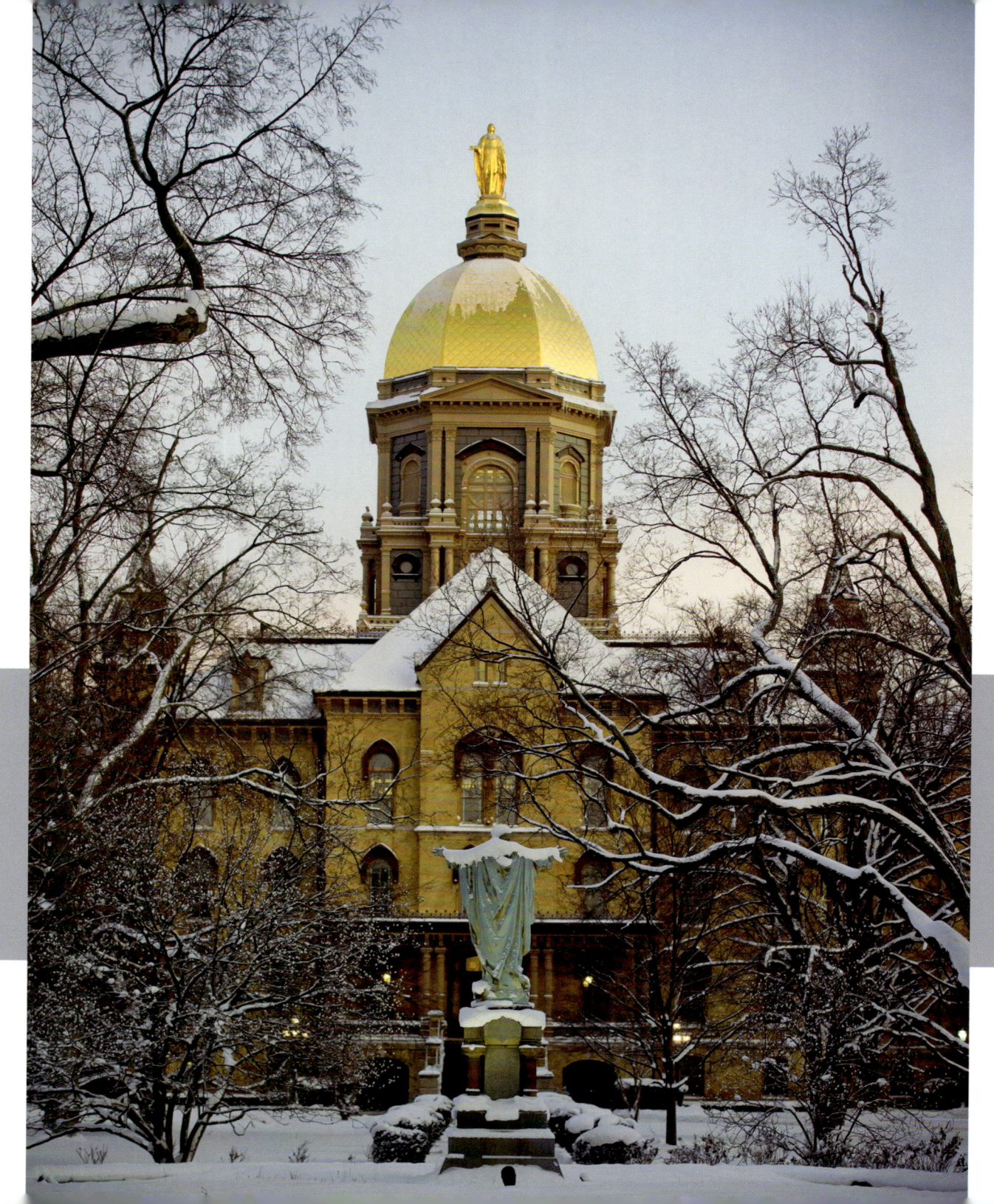

But just now . . . and just so many times, how I long for the Grotto. Away from the Grotto Dooley just prays. But at the Grotto, especially now when there must be snow everywhere and the lake is ice glass and that triangular fountain on the left is frozen solid and all the priests are bundled in their too-large too-long old black coats and the students wear snow boots . . . if I could go to the Grotto now then I think I could sing inside. I could be full of faith and poetry and loveliness and know more beauty, tenderness and compassion.

—Tom Dooley, celebrated humanitarian doctor,
in a letter to Father Hesburgh written
December 2, 1960, six weeks before his death

WINTER

Winter at Notre Dame can hurt. It can be a grim, siege-like assault on the senses, the psyche, the spirit, the soul. A pearl-grey permacloud can settle over the landscape for days, and the days can trudge by. Notre Dame winters seem to defy the laws of physics. There is no tailwind; the wind is always coming at you.

But I do love winter when the cascading snow is beauty in flowing motion, when the sky is blue and the air is crisp and tight as crystal, with snow blanketing the quads and rooftops, dolloped like whipped cream on tree trunks, limbs, and bushes. It can be bracing, and unearthly quiet— footsteps and voices muffled by the muting acoustics of snow. Sometimes, when the air is still and clean, I will pause to savor the elegance of this wintry wonderland, the purity and peace. The Dome is never brighter than on a glistening January day, the Grotto never more explicitly fervent than on a winter's night. I love walking campus in the dark of winter when even the shadows are illumined by winter's white countenance. The buildings, too, seem more inviting, as they offer warmth and refuge from frosted nights afoot.

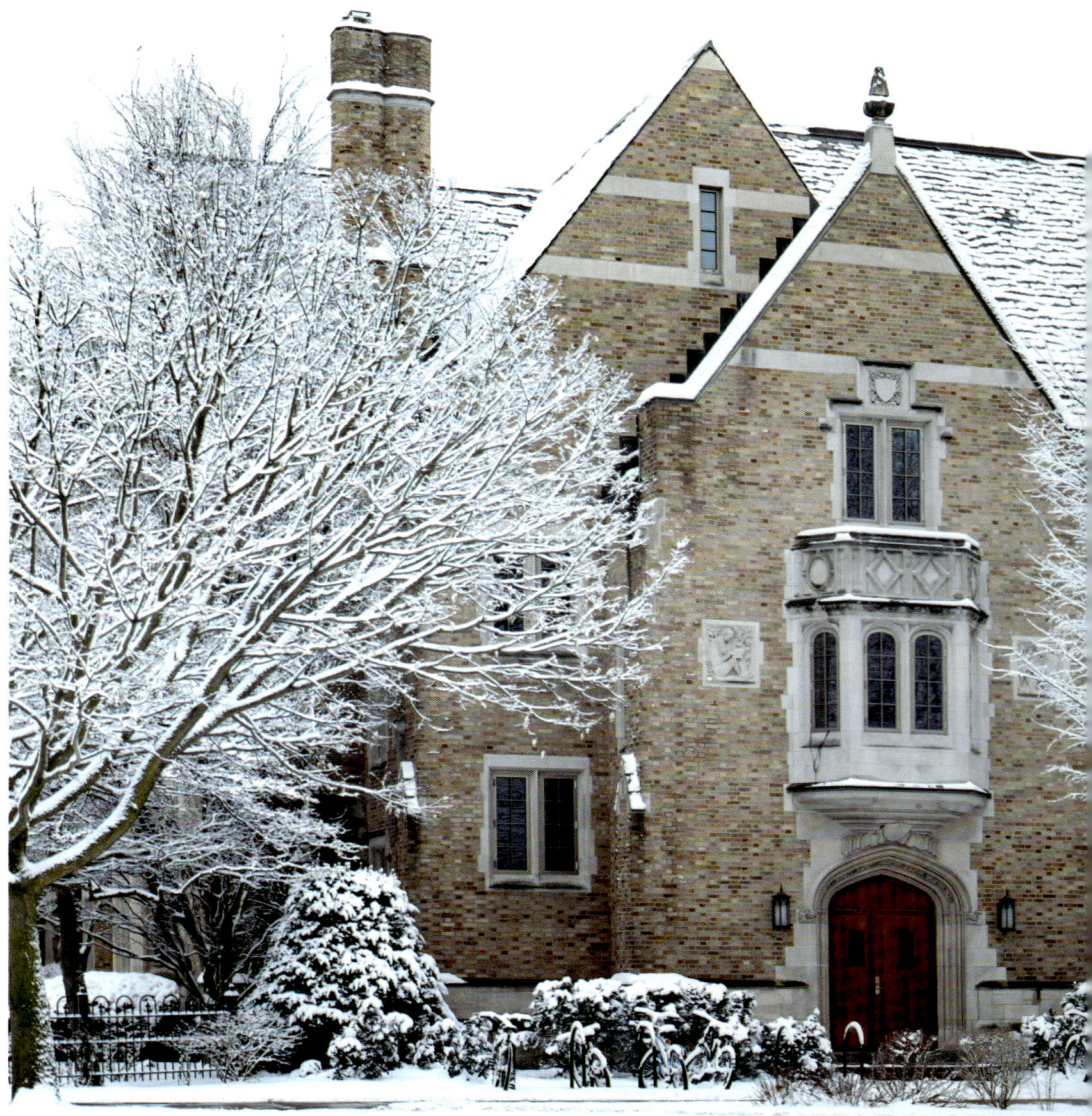

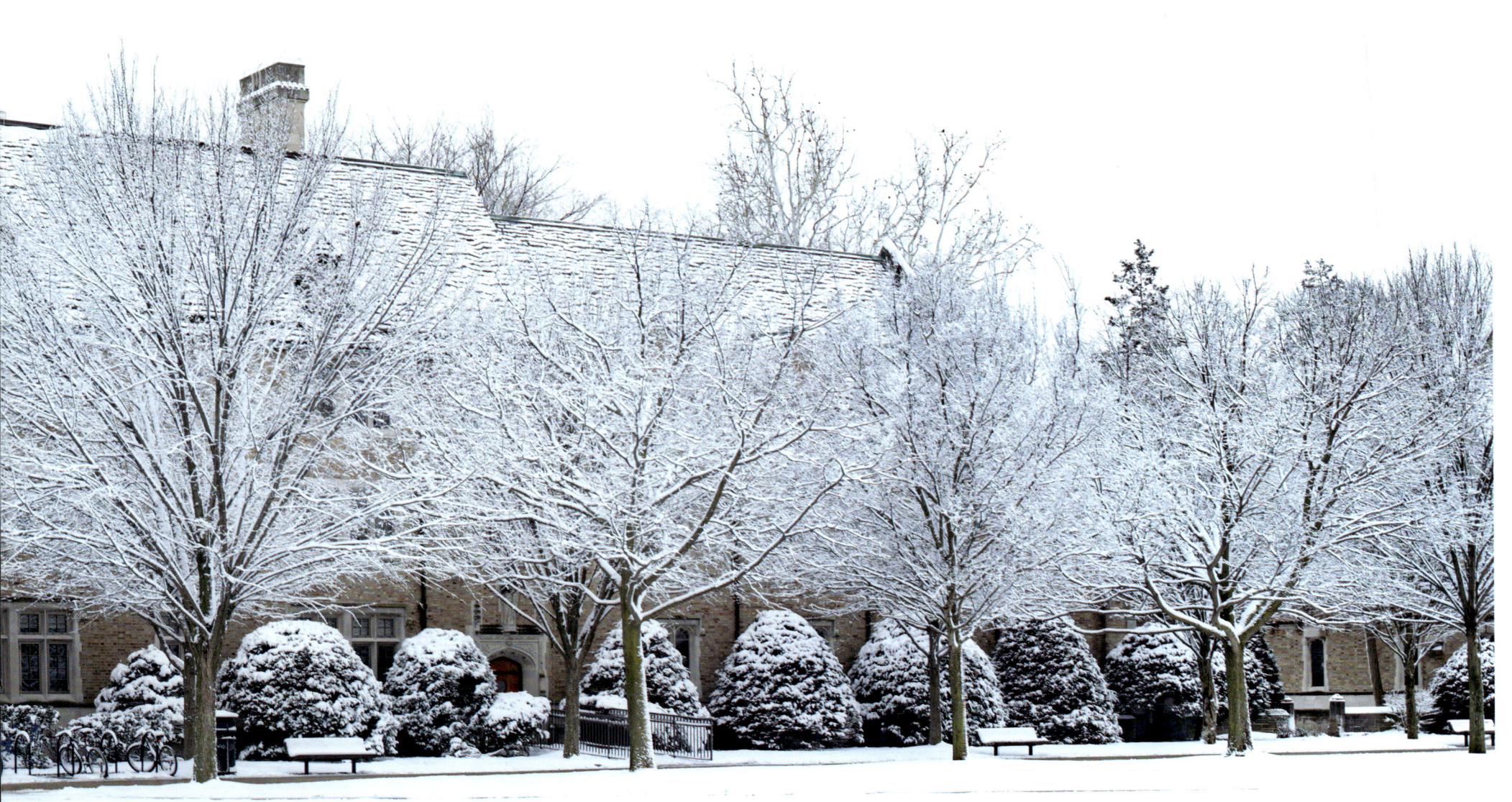

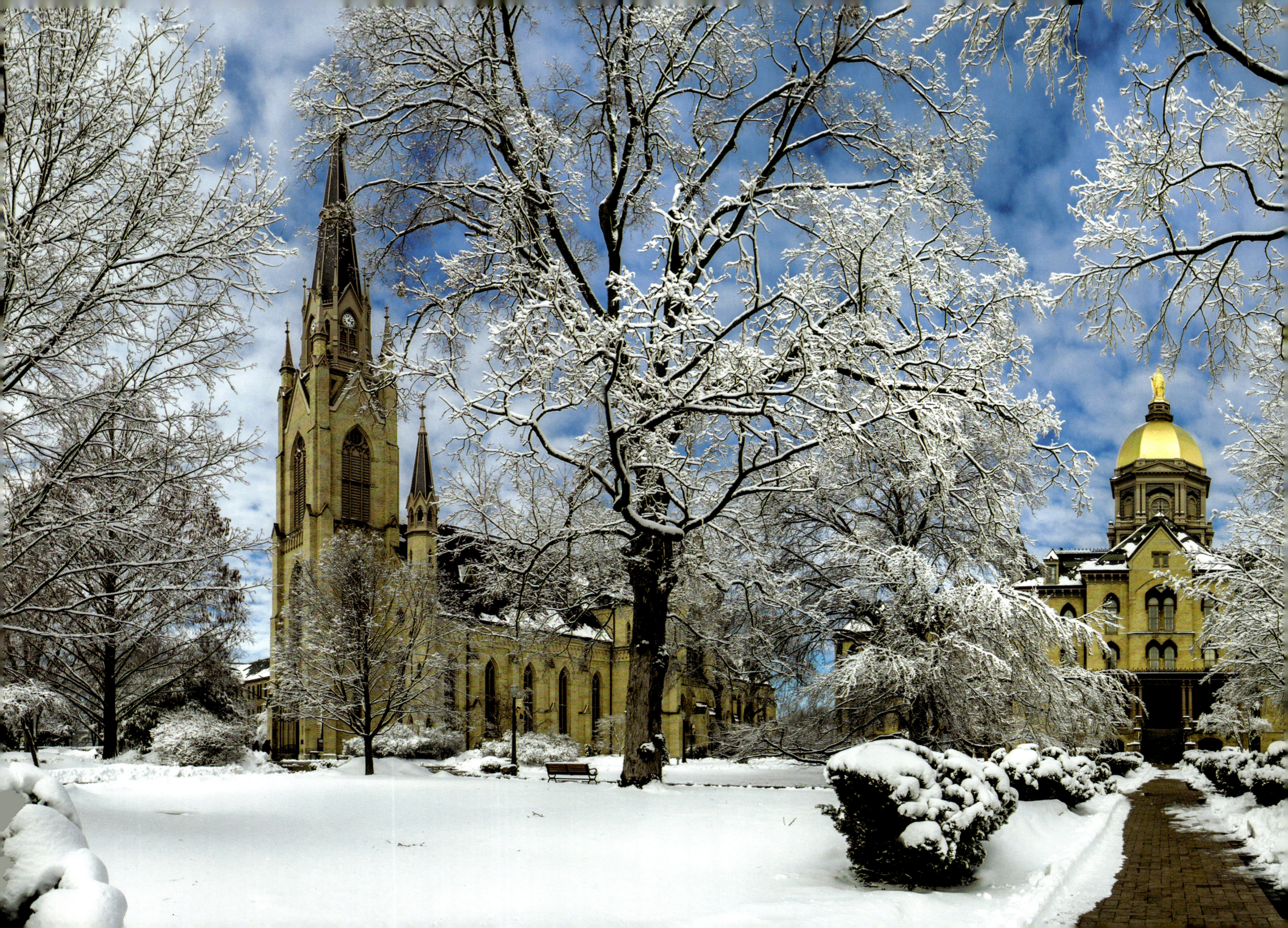

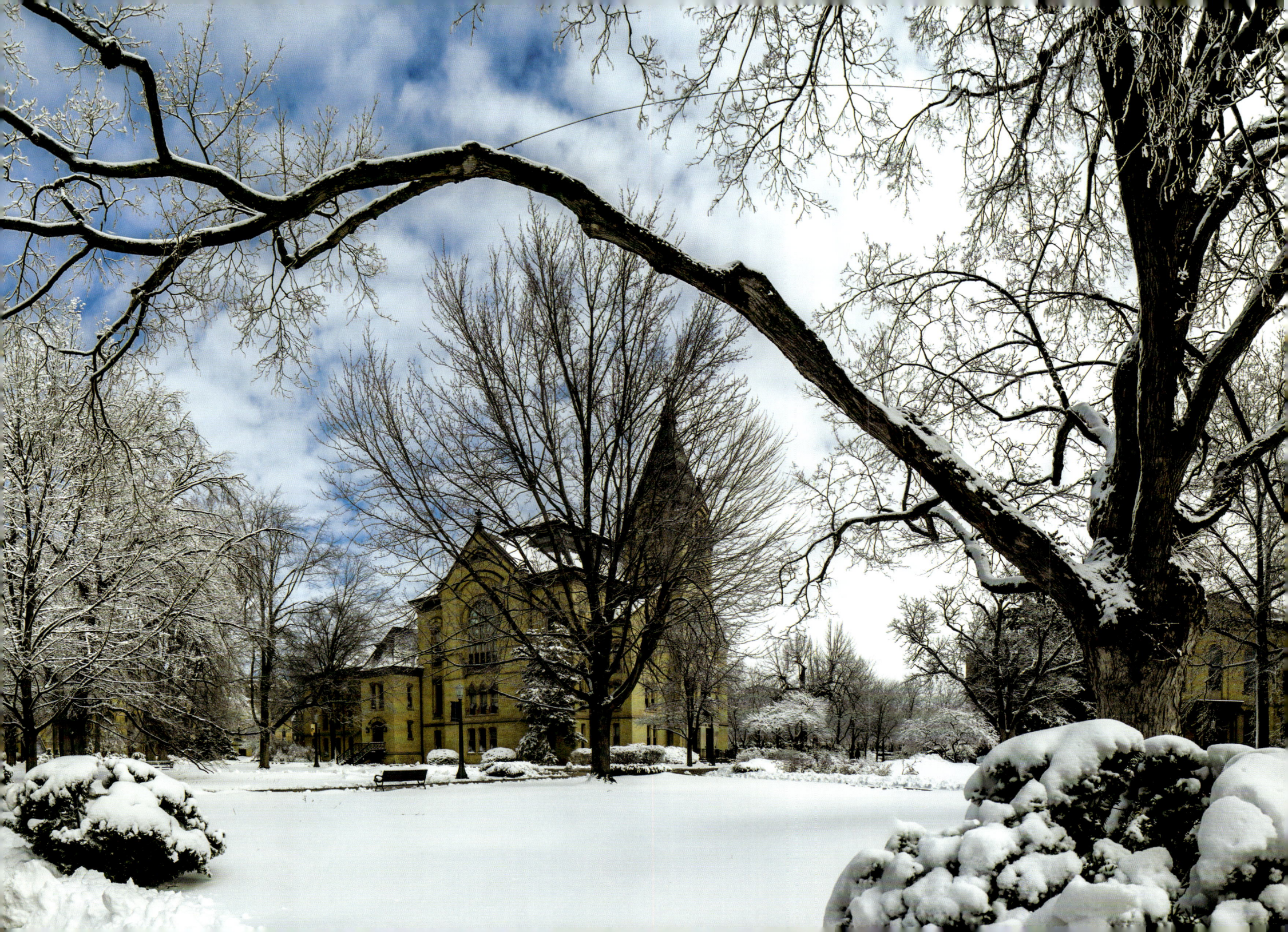

For those shuffling from one building to another in winter, silence envelopes the darkened campus. Light pools on the sidewalks. The lattice-work windows of residence halls glow reddish, gold, and amber. The sounds of music and laughter emanate from the cozy confines where roommates study, tease, and taunt, sometimes console in hushed tones. Real living takes place here, where bunks and lofts, rectors and friends and desks and all manner of electronic devices crowd into these flourishing cells of human habitation. Indeed, this just might be the very place where the real education takes place, where the ideas, dreams, and theories get plumbed and tested to see if they mesh or clash with the inescapable, in-your-face reality of living life in earnest.

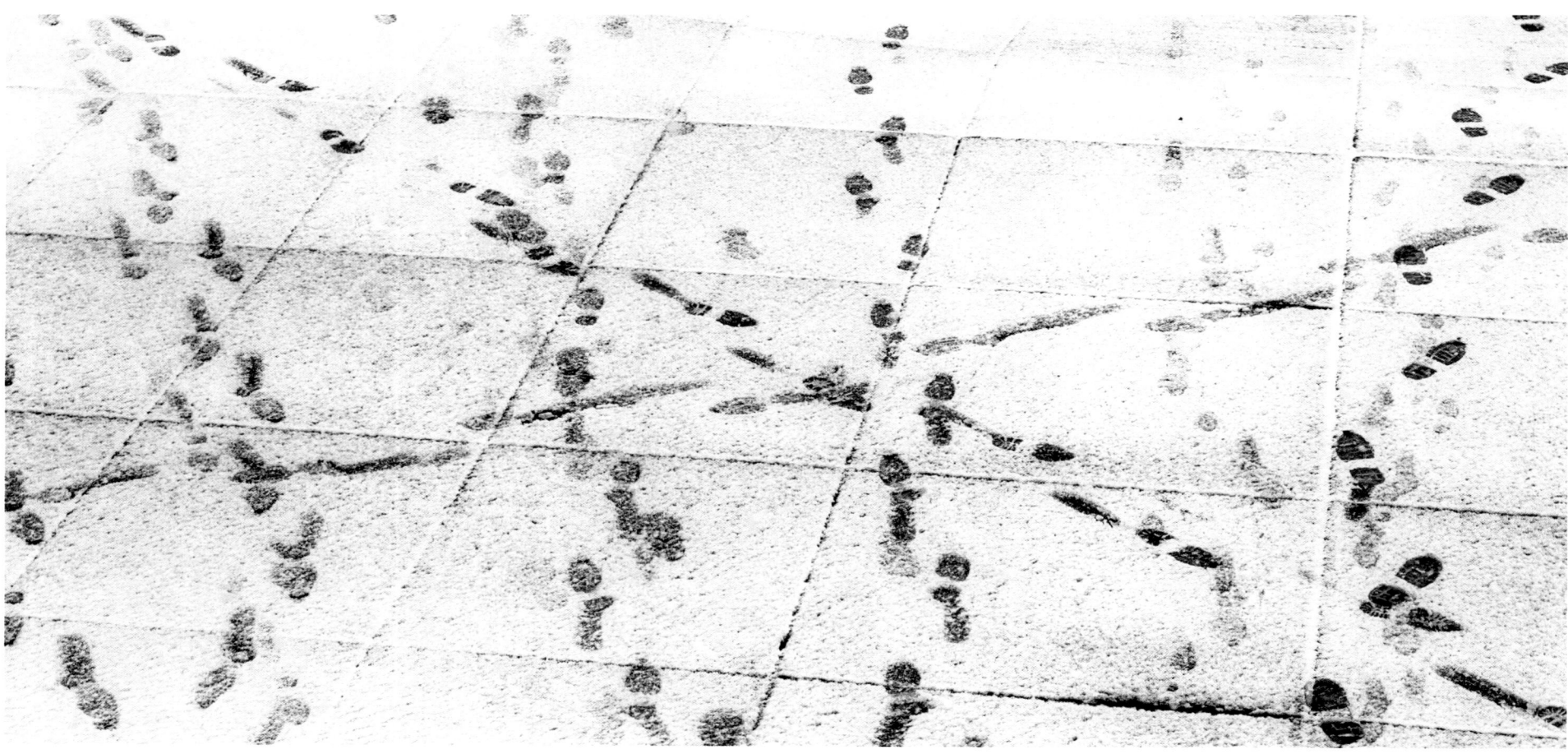

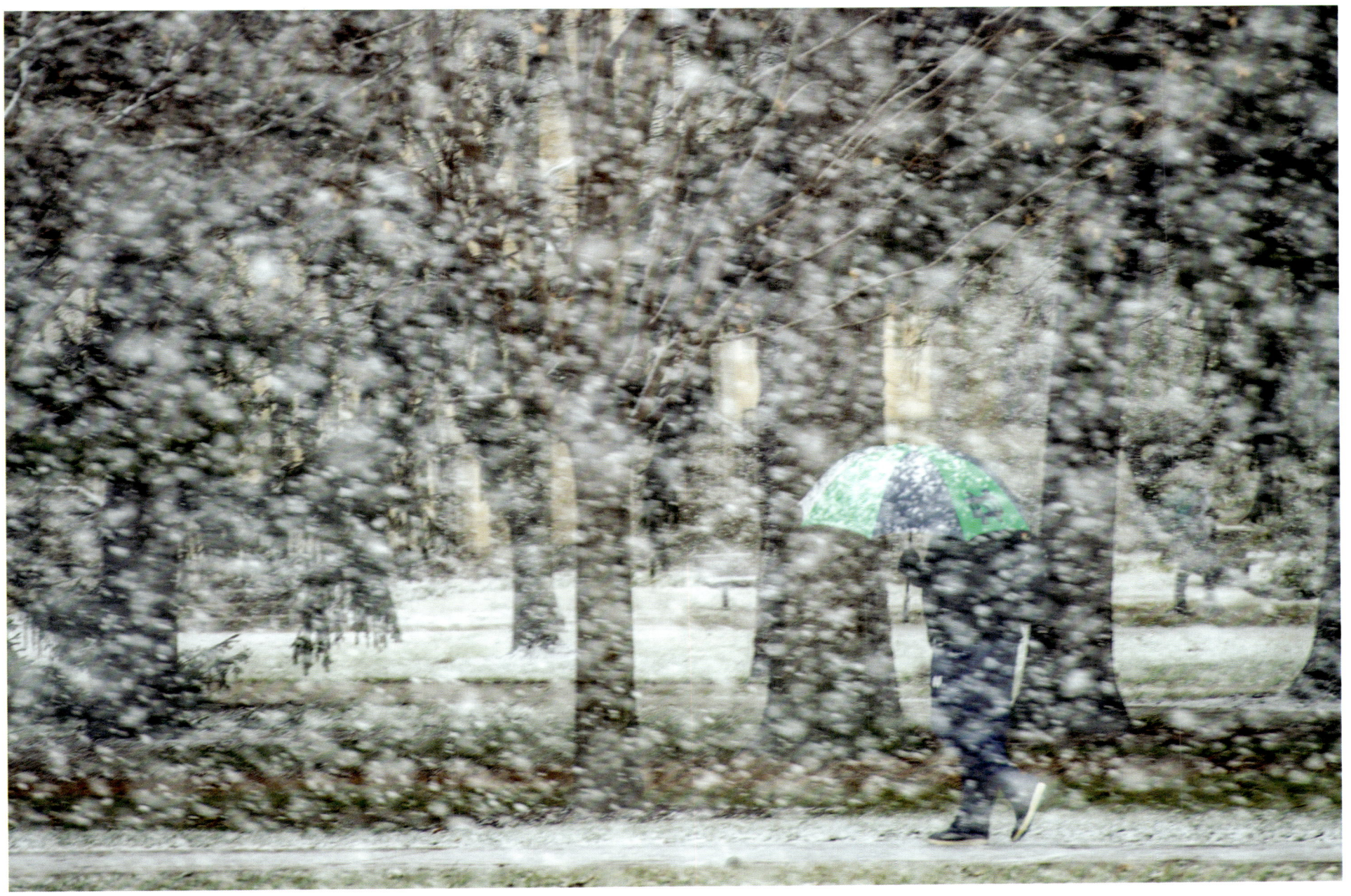

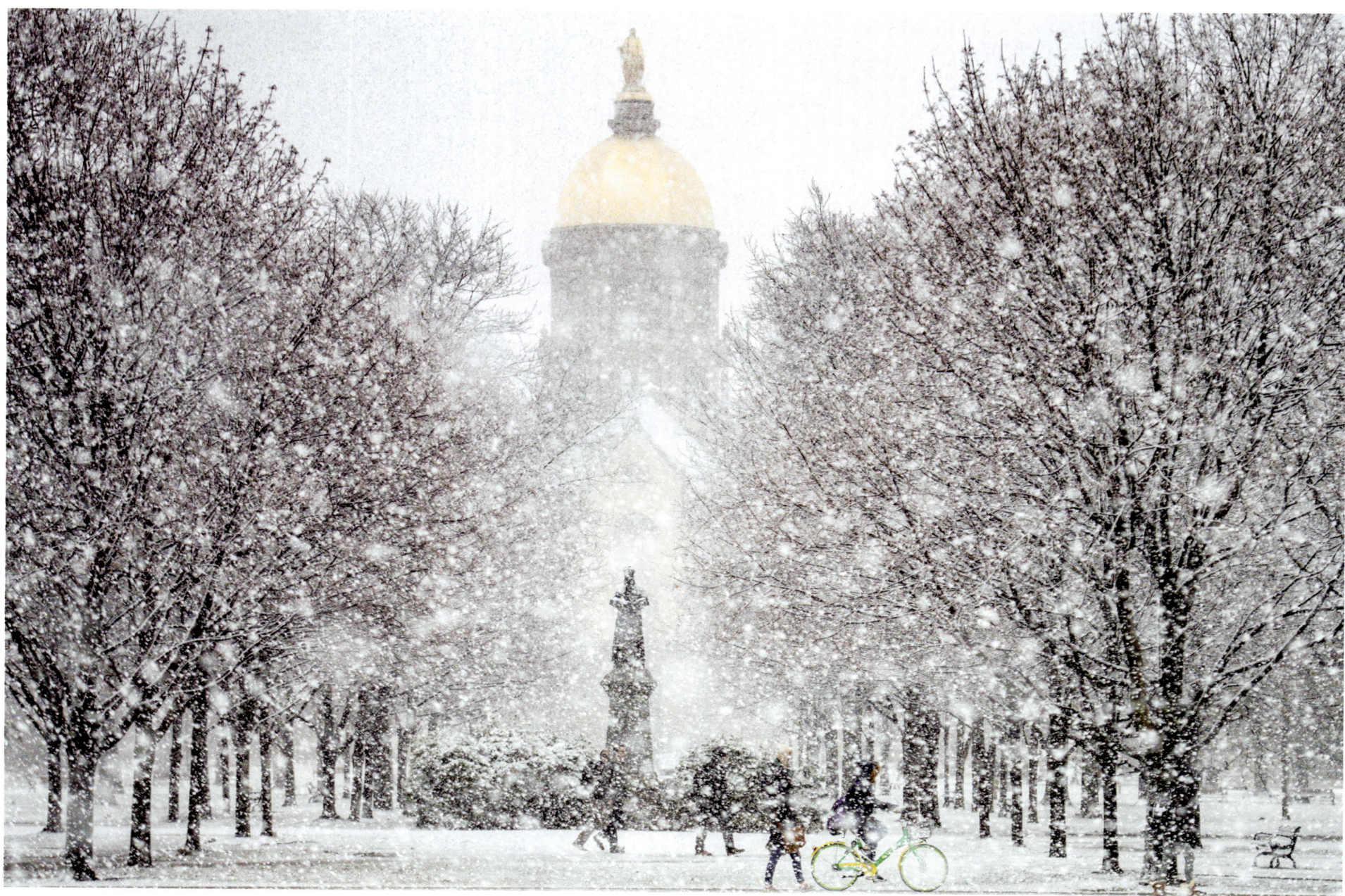

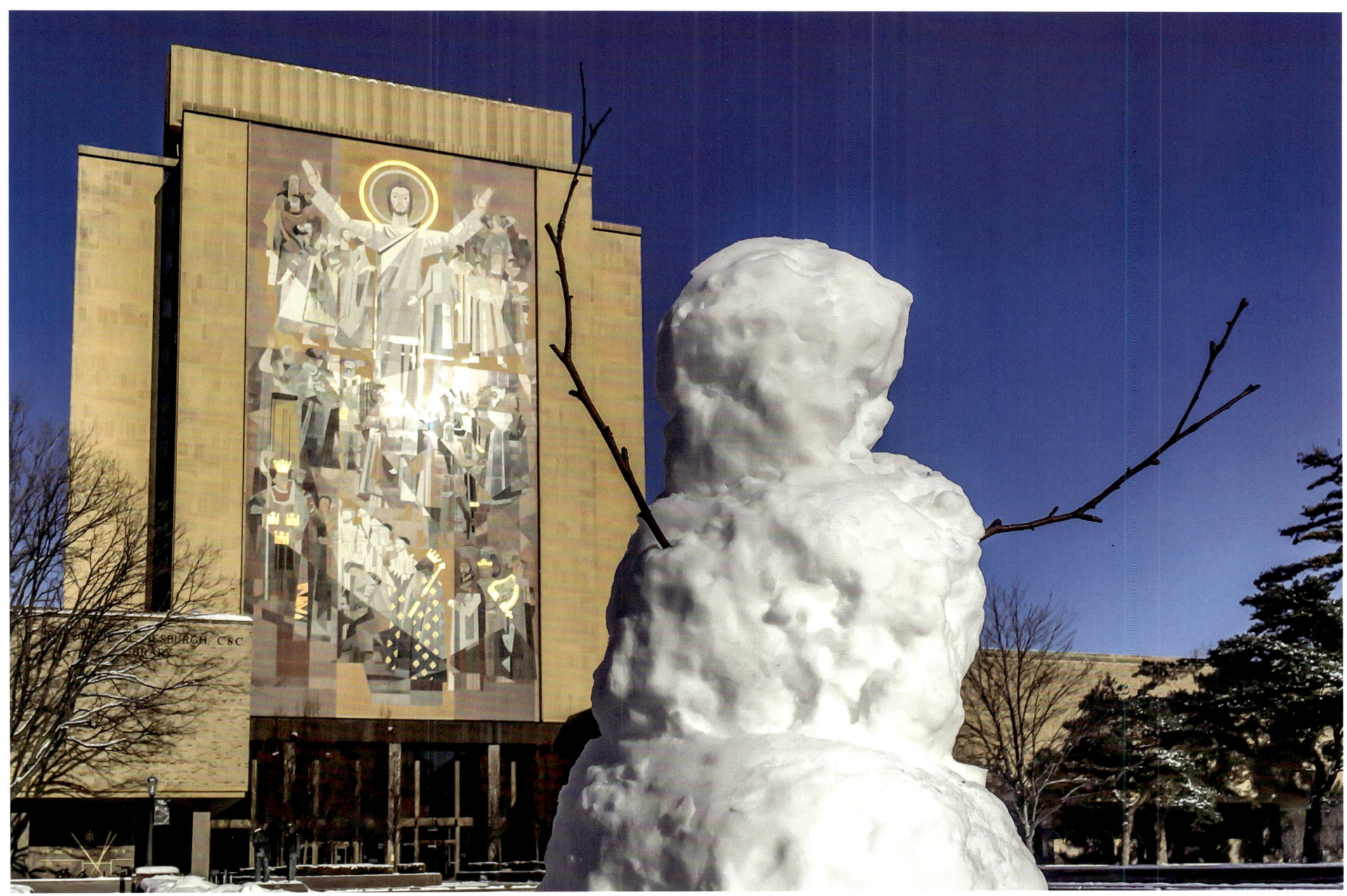

In the beginning Notre Dame was to be its own place. It had its own farm and farm animals, crops, butchers, kitchens, brick works, stables, tailors, cobblers, bakers, cooks, priests, teachers, and students—a hummingly self-sufficient little enterprise carved into the Indiana wilderness. Today Notre Dame, having shed its monastic mindset, is still remarkably self-sufficient, taking care of its own utilities, running its own police and fire departments, providing its student body with all the twenty-first-century amenities, giving them all the advantages of a holistic, cutting-edge education while also operating a vastly complex corporate enterprise in support of this thriving community of scholars.

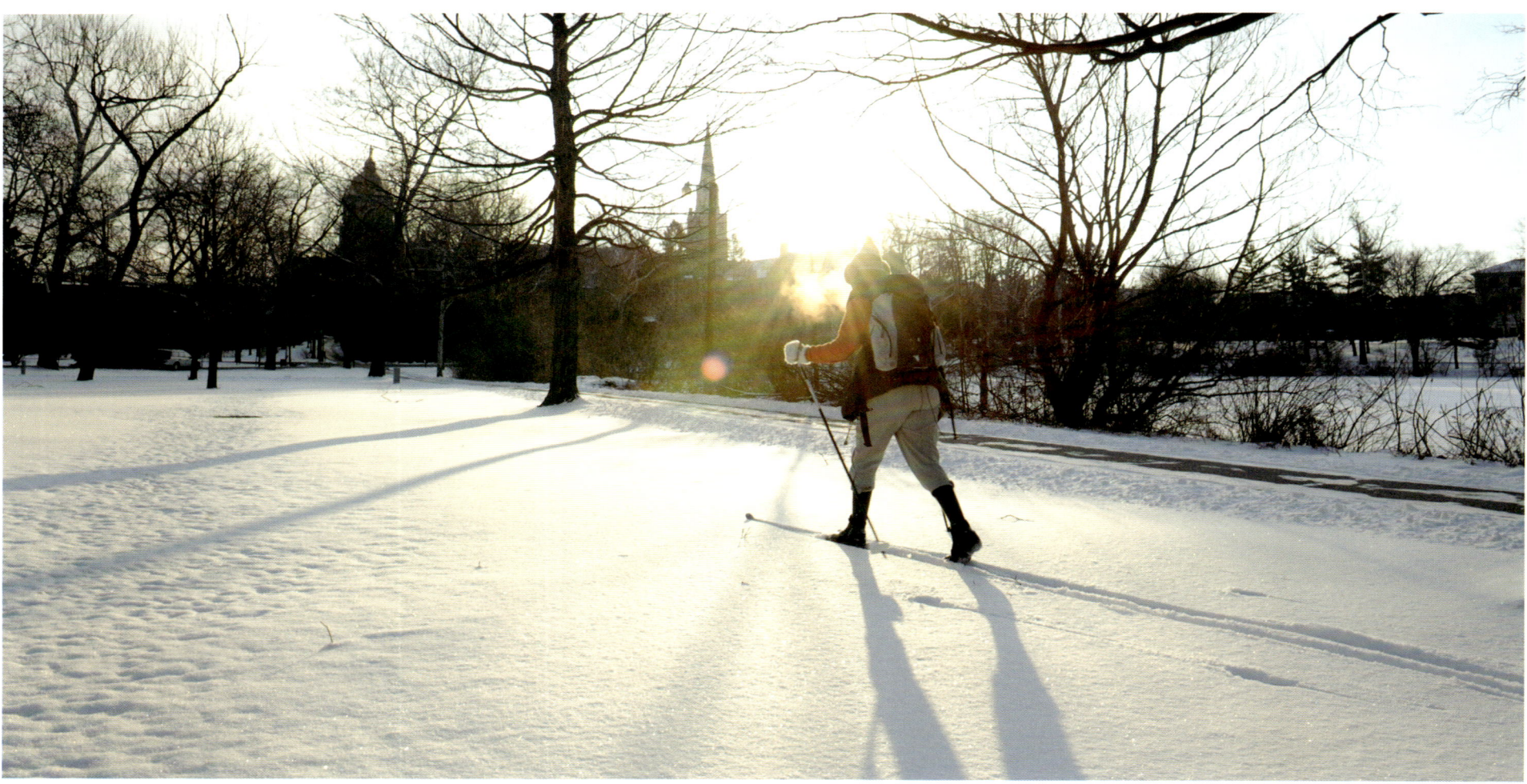

And yet all is peripheral to the education of students. Whether in the classroom or lab, hallway talk or conversation over coffee, the analysis of a senior thesis or the gentle coaxing of gleaming insight from a first-year seminar, that personal transaction between teacher and pupil is at the heart of all that happens here.

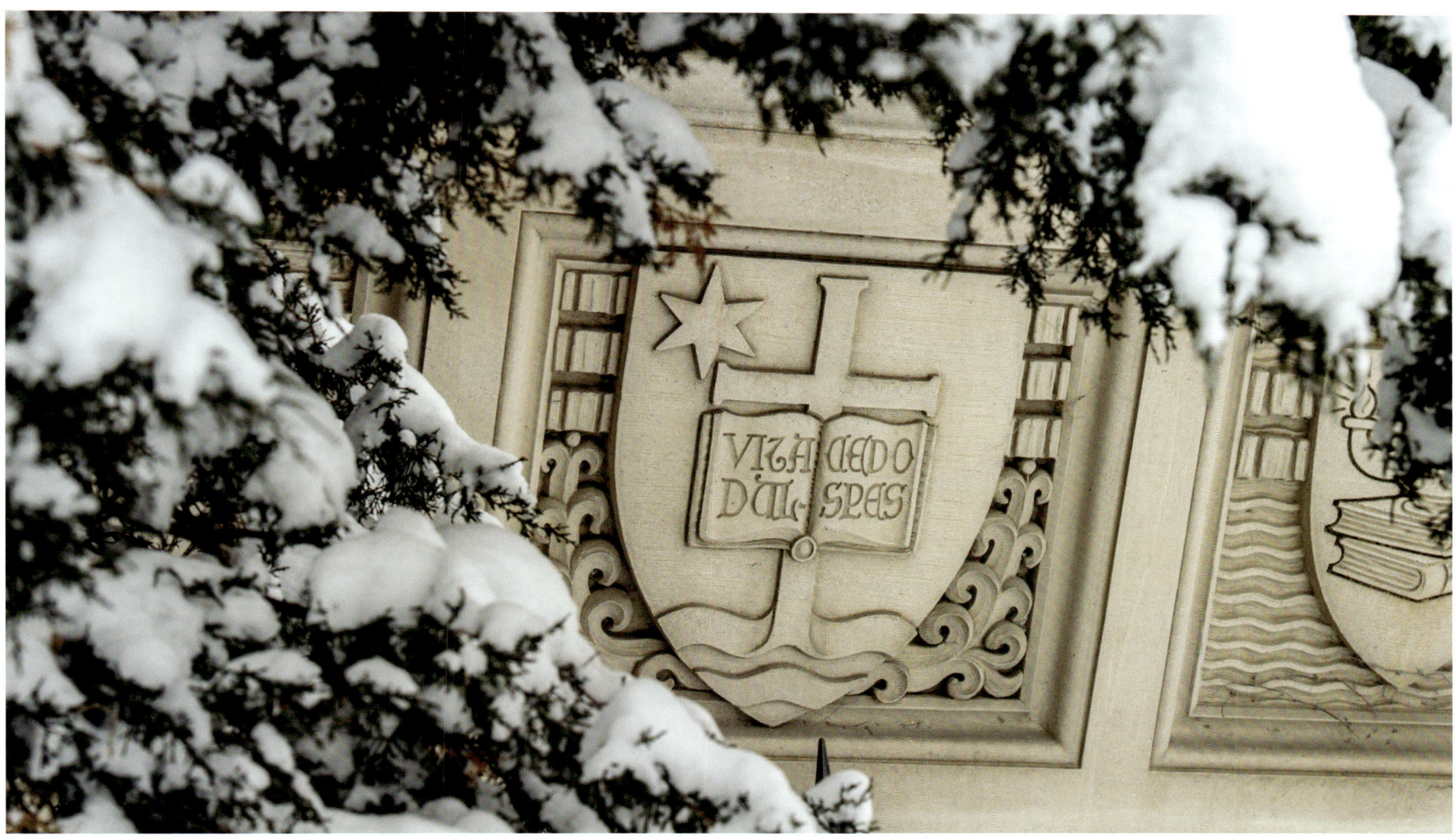

Each class I have taught over the years has had "writing" in its title. It has been so for decades; it is a kind of writer's workshop. It is grounded in journalism, in the elements of all good writing. But it's really about clarity of thought and self-expression, about the importance of communication and mining for truth as we fashion sentences and find the right word and tell our stories to each other. I do not teach or profess; I am a facilitator, a midwife, a fellow pilgrim, one of them. We look at essays, articles and stories, poetry and passages from books. We read and critique each other's work. We are all in this together. There is a pantheon of giants who have come before me. I try my best not to let them down. Or fail the students sitting before me—so eager and earnest, so incredibly smart and ambitious, so wanting to please, to do what's right, to learn and move on. So even though each class has "writing" in the title, the time together is also spent trying to figure out life and ourselves, to say and write what we mean, to know how we really feel, to convey what we've really experienced, to raise our hands and speak to the world, the words we pull from our minds and hearts. And this happens all over campus, I think, even in classes not about writing.

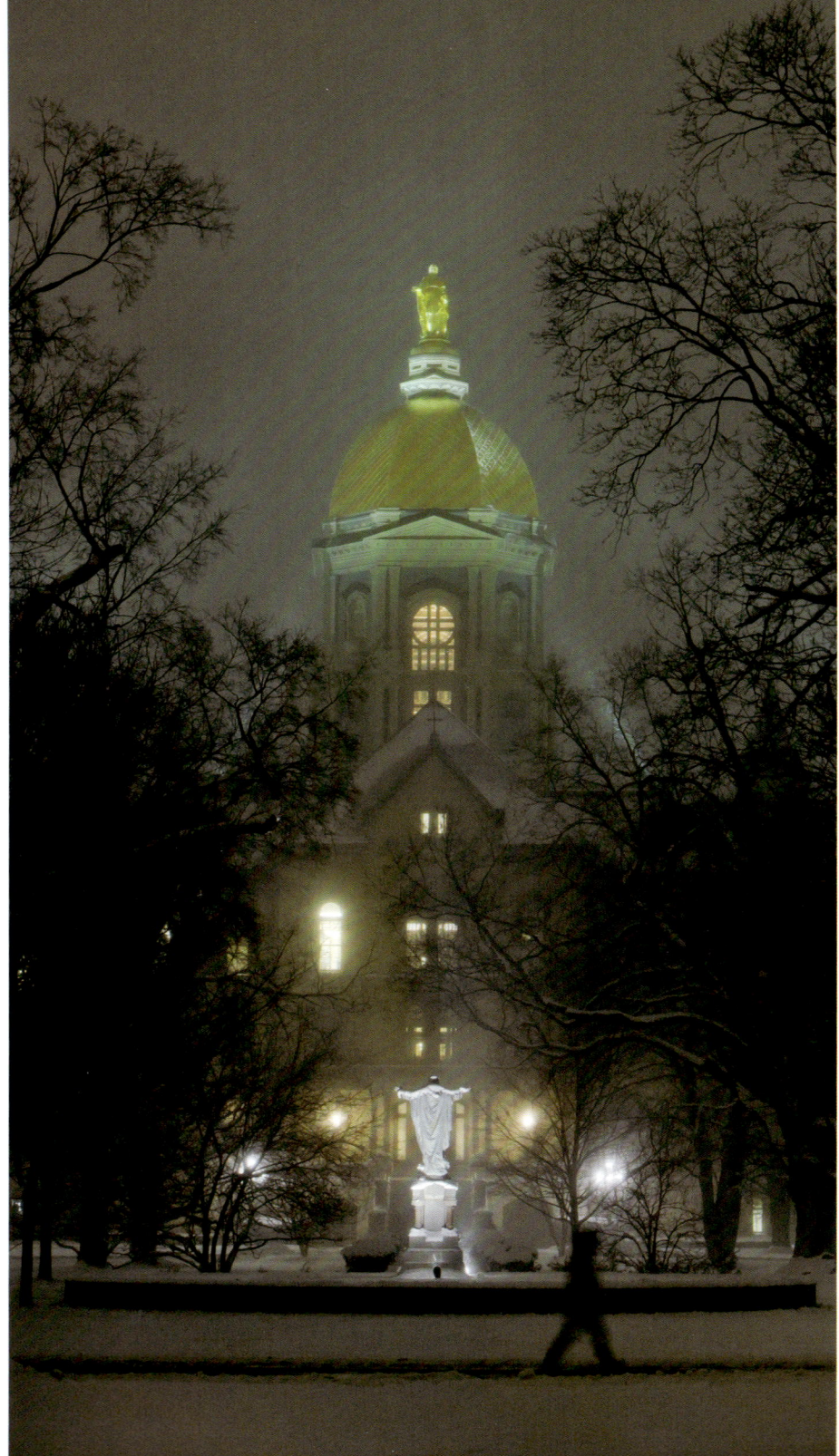

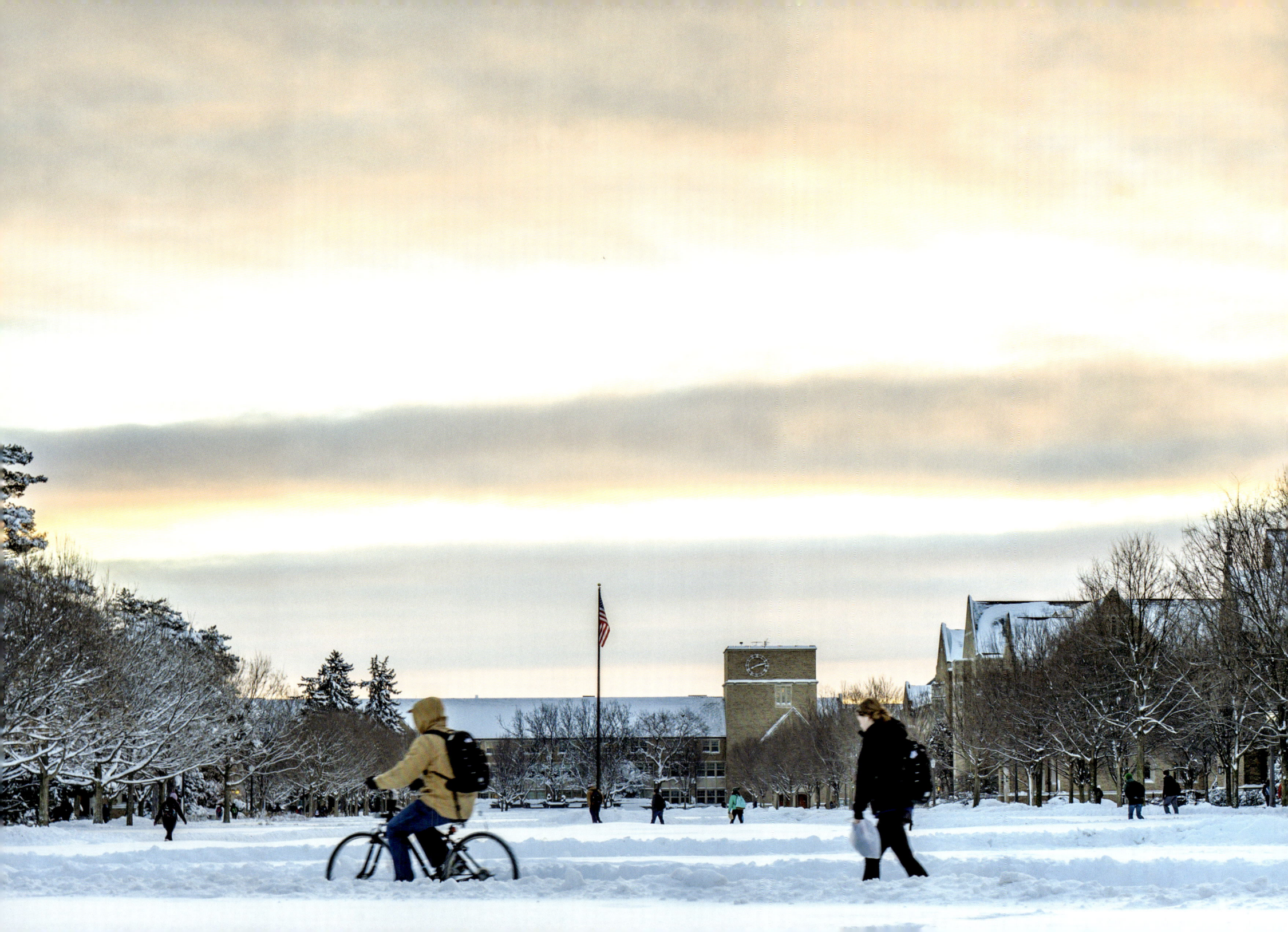

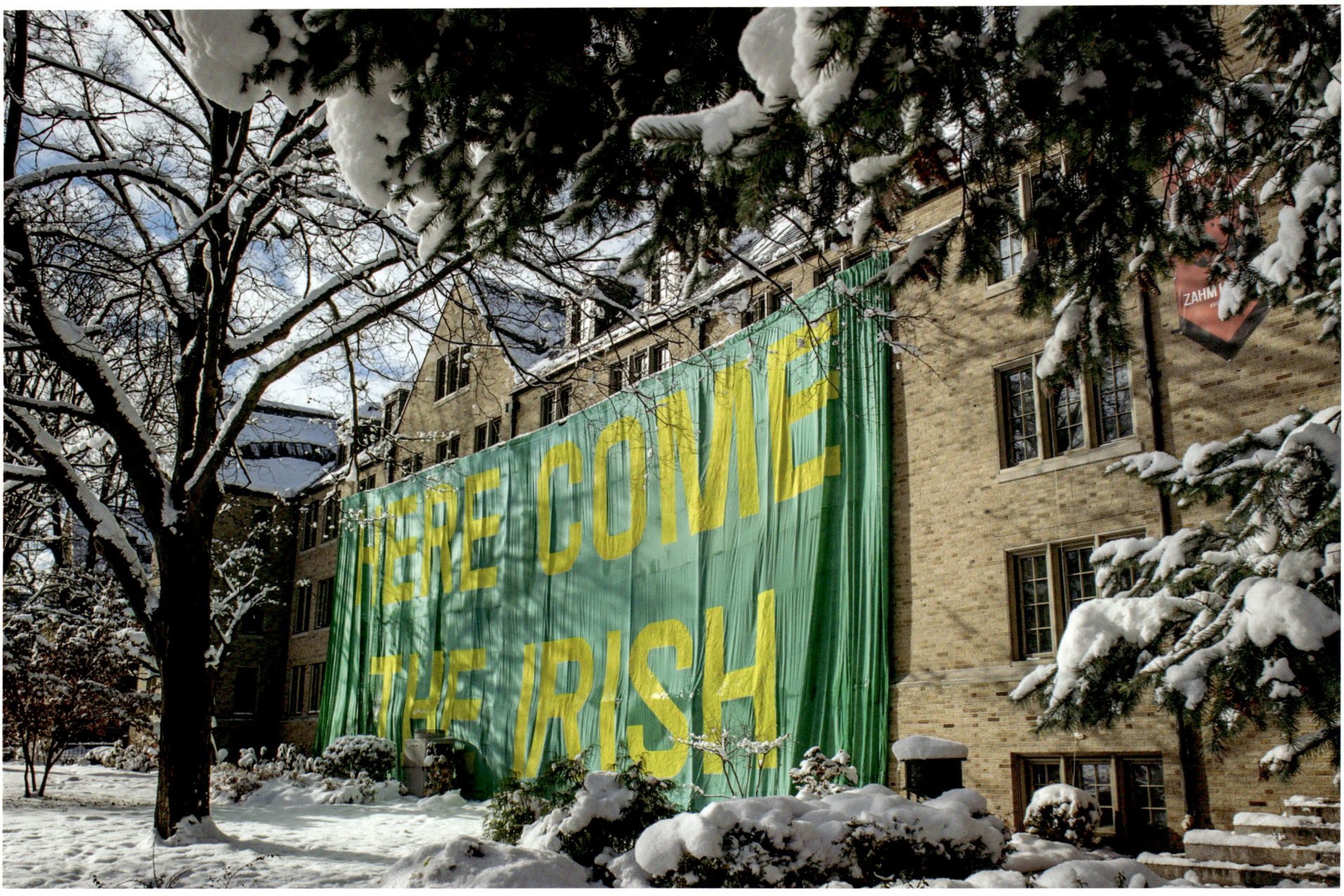

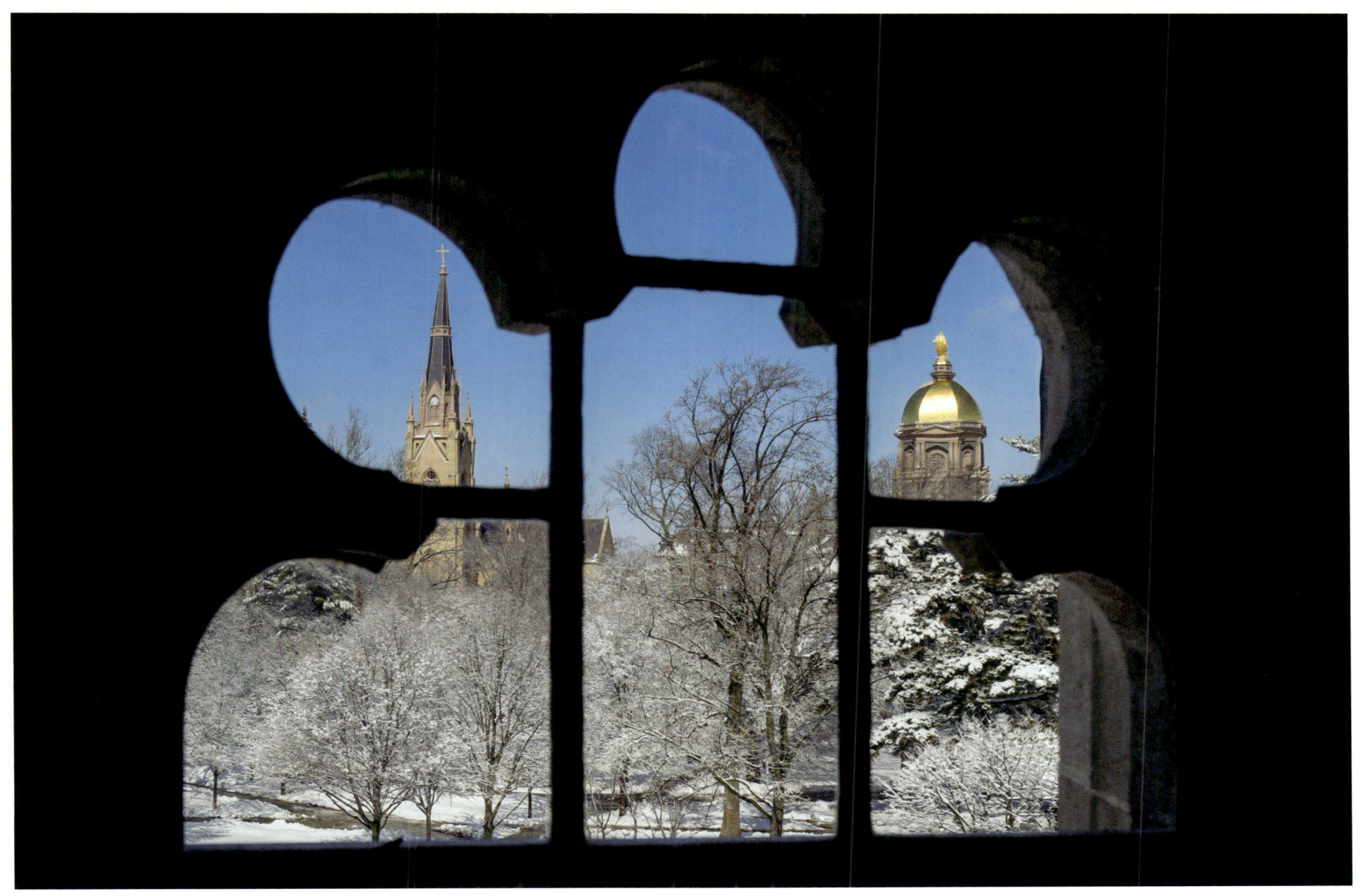

While some have suggested that the university's academic aspirations have been hurt by its distance from the great cultural centers and by not readily interlacing with a dynamic urban environment or "college town" atmosphere, the setting has its own merits. It is park-like and pastoral, a wellspring of nature's beauty. The statues, architecture, chapels, and religious iconography are quiet reminders of those eternal questions and concerns so easily lost in contemporary society. It is a place of both solitude and intimate community. A place that encourages a late-night walk or strolling conversation about those timeless issues that have confounded humans for millennia.

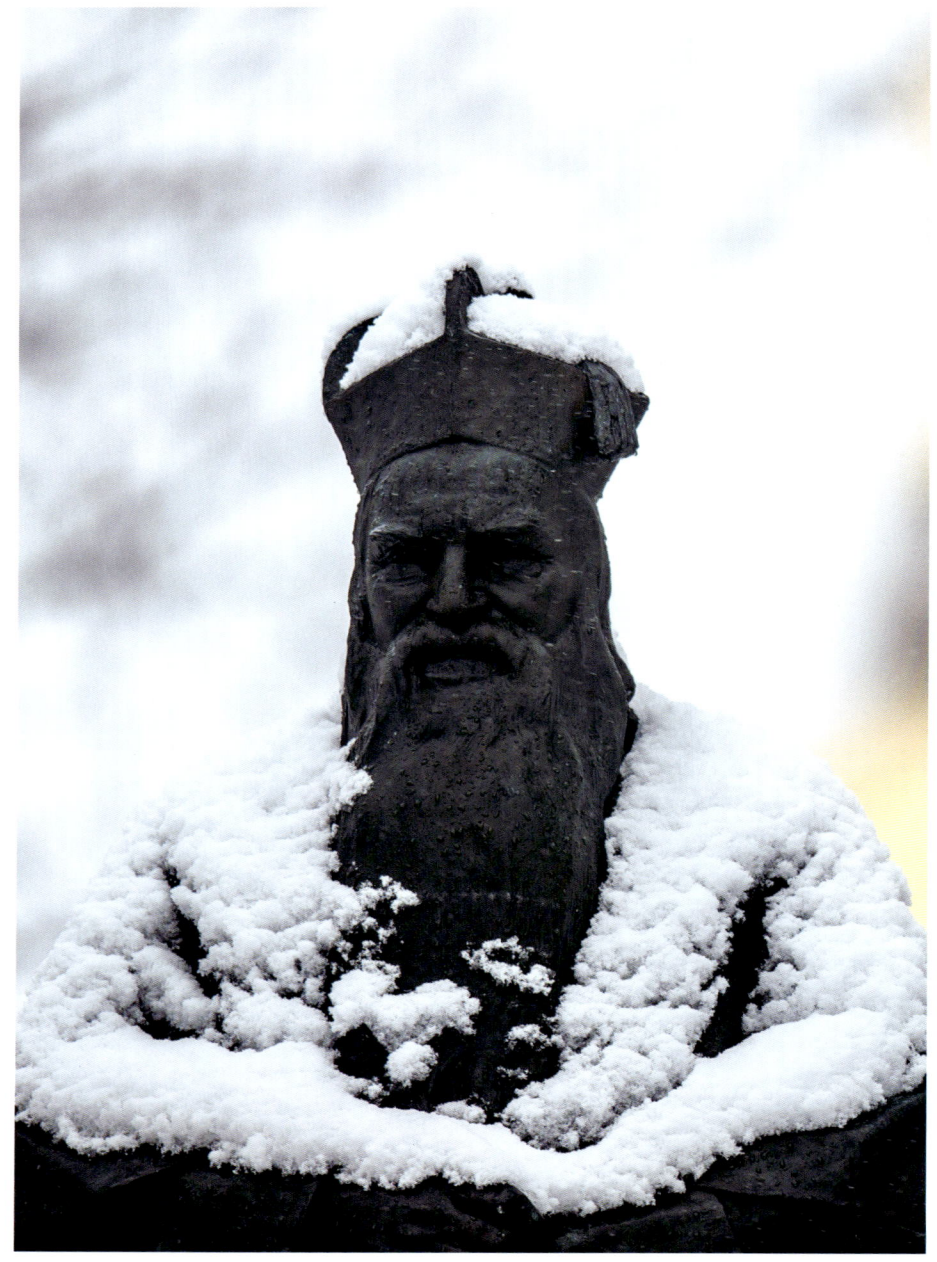

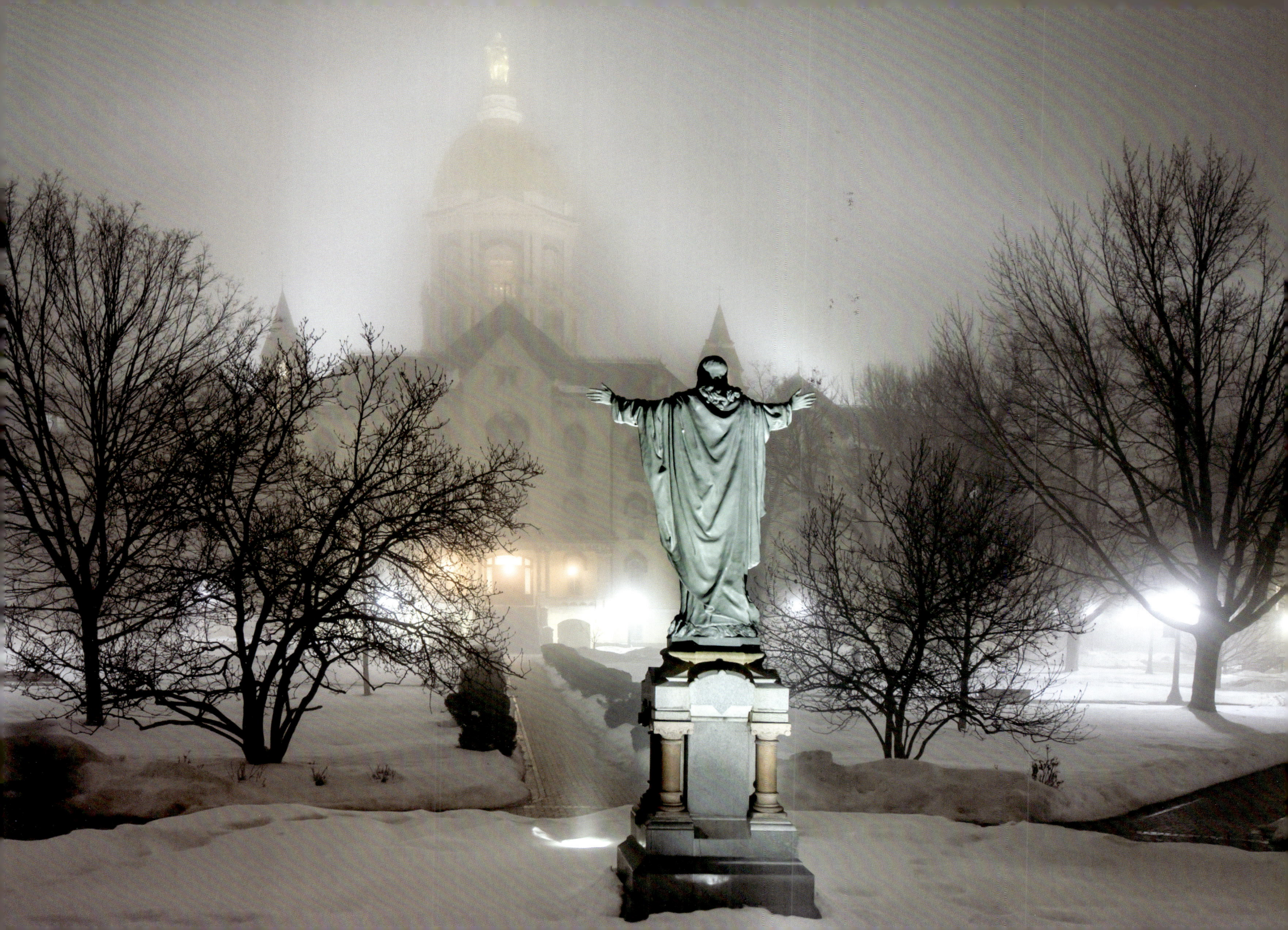

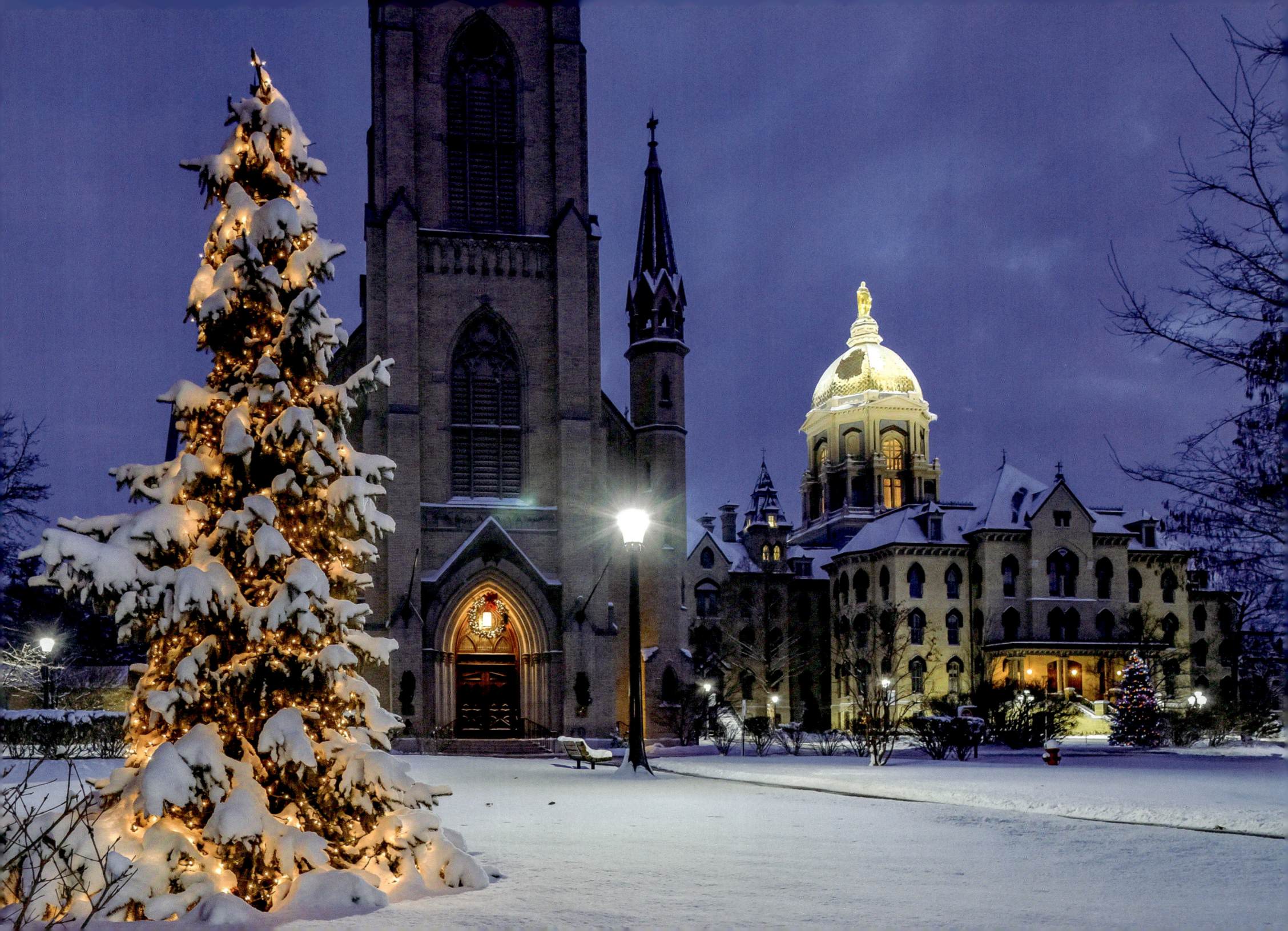

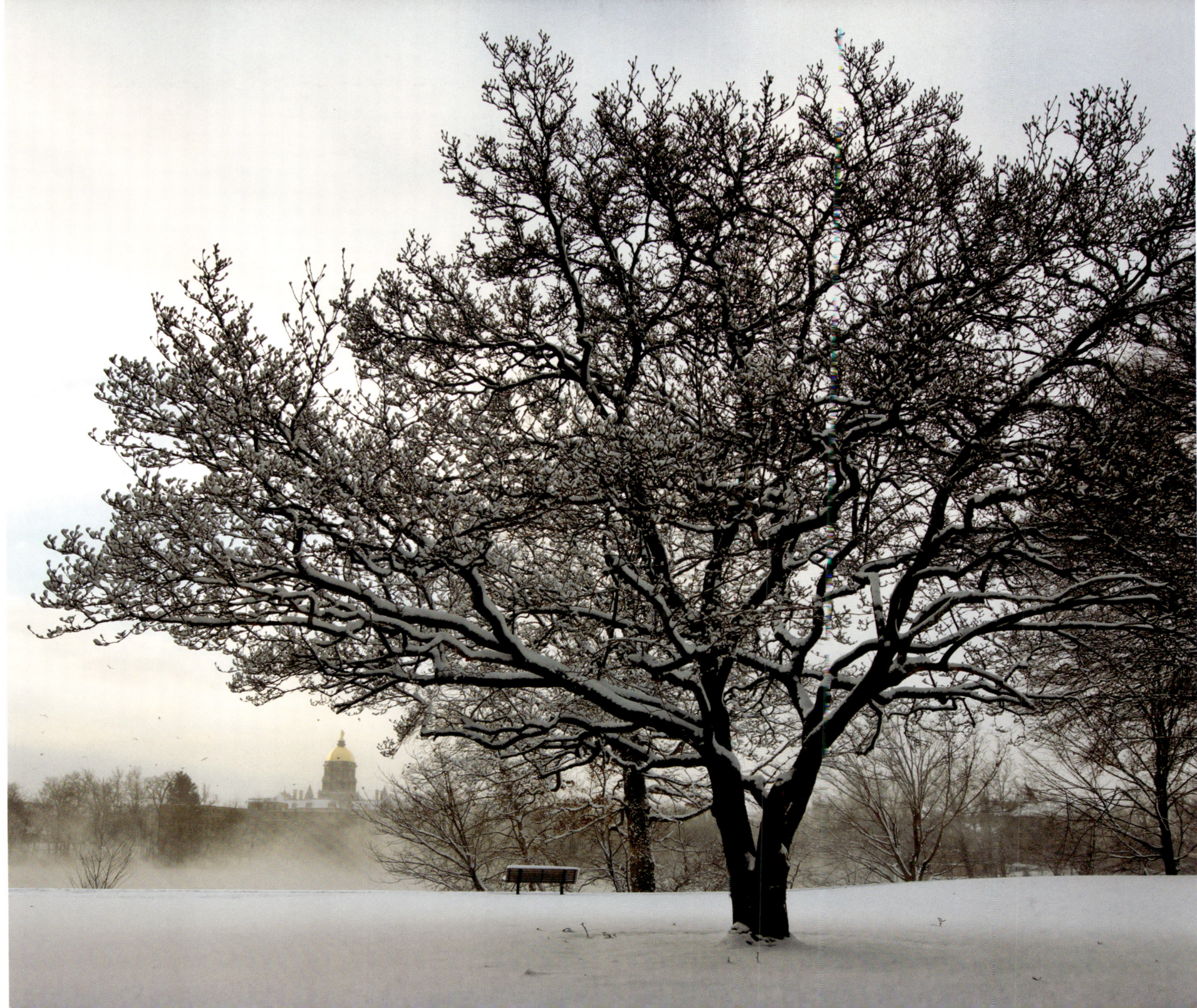

"We do mean to be a great university," Father Hesburgh stated in a 1977 document outlining his vision for Notre Dame's future. "We are open to all the great questions of our times. We are confident enough, of ourselves and our students, to look at a wide variety of possible answers and to be assured that new light will be brought to bear upon these problems as we discuss them in a Christian context. We have no problem with other universities choosing to do their discussing in what might well be a more restrictive context, more secular, less religious, more purely or exclusively scientific and technological. So be it. But we need not be defensive in placing the same discussion in a different context, more universal (which is the meaning of catholic), more Christian, more moral, more spiritual, more open to the transcendental, to God, but no less intellectual. We do what we do freely, and in the conviction that the times, and especially the future, will need such an approach."

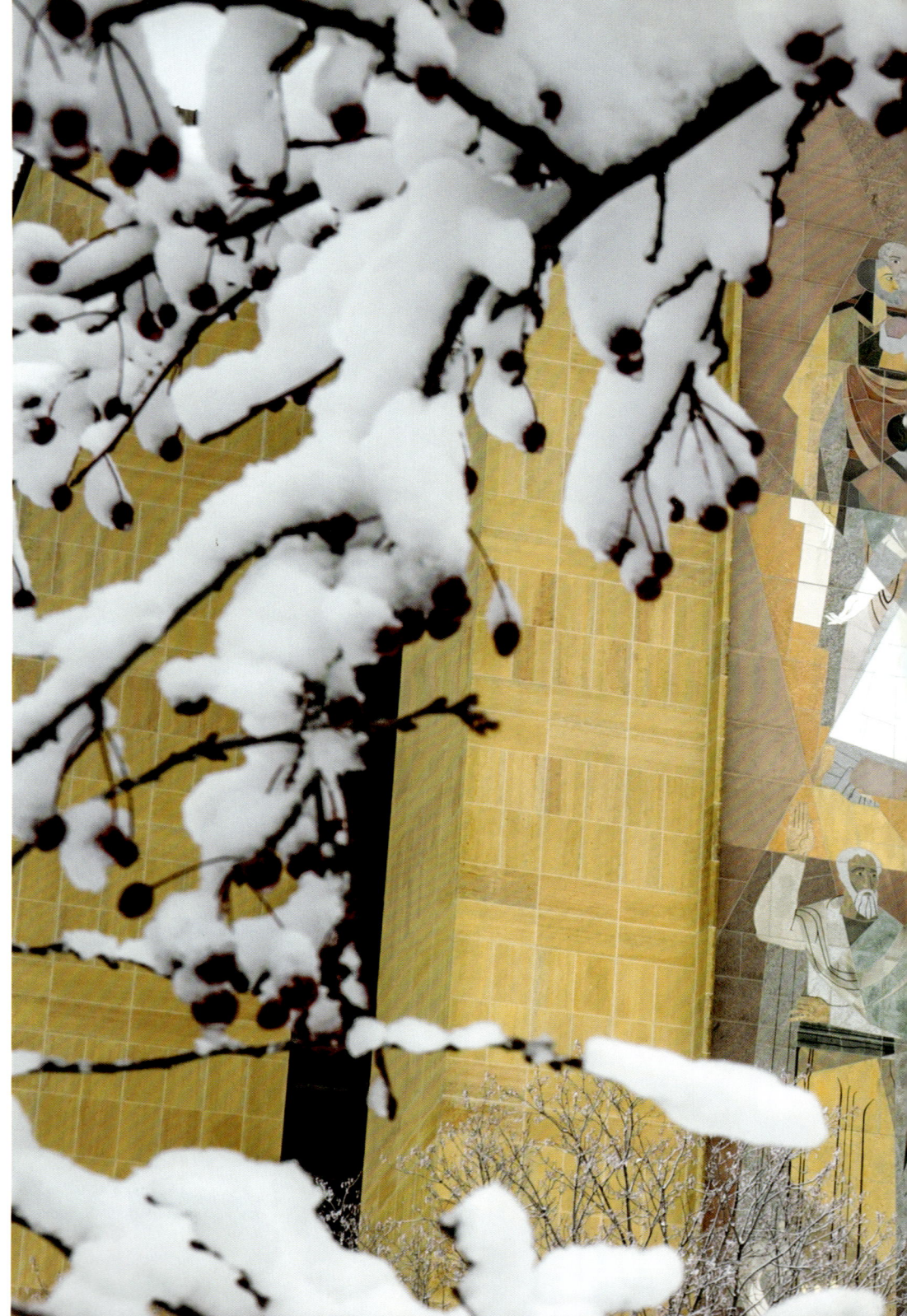

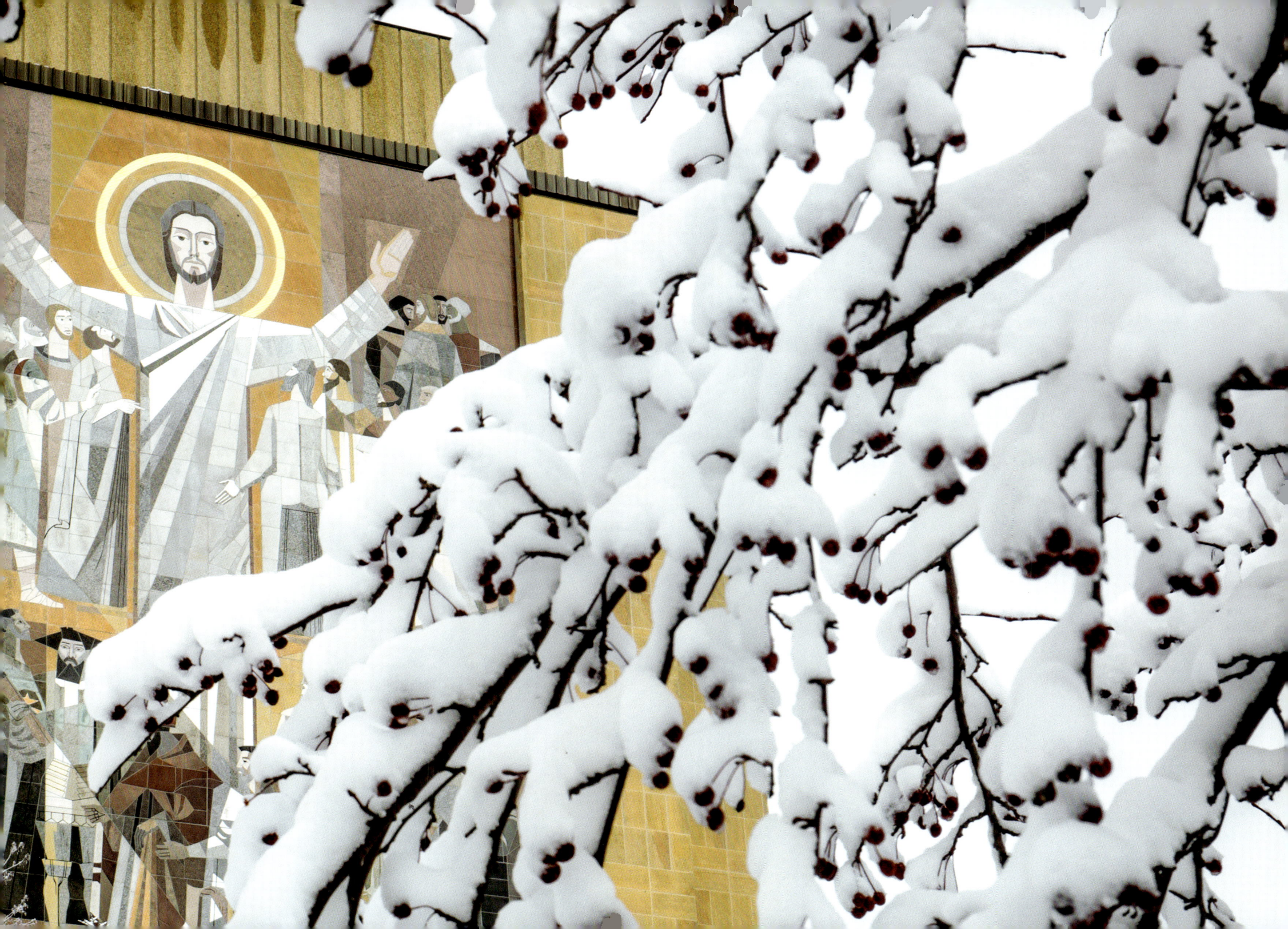

Notre Dame is a keenly nocturnal creature. So much happens after the sun goes down. Students seem to move under cover of dusk. Treks to the library or LaFortune or Duncan Student Center. Heading to movies or lecture. The Keenan Revue, Black Cultural Arts Festival, SYRs, something doing at DPAC, Legends, or Washington Hall. Trips to the neighborhood bars, off-campus harbors. Food sales. The hectic humming in the *Observer* offices, middle-of-the-night daily newspaper production. Bone-chilling tromps on snowy nights to basketball games at the Joyce Center. Late-night studying, hanging out, video games till all hours, communal TV watching, reading, meeting, gathering. Rolfs and the Rock pulsing, dancing with the combustion of youthful hyperactivity.

Students who stay on the trail throughout the day come alive at night, but not really till 10:00 or so, when the rest of the world is turning off, tuning out, turning in. The college-age cohort is on a different clock, a different time zone. Midnight is early, hours to go before they sleep. Each day is a feast, a circus, a caravan packed to overflowing—so much to fit in . . . papers to finish, phone calls to make, exams to study for, good friends to laugh with. Tomorrow waiting.

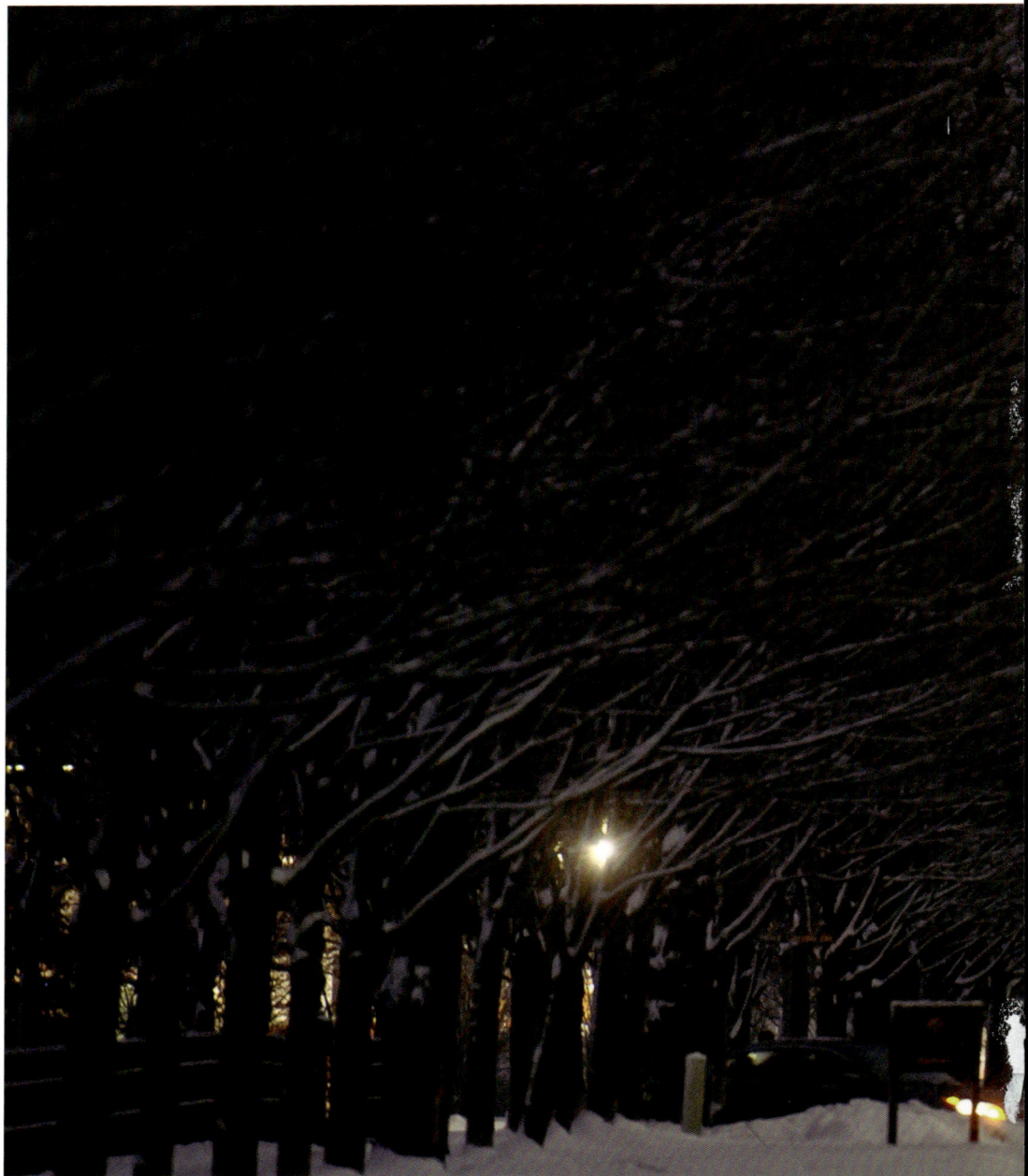

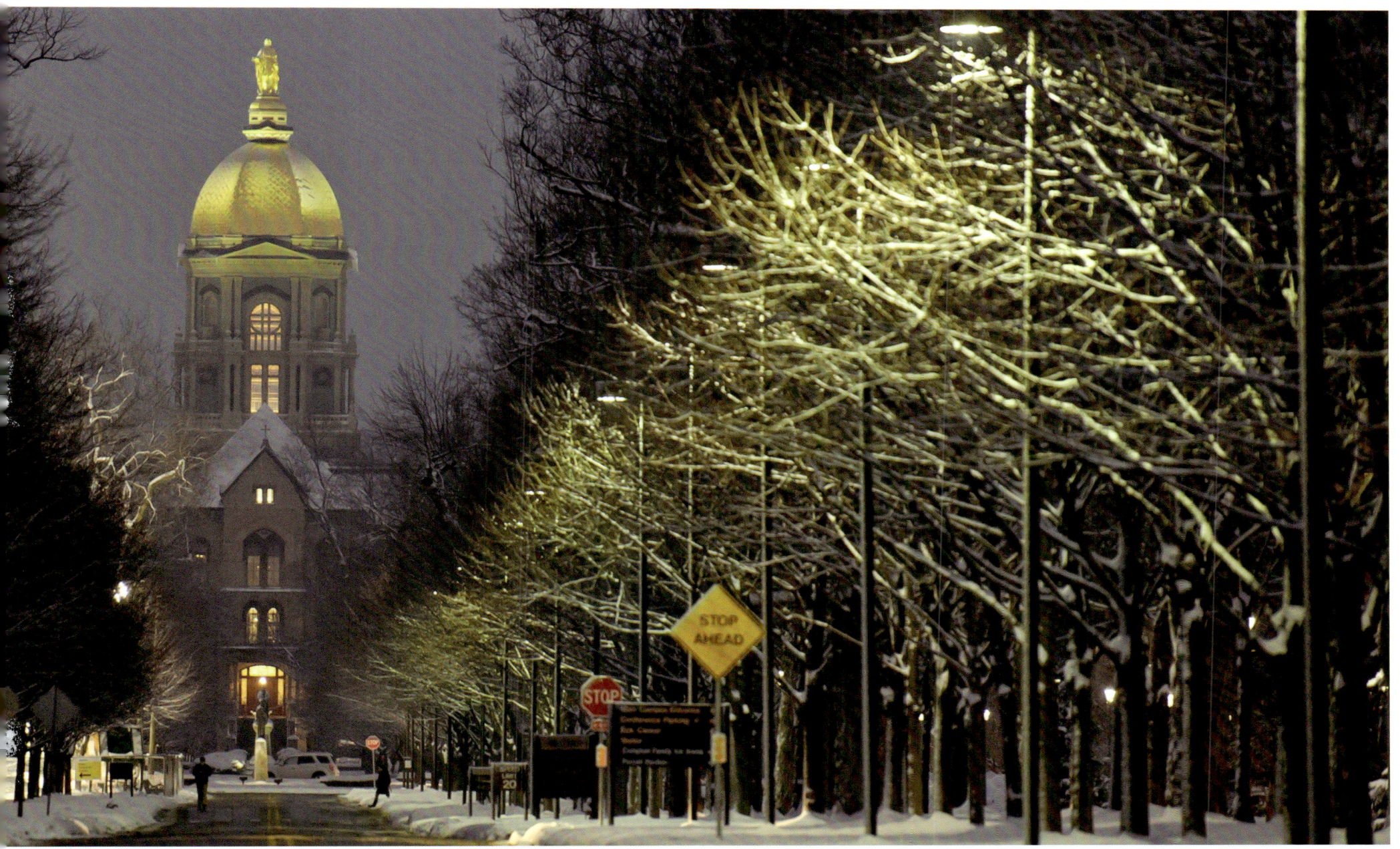

109

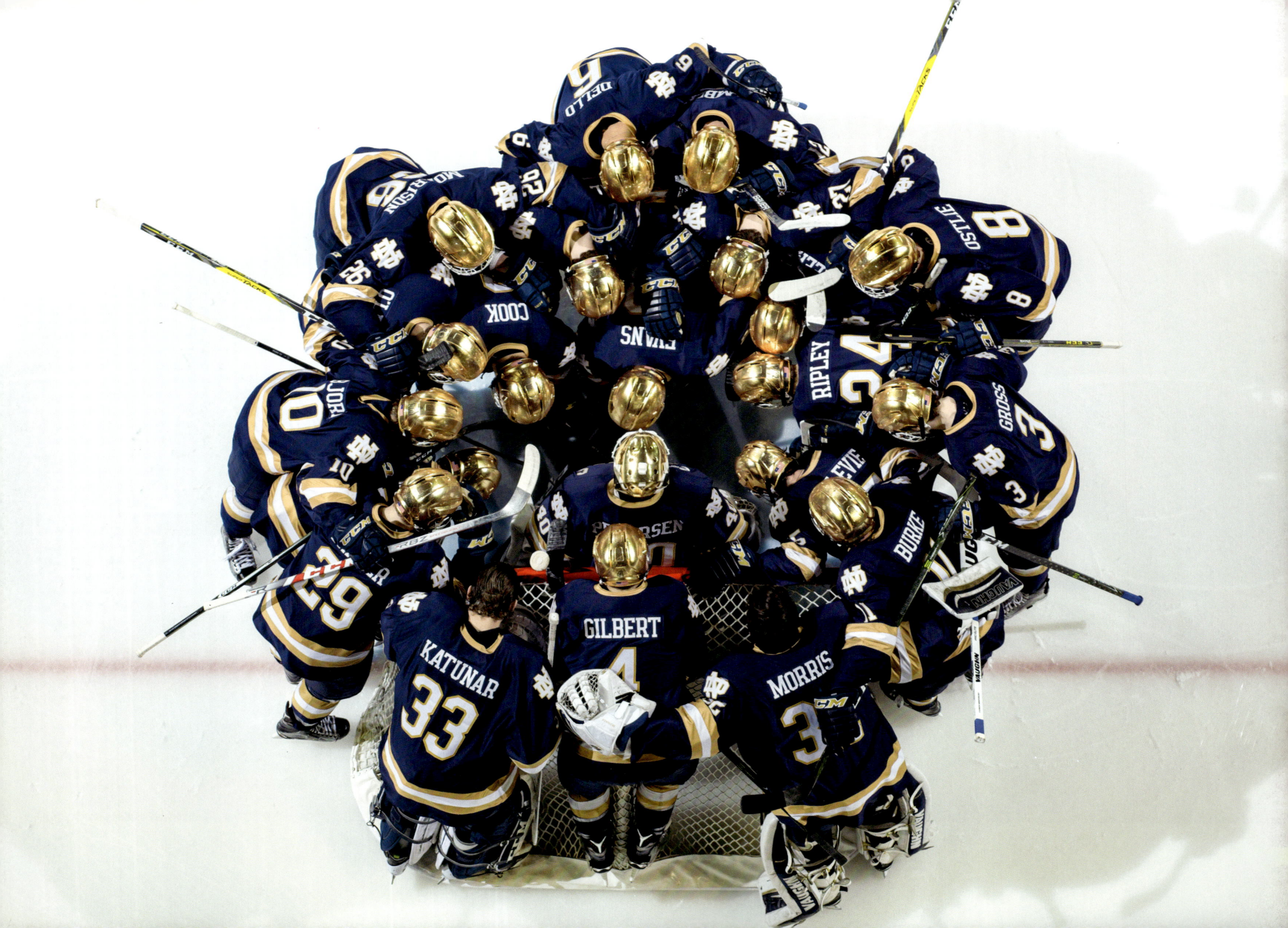

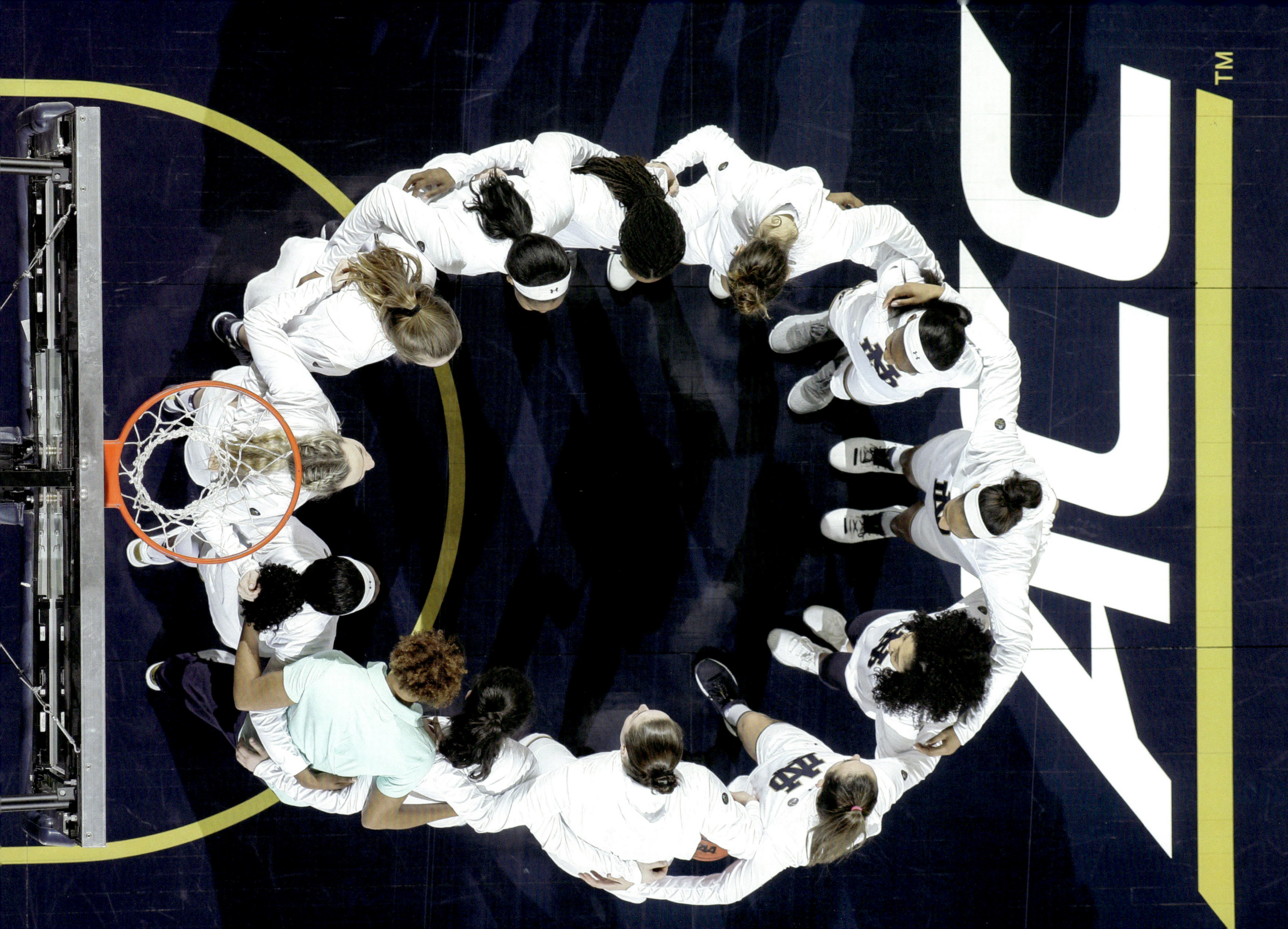

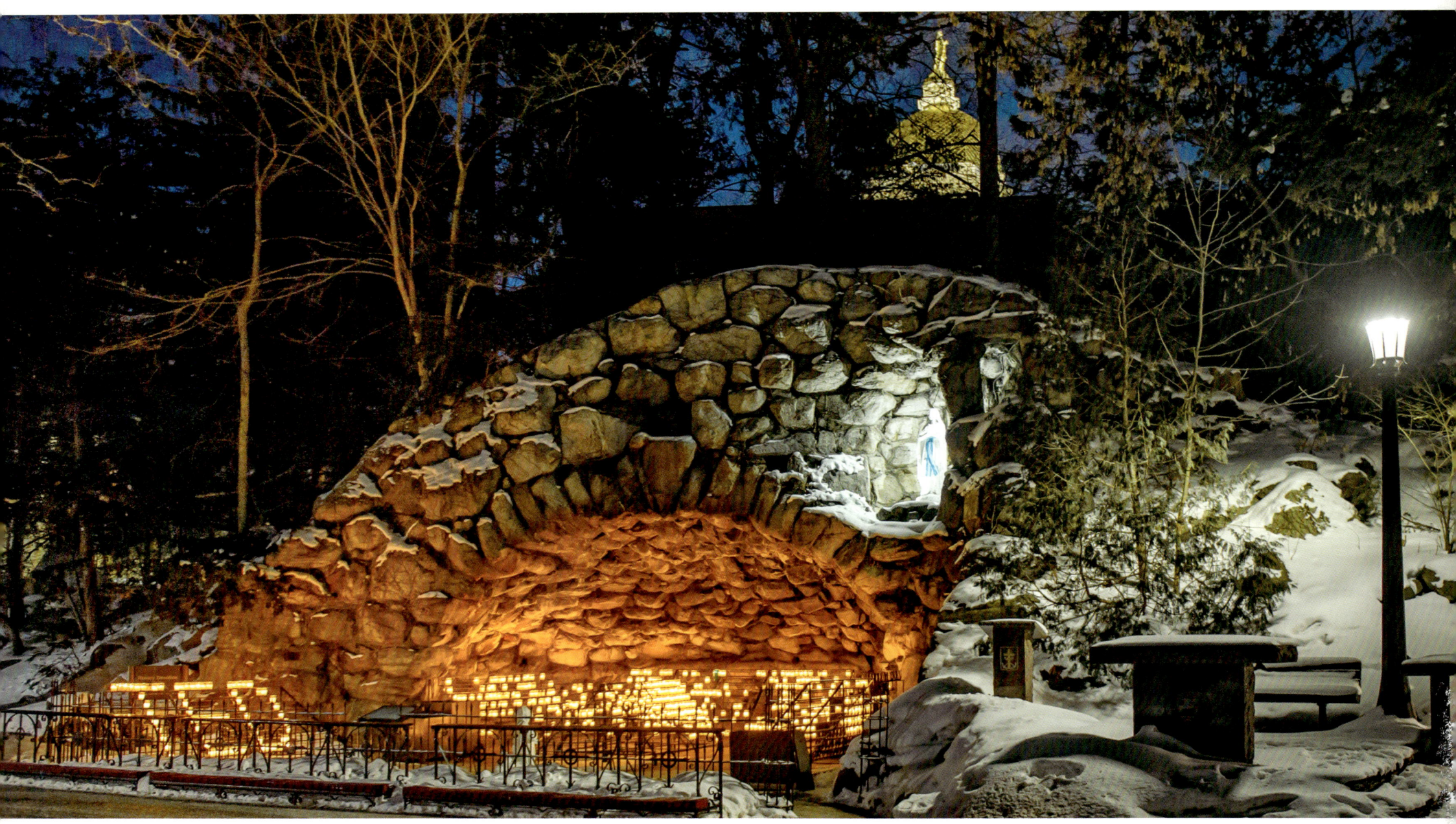

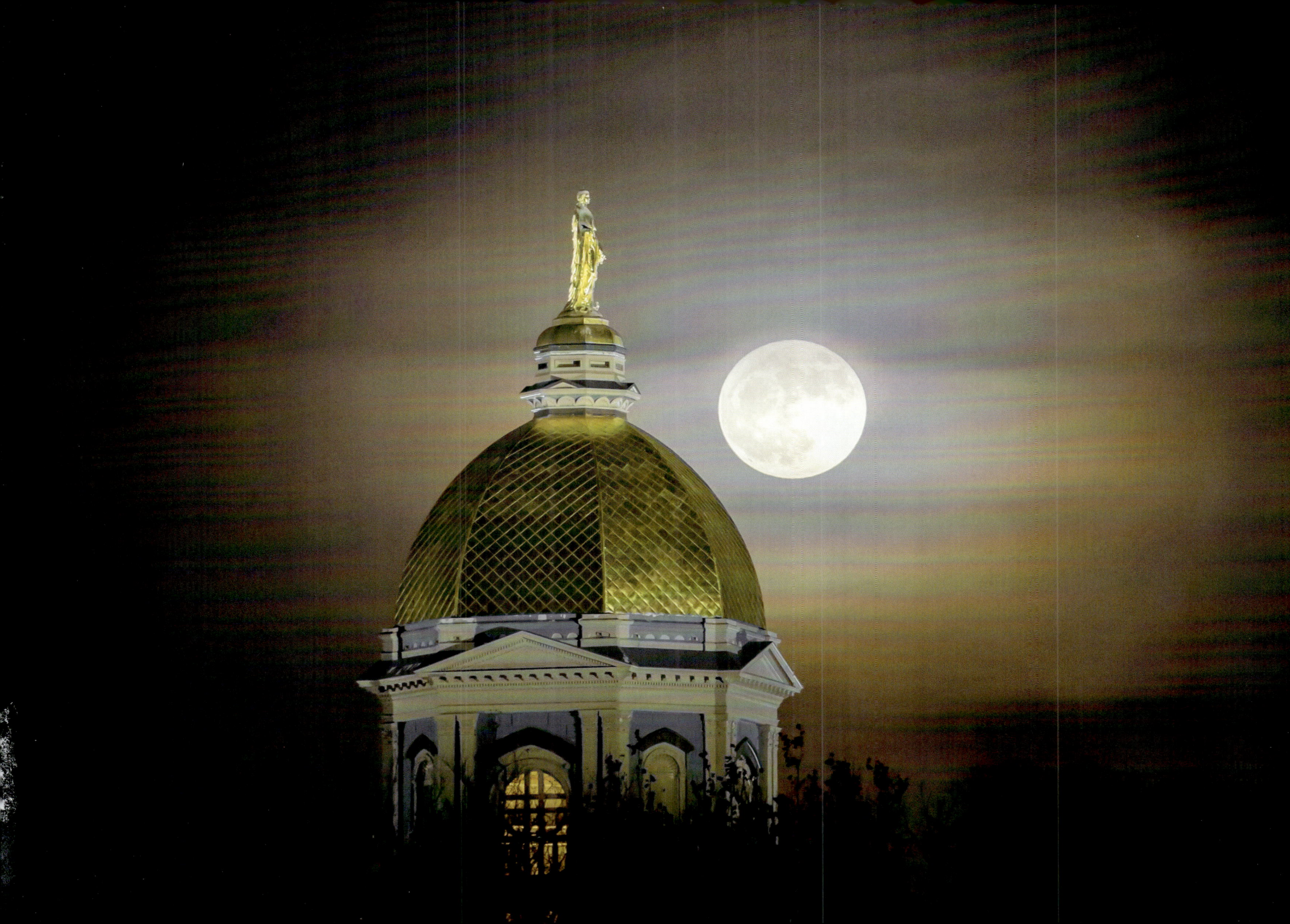

The Notre Dame winter, surely the target of most Domer complaints about life in this corner of Great Lakes frigidity, is a considerable ingredient in the powerful concoction that is Notre Dame. It shapes and layers so much of what happens here, enforcing the solitude and sanctuary that deepen the waters of college life.

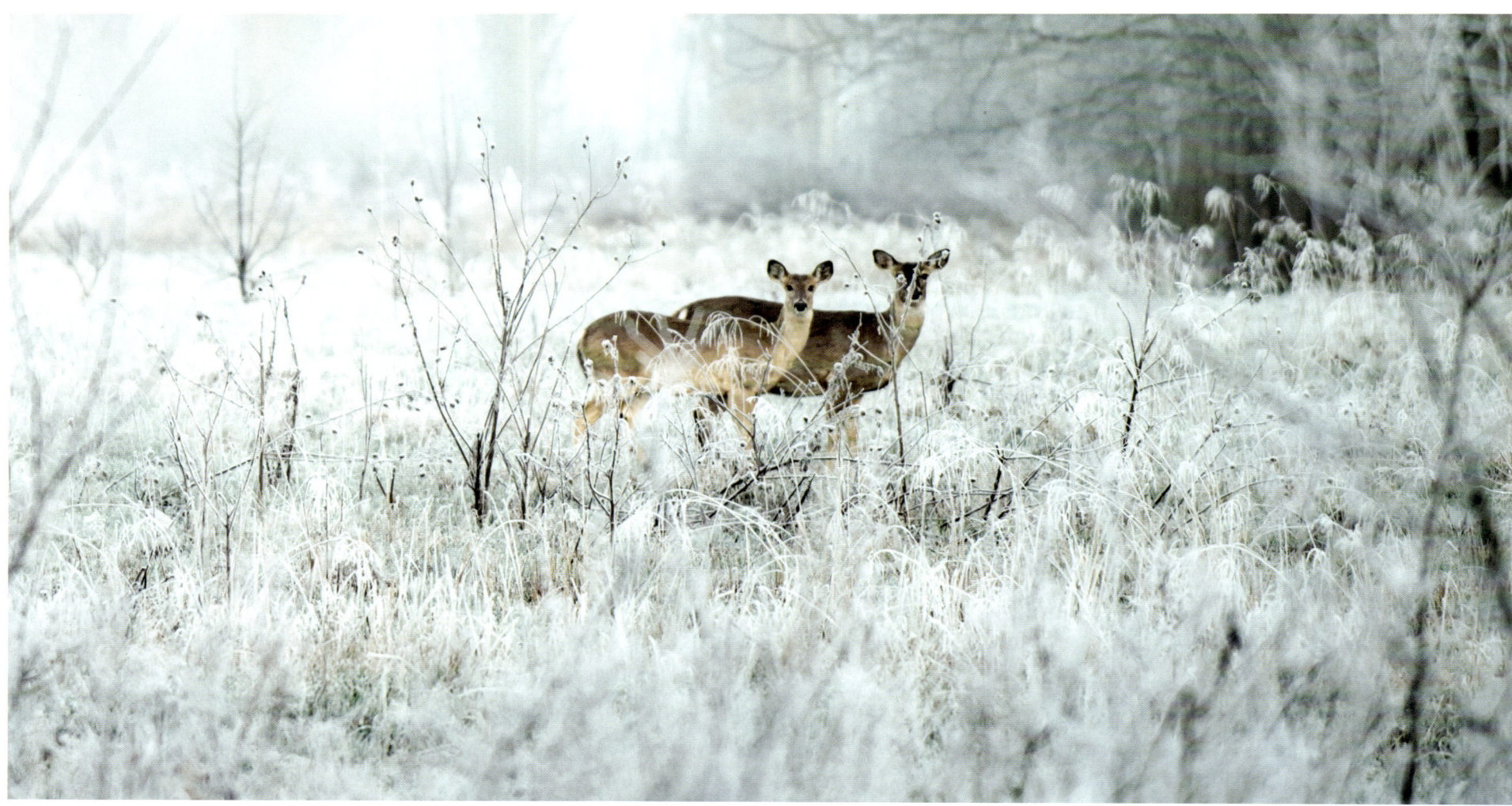

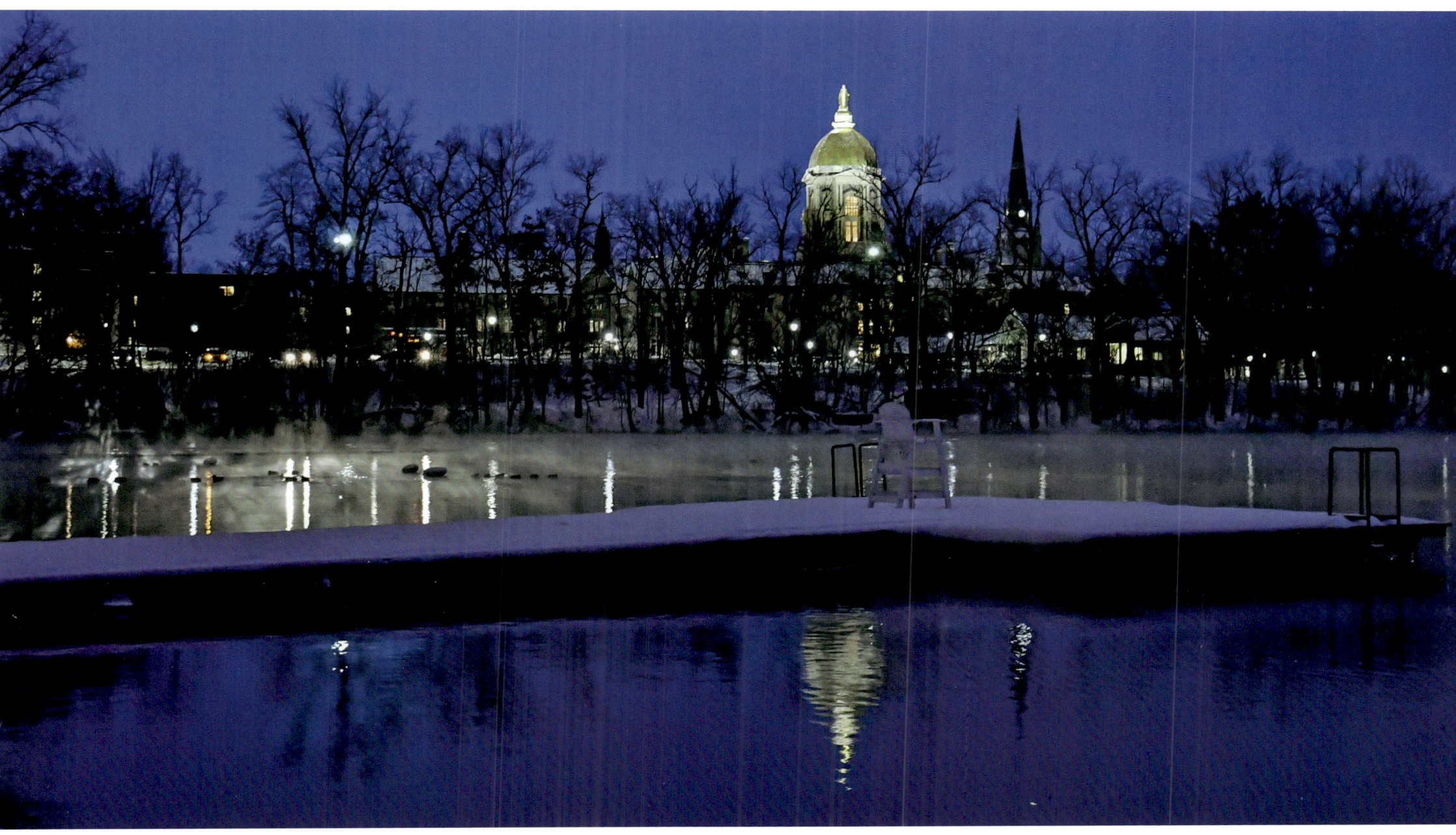

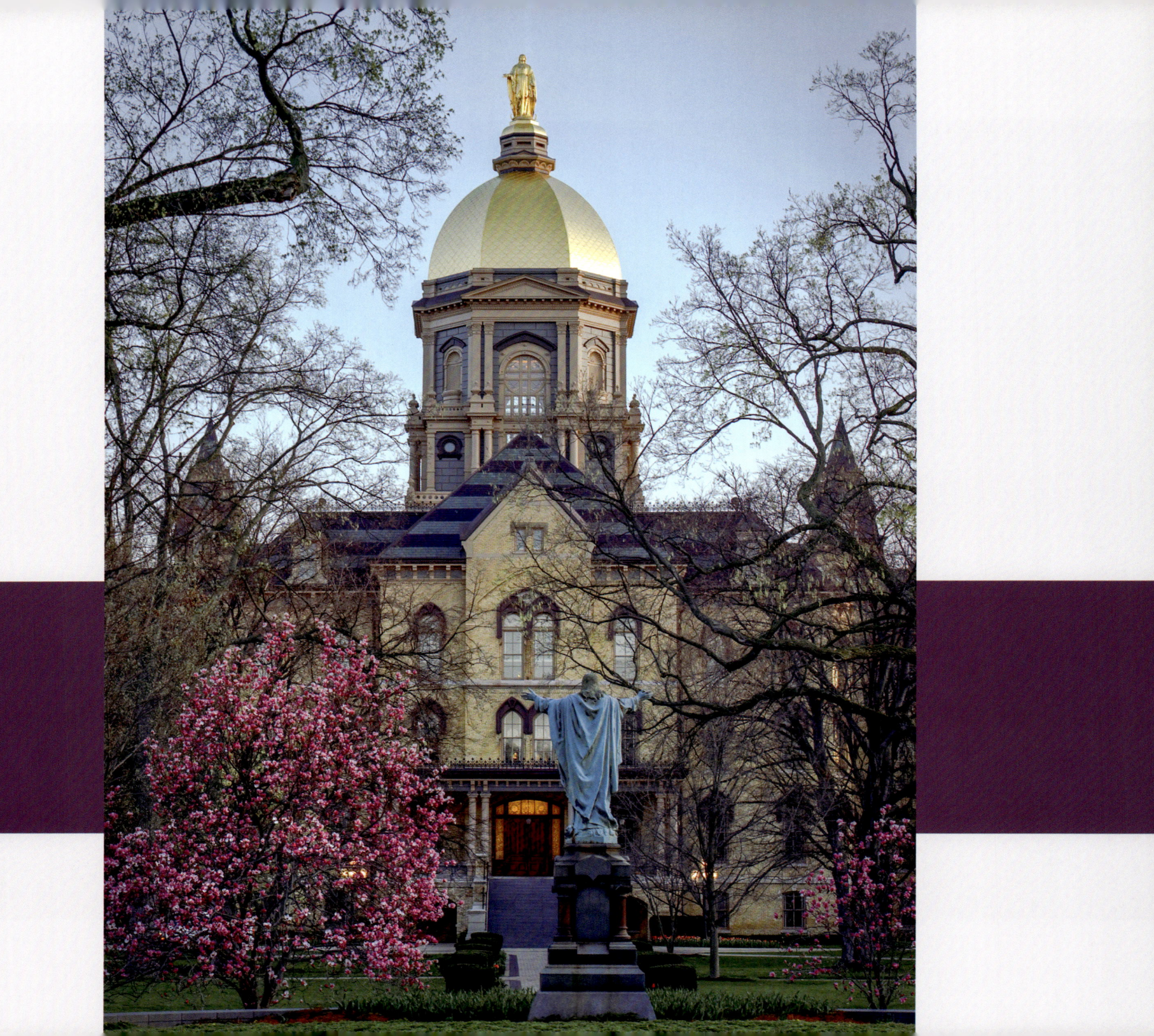

The campus is ablaze with light in every growing thing and in every radiant person made in the image of God. It may not be a stretch to see the campus as a garden of God's own making, through our own shaping of it, sometimes more and sometimes less than we had hoped.

—Rev. Nicholas Ayo, C.S.C.,
The Heart of Notre Dame

SPRING

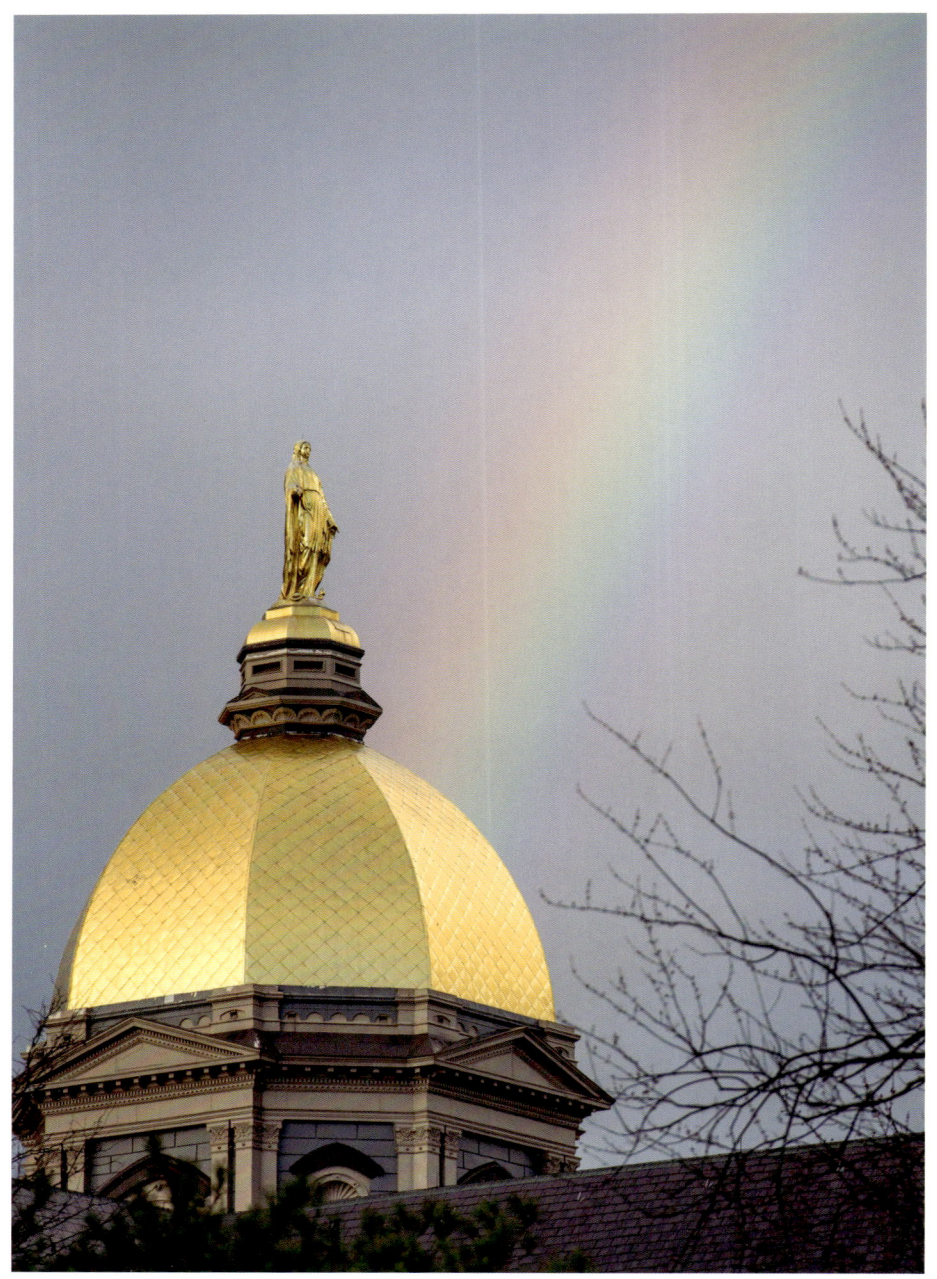

Spring is an awakening, a coming to life; even the air seems to exhale a sigh of relief as winter fades, snow melts, and sunlight lingers on the quads past dinnertime. Students linger, too, as the initial charms of spring fever beckon and dull their appetites for study, for heading indoors, for sequestering themselves in cubes and carrels made for work and concentration. Footsteps are lighter, voices livelier as they drift in packs out of the dining hall, or during those afternoon migrations exiting McCourtney Hall or Galvin, or navigating the traffic flow in DeBartolo's teeming hallways. If winter has a grip on campus, then spring releases the lock, pops open the lid, unfurls the sail. The exuberant vitality of youth gets loose. And it's contagious.

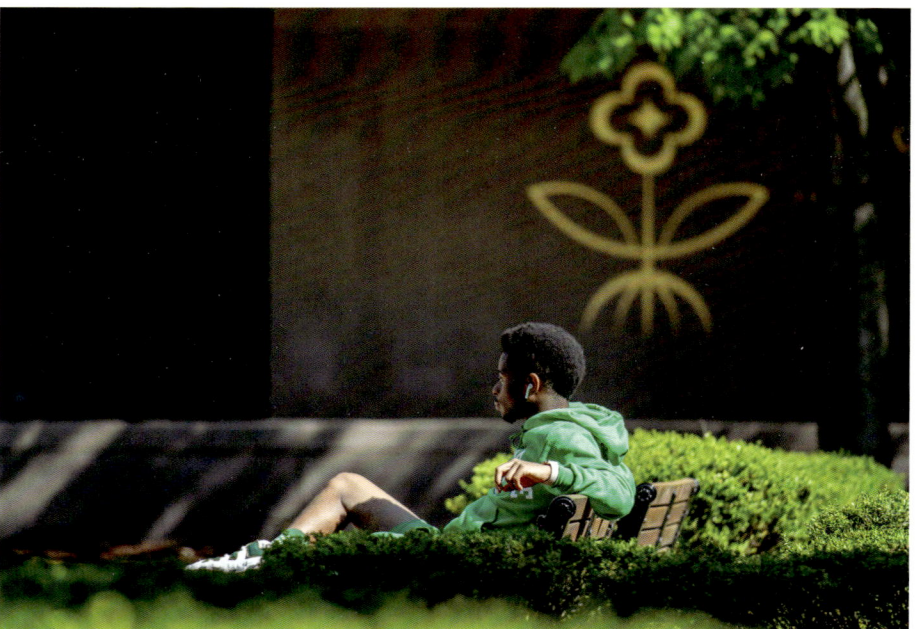

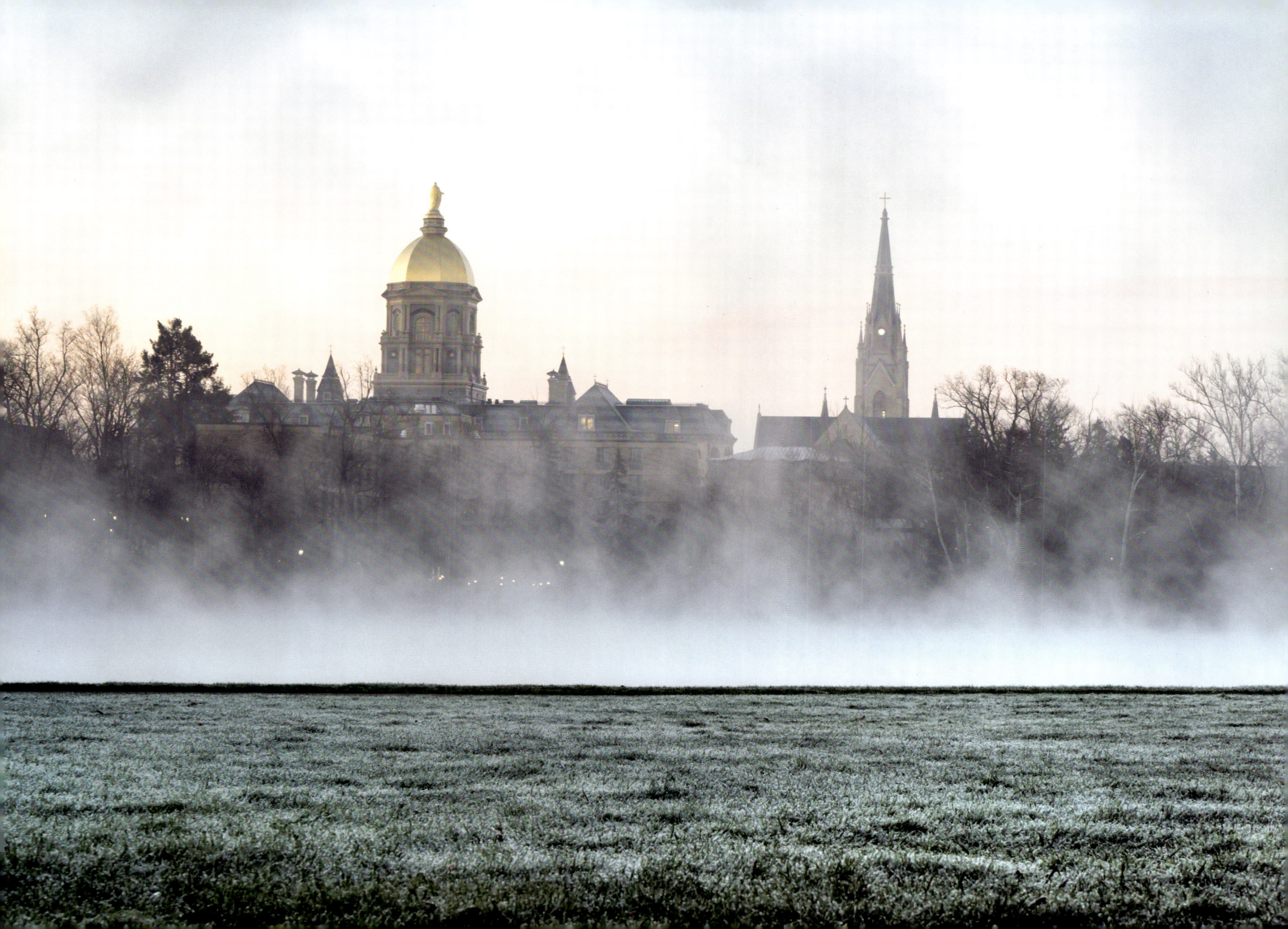

And there is that one day—it happens every year—when spring fully arrives one airy afternoon, and all the housebound come outdoors, the quads come alive. The lacrosse sticks are pulled out, and a baseball and gloves. Frisbees fly through the air. There's volleyball behind Morrissey and blankets in front of Farley where students stretch out and pretend to read.

Spring is festival season. Mud pits, the Fisher Regatta, An Tostal, Bookstore Basketball. Runners race about the lakes, profs take their classes outside, sit in circles under green trees. There's a happy chase through spring semester, so young minds must be keen and quick and sharp in this *carpe diem* season of flight and illumination.

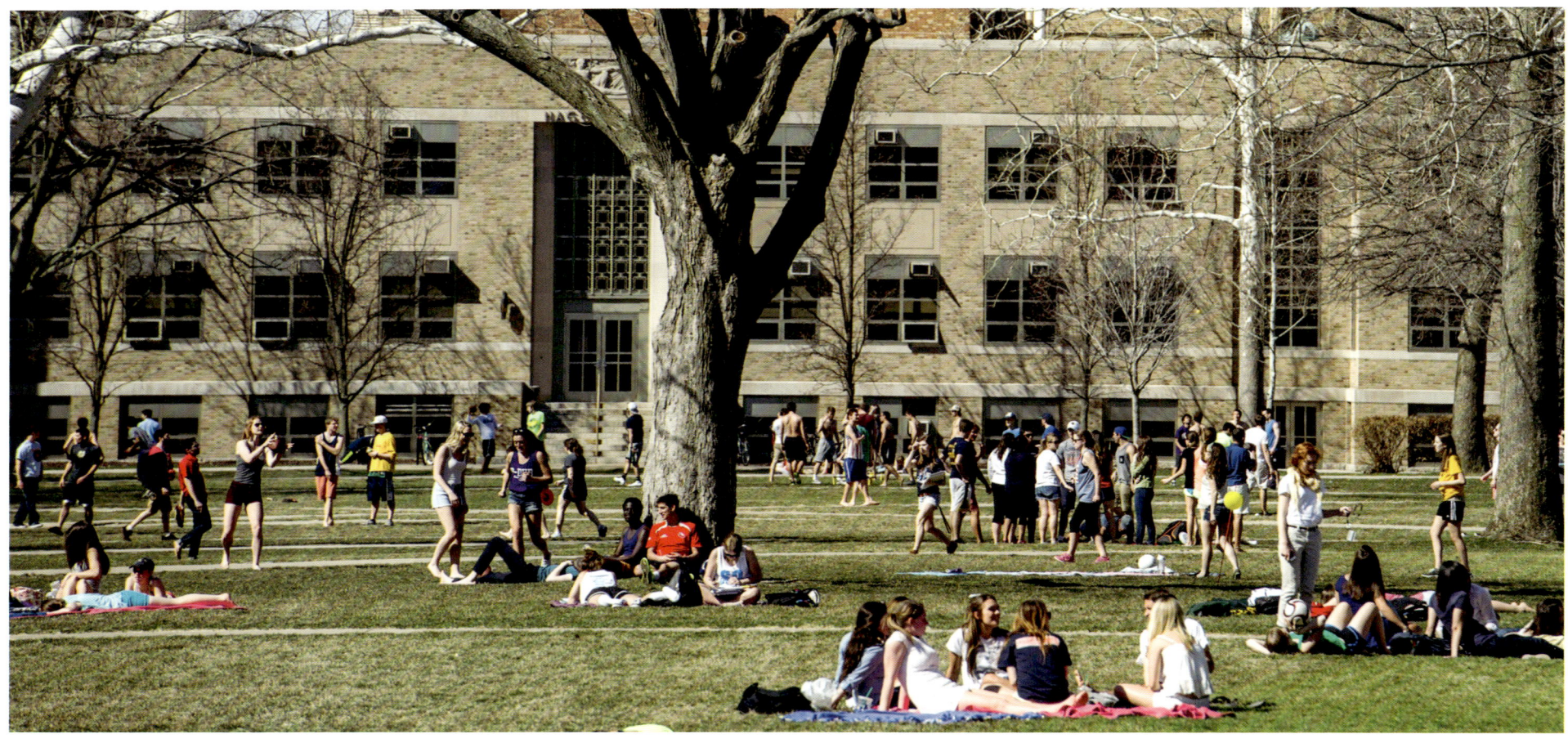

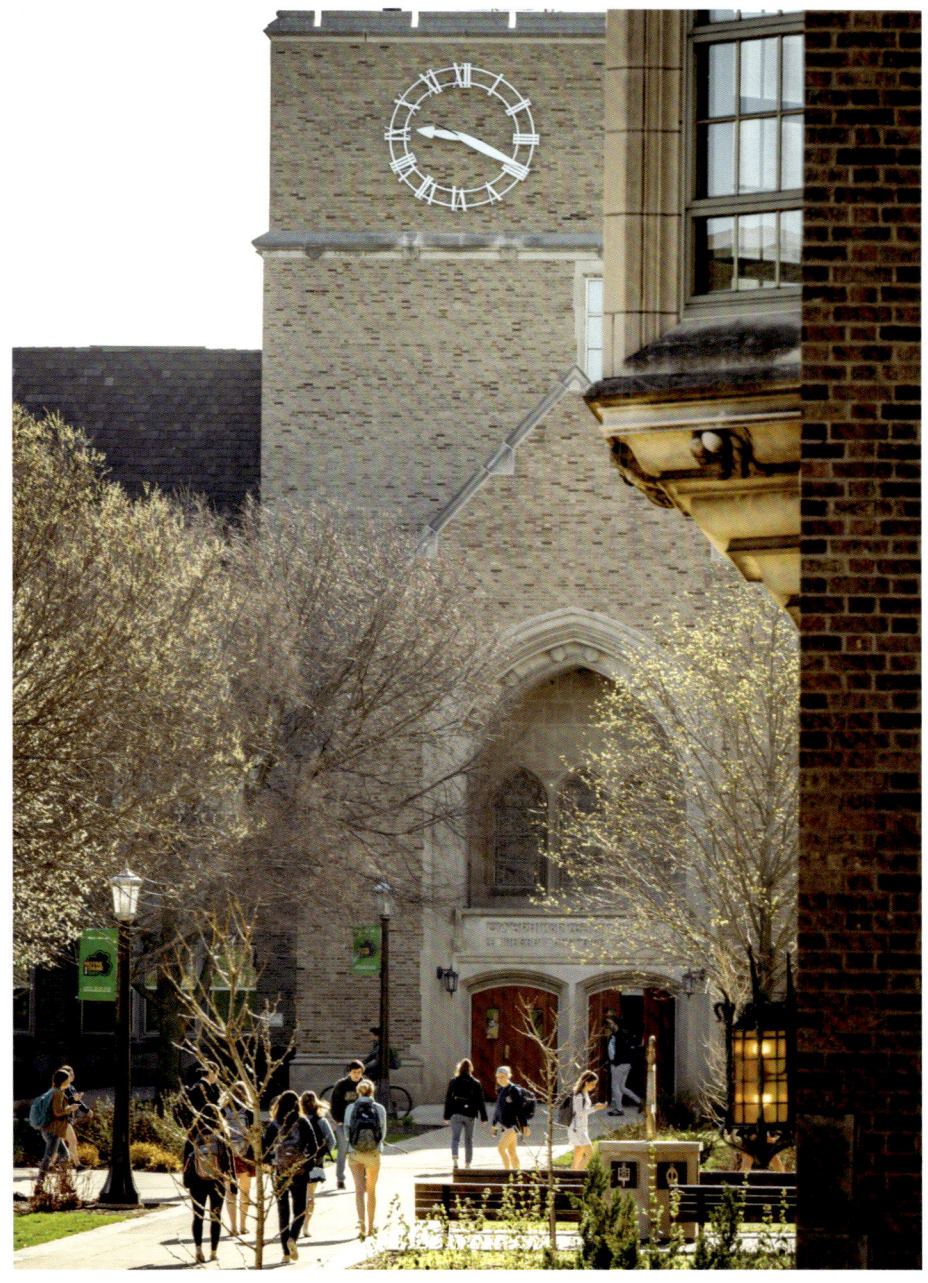

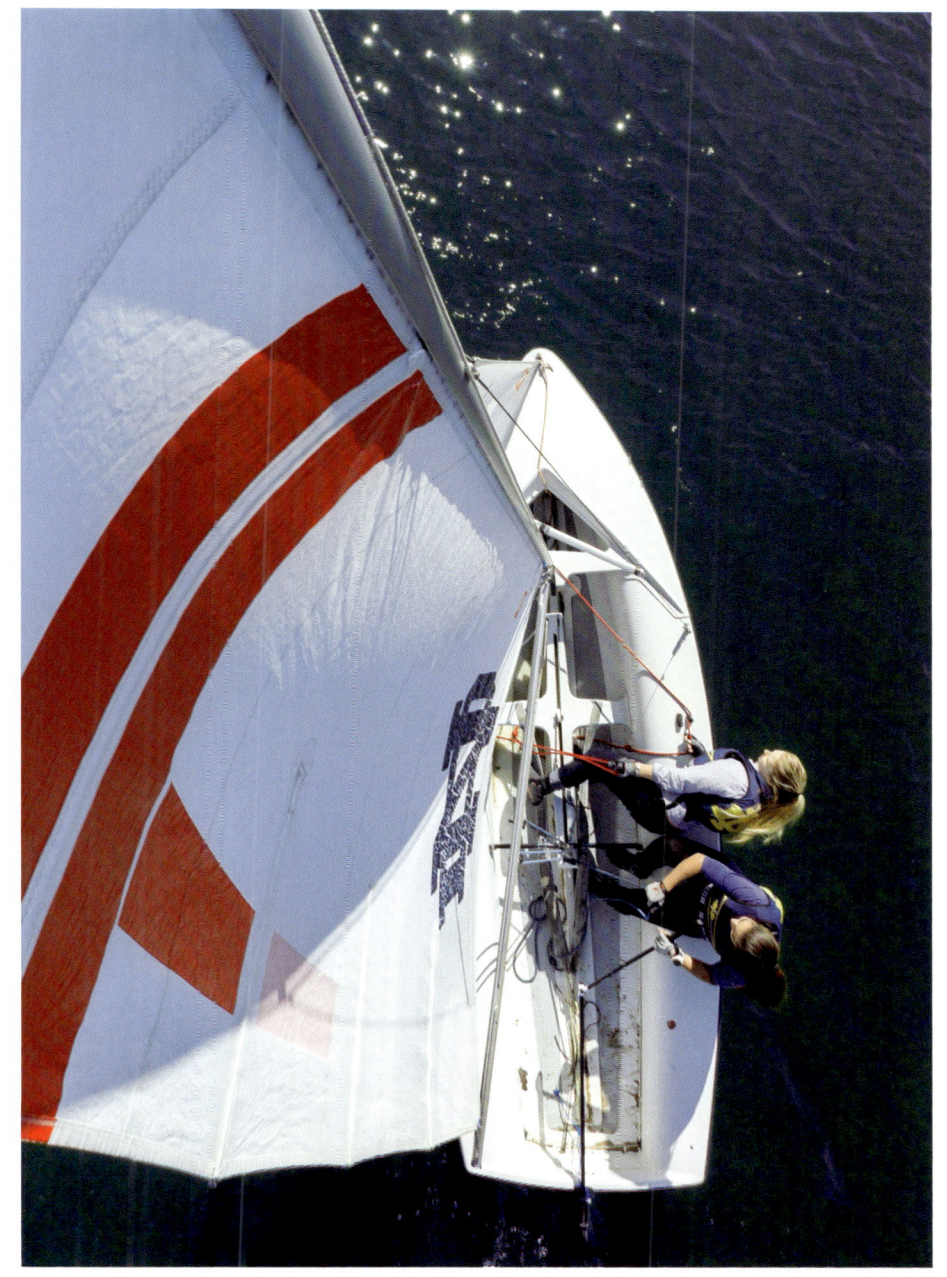

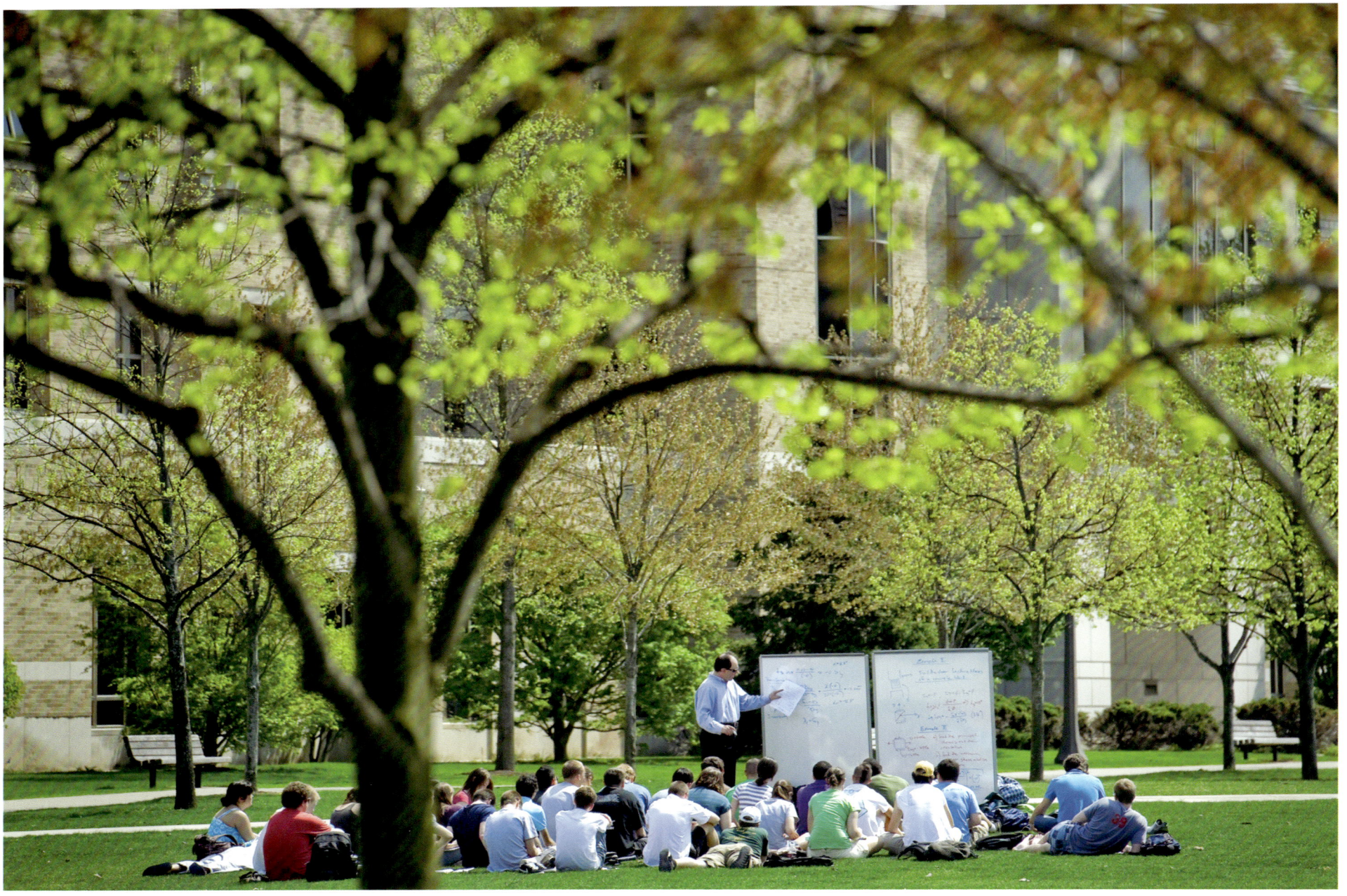

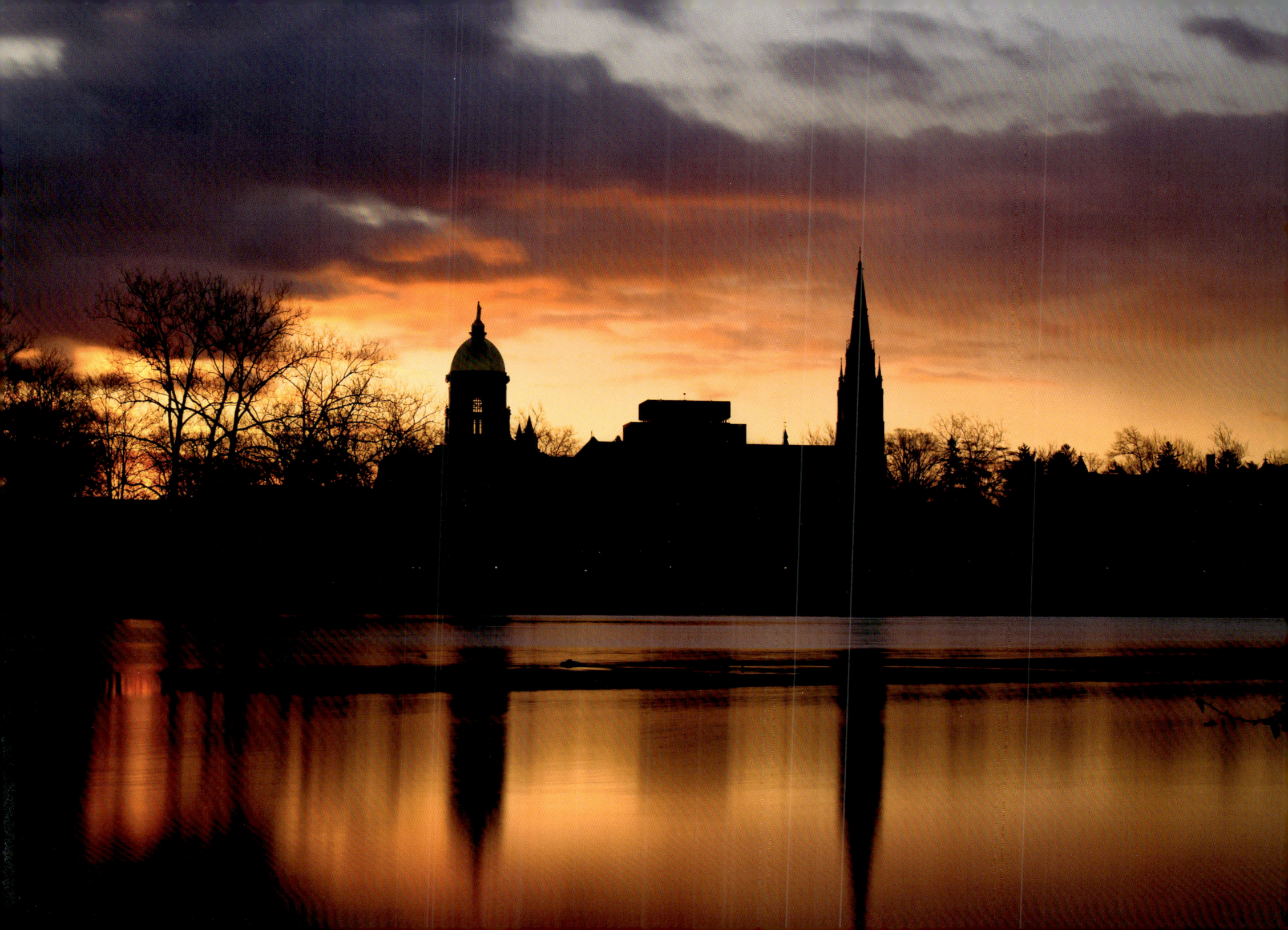

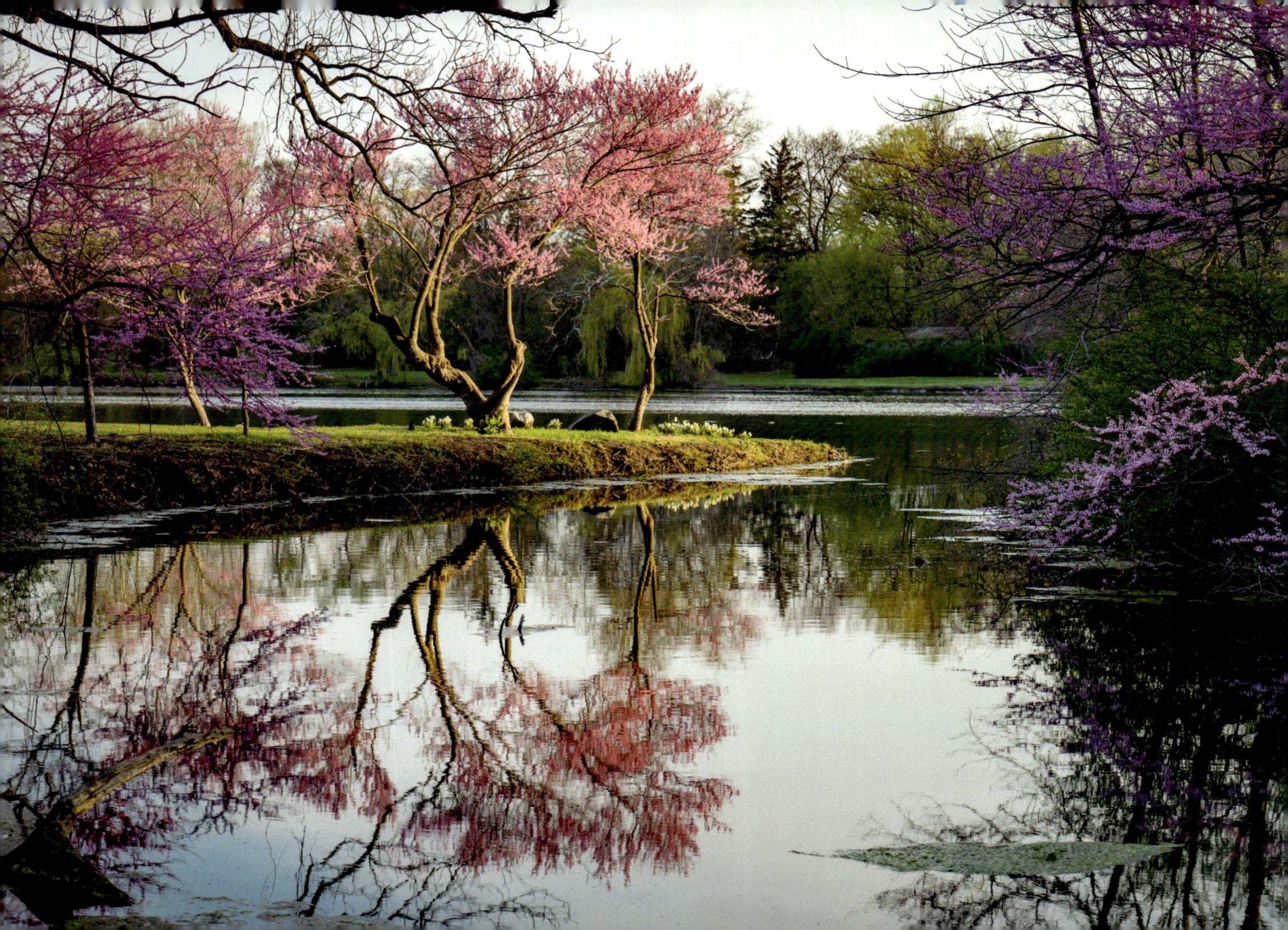

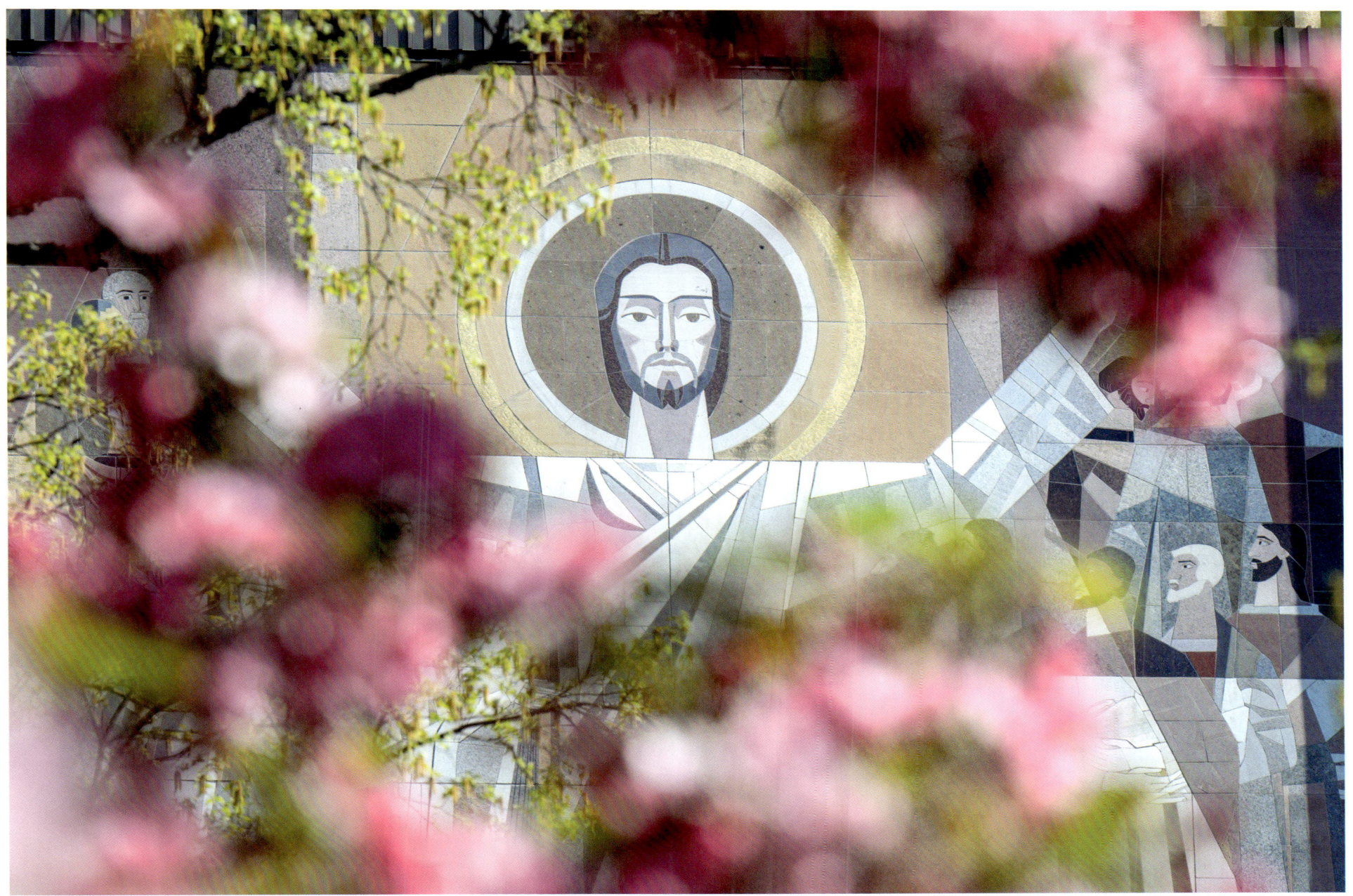

Notre Dame is different from many schools with similar academic aspirations. It is undeniably Catholic, and its Catholicism pervades the place. The manifestations of faith are obvious: crosses and statues, the Grotto, the Mestrovic sculptures outside O'Shaughnessy, Mary atop the Dome, the giant mosaic of Christ on the Hesburgh Library, a crucifix in every classroom. Each residence hall has its own chapel, and the weekly masses infuse each with a sacred intimacy. Questions of faith, morality, and ethics are topics for classroom debate as well as informal dialogue—in hallways, over lunch, late at night, on the pages of the *Observer*. Theology and philosophy are required academic offerings. Campus Ministry, the Center for Social Concerns, and other institutes uniquely foster faith lives. The student body is decidedly Catholic; they are impressively involved in volunteer efforts. Much scholarship is mindful of issues of right and wrong, doing the right thing, cultivating Catholic social teaching and a Christian conscience. Despite the occasional calls to be vigilant in nurturing this crucial element of the Notre Dame ethos, the university's Catholicism is healthy, vibrant, and diversely textured.

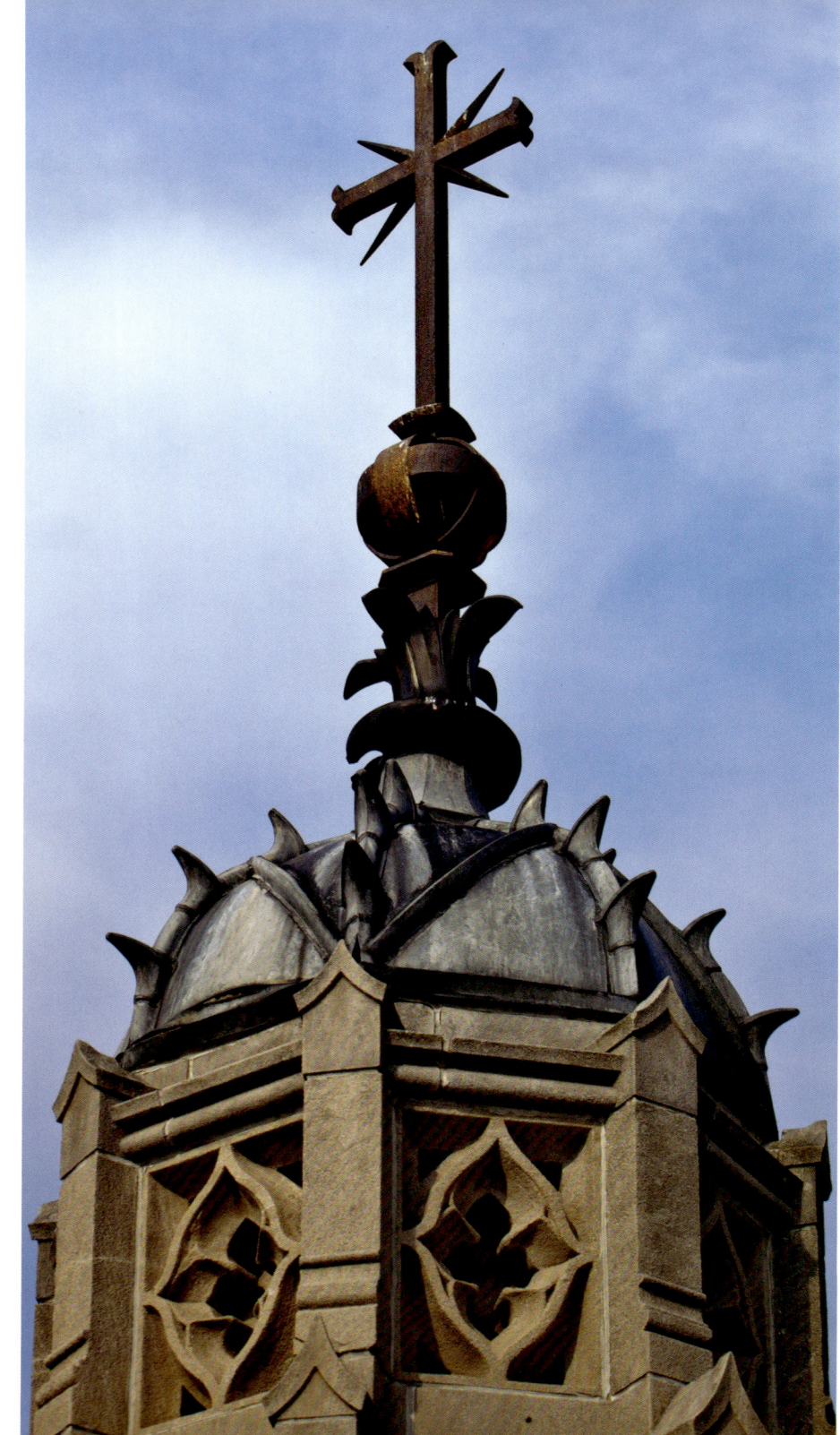

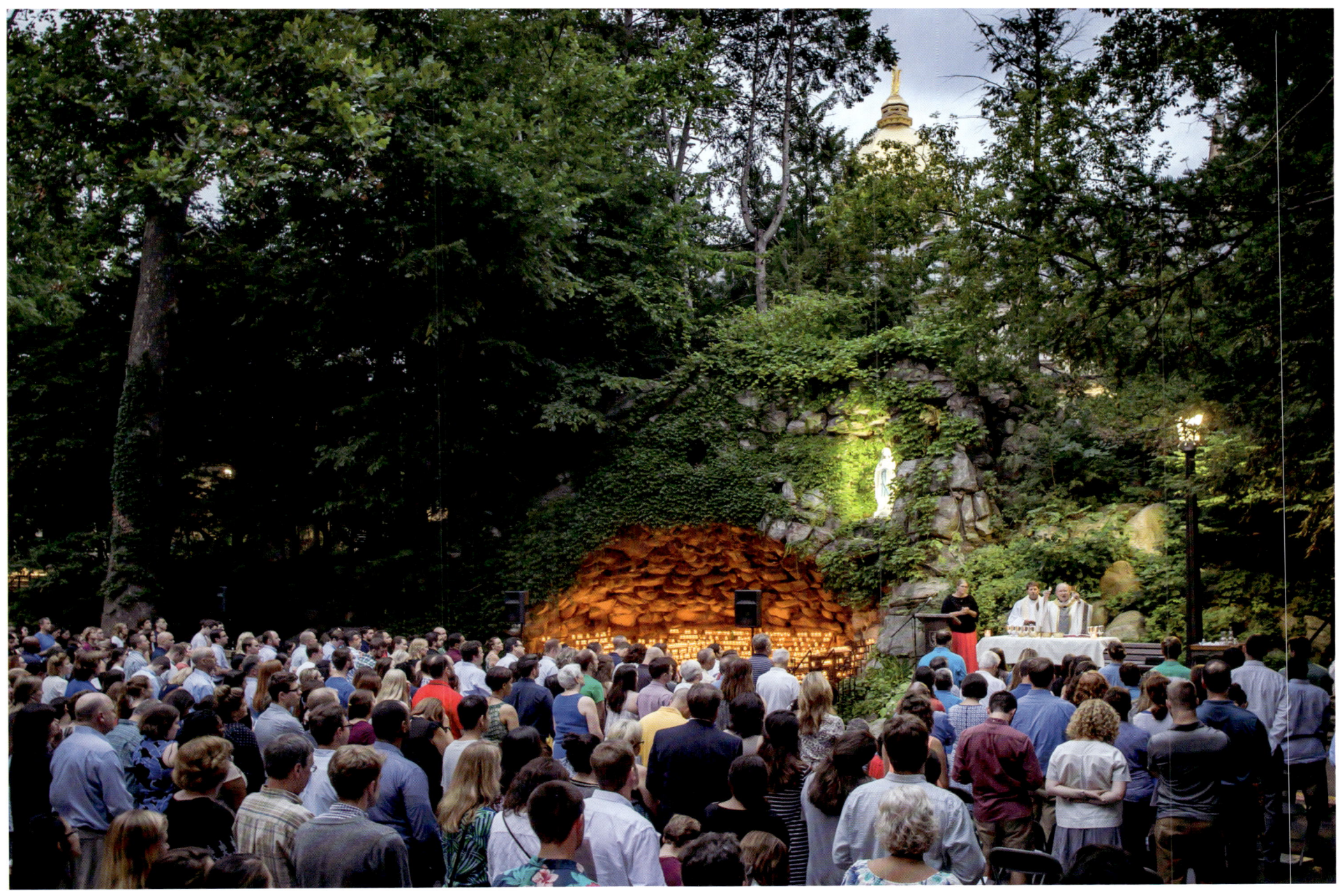

Yet there is little doubt that the university's academic ambitions can pose rival demands to its fundamental Catholic traditions. The result is a creative tension that has animated the campus conversation for decades. How does one give free rein to the intellect, the scientific method, to free will and reason, to the very ideals of the secular academy while simultaneously following the tenets of faith and morals and religious teachings that go back millennia? That's an essential question whose complex and ever-evolving answers articulate Notre Dame's very nature.

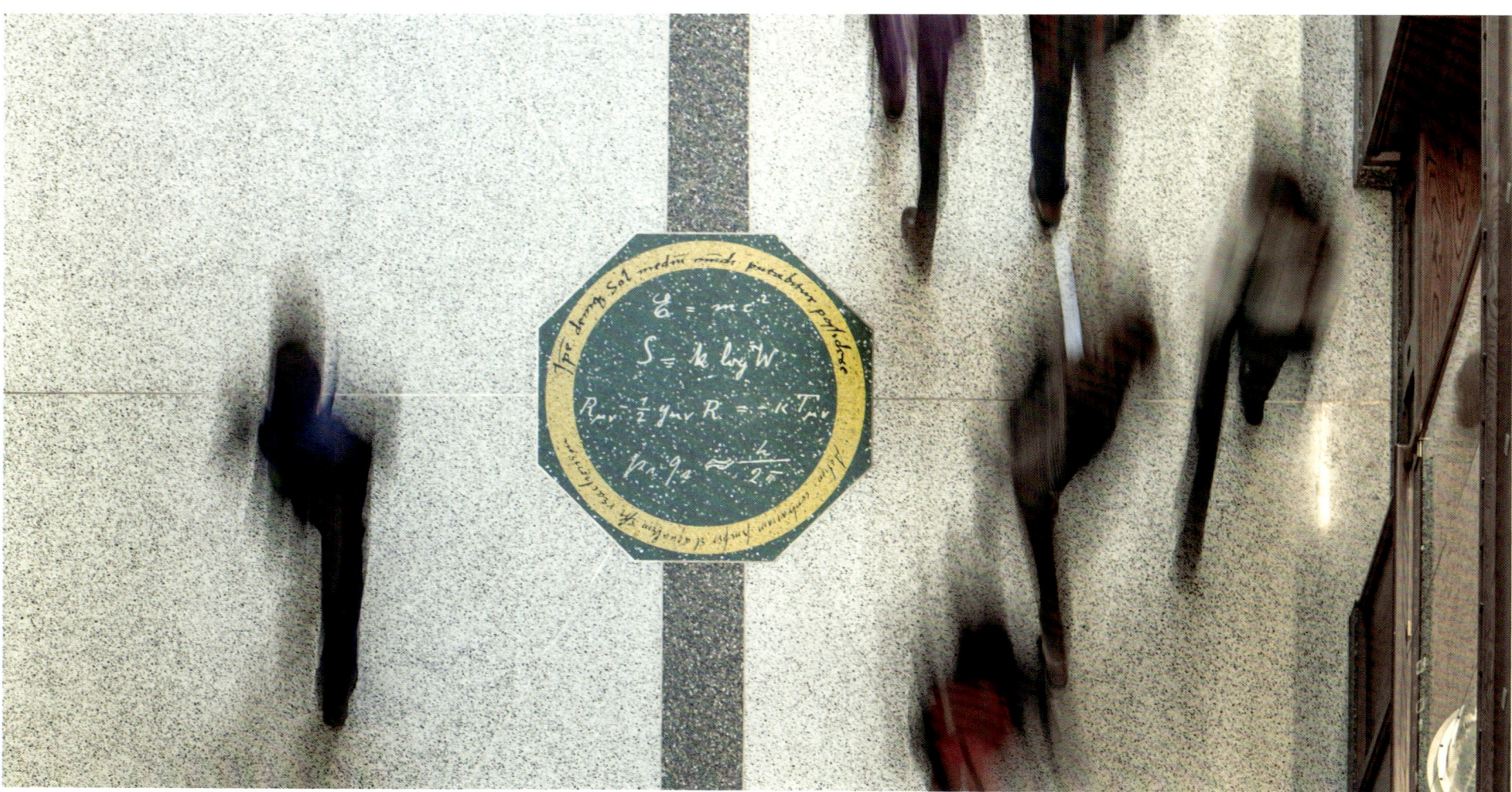

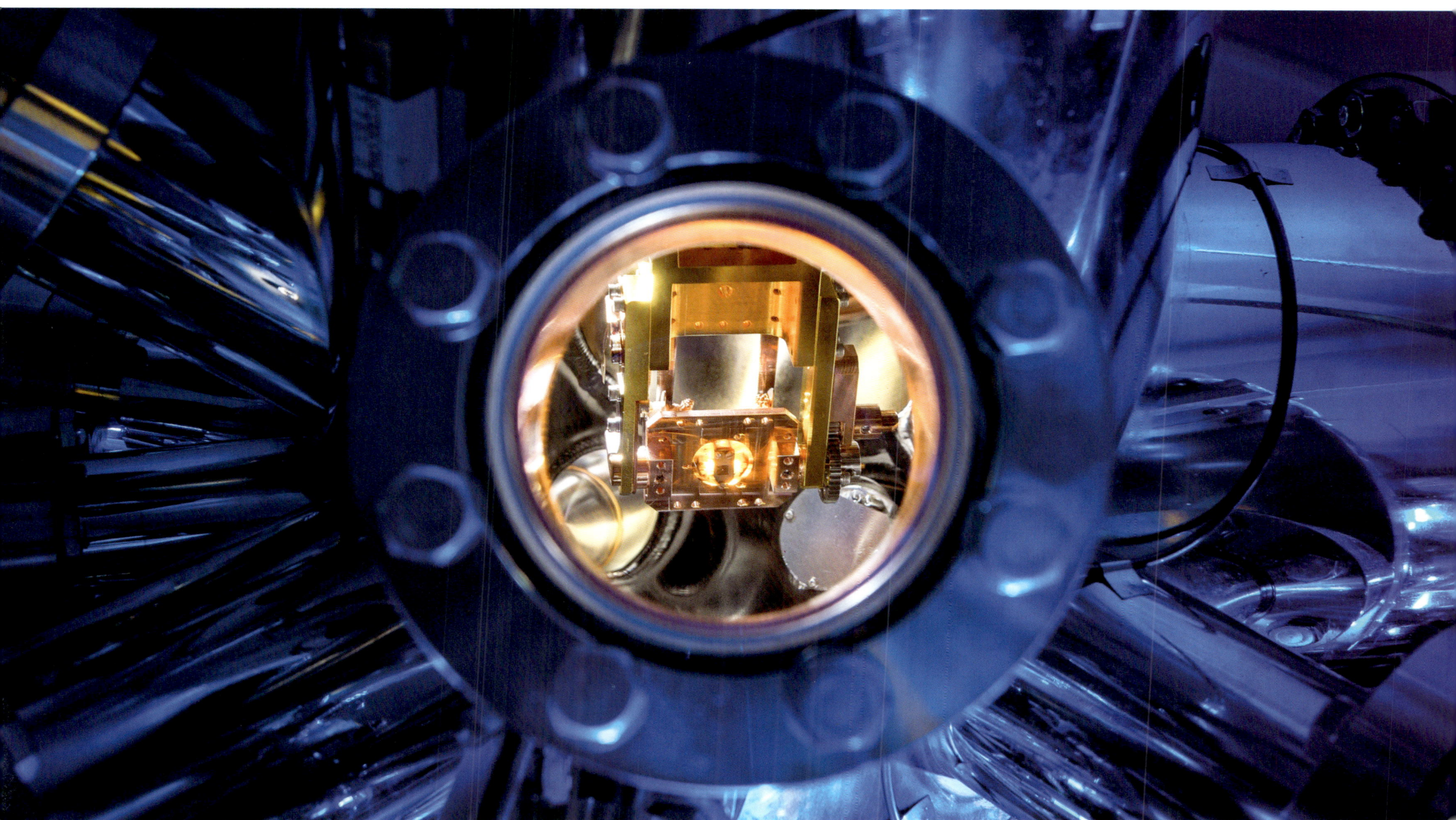

"Notre Dame is different," said Father John I. Jenkins, C.S.C., during his inaugural address in 2005. "Combining religious faith and academic excellence is not widely emulated or even admired among the opinion-makers in higher education. Yet, in this age especially, we at Notre Dame must have the courage to be who we are. If we are afraid to be different from the world, how can we make a difference in the world?"

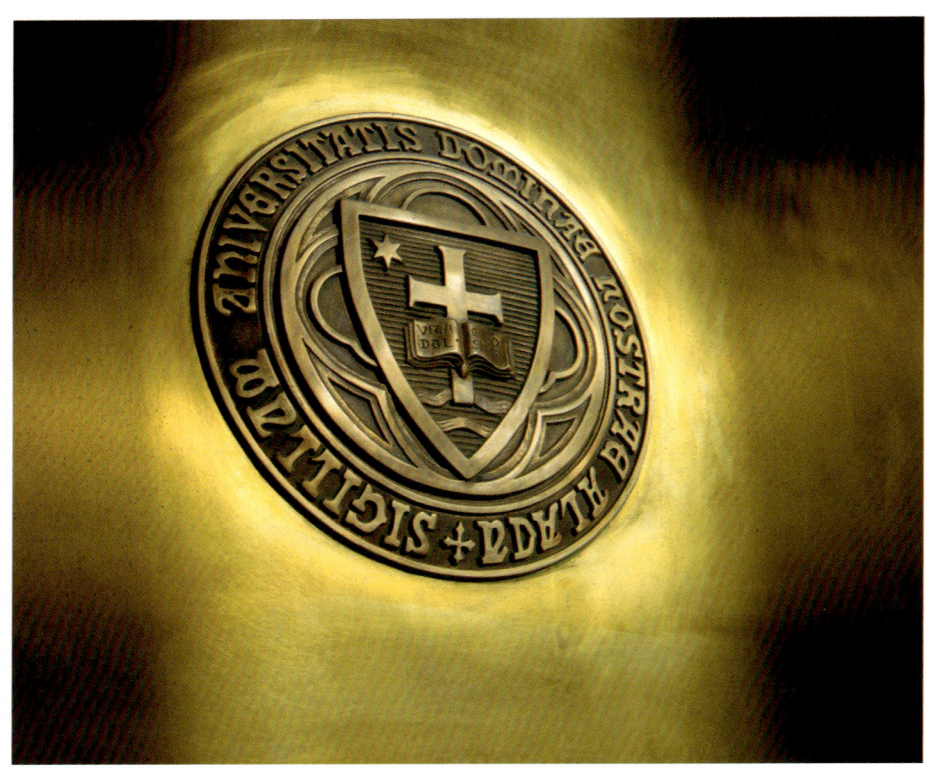

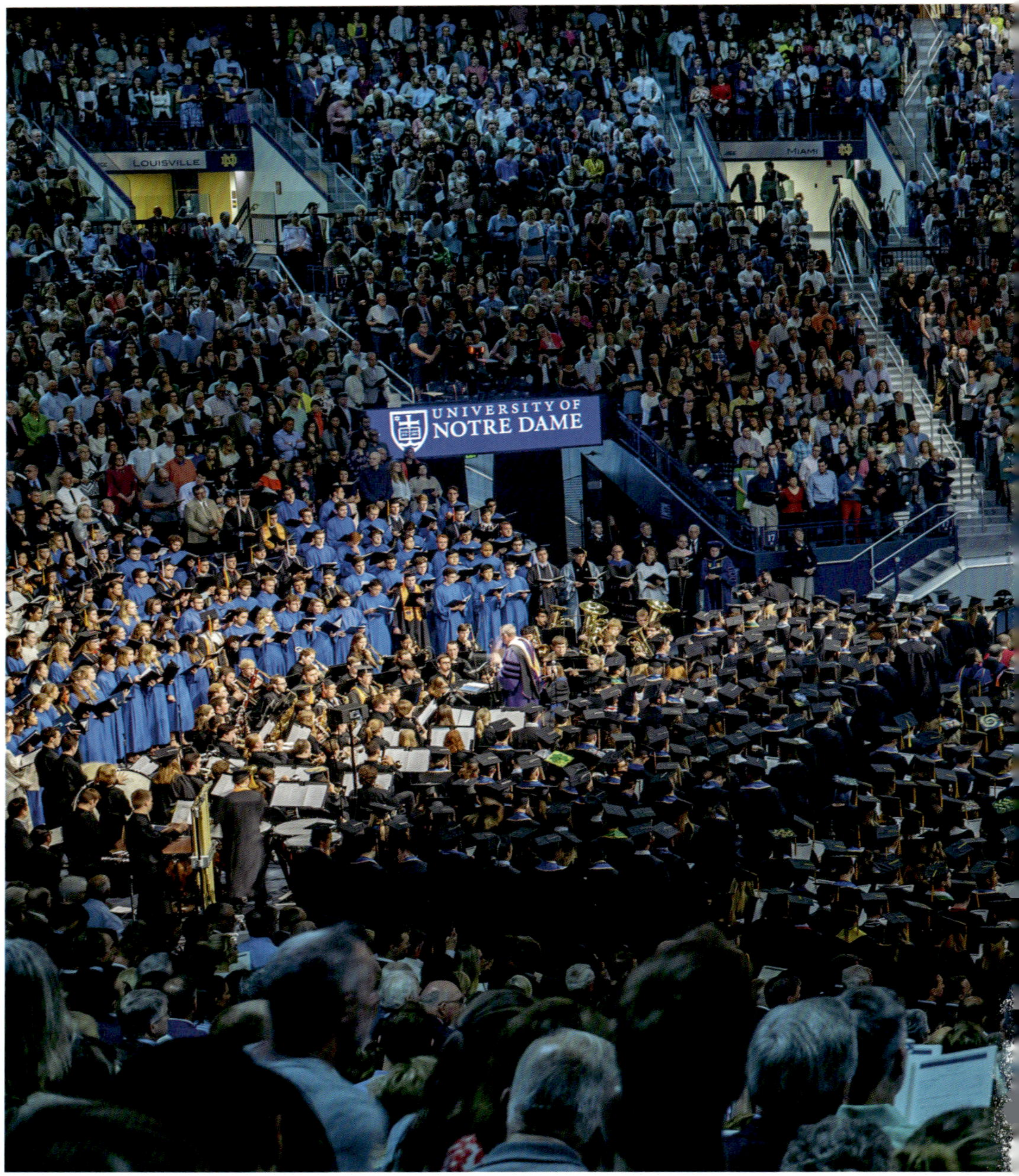

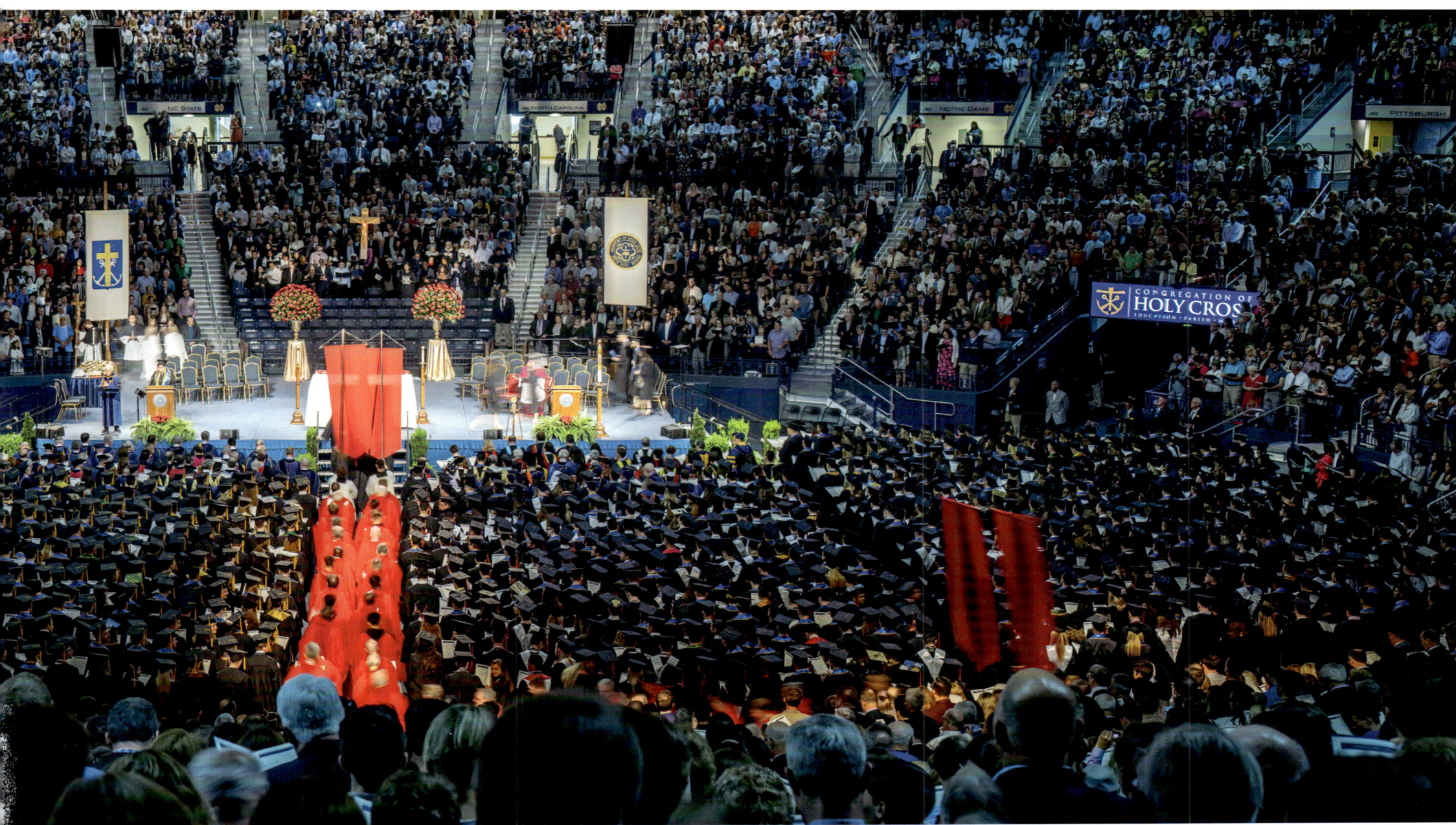

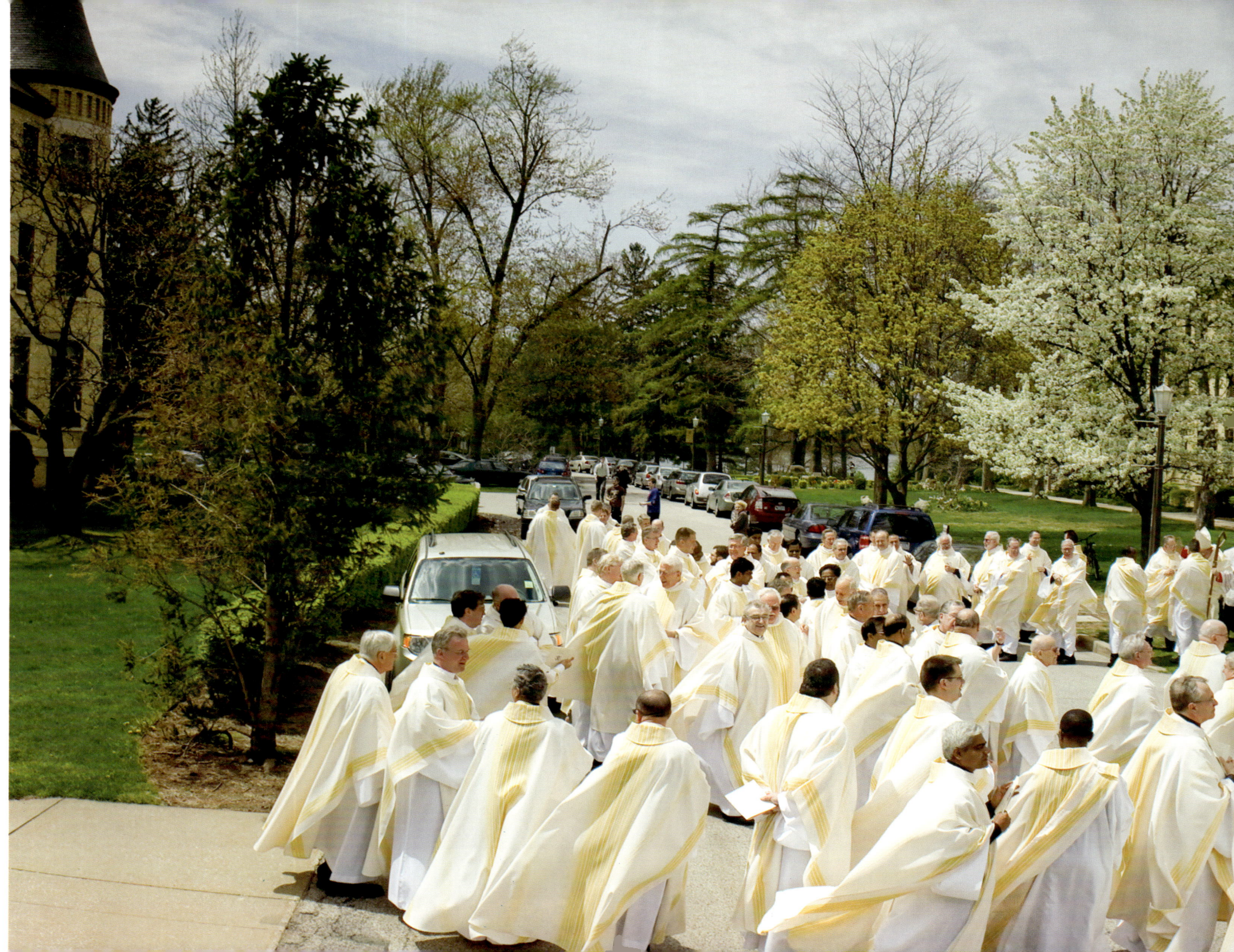

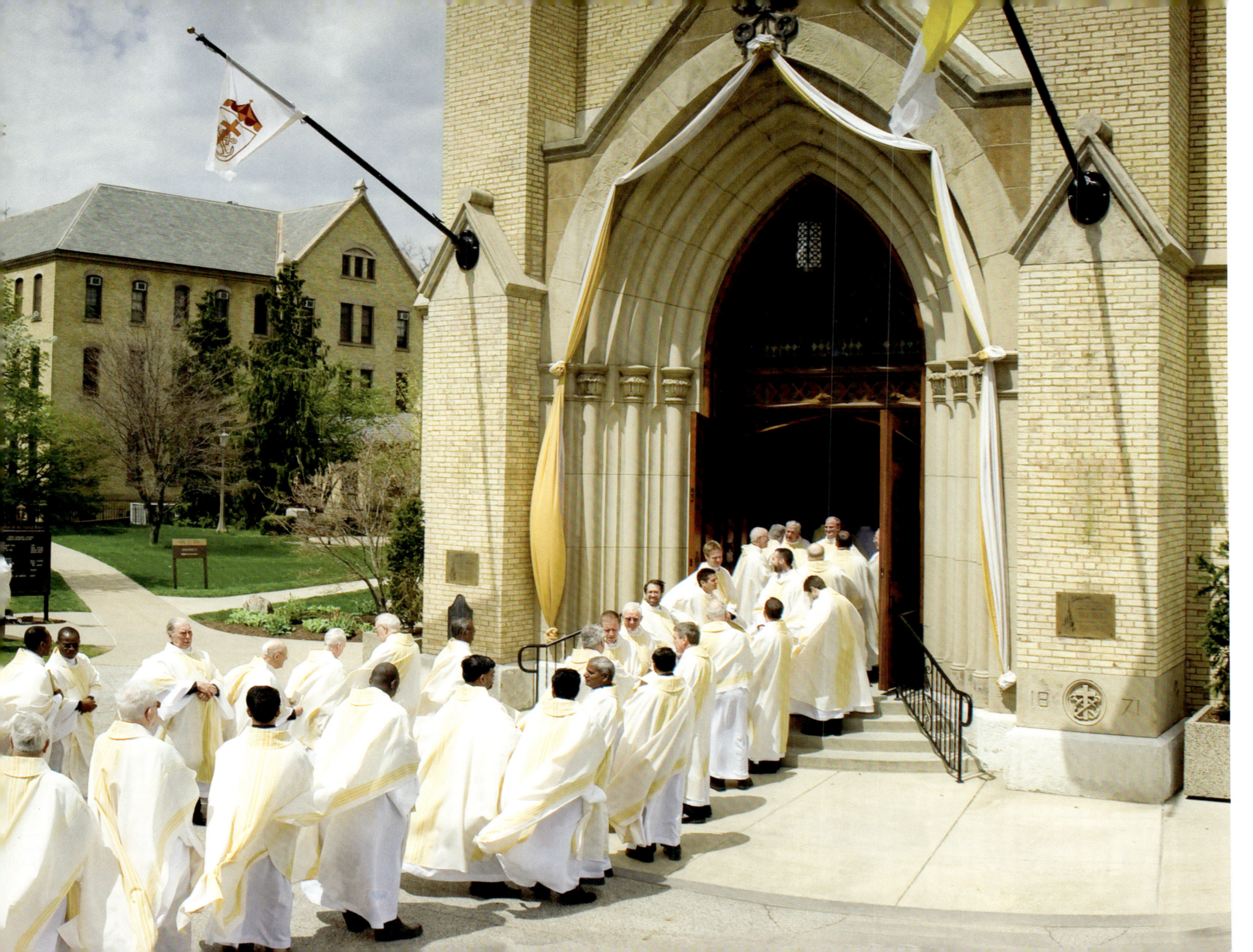

Academics is not the only area where competing goals, values, and principles rub against each other at Notre Dame. How does the institution, for example, maintain its sense of community and humanity as it experiences astounding growth? How does it care for students entrusted to its guidance and supervision while fostering their maturity, independence, and intellectual investigations? How does it embrace diversity and the competing influences of contemporary culture while holding firm to its Catholic character? How does it boldly enter the future while embracing, even clinging to the foundations that have girded its past?

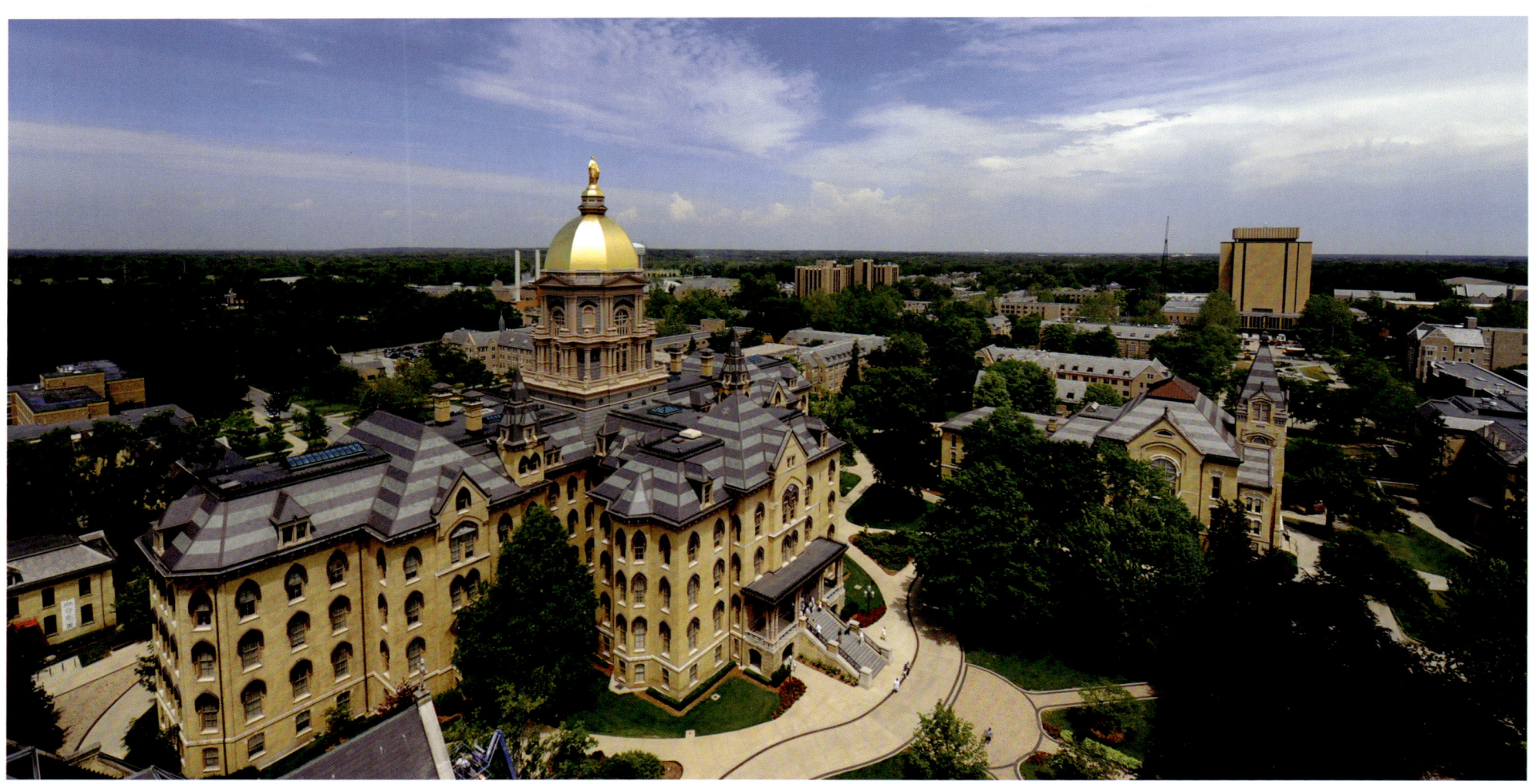

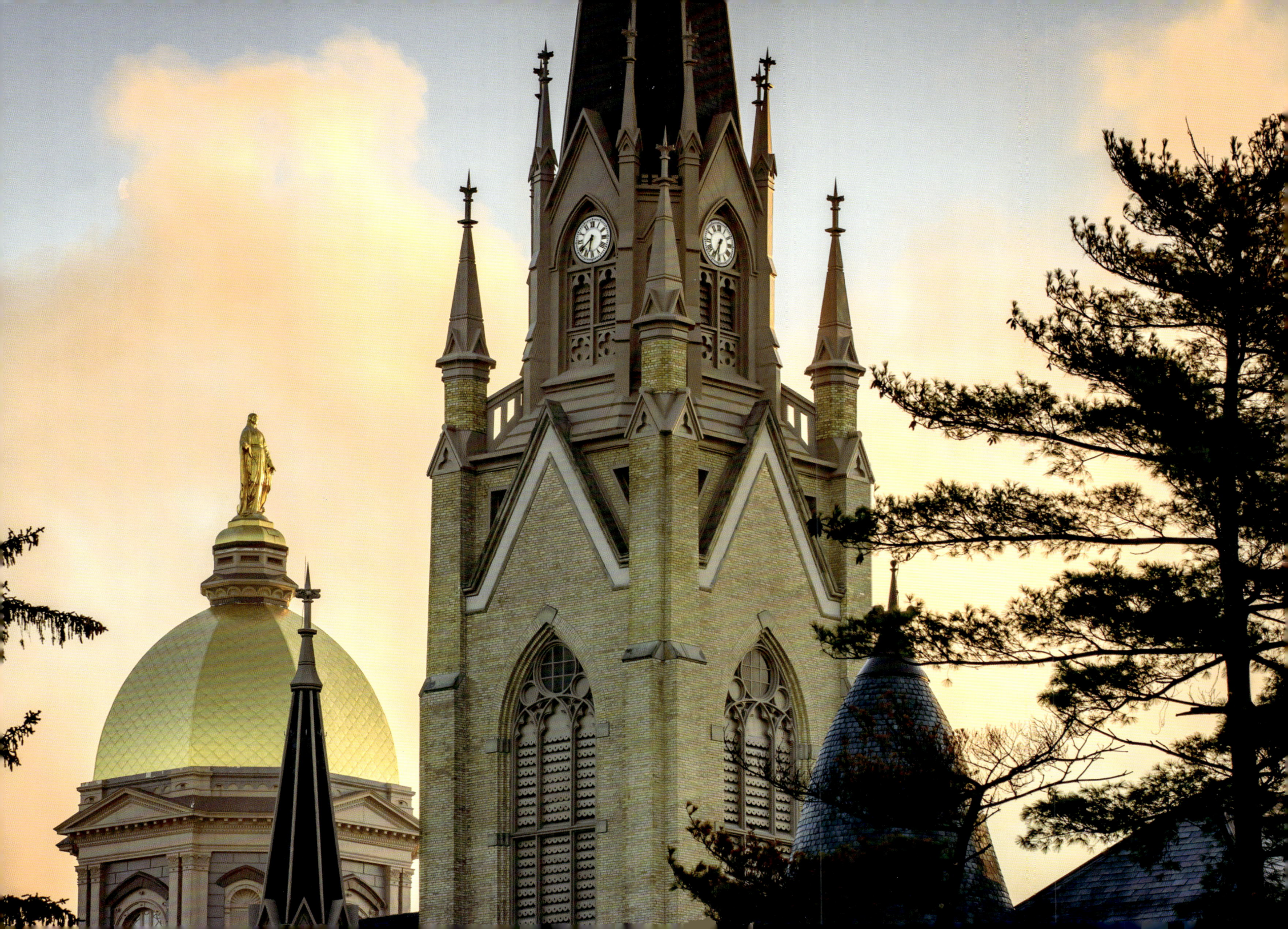

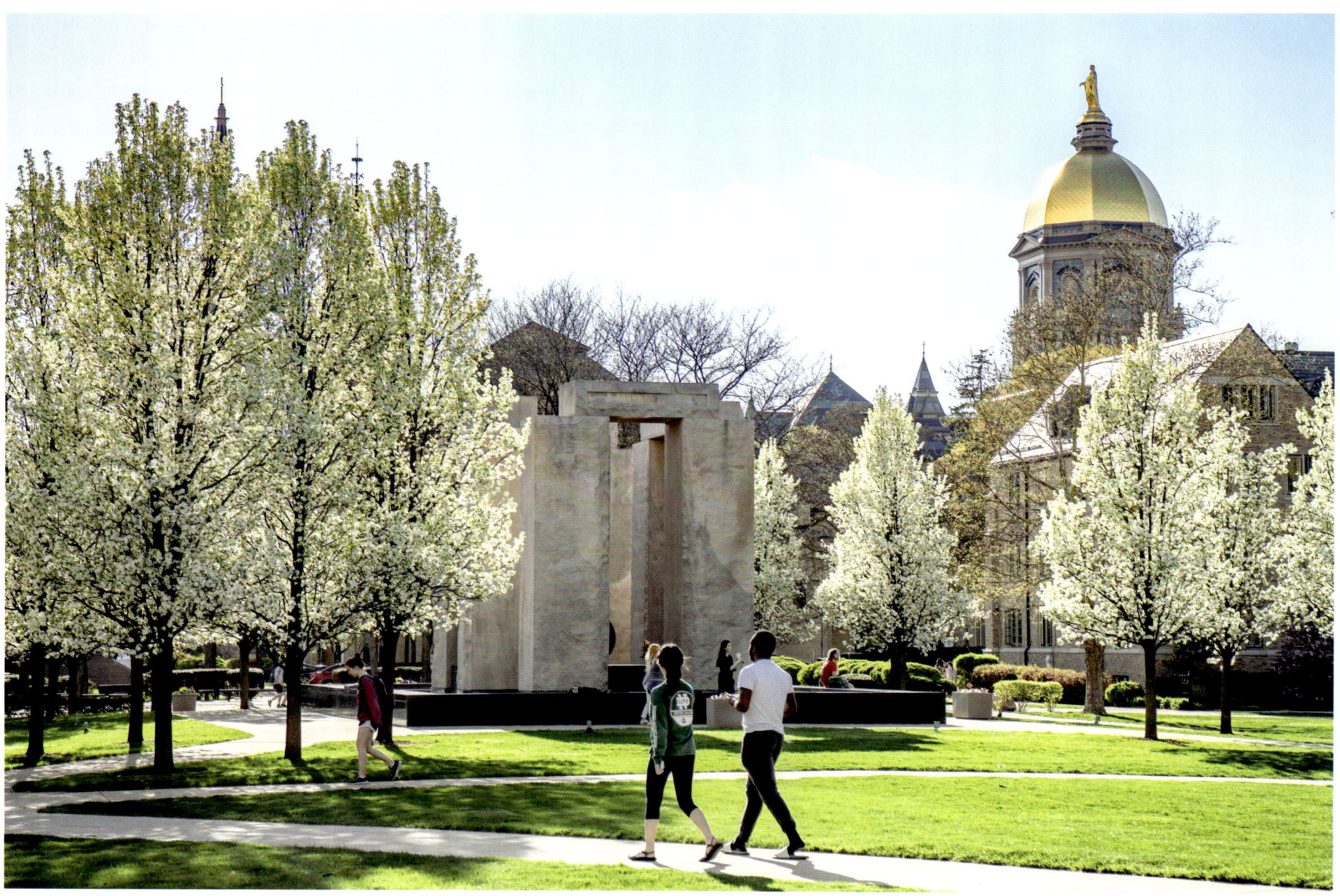

"The struggle to be a great Catholic university in a world that has become both increasingly secular and more radically religious has placed Notre Dame in a unique positon at the heart of the most complex issues facing our society," Father Jenkins acknowledged at his inauguration. "We have not just an opportunity, but a duty to think and speak and act in ways that will guide, inspire and heal—not just followers of the Catholic faith, but all our neighbors in the nation and the world. . . . Notre Dame will provide an alternative for the twenty-first century . . . where technical knowledge does not outrun moral wisdom . . . where our restless quest to understand the world not only lives in harmony with faith but is strengthened by it."

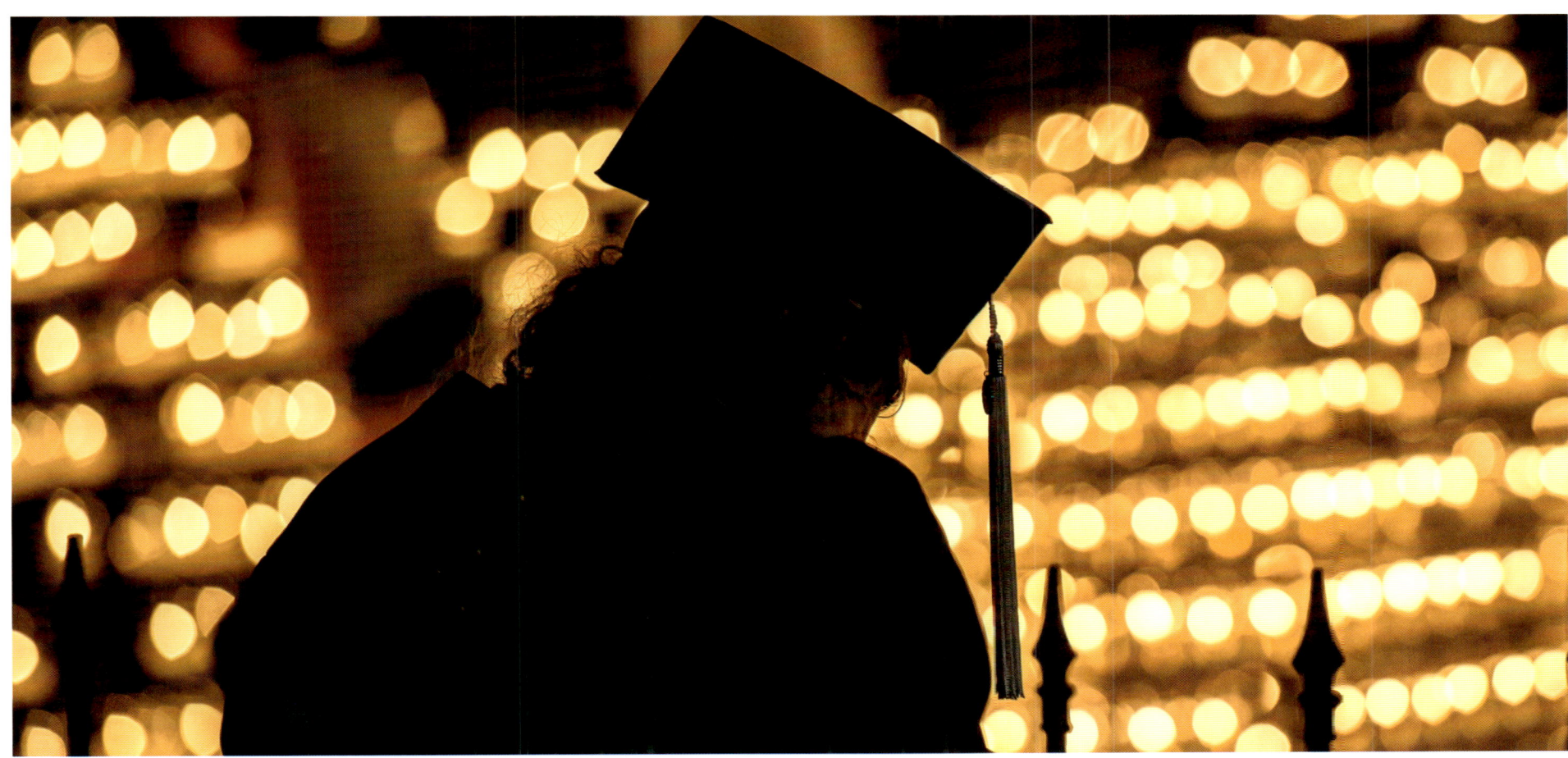

What I loved most about my undergraduate days at Notre Dame was the dialogue, the continuous conversation, that tension between tradition and exploration. I loved reading books and going to class, hearing lectures, getting exposed to divergent views, opinions, and beliefs, listening to guest speakers and scholars, and taking those conversations back to dorm rooms or to Louie's or Rocco's where we'd drink beer, eat pizza, and talk about God and sports and the meaning of life and what we'd do to make the world better.

For me, Notre Dame was the confluence of freshman biology, Mark Twain and Willa Cather, Taoism, Shakespeare and the koans of Thomas Merton. It was Collegiate Seminar—that two-semester "great books" course in which twelve or fifteen of us met in the Farley Hall lounge for three hours each Monday night to explore the week's readings. We talked Plato and Freud, Black Elk and Confucius, Augustine, Aquinas, and Karl Marx, arguing about war and peace and God, corporate America, evolution and materialism, the role of government and how to get along . . . then going back upstairs to test our good intentions in the smelly, warty mix of all-male communal living.

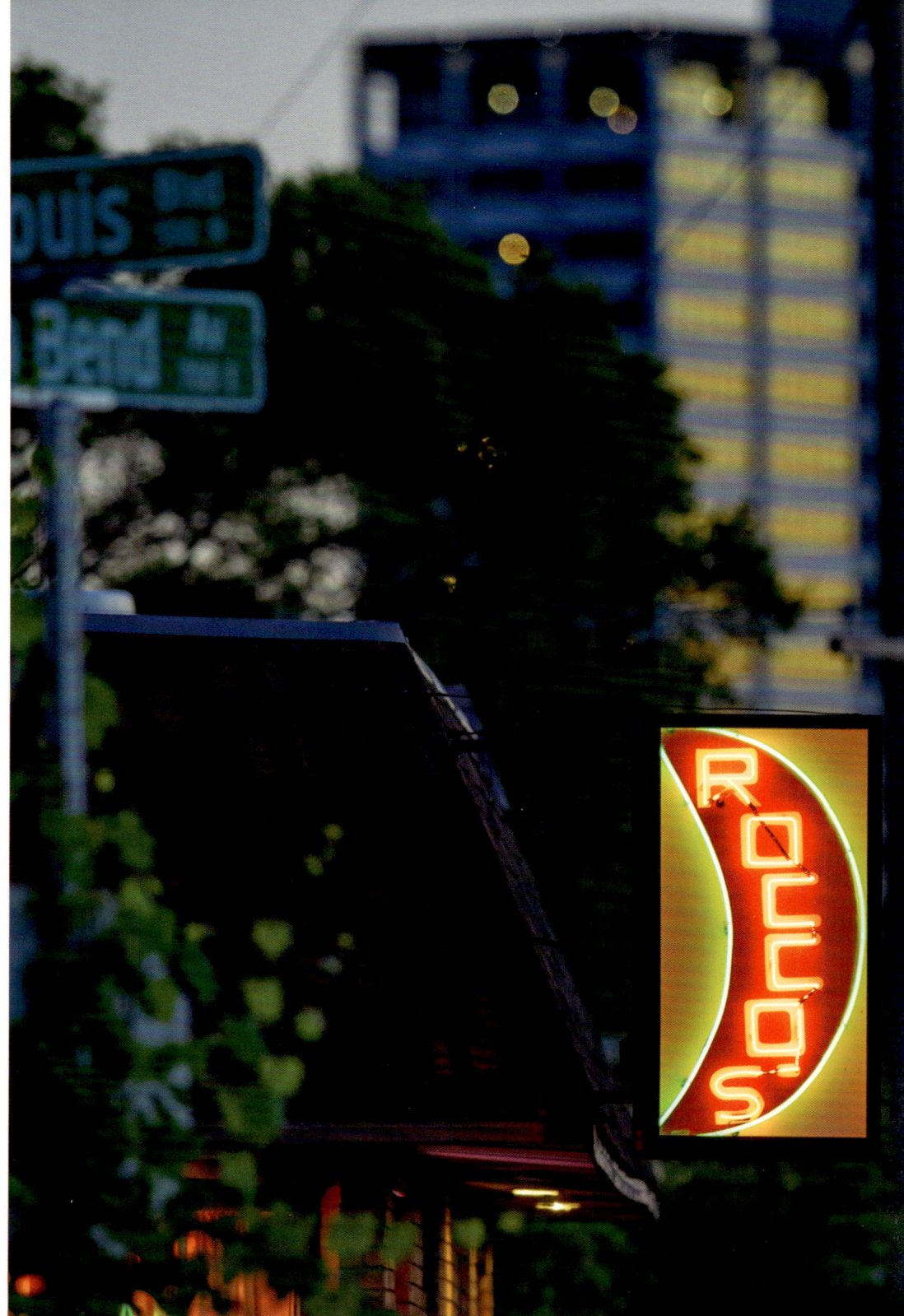

"The characteristic spirit of this University seems to me one of considerable intellectual tension," Richard Sullivan wrote in *Notre Dame*: *Reminiscences of an Era*. "The people here strike me as exhibiting a remarkable concern—I should say a primary concern—for ideas, principles, values, theories, facts and the terrific illumination generated by the friction and occasional collision of all these. The very fury with which we quarrel confirms me. Clash of conviction is the honest noise made by intellects in action. And at Notre Dame there is perhaps an increased volume and a special clarity because here, clashing, we still speak a common language and share a common faith and intention. We have, as they say, a core."

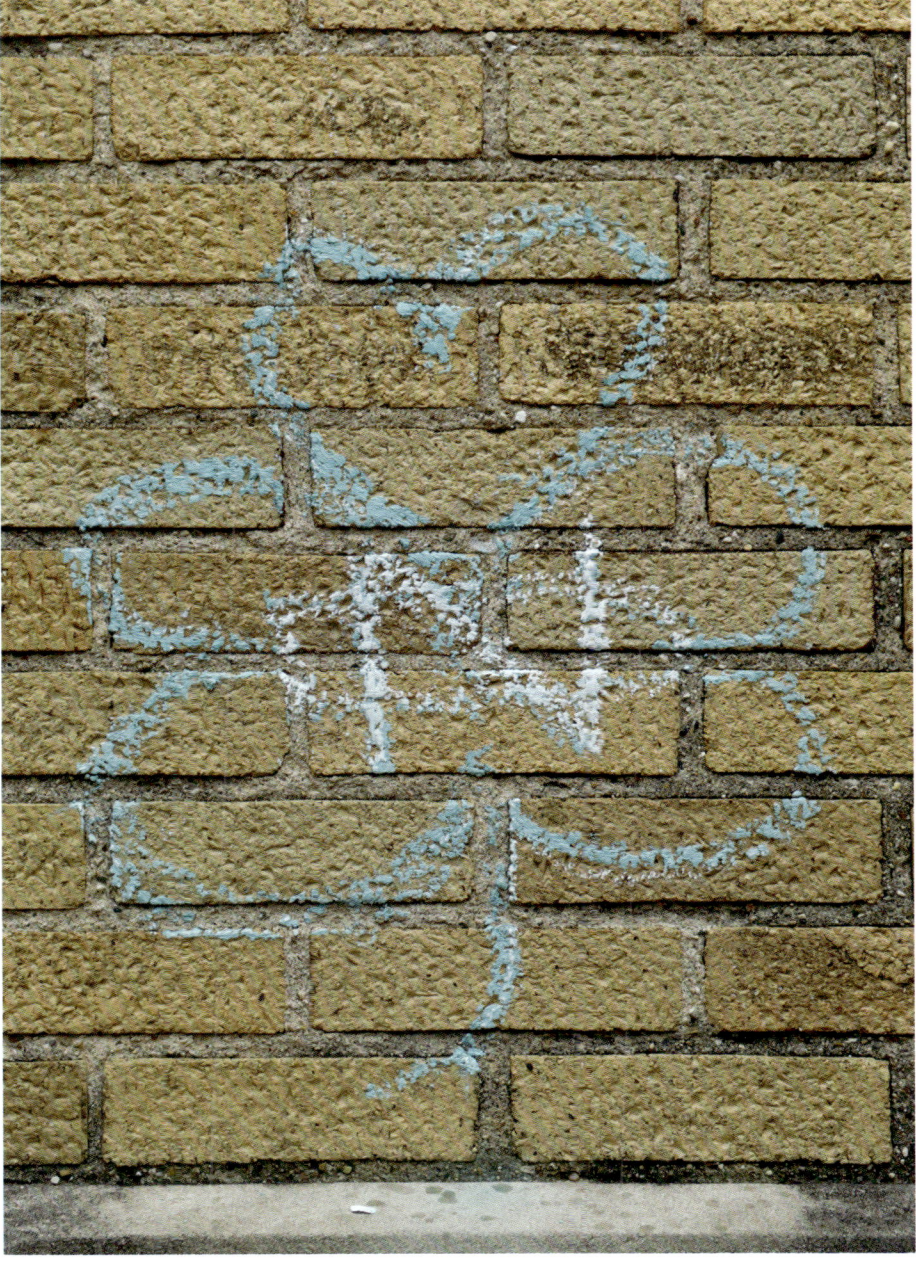

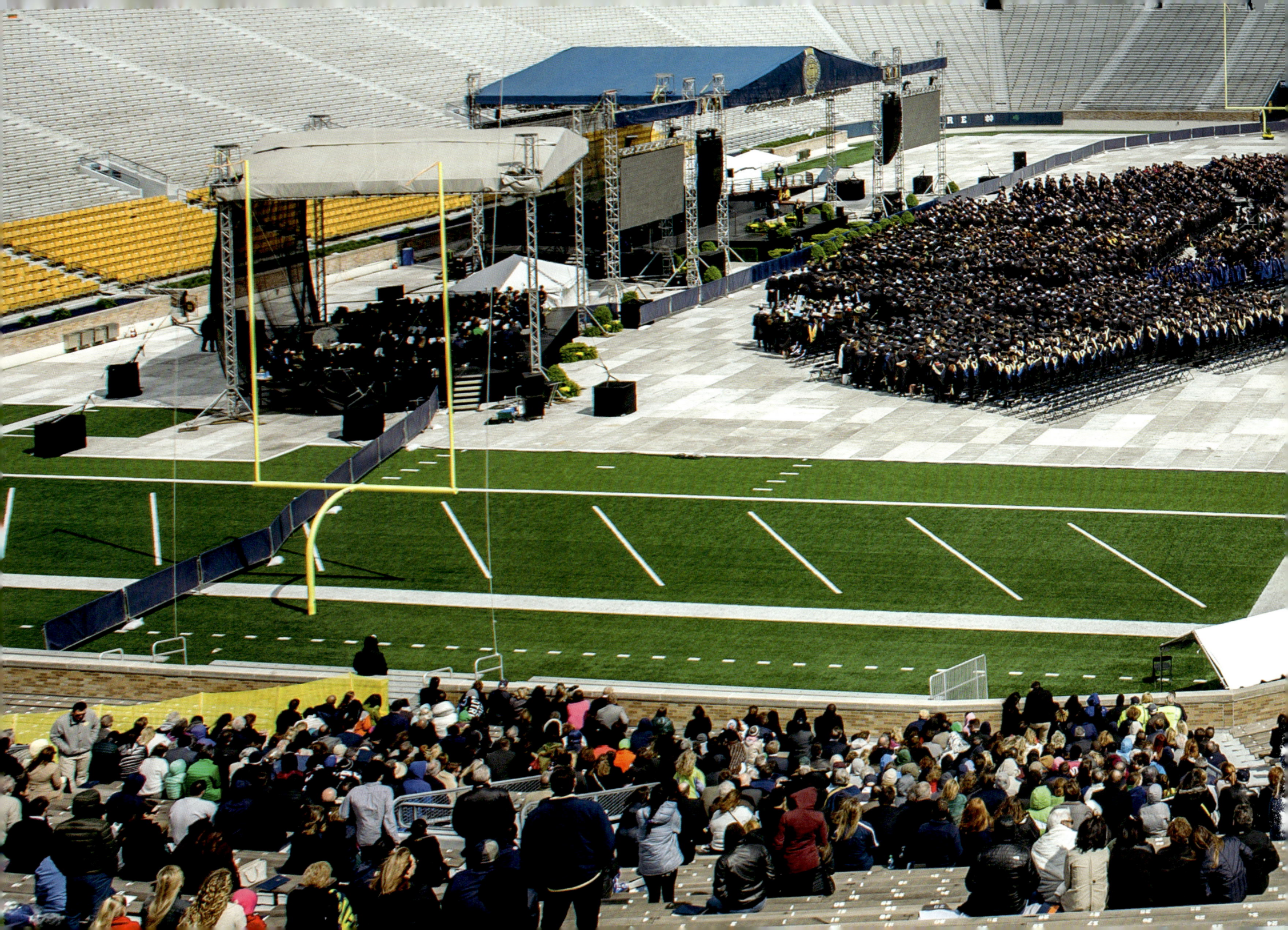

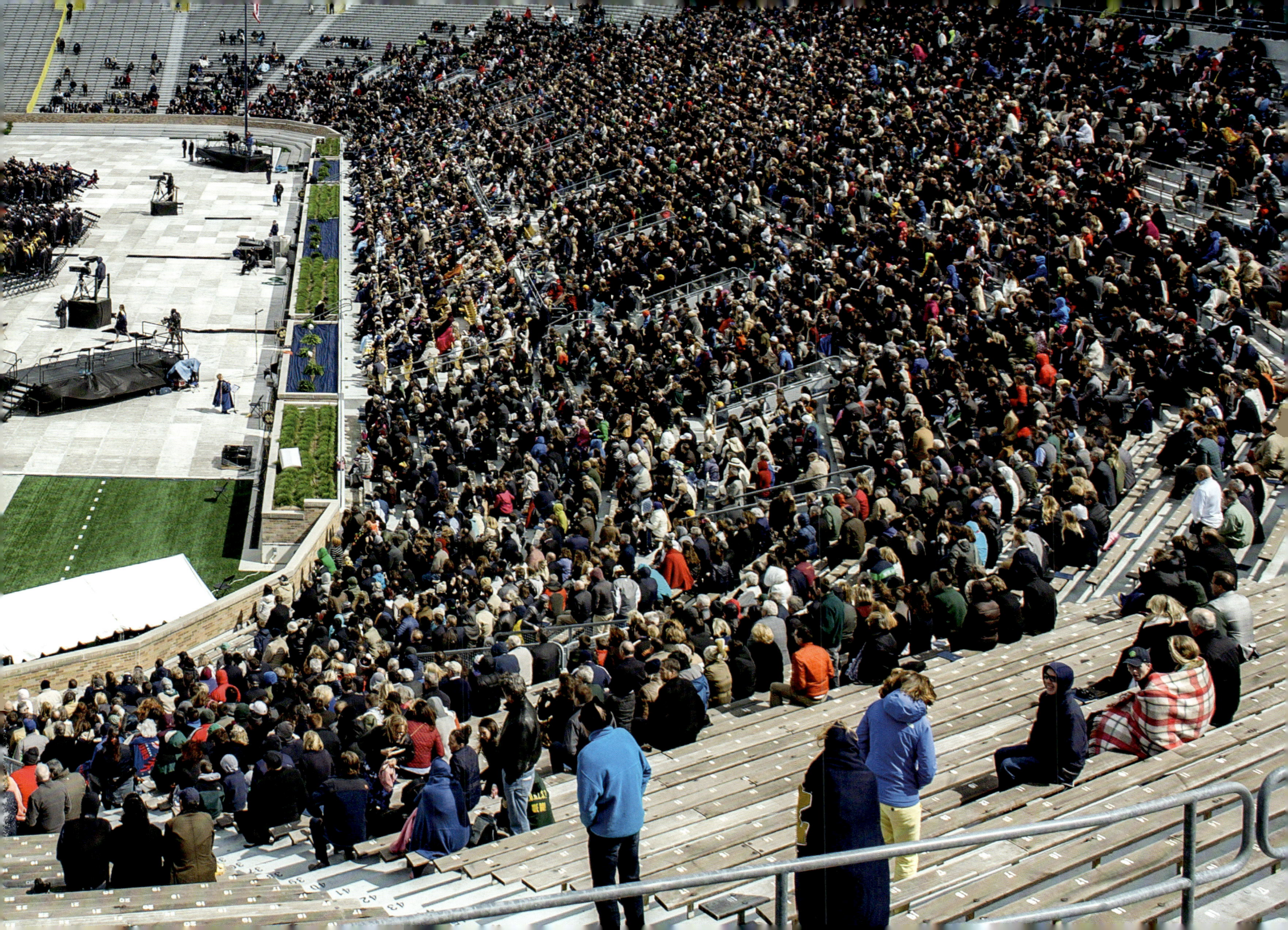

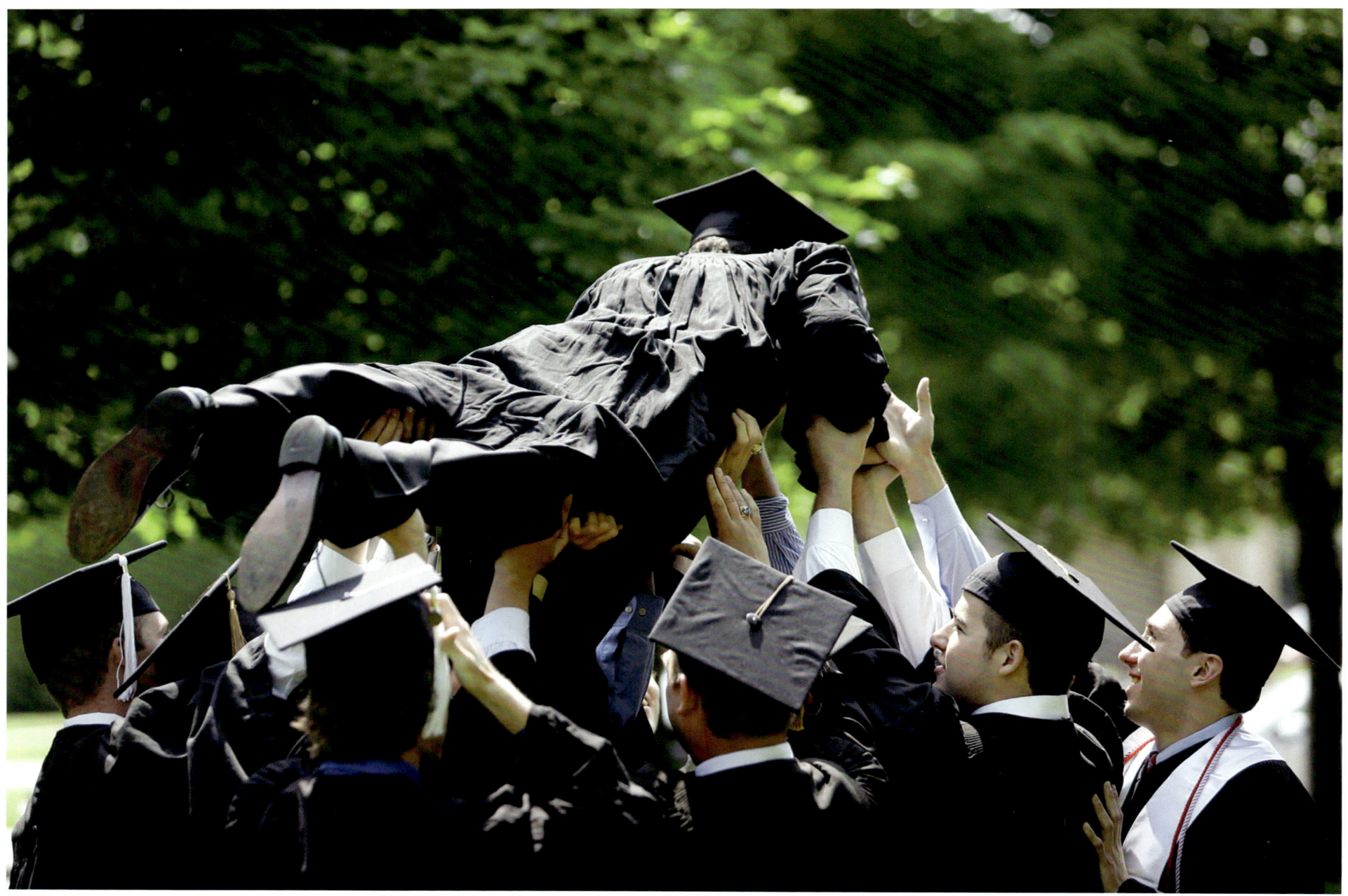

142

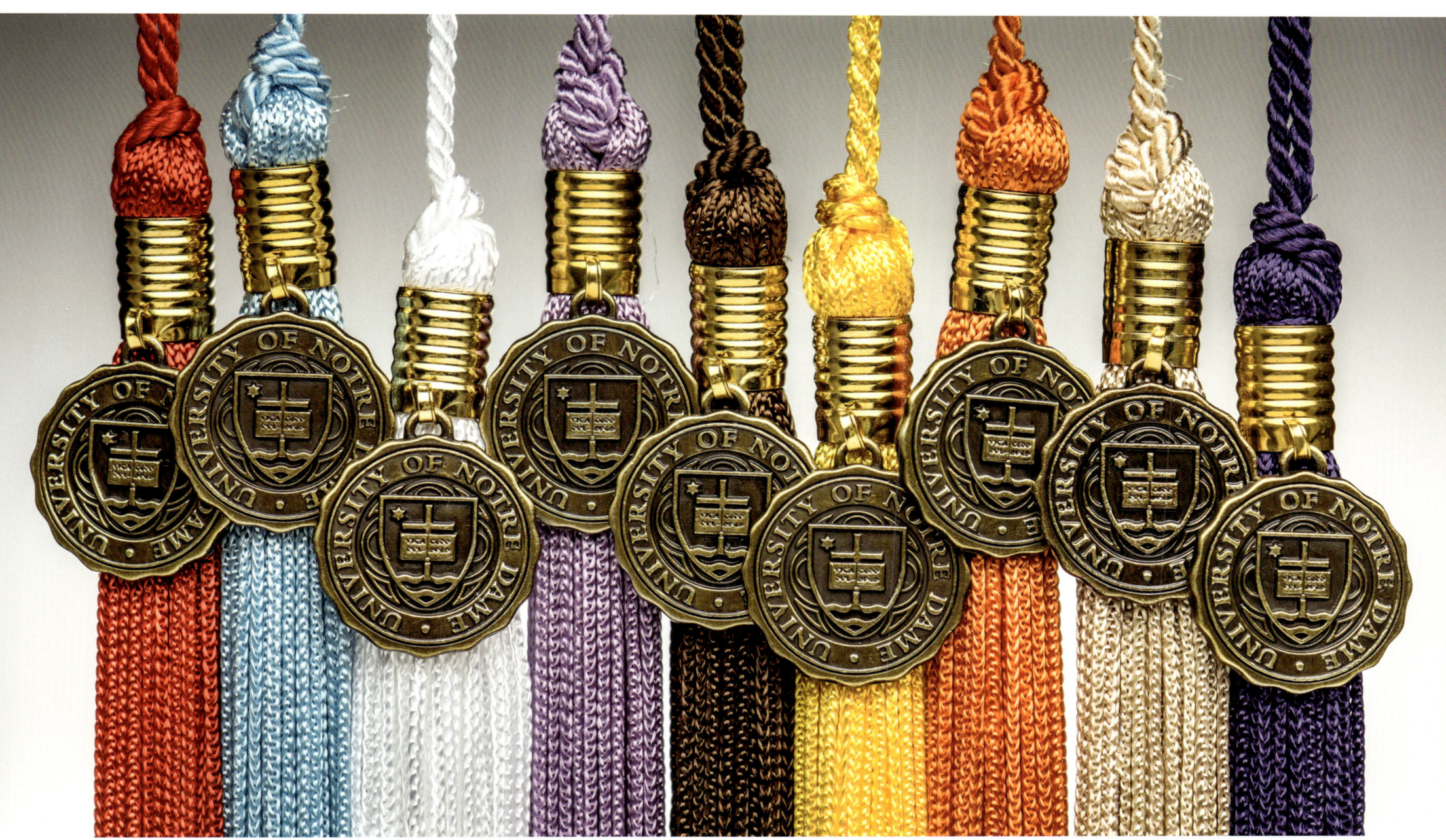

143

It was spring semester senior year when the meaning of Notre Dame was most poignantly distilled for me. Each afternoon, Monday, Wednesday, and Friday, I went to Chris Anderson's abnormal psychology class. There I learned the truth about human nature—behaviorism and B. F. Skinner, the mechanistic body and our computer brains, some advanced species that's merely the most complicated offspring derived from countless random acts of evolution. And I walked out of there thinking, yes, that is all there is to us. There is no soul; the rest is all wishful thinking.

Then I walked over to Father John Dunne's theology class and listened to his lectures on the spiritual essence of life, the unseen and invisible, the mystical and the supernatural, and his moving examination of the path of the heart's desire. And as he paced back and forth, delivering truths like nuggets of flame, citing the wisdom of Rilke, Kierkegaard, and Kazantzakis, he would lift us and inspire, and paint whole new vistas of the wonders of infinite human nature.

For thirty years now that juxtaposition has stood for me as the most eloquent definition of my Notre Dame education—the sometimes uncomfortable meeting of the intellectual and the spiritual, the crossing of the transitory and eternal, the dazzling facets of truth that come from living the right questions. Notre Dame is a place where the ultimate and most elemental answers matter.

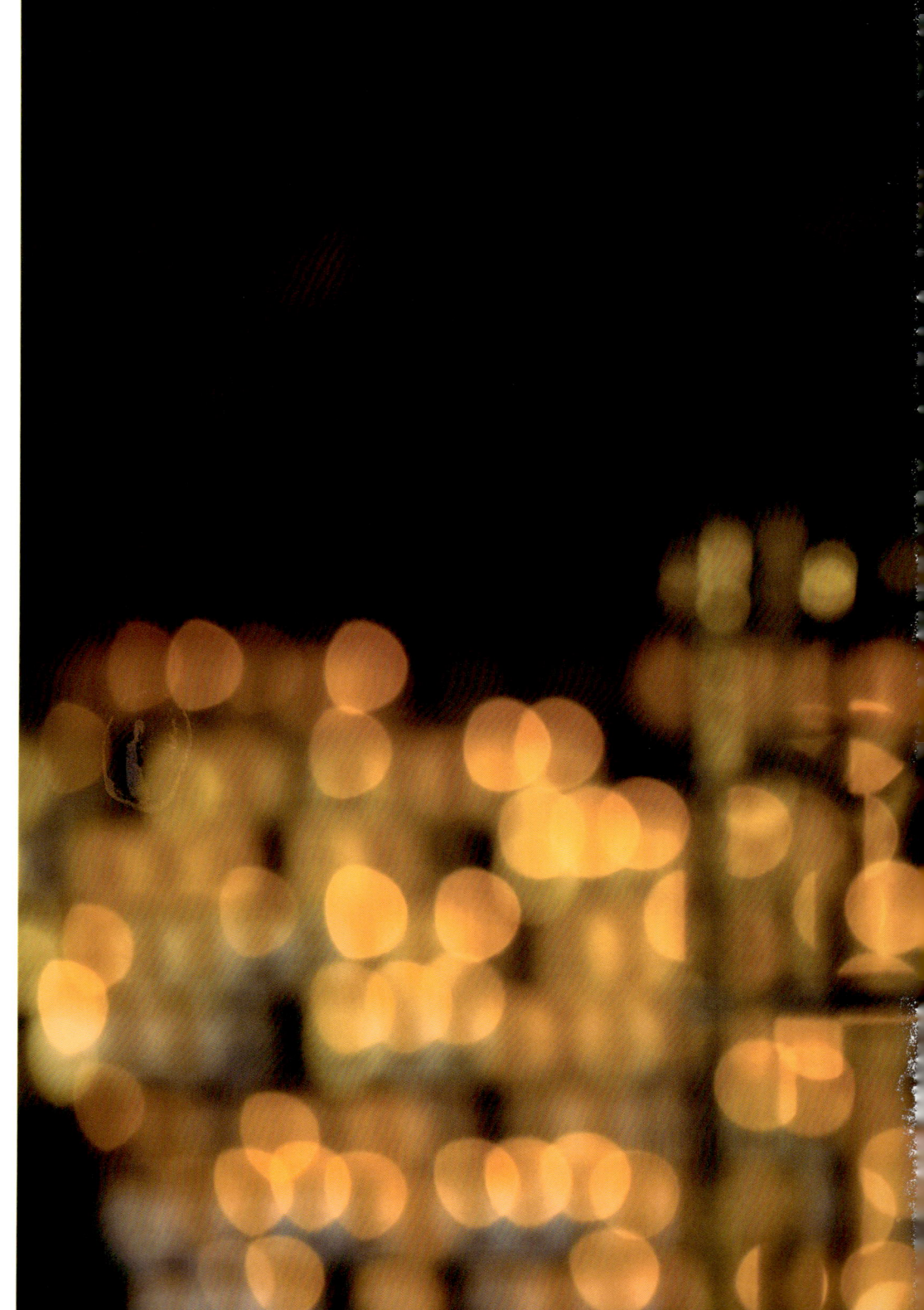

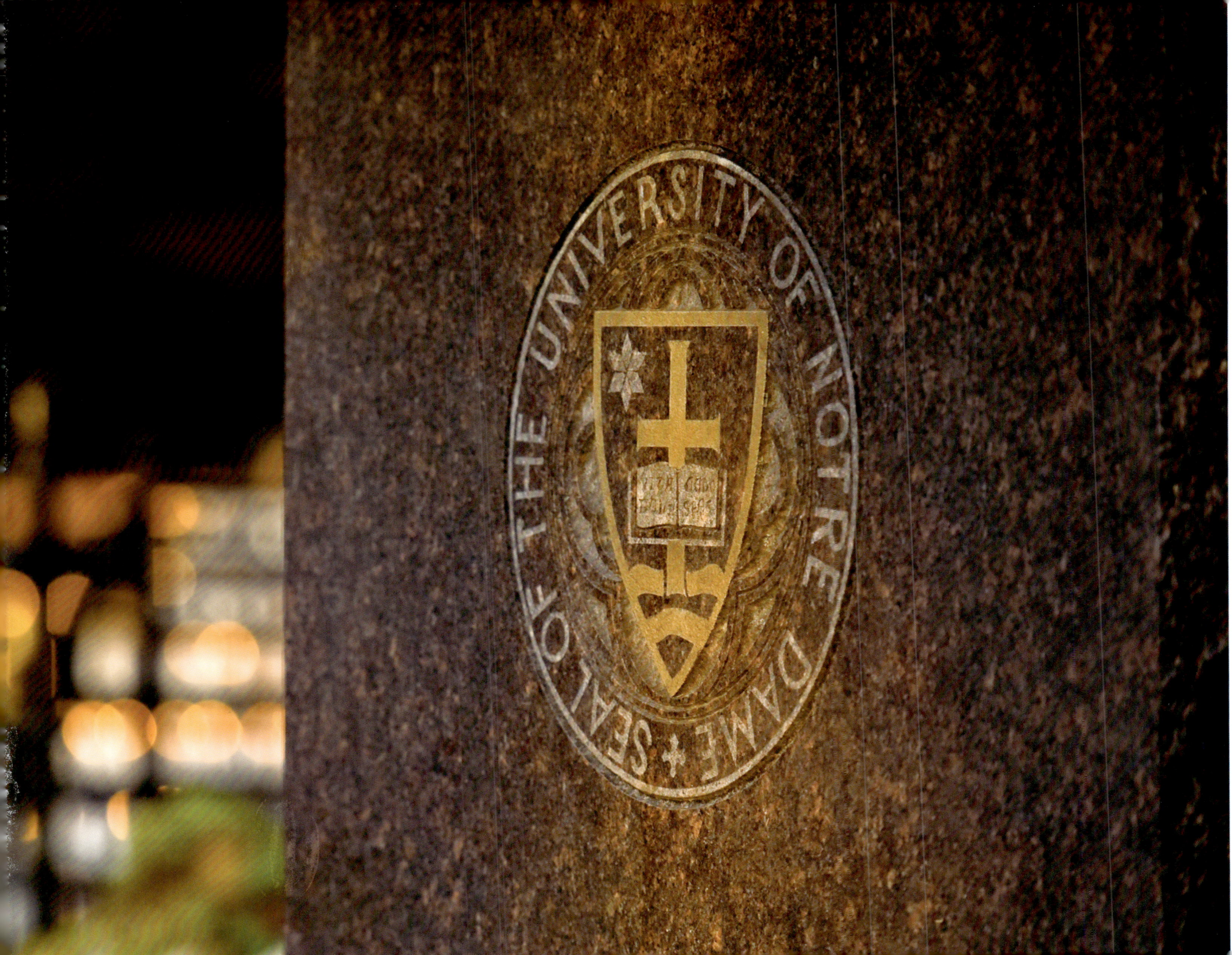

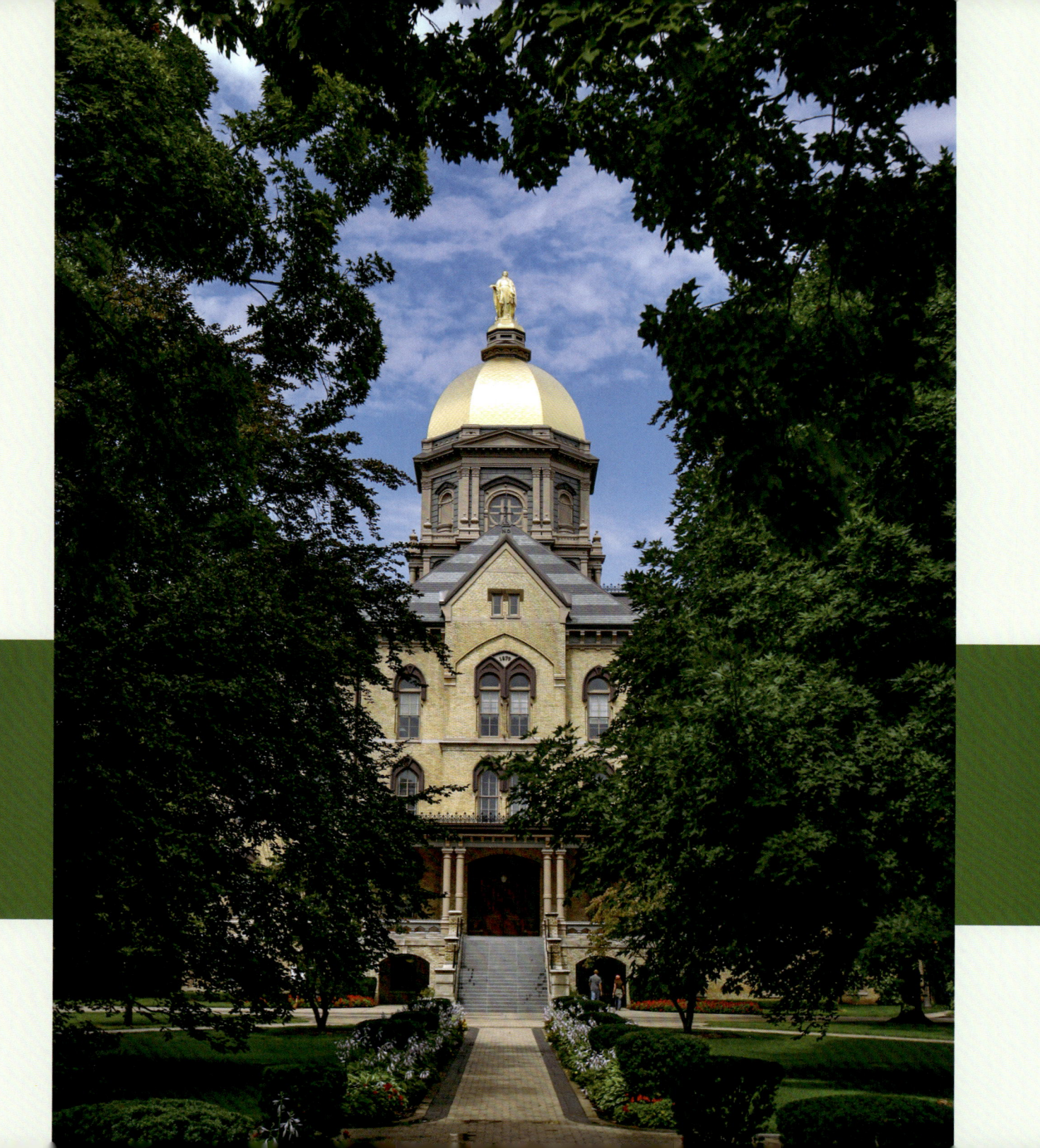

*When this school, Our Lady's school, grows a bit more, I shall raise
her aloft so that, without asking, all men shall know why we have
succeeded here. To that lovely Lady, raised high on a dome,
a Golden Dome, men may look and find the answer.*

*—Rev. Edward F. Sorin, C.S.C.,
in 1844, two years after
the university's founding*

SUMMER

There are those who jest they prefer the campus in summer because there are fewer students here. They know full well that Notre Dame belongs to its students. Even those who live and work here for decades know that it is not really their place. It exists for the students, and it is theirs for a fleeting glimpse of years—a once-in-a-lifetime passage of startling experiences, life-changing journeys, and the powerful assault on the mind, heart, and spirit that is college life du Lac.

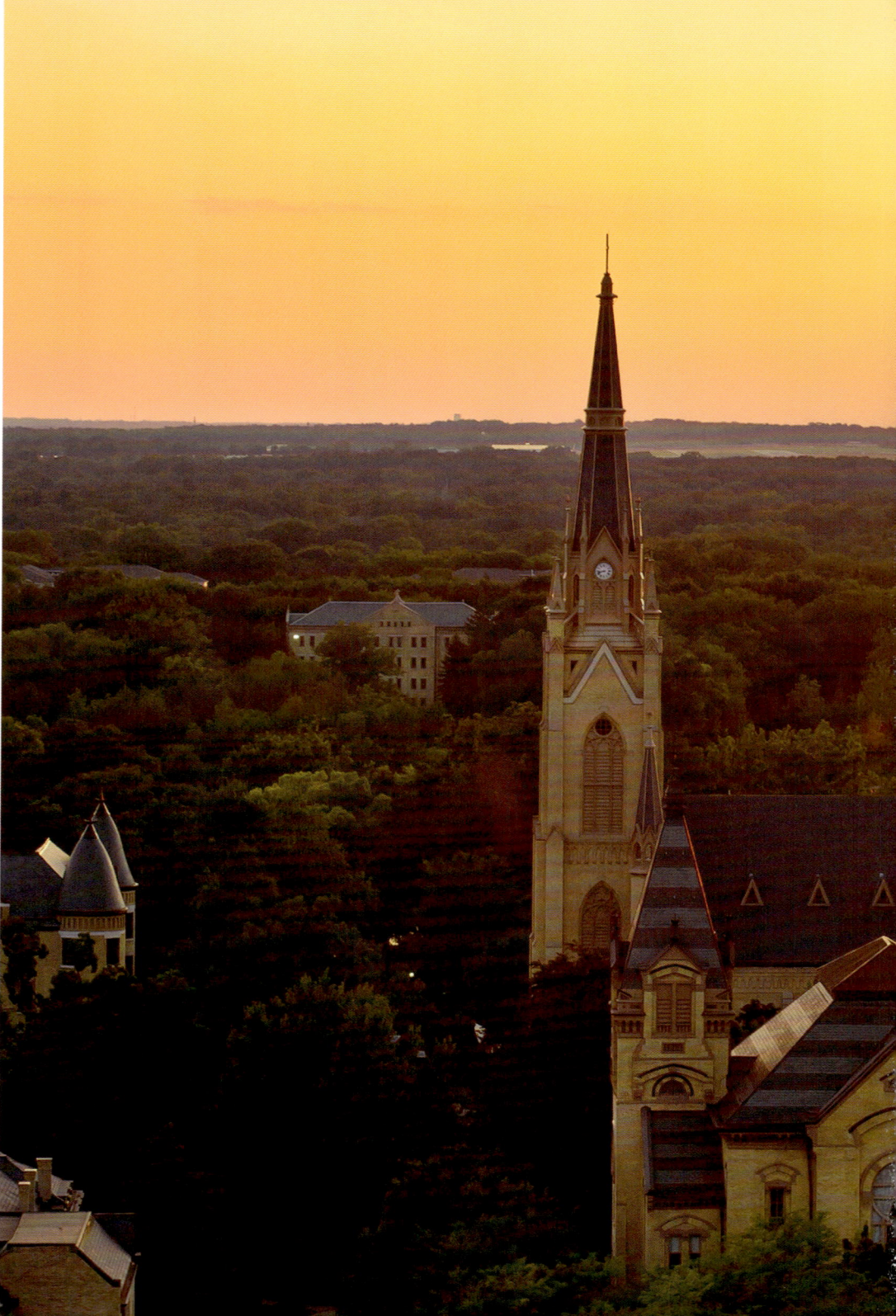

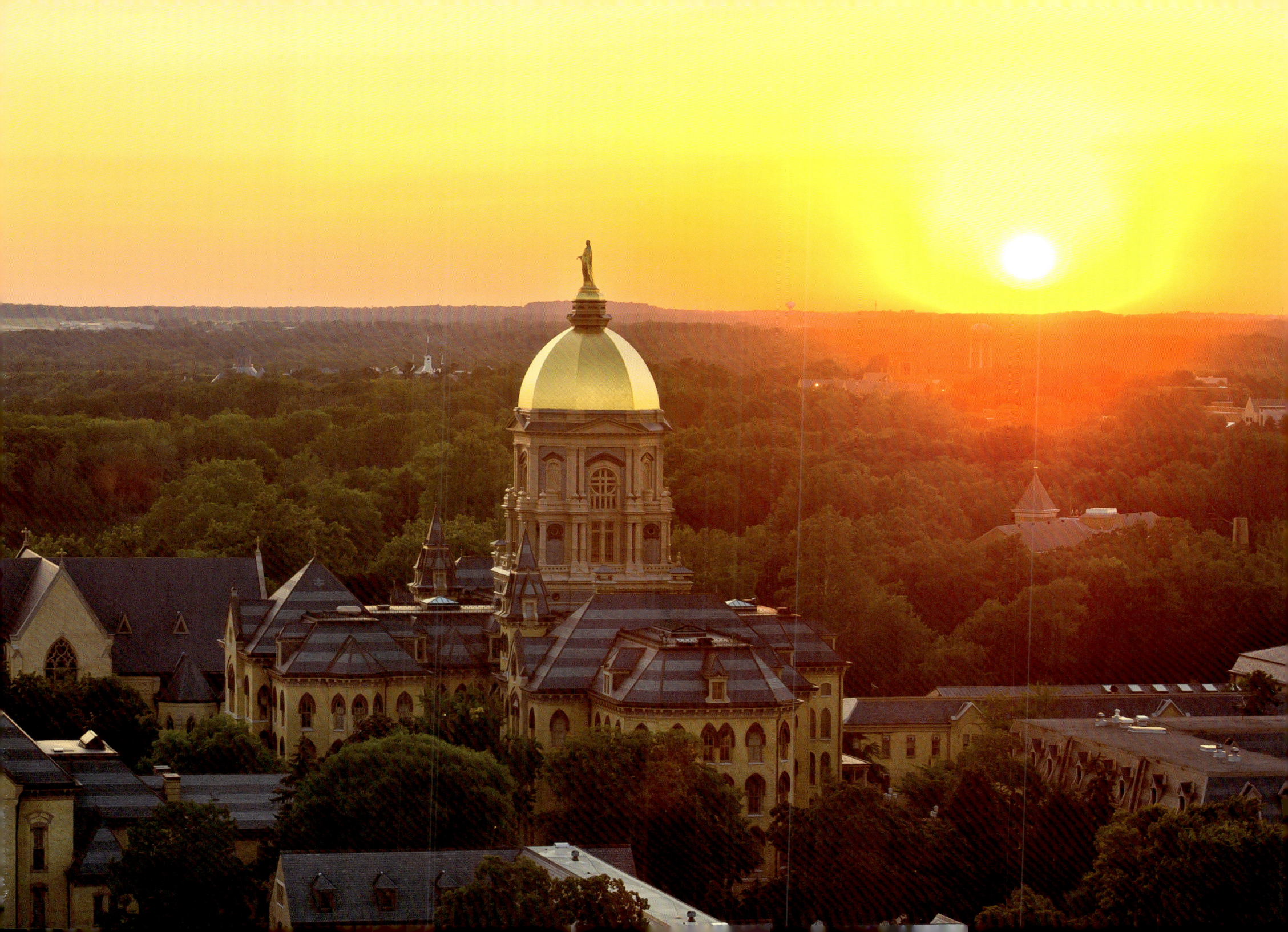

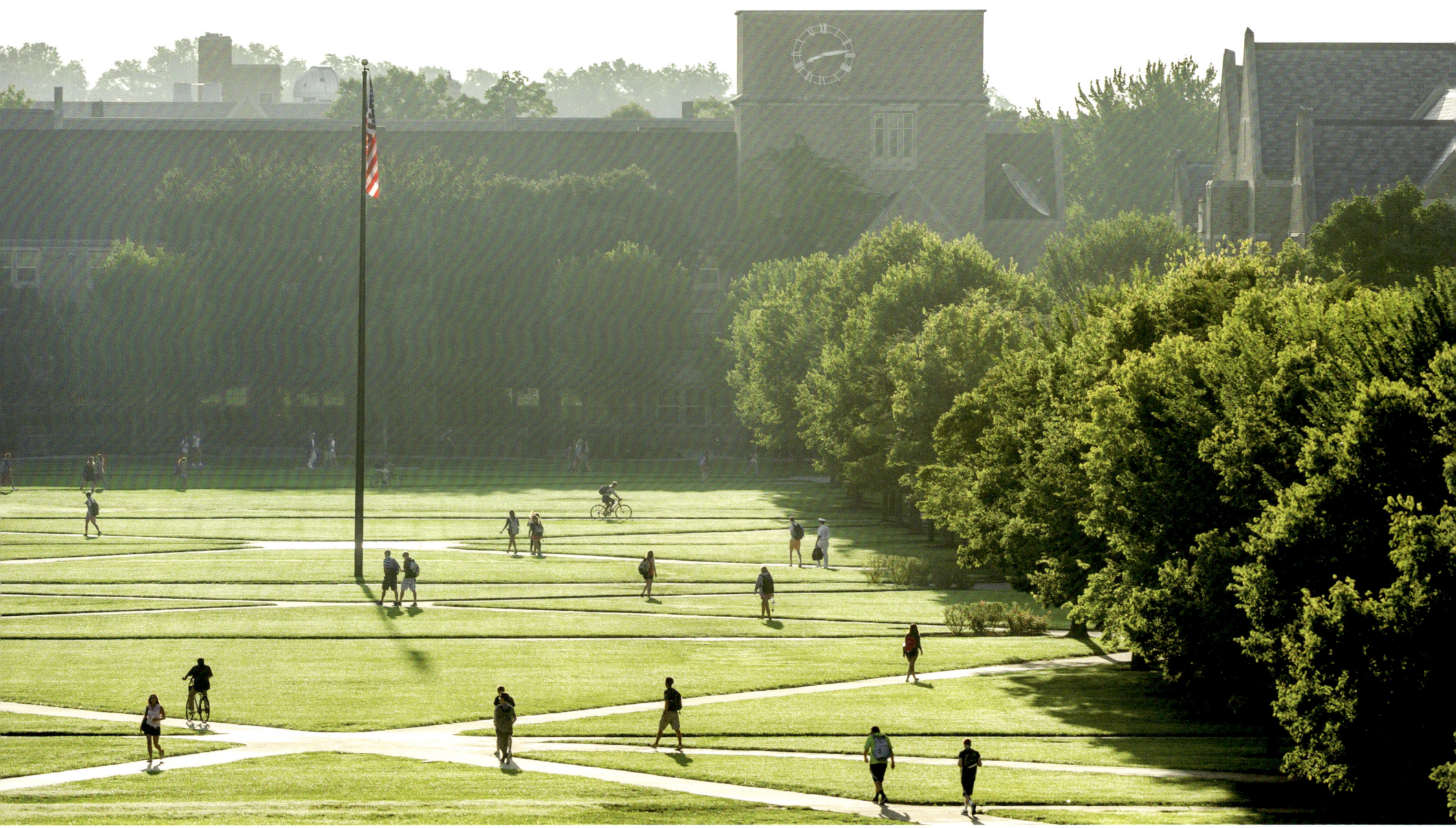

But summertime Notre Dame is a more restful place, with a slower pace, and more time to really see and feel the campus. The place is green and lush, with a million flowers and trees in bloom. Students remain, of course—those here for summer session, the graduate students whose heads-down pursuits in libraries and labs require a warrior's unrelenting diligence and endurance. There are cohorts, too, of students in Notre Dame's Alliance for Catholic Education, one of the university's most powerful exports, sending young hearts and minds to teach in under-served Catholic schools throughout America. There are still others en-rolled in special educational sessions and programs of religious formation. But summer is clearly a season of relative quiet on a campus that hums and drives and hustles most of the year.

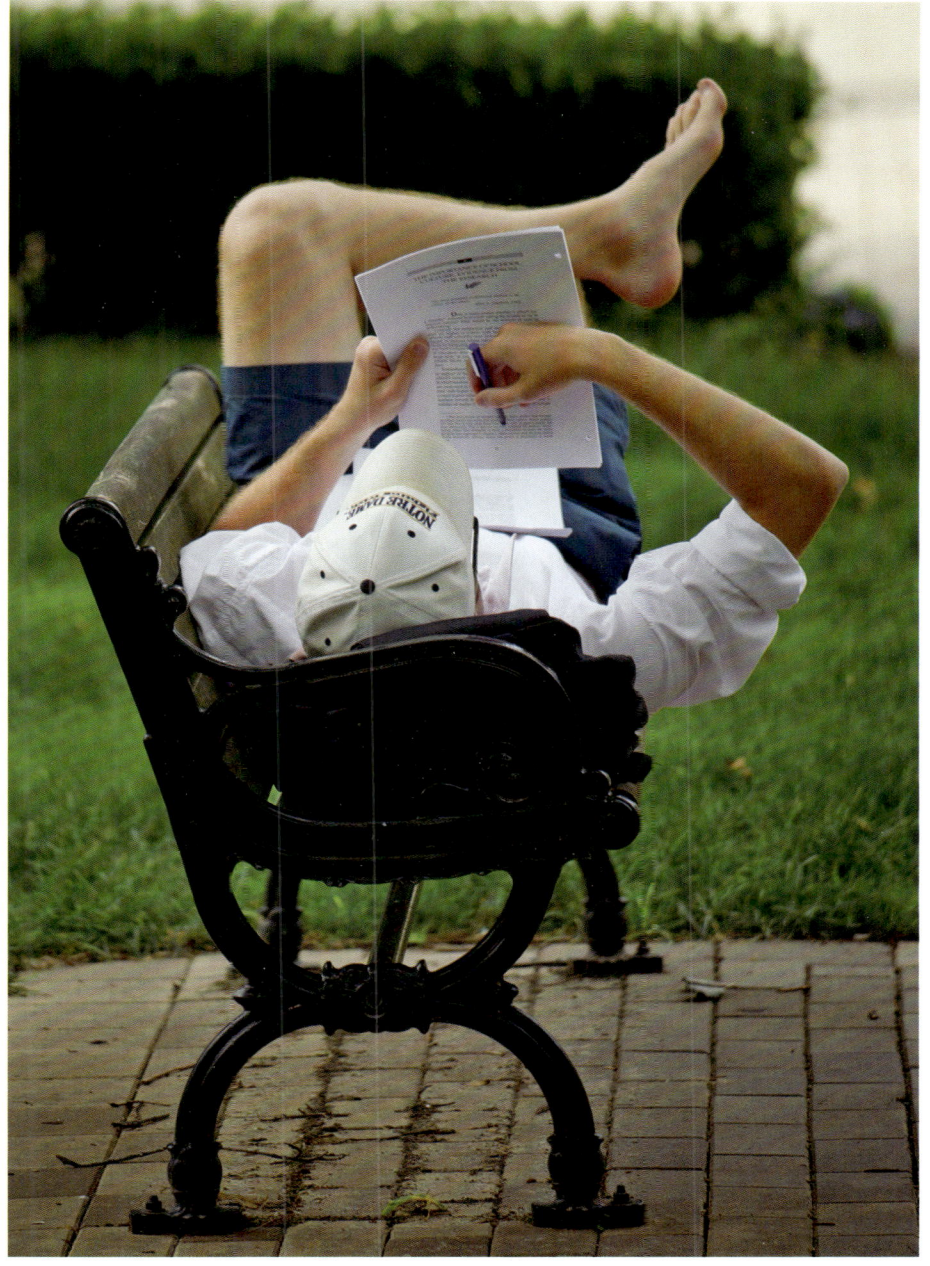

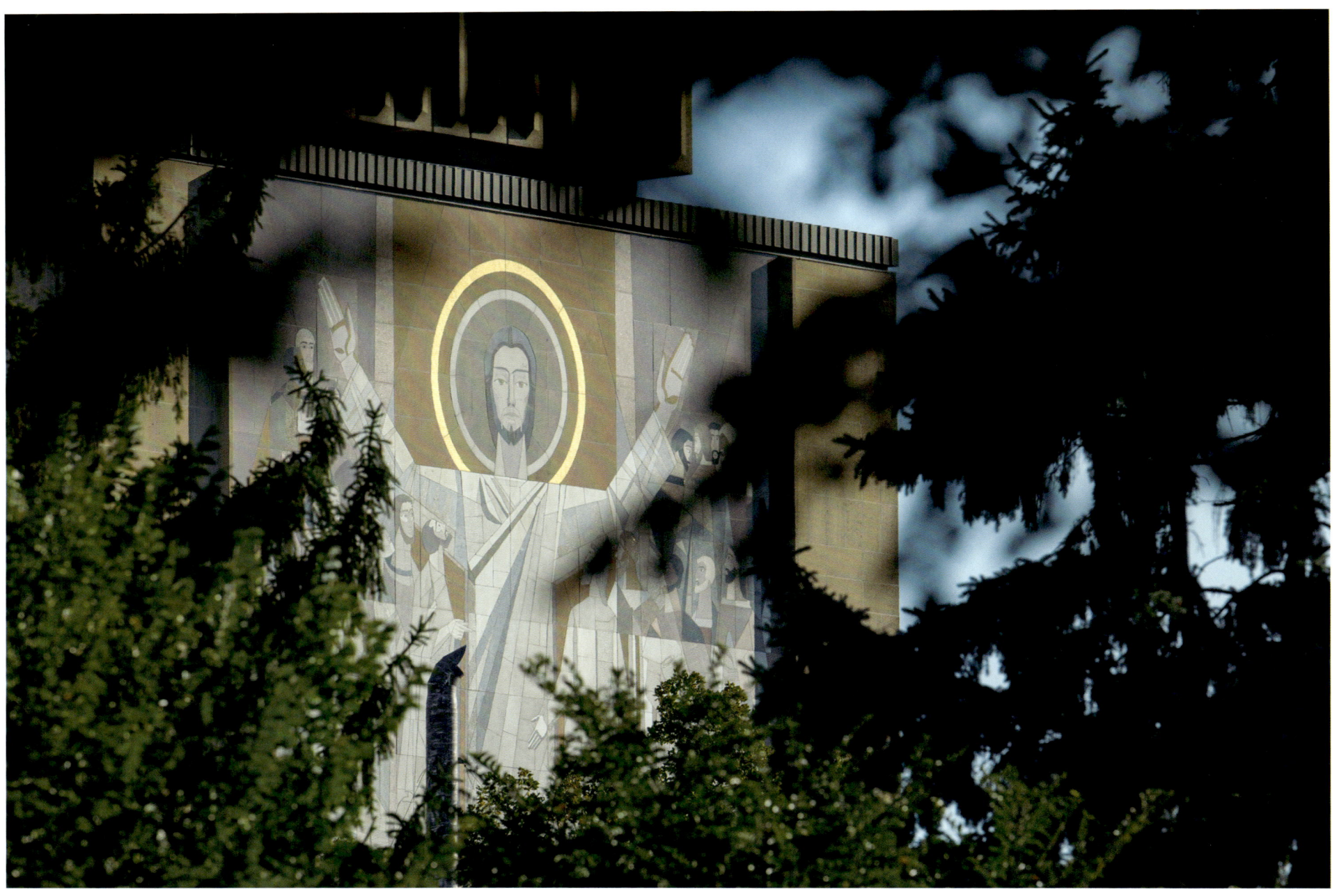

The Grotto is always there for the pausing and praying. There are stories of miracles first petitioned there, and moments of earnest solitude when prayer feels like the only recourse, when what is far comes very close and the pressing weight is lifted off. Candles tremble and persist in wind and rain. The moon-faced clock in the Sacred Heart steeple keeps watch. The Dome is a yellow lighthouse; birds and bats play in its aerial glow. On starry nights and under cover of cloud the Grotto offers solitude and serenity, and the warm, whispering breeze on your face. I too went to the Grotto on the night I spoke my life's most fervent prayer.

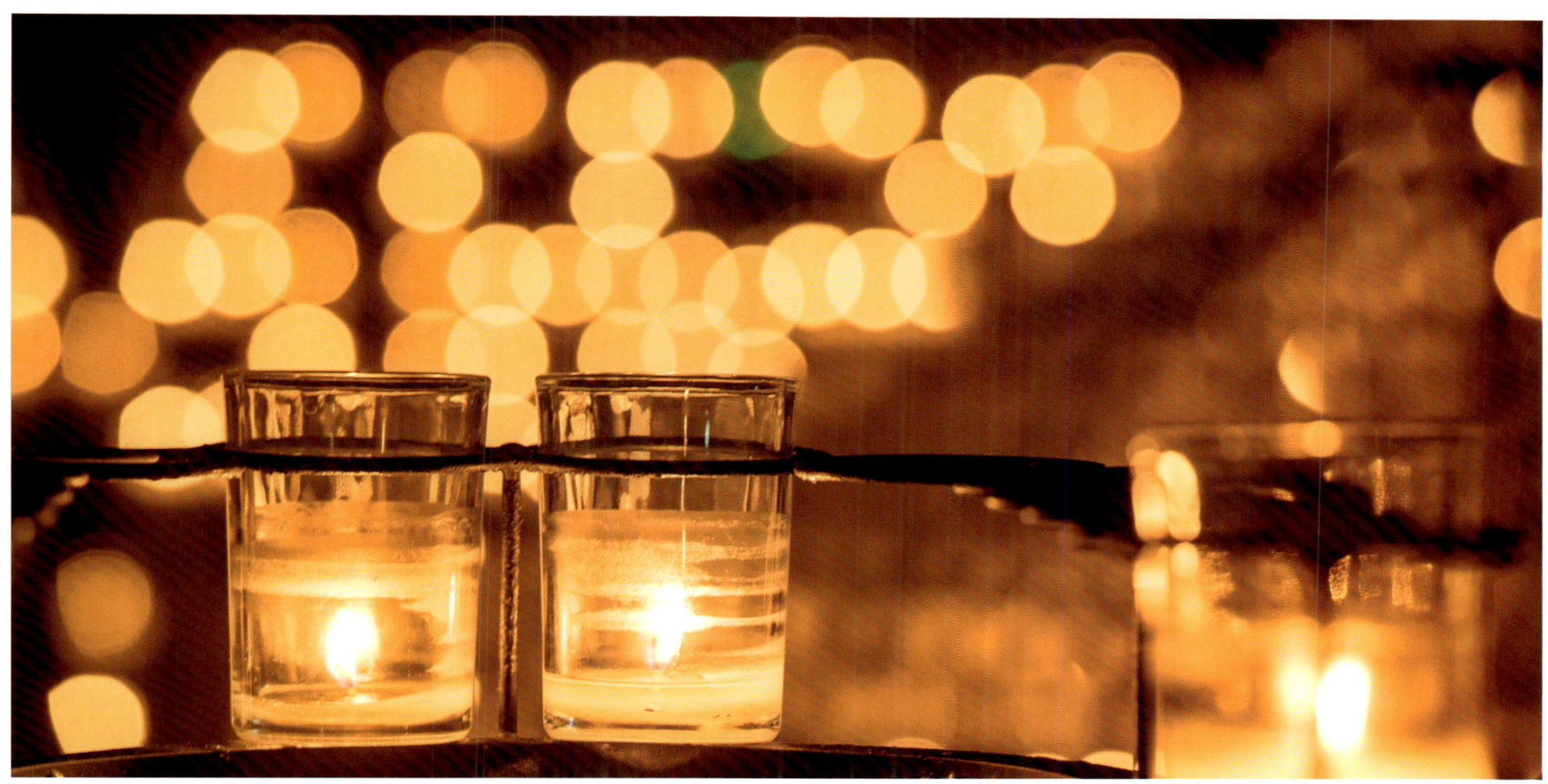

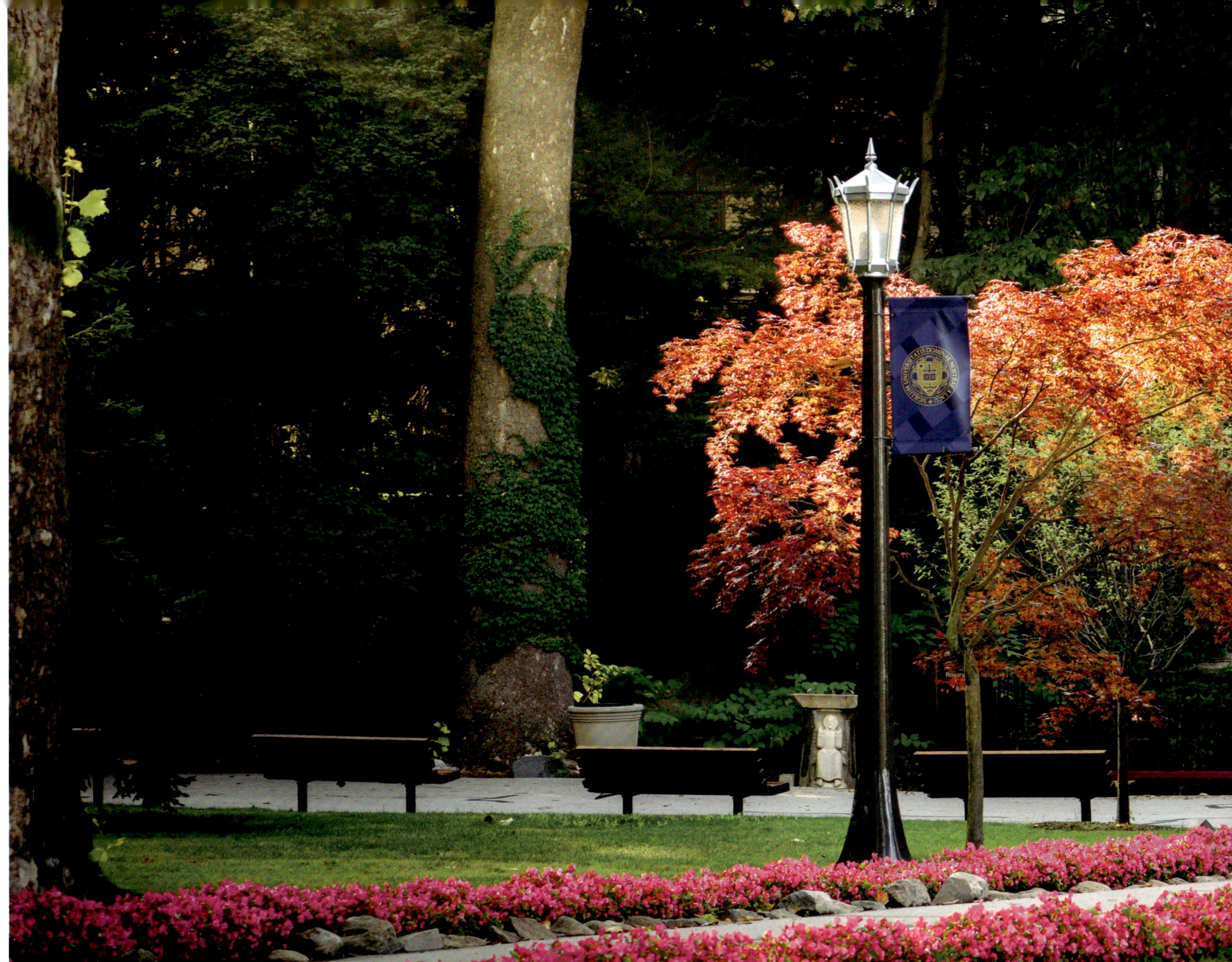

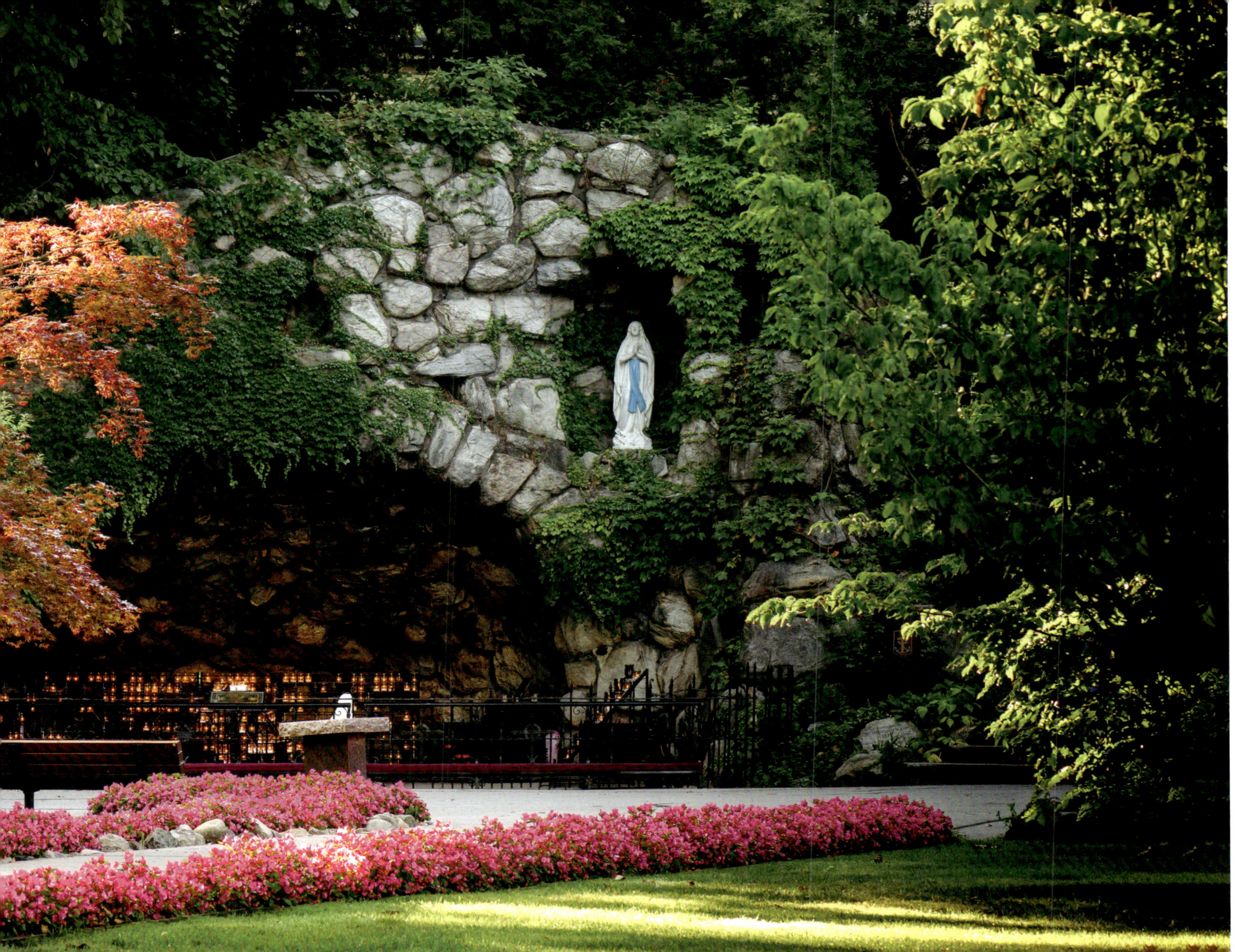

"Religion has been Notre Dame's abiding strength," Ed Fischer '37 once wrote. On the faculty for thirty years, the venerable professor added, "Since there are fashions in theology as in everything else, the religious mood is not the same today as it was fifty years ago, and fifty years from now it will not be the same as today. But no matter what the mood of the hour, Notre Dame always stands as a witness to the unseen. A sensitivity to 'beyondness' saturates these acres. Because of an alertness to the transcendent, Notre Dame has not lost its sense of mystery. It never tried to fool students into believing that knowledge solves mysteries of any real depth."

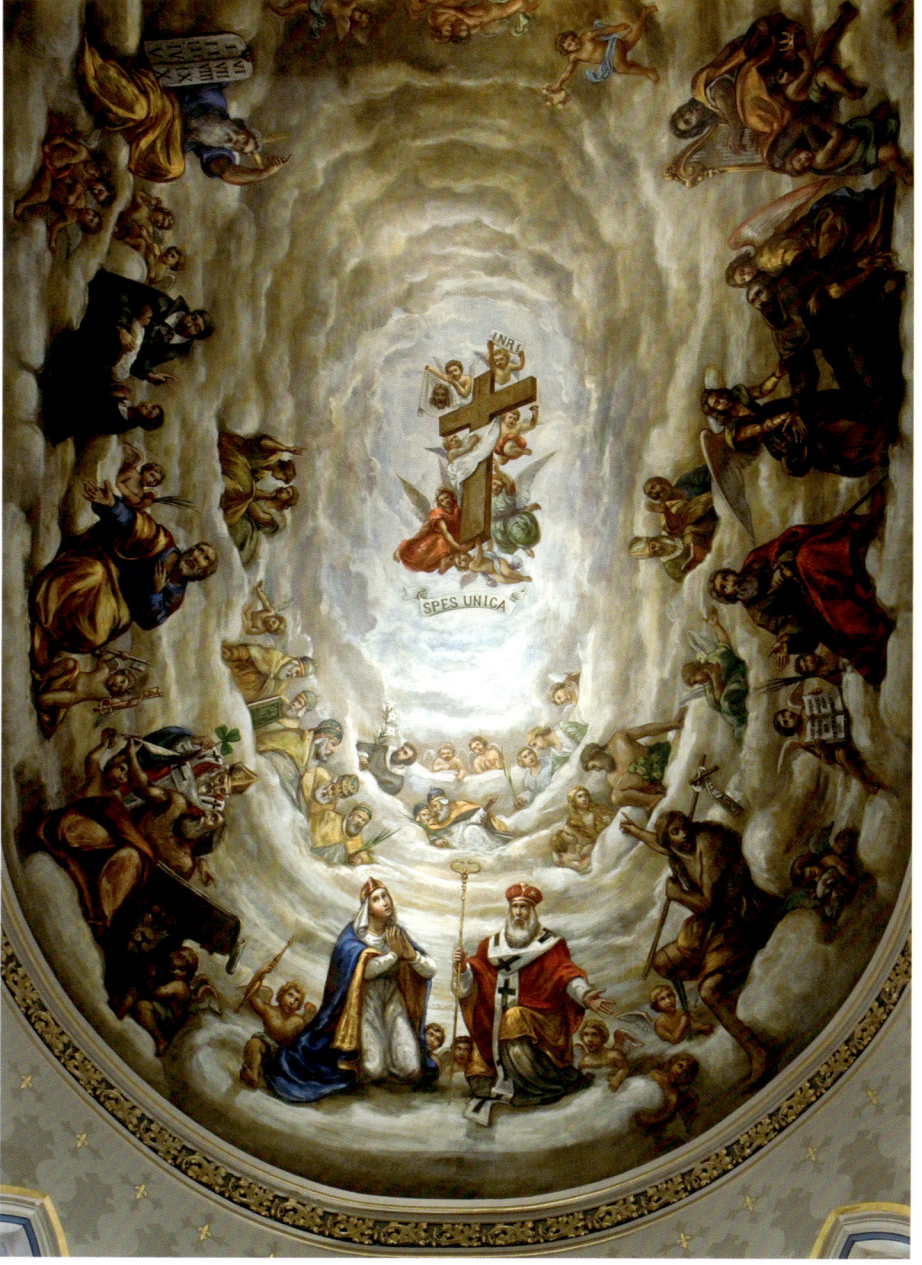

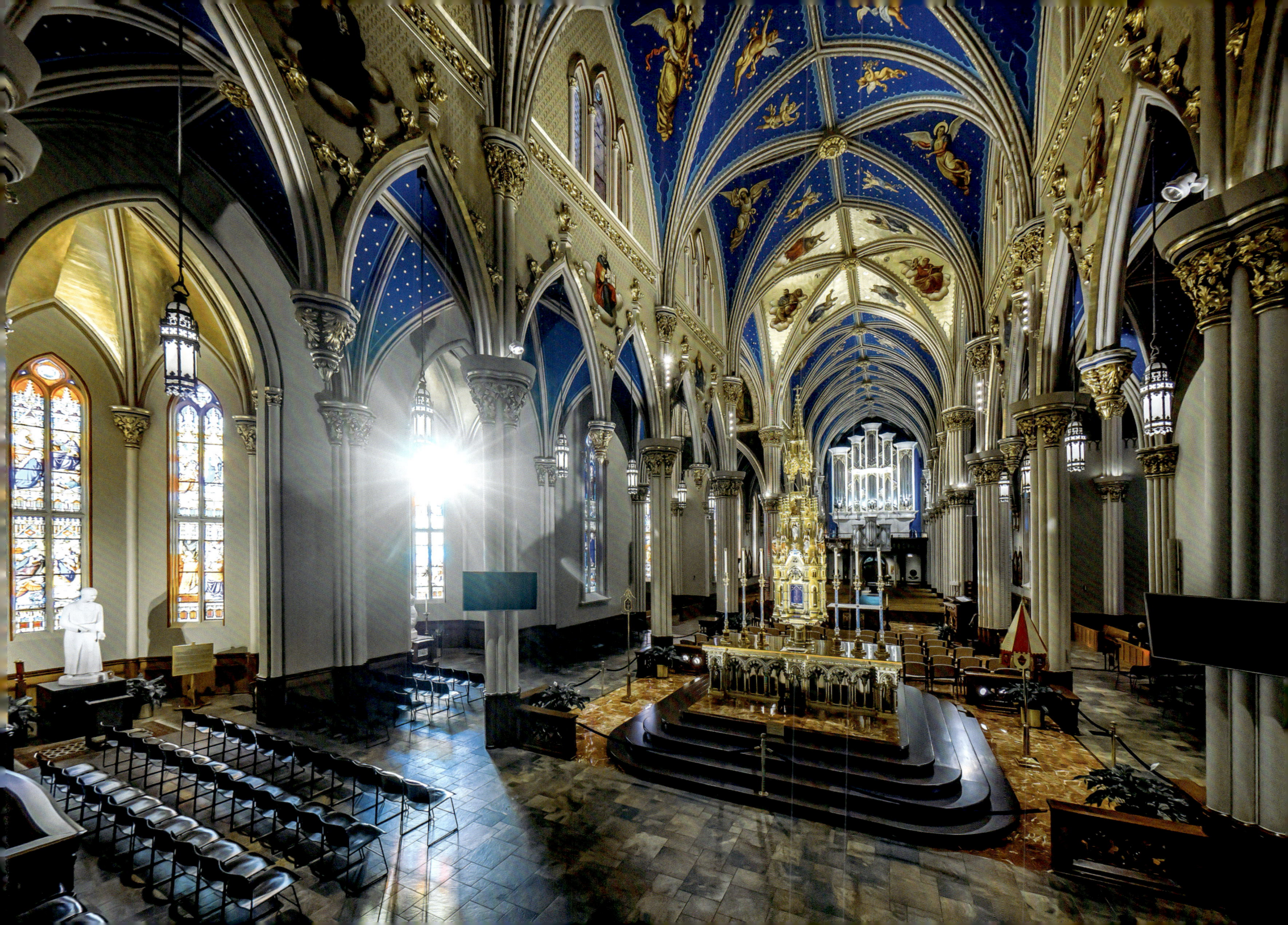

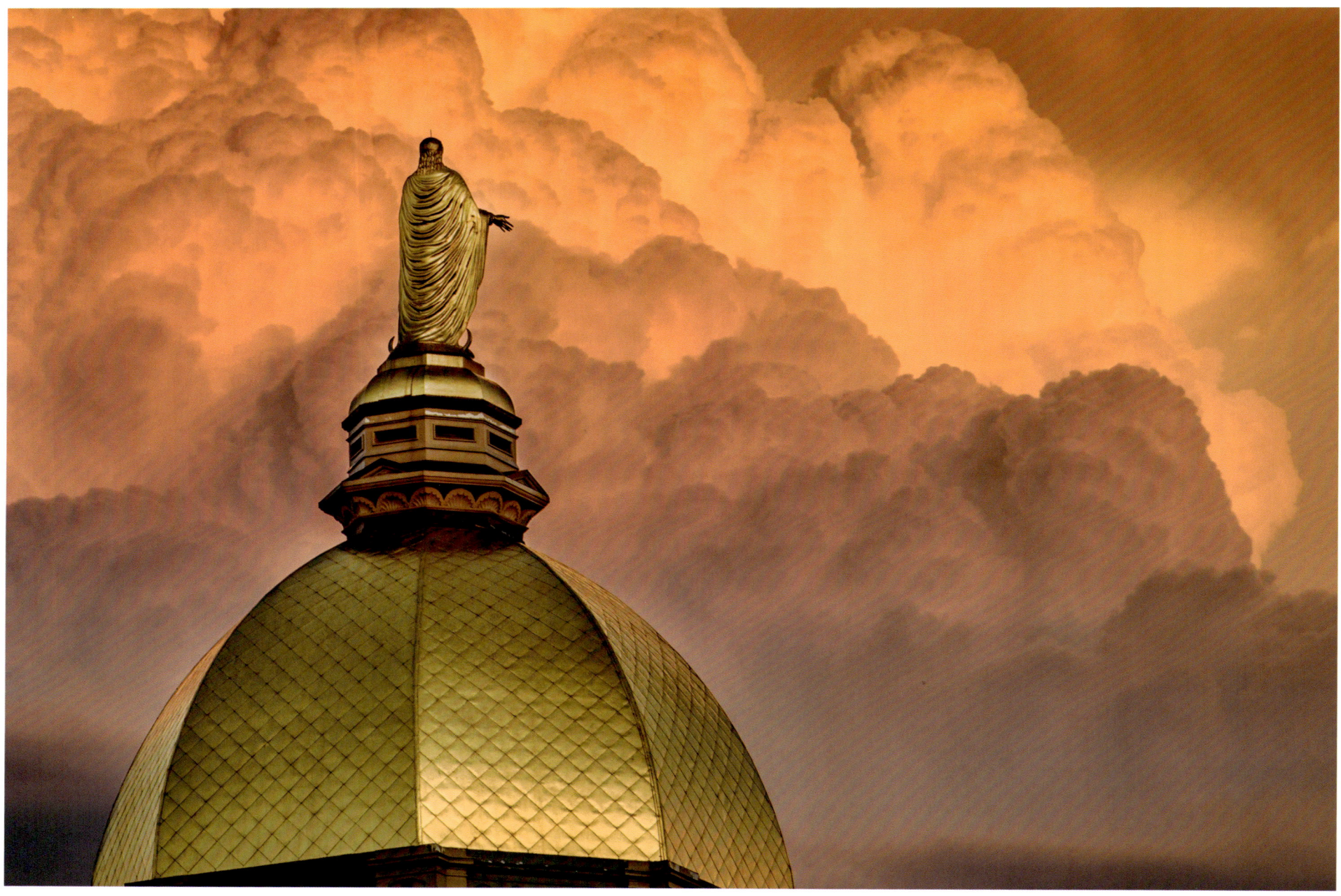

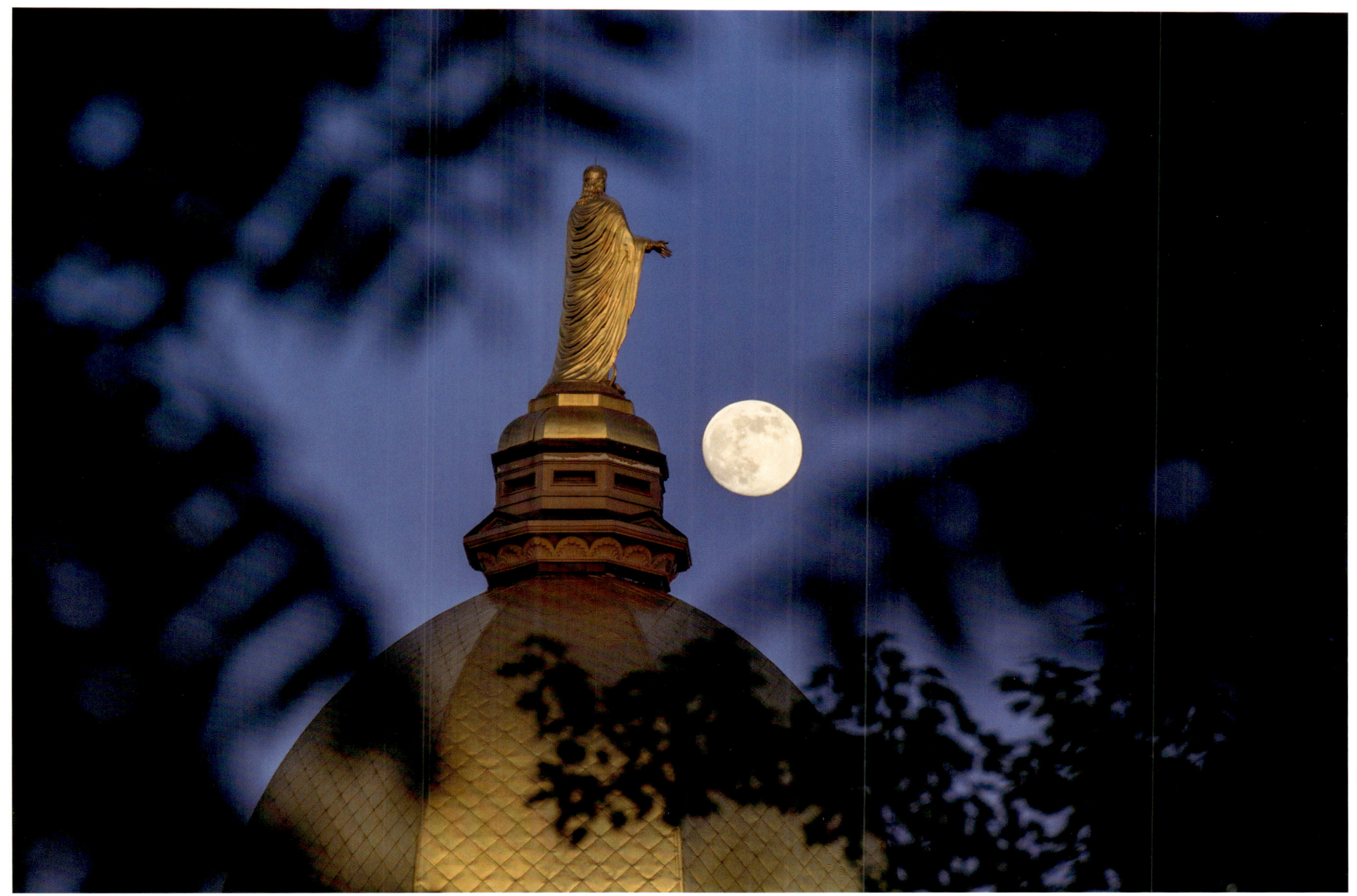

In his later years Emil T. Hofman, the legendary, tough-love chemistry professor and mentor to many, would sit daily on a bench in front of the Main Building. Some would stop and talk, but mostly, he said, he was there to sit, remember, and watch for the departed phantom friends, colleagues, and students he might glimpse on the pathways there. I can still see Father Griffin walking with his cocker spaniel—Griff known best by his *Observer* column, popular Masses, and compassionate care of souls whose longings he shared from his own restless walk of faith. I think, too,

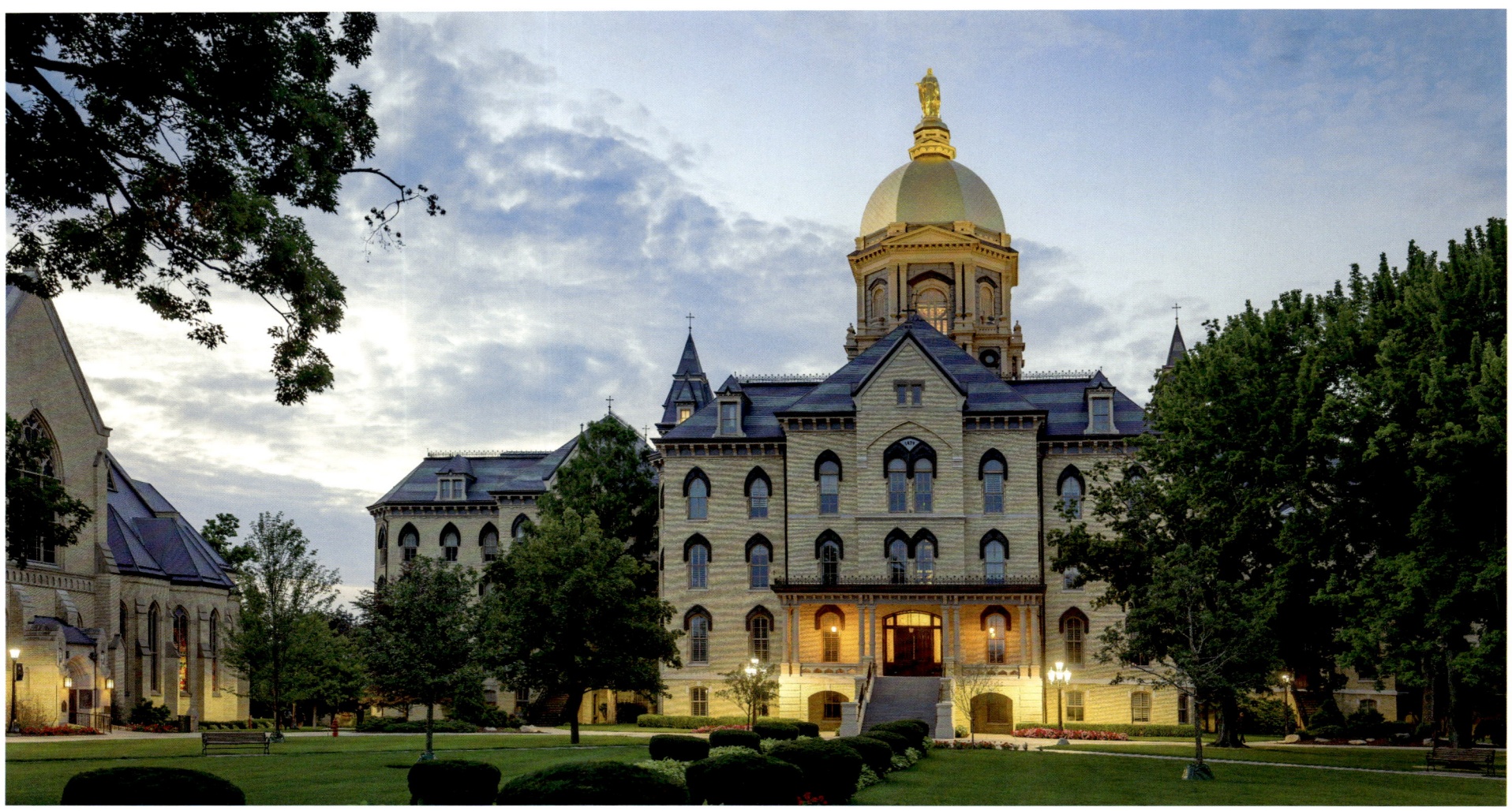

of Joe Evans, sitting on the low wall beside the library, reading his newspaper in the afternoon light, making himself fully available to students, a source of wisdom, love, and the humanness of education. Or Al Sondej collecting coins outside the dining halls every night to help feed the world's poor. Or Sister Jean Lenz, making her way from Farley Hall where she was its longtime rector in the early years of coeducation to her Student Affairs office in the Main Building where she shepherded young women through those pioneering days. And I cannot think of Jean without remembering the night she stood her ground at Farley's door against a mob of male streakers trying to enter there—part of the folklore that speaks of the place.

All those who pass this way populate campus with their own mental scrapbook of images, classmates, friends, and faculty members. And all those memories, snapshots, and characters become part of the culture that lives on in each of us.

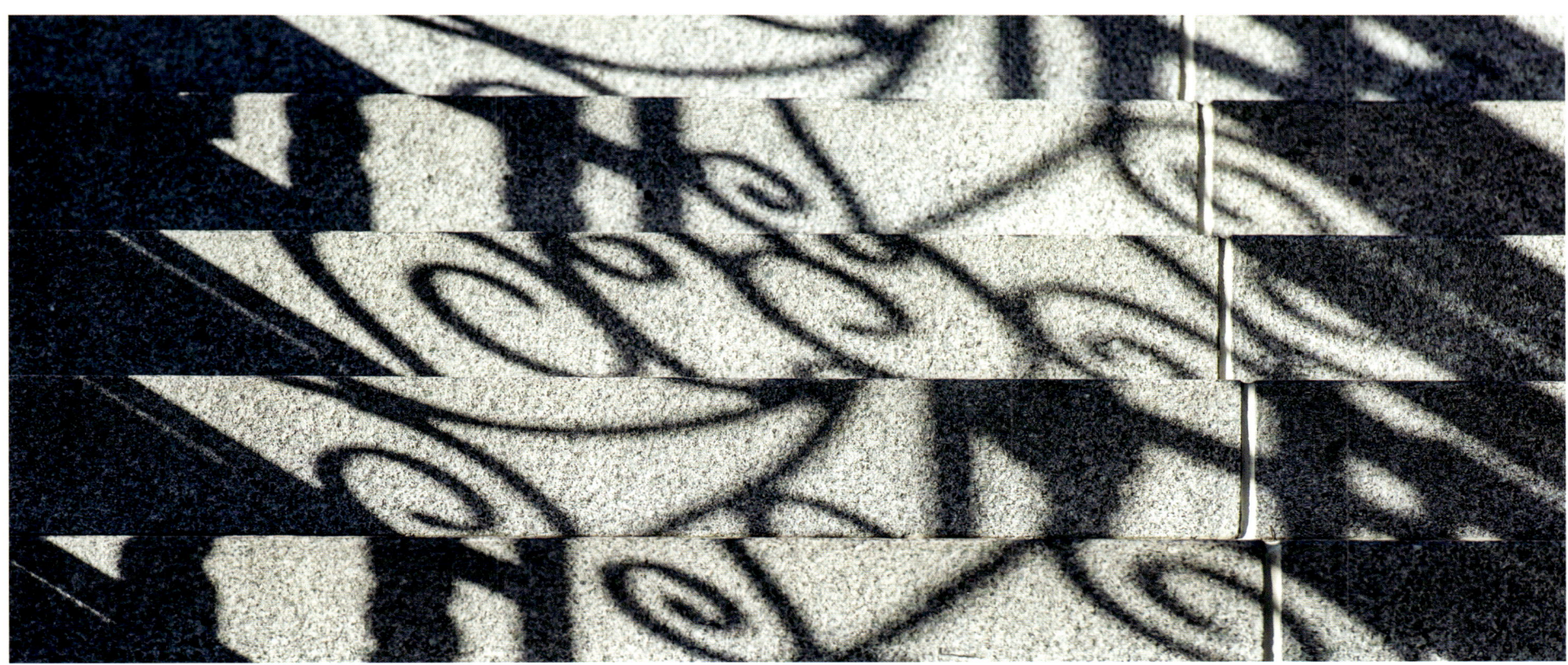

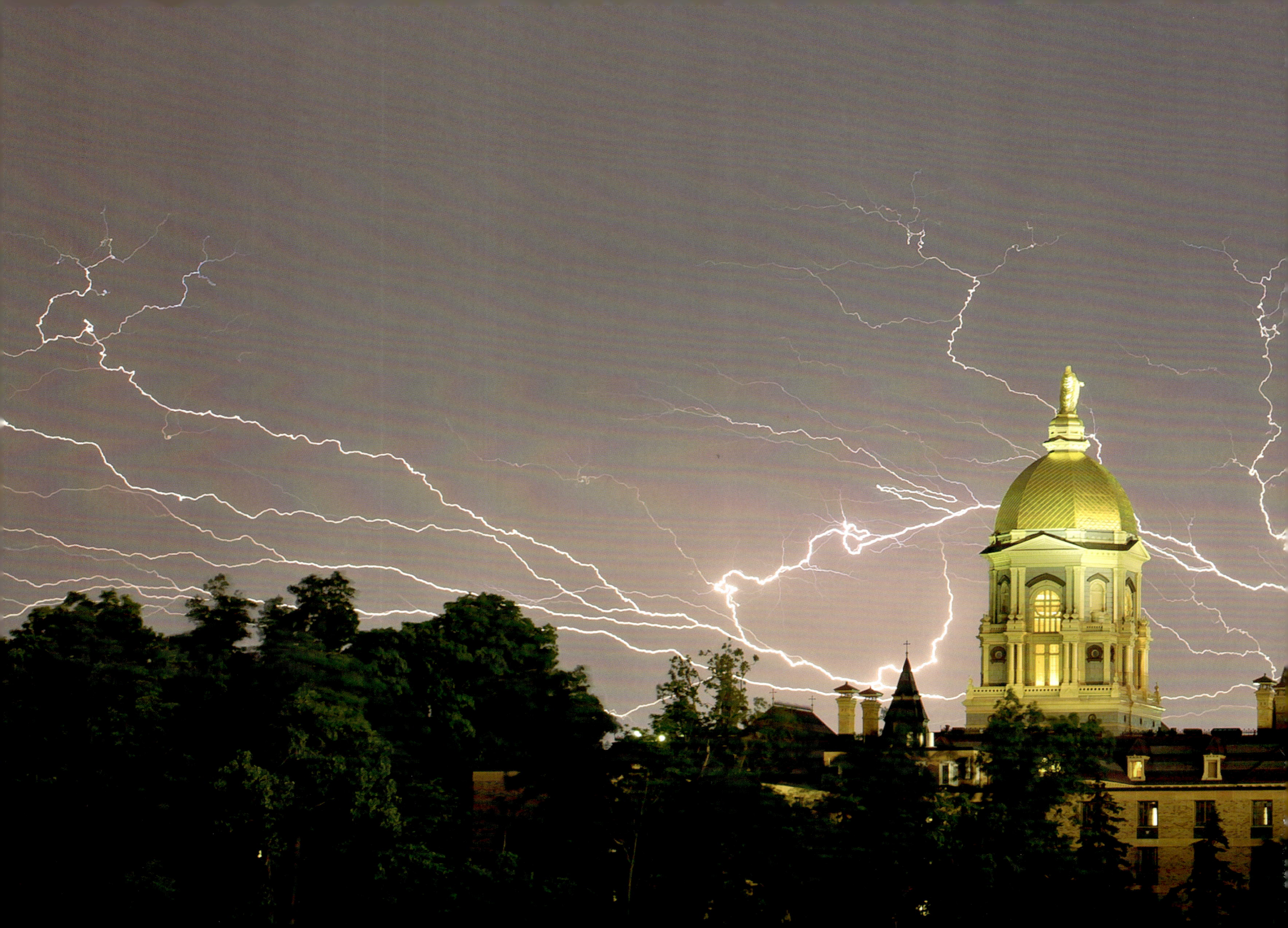

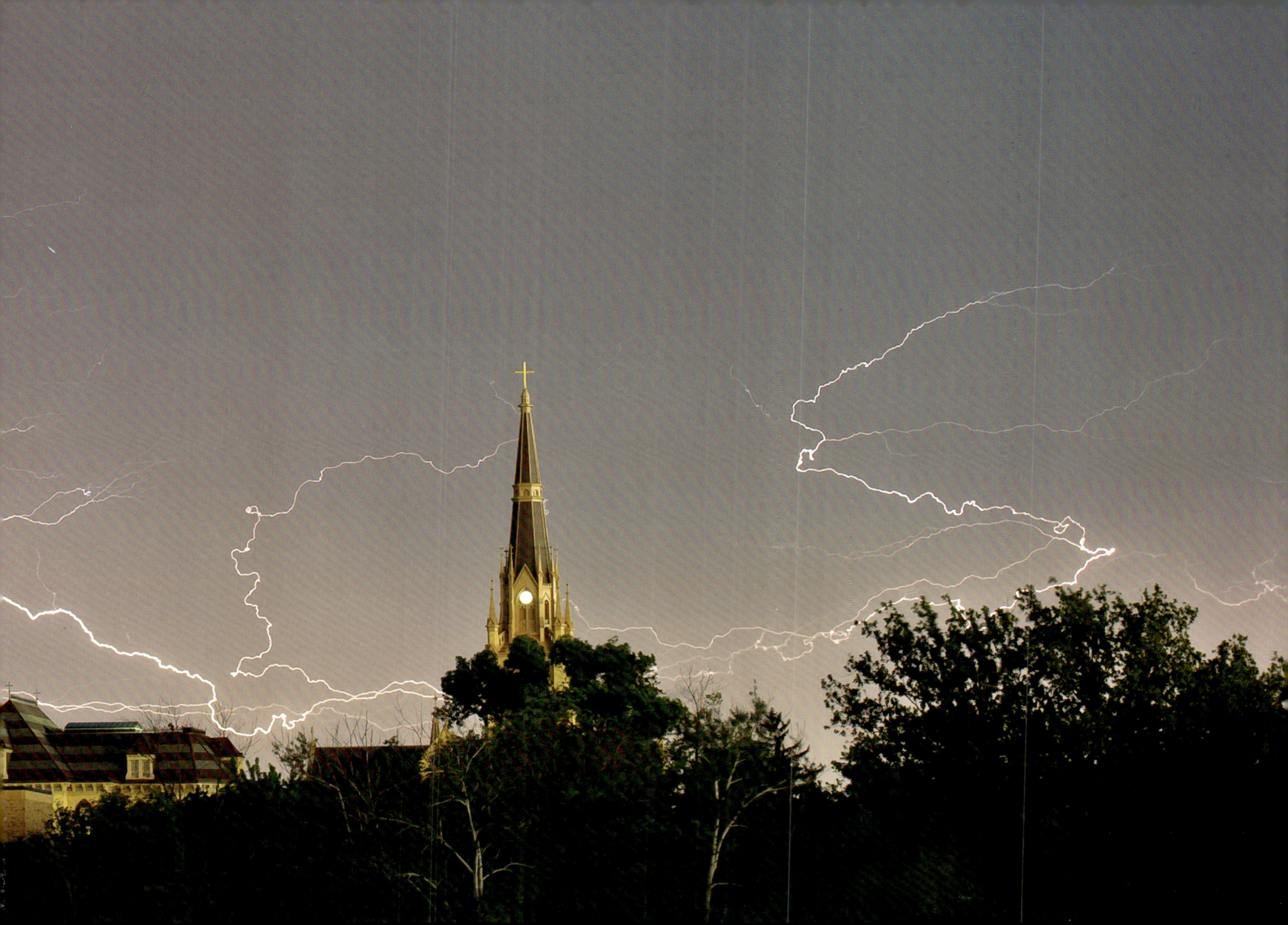

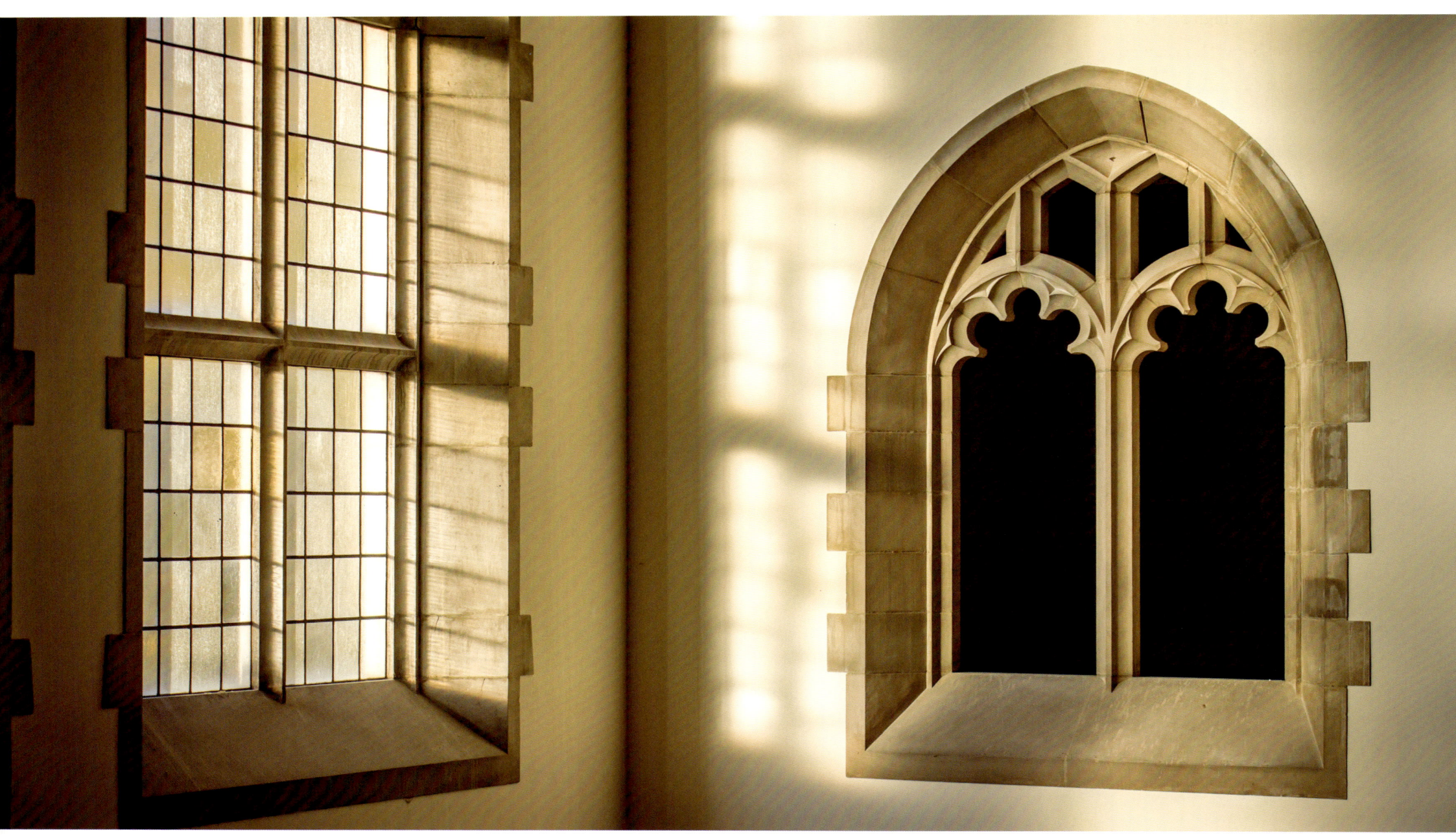

I once told a high school senior who was trying to decide whether or not to enroll here, "You can go to college anywhere and get a good education, but Notre Dame will change your life." I tried to say why, but quick and concise reasoning escaped me. I fumbled with inept words and phrases, and later remembered something Richard Sullivan once told me: "Some things go beyond words. There are elusive yet obvious feelings, even facts, you cannot find words for. You can only suggest them. Poems can be written about Notre Dame, but not definitions."

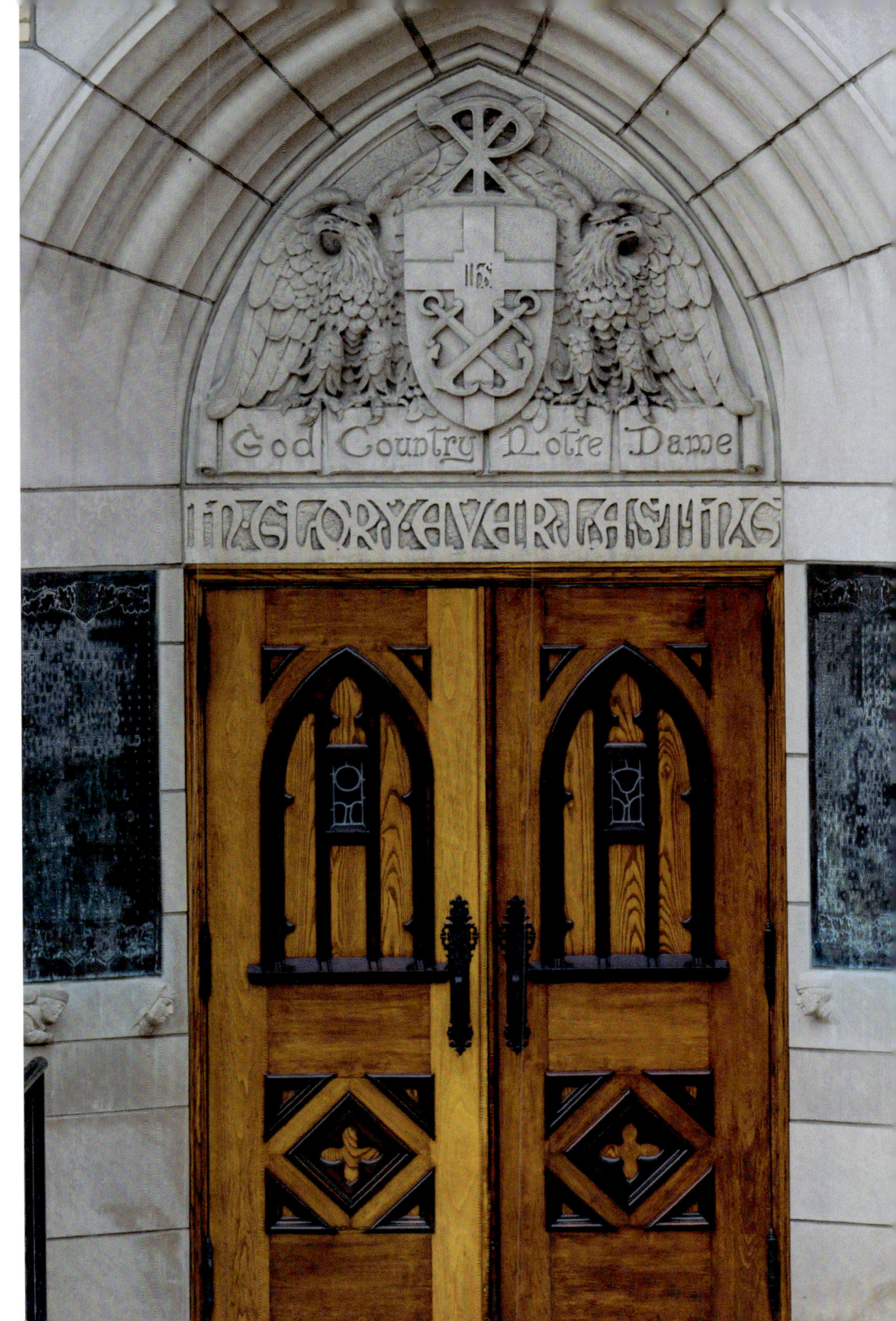

It turned out that my student days were not the best four years of my life after all. But there has never been a time in my life that was so carefree and so fun, a time so full of such genuine camaraderie and intimate friendship, of such exciting personal explorations, the robust feeding of intellectual cravings, the wide-open pursuit of dreams, meaning, and idealism, the sweet sense of life on the doorstep, horizons all clear and promising, beckoning.

Notre Dame may belong to its students, but its graduates will belong to Notre Dame for the rest of their lives.

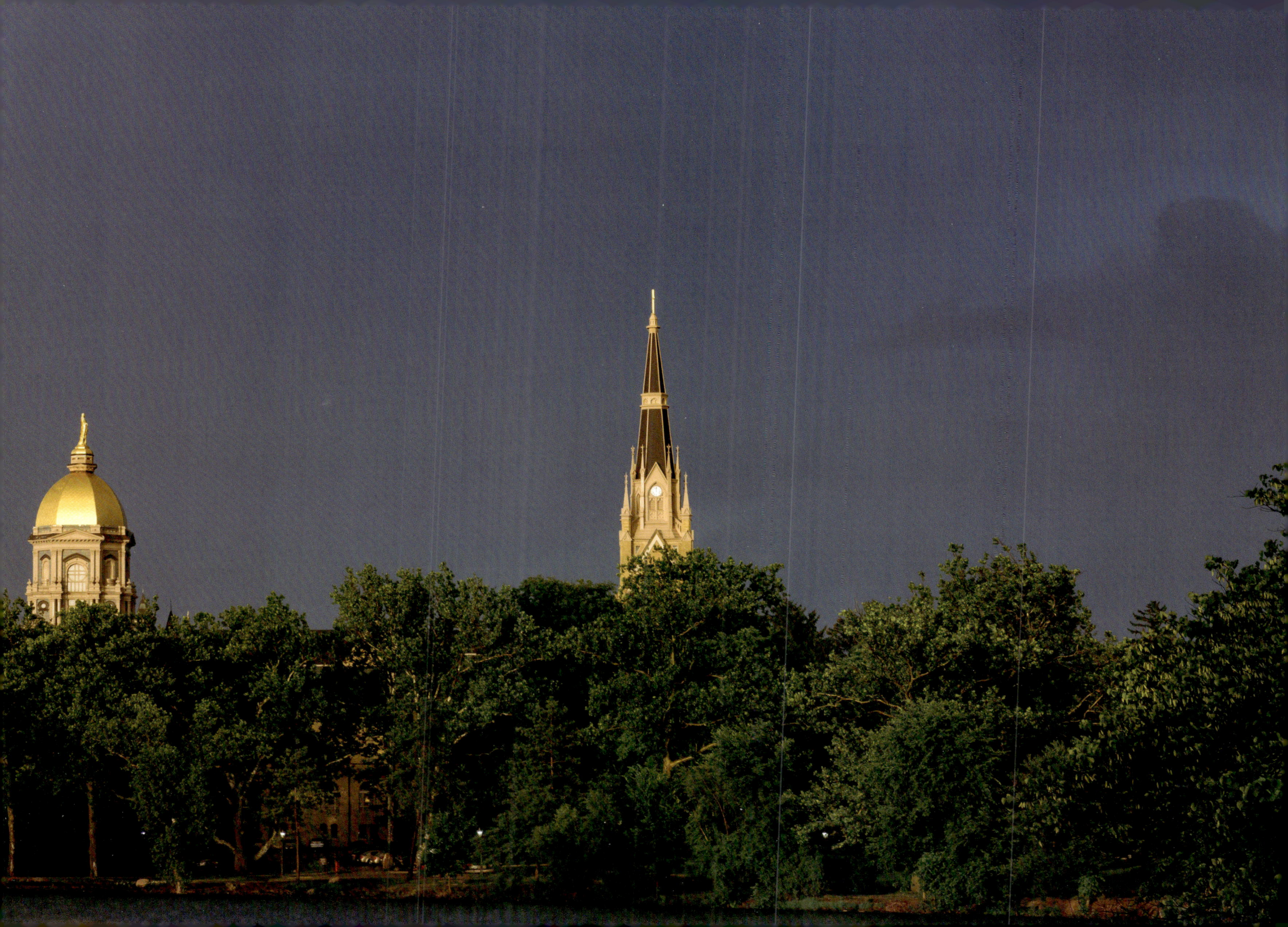

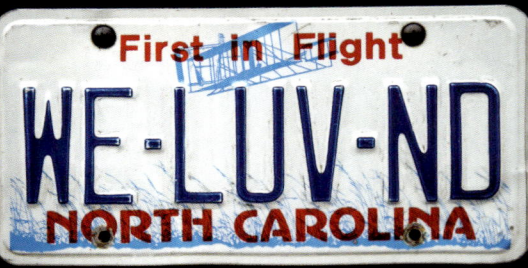

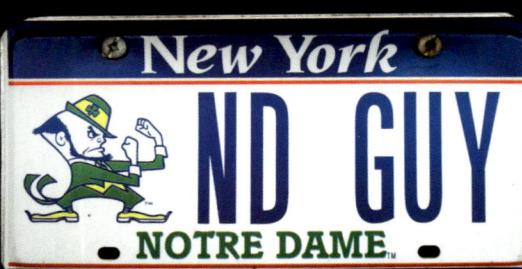

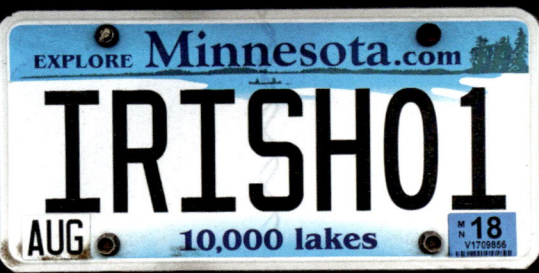

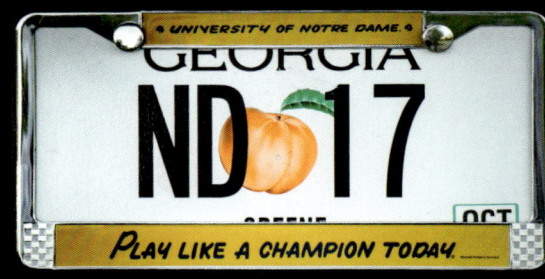

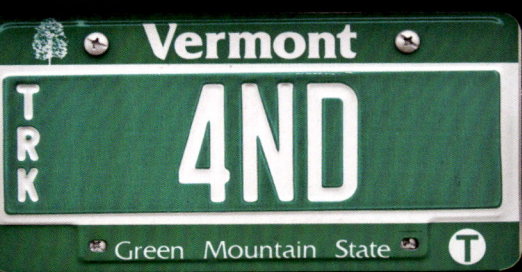

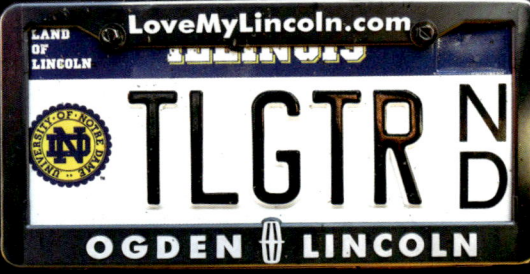

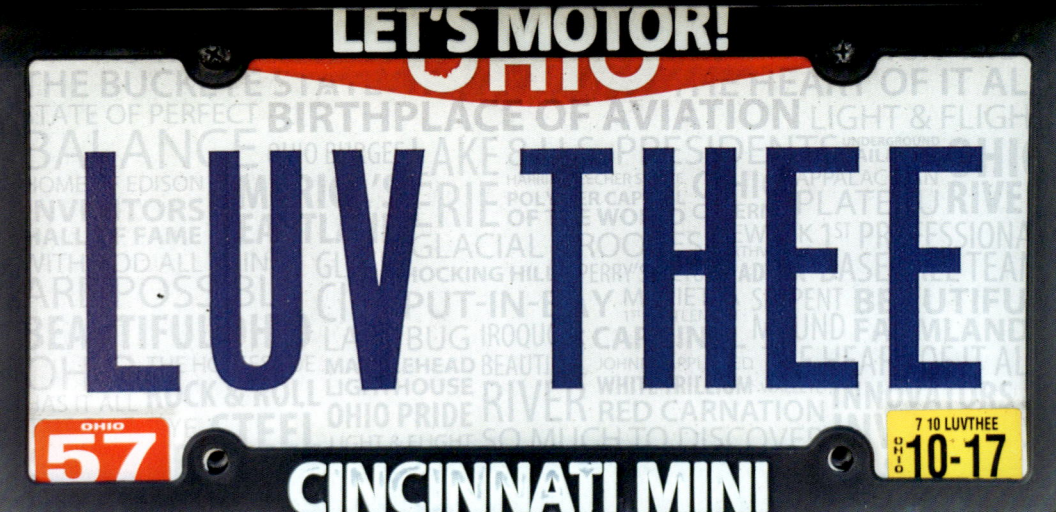

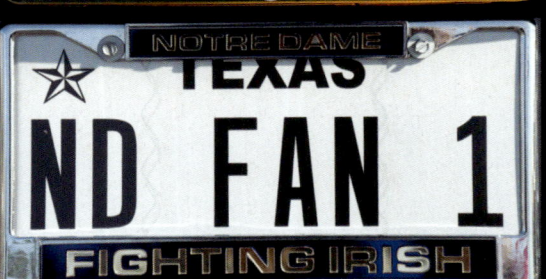

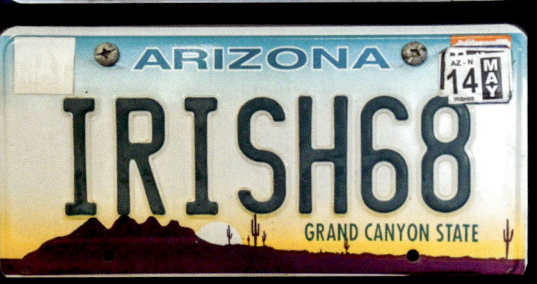

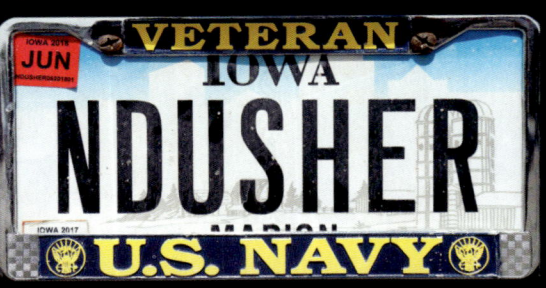

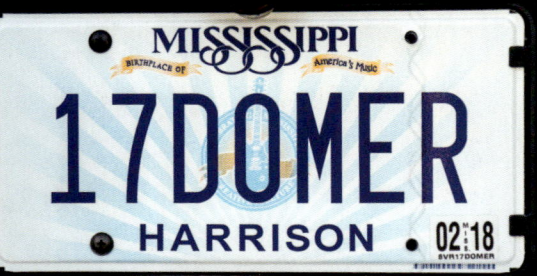

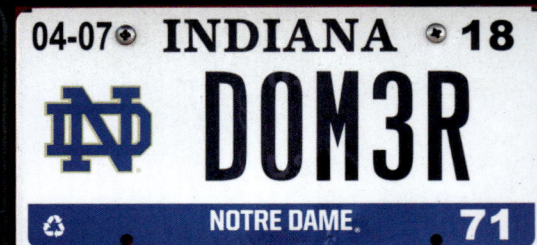

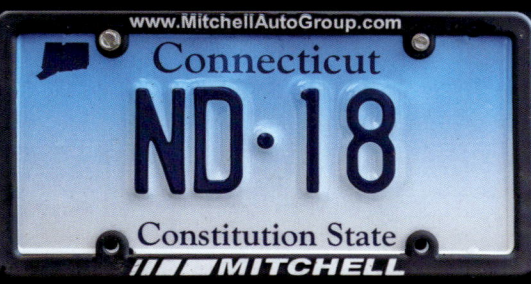

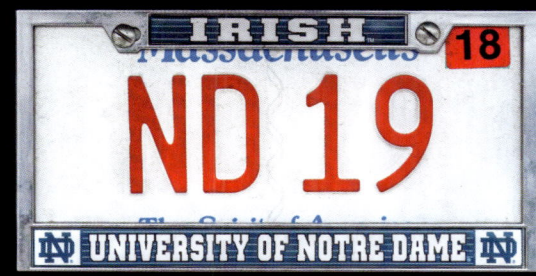

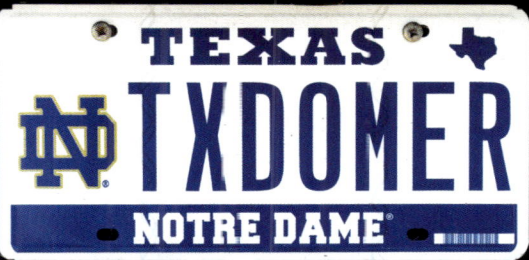

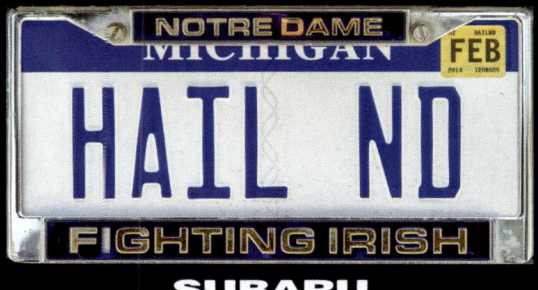

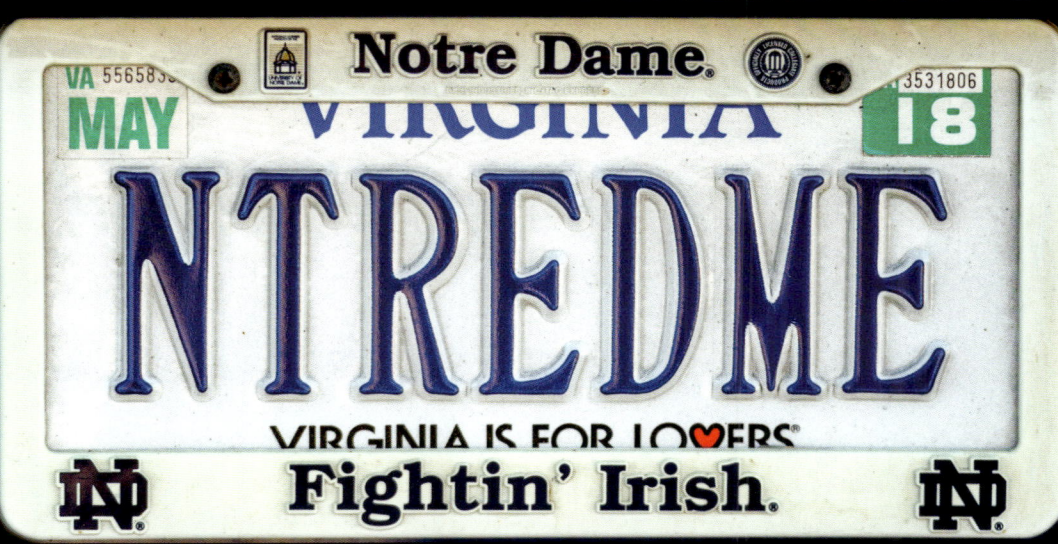

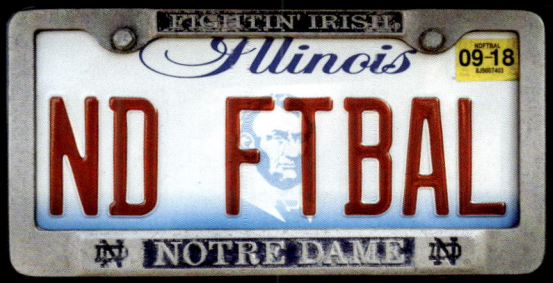

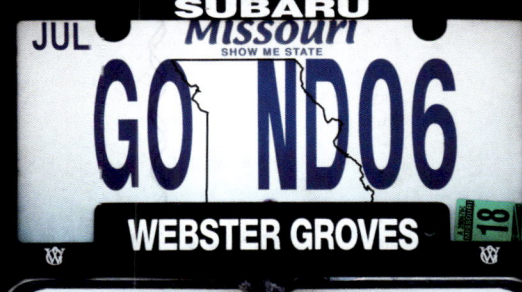

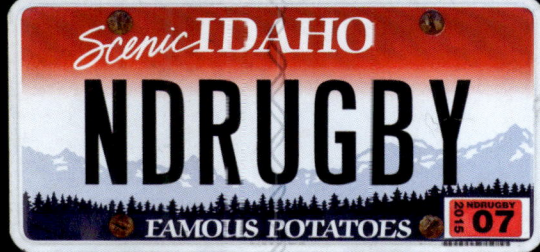

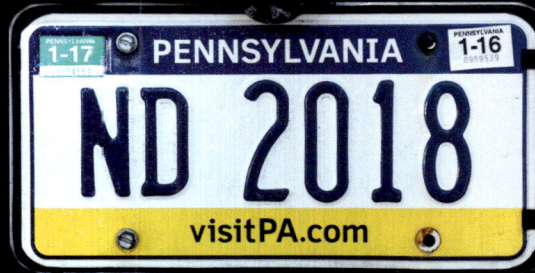

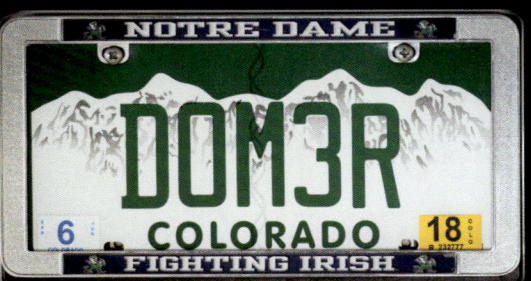

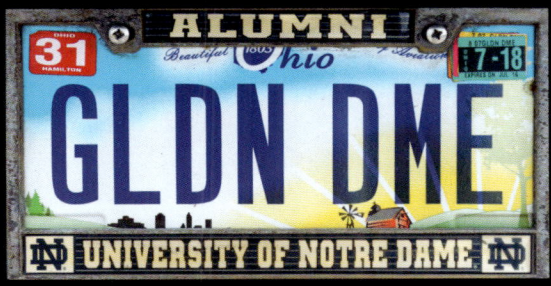

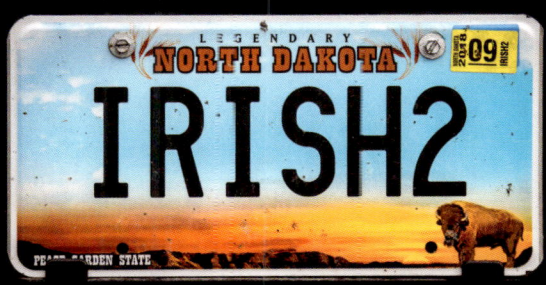

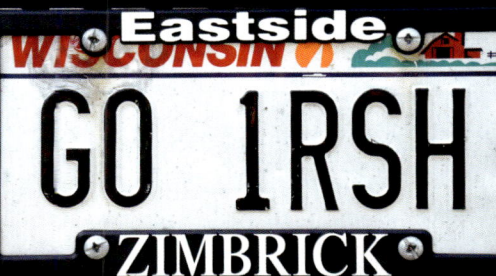

"If you want to belong," Father Robert Griffin, C.S.C., once wrote, "you have to learn the myth. You have to wrap your heart and mind around it. You have to believe the meanest rocks of the place tell a story. . . . Behind the myths is a cast of hundreds, working in loyalty for the Notre Dame of their dreams, in a love affair that lasts a lifetime."

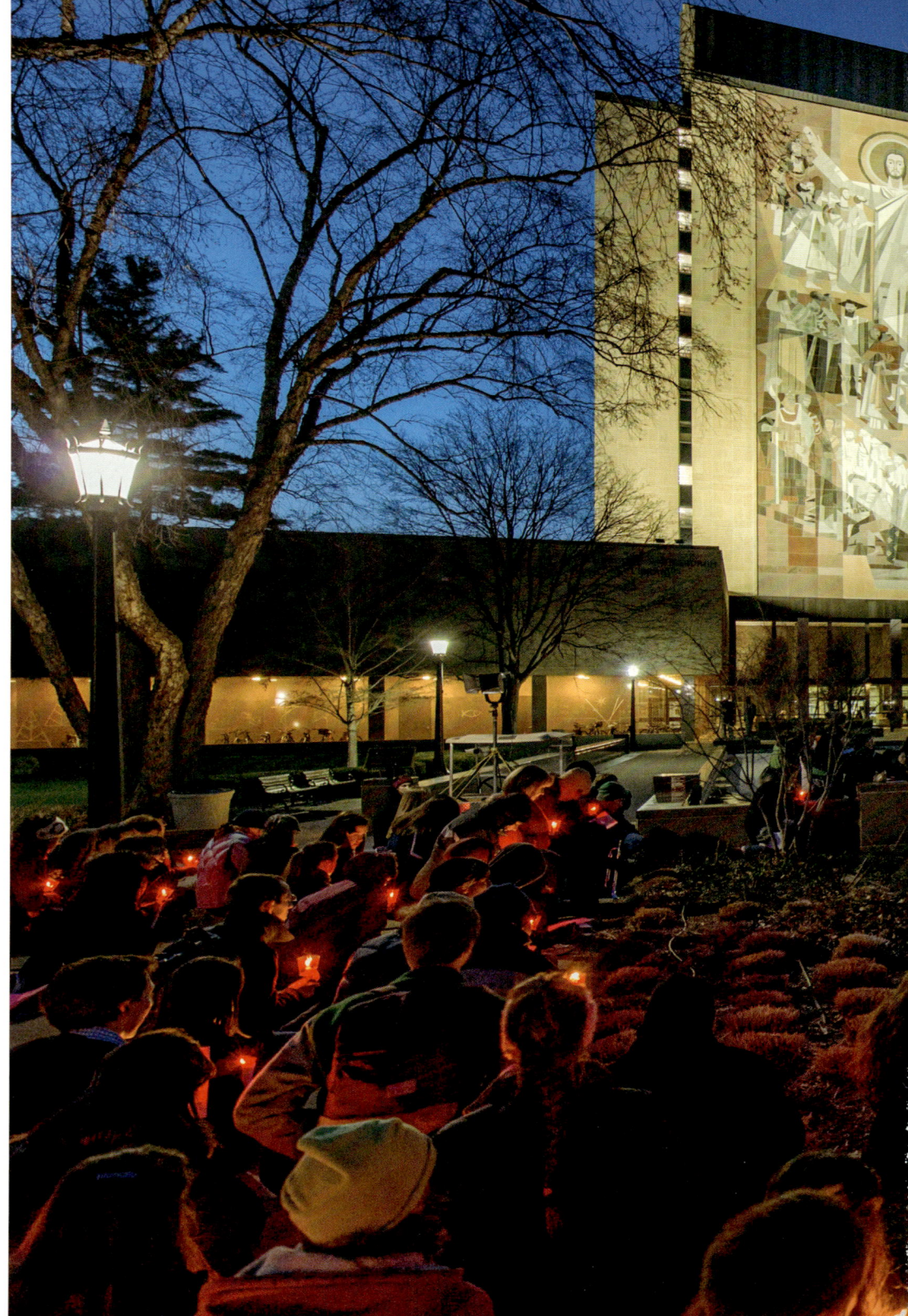

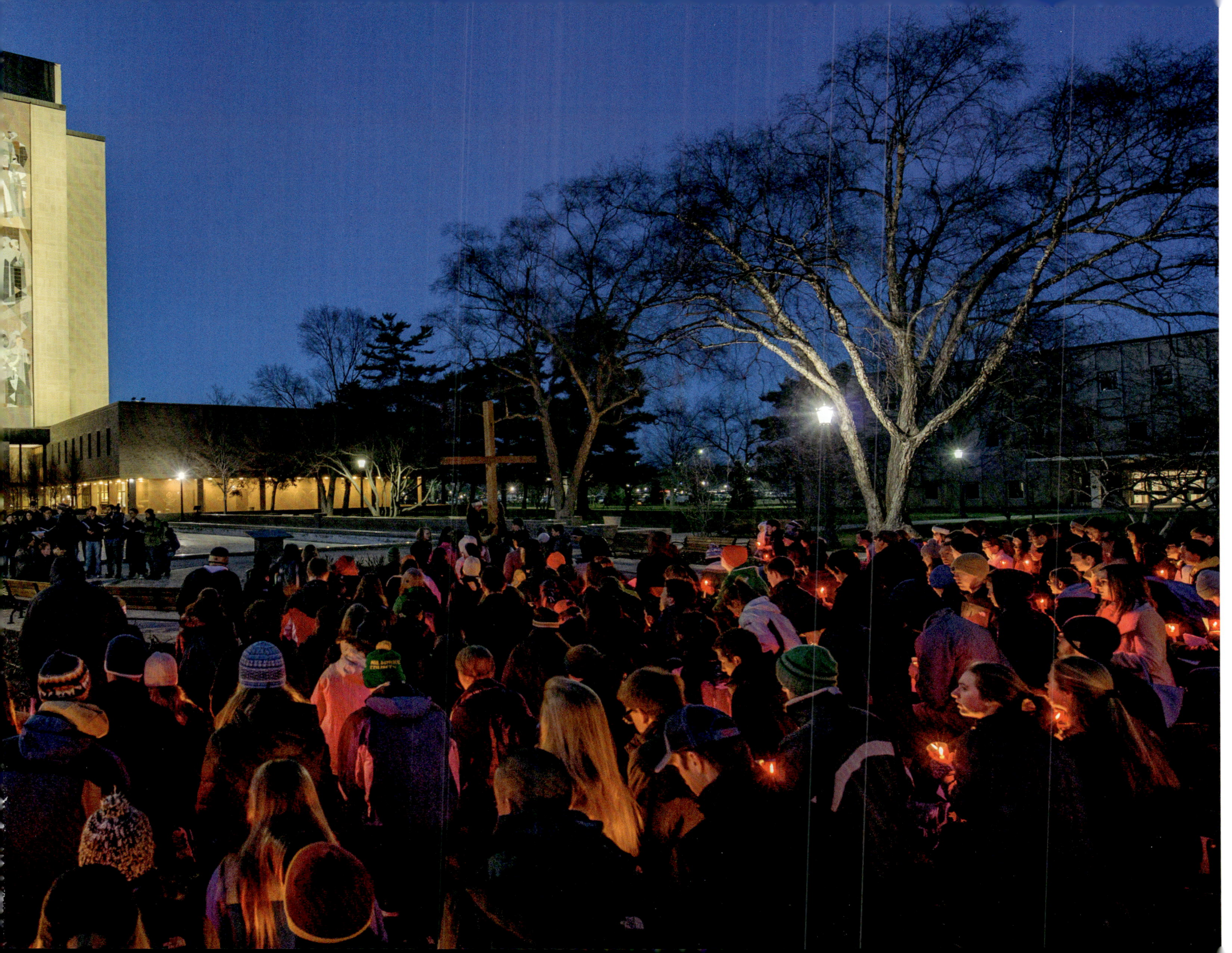

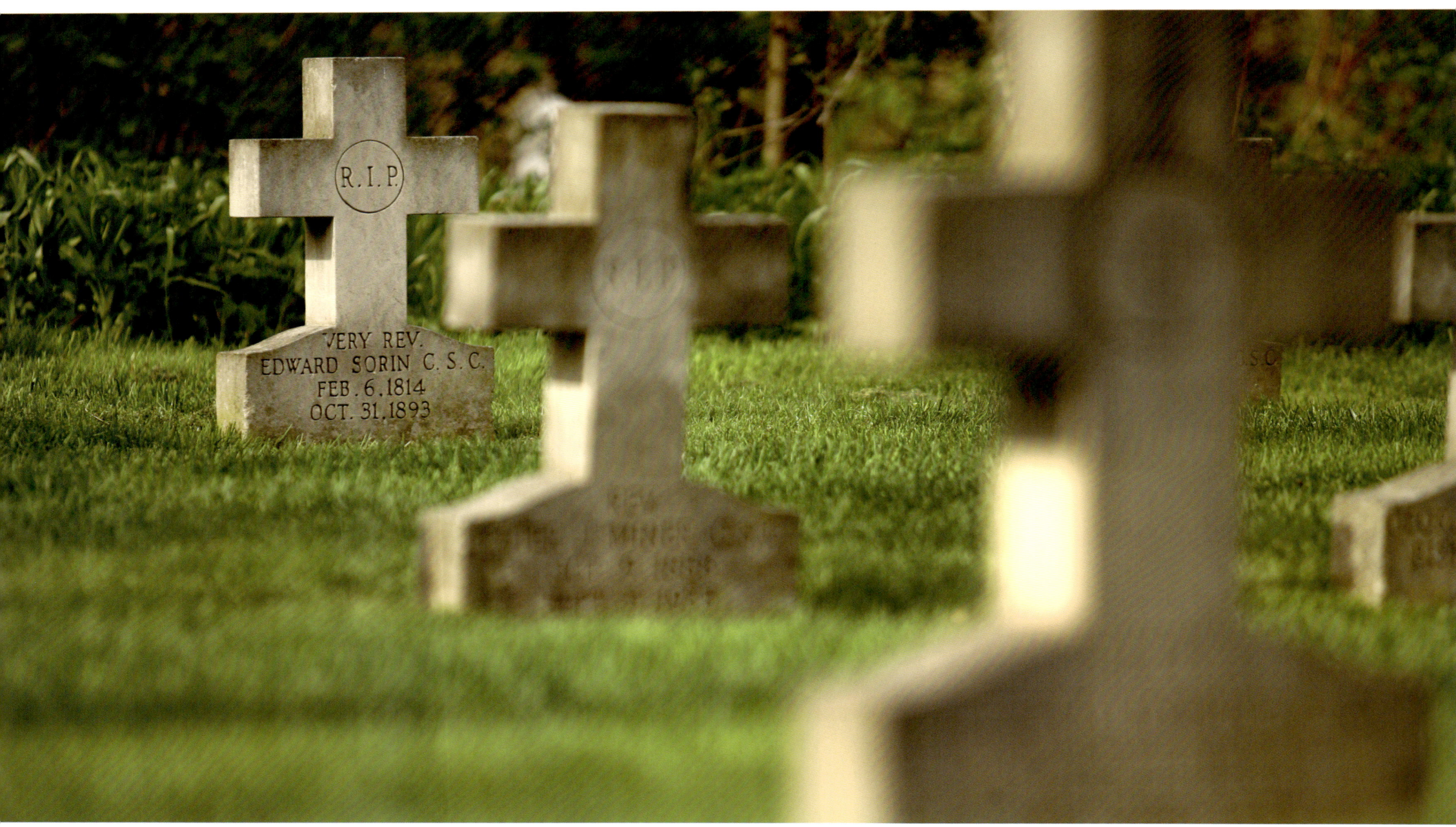

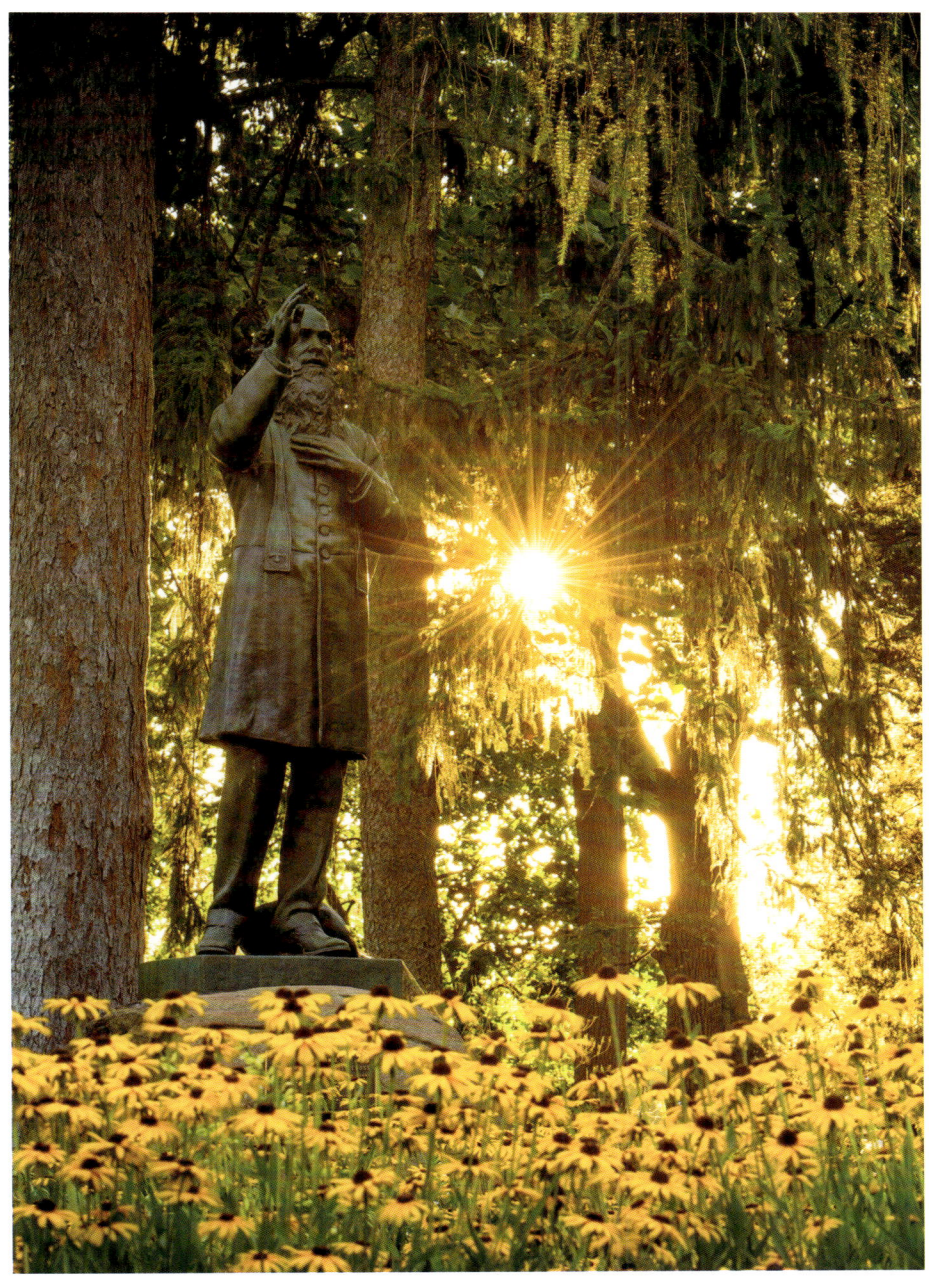

There's a road that runs between the two campus lakes, heading west from the Grotto, that candlelit sanctum tucked into the hillside there. Along the road and up the hill is the community cemetery, the uniform rows of white stone crosses that mark the resting places of Holy Cross priests. They're all the same. Generation upon generation of priests and brothers who gave their lives to this place. It is both a corporate and a human statement. Of sacrifice and service. The making of Notre Dame by the men whose holy mission was to nurture, nudge, and lead.

The cemetery is up the hill from the lakes where I walk; many of the names are familiar, some were friends, some were legendary, some unknown to me. It would not be fair to attempt a litany, a roll call of saints, a roster of favorites. The point is that, from the beginning—from the time Sorin and his band of Holy Cross brothers first tromped around these lakes—until today, the Congregation of Holy Cross has been most responsible for what this place is.

In the early years, for the first hundred years and beyond, the C.S.C.s staffed, administered, and managed the university. They filled the classrooms, celebrated the Masses, counseled students and lived in the residence halls where so much of a Notre Dame education took place. They set the tone, established the educational philosophy, Catholic character, and communal care that still permeates the university today. This approach is not just a legacy, an inheritance to be treasured as an antique. It is as vital and real today as it was in Sorin's day, or O'Hara's, Zahm's, Hesburgh's, and Malloy's.

Notre Dame is a place so rich, nuanced, and complicated that it defies a tidy explanation, and that is perhaps truer today than ever. But on those days I walk the lakes or make my way across campus I am still fascinated by this very human institution called Notre Dame, and am grateful to all those I have known here. We are all wrapped in the spirit and blessed by its graces.

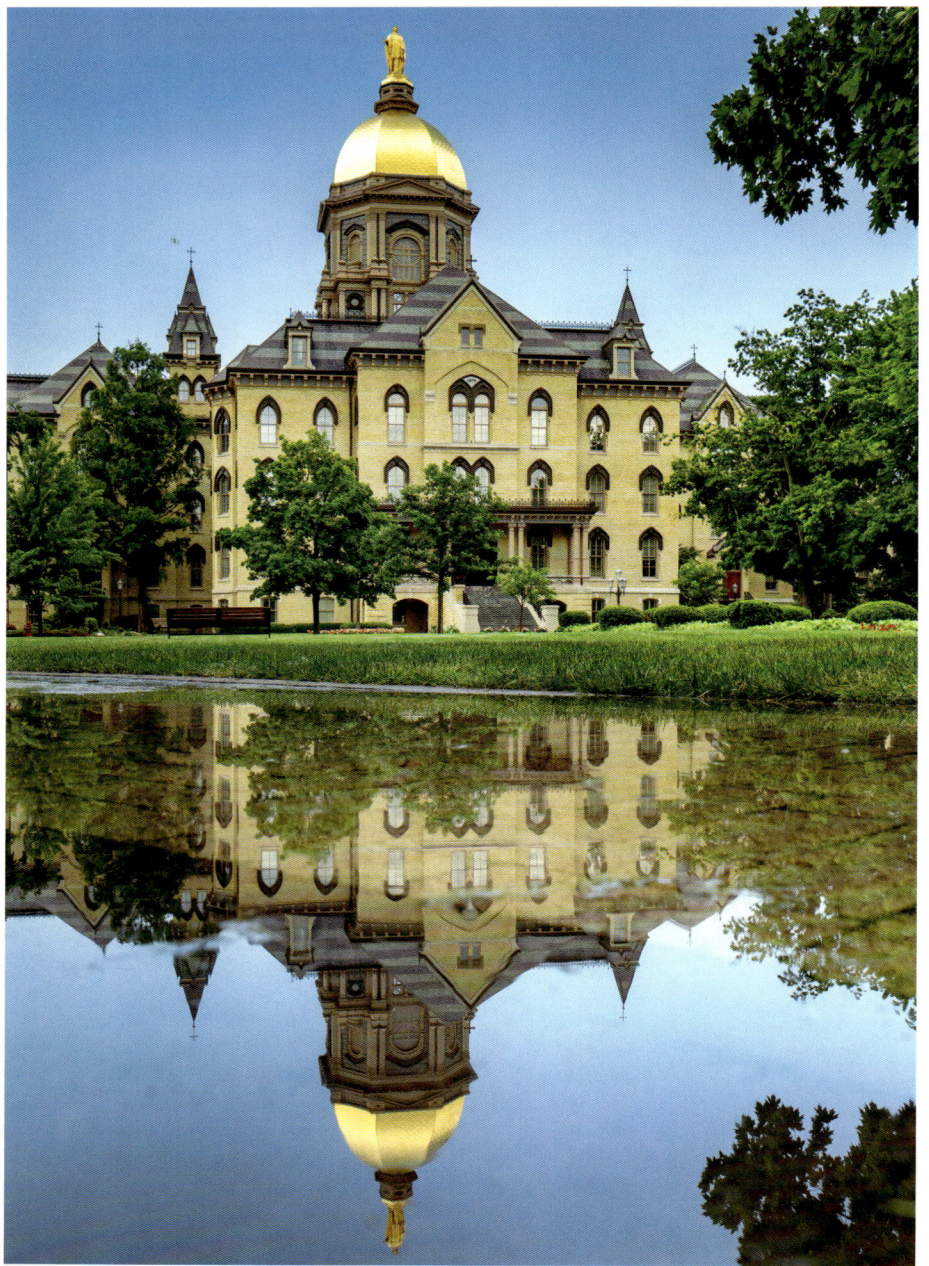

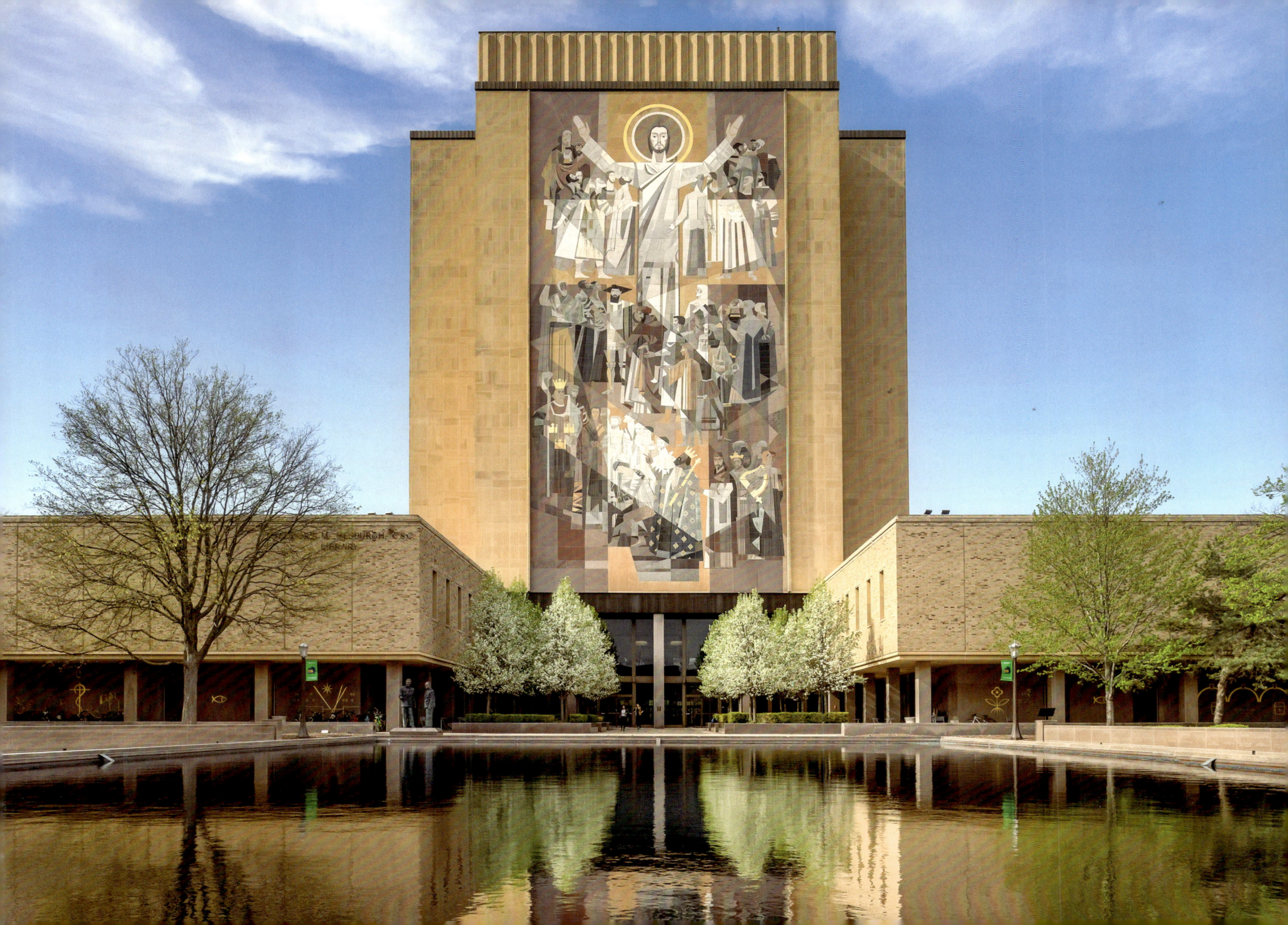

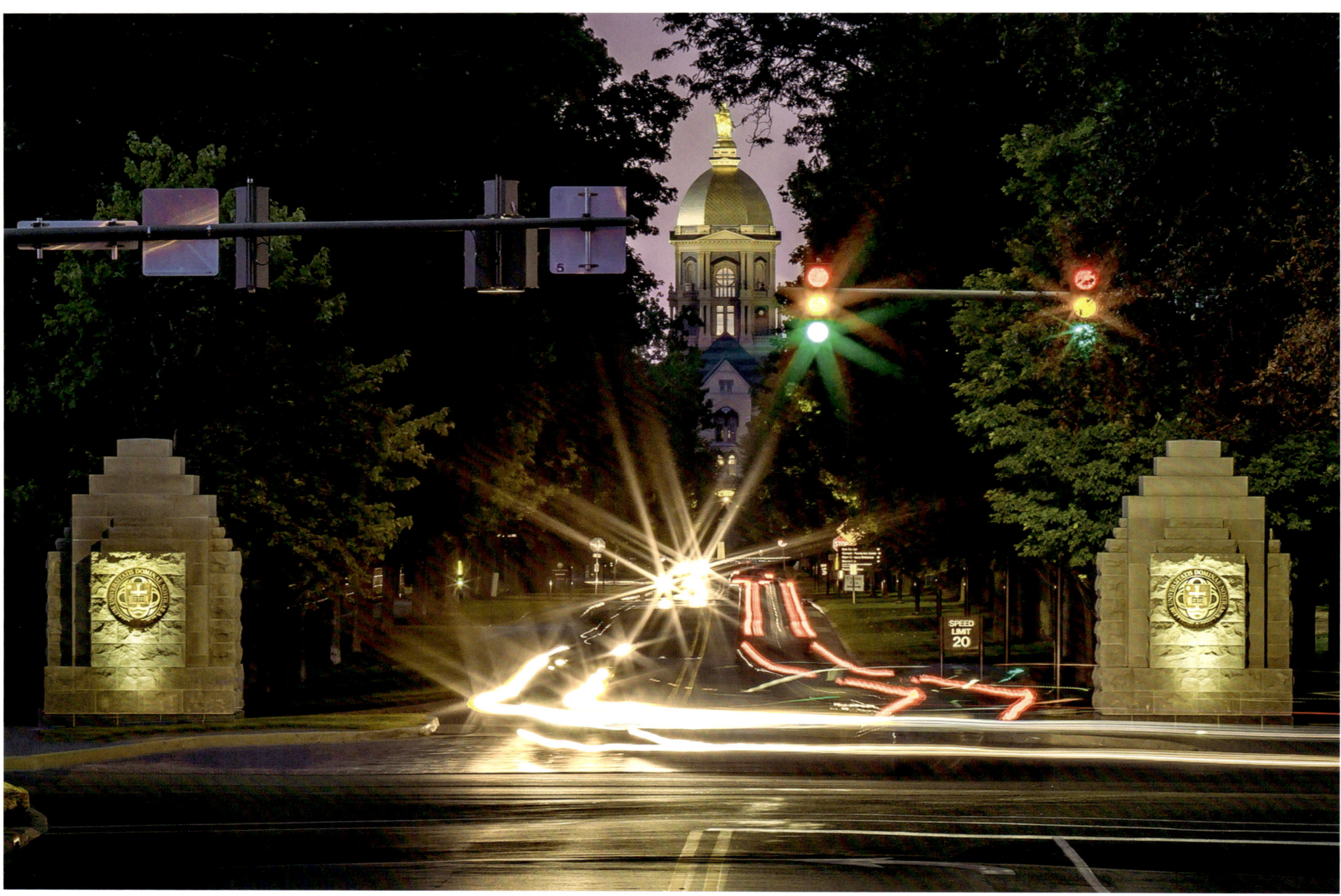

INDEX OF PHOTOGRAPHS

All photos in this book are available as prints at photos.nd.edu

16: Sept. 16, 2014; University seal detail on Howard Hall, "Vita Dulcedo Spes," Latin for "life, sweetness, hope."

17: May 30, 2018; Corbett Family Hall.

18: April 14, 2016; Globe in Hurley Hall.

19: Sept. 25, 2011; Main Building at dusk.

20: Howard Hall, fall 2008. [No date included.]

21: March 25, 2012; Stone from Lourdes, France, at the Grotto.

22: April 15, 2018; Rev. Pat Reidy, C.S.C., celebrates Sunday evening Mass in Our Lady of Guadalupe Chapel in Keough Hall.

23: Detail of Mary statue atop the Golden Dome. [No date included.]

24: Oct. 11, 2016; Downspout on the side of Cushing Hall of Engineering.

25: Sept. 2, 2017; Notre Dame Stadium on a game day.

26–27: March 13, 2018; Ducks on St. Mary's Lake after a snowfall.

28: Nov. 15, 2016; Campus skyline.

29: April 27, 2015; Dome in spring.

31: July 26, 2016; Sunrise over St. Mary's Lake.

AUTUMN

32: Nov. 14, 2007; Dome in fall.

34: Aug. 19, 2011; Move-in 2011.

35: Aug. 17, 2012; Move-in 2012.

36: Aug. 19, 2011; Move-in 2011.

37: Aug. 27, 2013; 2013 Opening Mass.

38–39: Sept. 15, 2015; Students walk across South Quad between classes.

40–41: June 29, 2010; Clean Room in Stinson-Remick.

42: Nov. 15, 2016; Basilica steeple and setting moon.

43: Oct. 28, 2016; Main Building surrounded by fall color.

44: Nov. 7, 2017; Main Quad fall 2017.

45: Oct. 8, 2014; Lunar eclipse, also referred to as a "Blood Moon."

46: Sept. 26, 2016; Dome through stained glass window in the Lady Chapel of the Basilica of the Sacred Heart.

46–47: Nov. 2, 2015; Fall color on Main Quad, 2015.

48–49: Oct. 11, 2012; Jogging path around St. Joseph's Lake.

50: Oct. 7, 2015; Cedar Grove Cemetery aerial.

51: Log Chapel in fall. [No date included.]

52: Nov. 4, 2013; South Dining Hall dining room.

53: Aug. 20, 2012; Jordan Hall of Science.

54: Sept. 24, 2016; A pennant at Notre Dame Stadium flies prior to the football game against Duke.

55: Nov. 3, 2016; Statue known as No. 1 Moses or First Down Moses outside Hesburgh Library.

56–57: March 29, 2012; Basilica of the Sacred Heart.

58: Oct. 13, 2012; Carroll Hall on a Football Saturday.

59: Oct.: 11, 2016; Visitation statue outside Eck Visitors Center and Bookstore.

60: Nov. 3, 2010; Carving in a tree near St. Joseph's Lake.

60–61: Sept. 2, 2017; Notre Dame Stadium on a game day.

62–63: Sept. 17, 2016; Sunset over Notre Dame Stadium.

64: Oct. 22, 2011; The Goodyear blimp flies past the Golden Dome.

65: Sept. 5, 2015; Notre Dame vs Texas.

66: Oct. 11, 2014; Midnight Drummers Circle, held in front of the Main Building the night before a home football game.

67: Sept. 10, 2016; A visitor makes a video of the Main Building on a game day.

68: Oct. 22, 2011; The Notre Dame Marching Band performs their pregame Concert on the Steps at Bond Hall.

69: Oct. 4, 2014; "Trumpets Under the Dome," a brief performance of the Alma Mater and the Notre Dame Victory March by the trumpet section of the Notre Dame Marching Band in the Main Building rotunda on football Saturdays.

70: Oct. 13, 2012; An Irish fan shows off his souvenir pin hat.

71: Sept. 2, 2017; Tailgating outside Notre Dame Stadium before the Temple game.

72: Sept. 8, 2012; The Irish Guard march into the stadium.

73: Oct. 29, 2016; Notre Dame Marching Band's Concert on the Steps.

74: Aug. 30, 2014; Sign for vigil Mass outside Alumni Hall chapel.

75: Oct. 21, 2017; Notre Dame Stadium concourse.

76–77: Aug. 8, 2017; Notre Dame football locker room in Notre Dame Stadium following 2017 renovation and remodeling.

78: Aug. 8, 2017; Plaque in the Notre Dame football locker room in Notre Dame Stadium following 2017 renovation and remodeling.

79: Sept. 22, 2012; The Color Guard takes the field.

80: Sept. 19, 2015; Drum Major Brandon Angelini leads the band onto the field before the football game against Georgia Tech.

81: Sept. 30, 2017; The football team takes the field.

82: Oct. 17, 2015; The Notre Dame Marching Band takes the field before the game against USC.

83: Oct. 17, 2015; Celebration after an Irish score vs. USC.

84: Nov. 2, 2013; The Blue Angels fly over Notre Dame Stadium before the Navy game, 2013.

85: Sept. 23, 2013; The football team sings the Alma Mater with the student section after the win over Michigan State.

WINTER

86: Jan. 24, 2013; Main Building on a winter morning.

88–89: Feb. 4, 2018; Alumni Hall with snow.

90–91: March 12, 2014; Main Quad after a snowfall.

92: Feb. 24, 2016; Footprints in fresh snow.

93: Jan. 23, 2018; South Quad during a heavy snowfall.

94: Jan. 23, 2018; Main Quad in heavy snow.

95: Dec. 10, 2017; A snowman in front of the Word of Life mural, commonly known as Touchdown Jesus.

96: Cross-country skiing around St. Mary's Lake. [No date included.]

97: Feb. 2, 2015; O'Shaughnessy Hall detail after a snowfall.

98: Jan. 23, 2013; Main Building in a night snowstorm.

99: Feb. 2, 2015; Students walk to class on South Quad.

100: Nov. 14, 2014; "Here Come the Irish" sign on Zahm Hall.

101: March 12, 2014; Basilica steeple and Dome as seen through a window.

102: Feb. 25, 2016; Sorin statue after a snowfall.

103: Feb. 14, 2018; Main Building in the fog.

104: Dec. 25, 2017; Main Quad on Christmas morning.

105: Feb. 1, 2013; St. Joseph's Lake.

106–7: March 12, 2014; Word of Life mural after a snowfall, winter 2014.

108–9: Feb. 5, 2013; Notre Dame Avenue.

110: Feb. 17, 2017; The hockey team huddles before the opening puck drop.

111: Jan. 21, 2018; The women's basketball team huddles before a game.

112: Feb. 27, 2015; Candles at the Grotto are arranged to spell "Ted" in reaction to the death of President Emertius Rev. Theodore M. Hesburgh, C.S.C.

113: Dec. 3, 2017; Moonrise behind the Golden Dome.

114: March 29, 2016; Deer walk through a field on the north end of campus, which was whitened by frozen fog.

115: Dec. 16, 2016; Dock on St. Joseph's Lake on a winter morning.

SPRING

116: April 9, 2010; Dome in spring.

118: *(left)* March 26, 2017; Dome and rainbow. *(right)* May 8, 2018; Undergraduate student Brandon Hardy sits by the library reflecting pool.

119: March 29, 2016; St. Joseph's Lake at sunrise.

120: April 11, 2014; Students on North Quad.

121: *(left)* April 30, 2018; Students walk near O'Shaughnessy Hall. *(right)* May 8, 2017; Sailing on St. Joseph's Lake.

122: Class outside the Mendoza College of Business.

123: April 1, 2013; Sunrise over St. Mary's Lake.

124: April 24, 2016; St. Mary's Lake.

125: May 7, 2018; The Word of Life mural, commonly known as Touchdown Jesus.

126: July 3, 2012; Biolchini Hall of Law tower.

127: July 26, 2017; Alliance for Catholic Education Mass at the Grotto.

128: Feb. 18, 2015; Galleria of Jordan Hall of Science. For *Notre Dame Magazine*.

129: July 15, 2016; STM lab, Nieuwland.

130: Jan. 13, 2017; University seal on a door in the vestibule of Hesburgh Library.

130–31: May 19, 2018; Commencement Mass procession.

132–33: April 30, 2011; Concelebrants enter the Basilica of the Sacred Heart for the 2011 Ordination Mass.

134: Main Building as seen from the top of the Basilica. [No date included.]

135: March 29, 2016; Dome and Basilica on a foggy morning.

136: May 4, 2018; Clarke Memorial Fountain, commonly known as Stonehenge.

137: May 16, 2015; Prayer at the Grotto on the night before Commencement.

138: June 1, 2018; Rocco's restaurant, South Bend.

139: Sept. 7, 2011; Chalk drawing on Howard Hall.

140–41: May 15, 2016; Commencement 2016.

142: May 20, 2007; Grads celebrate with push-ups after Commencement.

143: May 13, 2015; Tassel colors representing areas of study, from left to right: Scarlet: Theology and Sacred Music Masters. Light Blue: Education (ACE). White: Arts & Letters. Lilac: Architecture. Brown: Fine Arts Masters. Golden Yellow: Science. Orange: Engineering. Drab: Business. Purple: Law

144–45: April 17, 2010; University seal on the altar at the Grotto.

SUMMER

146: Aug. 20, 2007; Dome in summer.

148–49: Aug. 16, 2013; Sunset over campus.

150: Aug. 27, 2014; South Quad on the morning of the second day of classes of the 2014–15 academic year.

151: July 10, 2013; Studying on a bench on Main Quad.

152: Sept. 16, 2014; Detail of Word of Life mural, commonly known as Touchdown Jesus.

153: Sept. 12, 2014; Grotto candles.

154–55: July 26, 2016; Sunrise over the Grotto.

156: Ceiling in the Lady Chapel of the Basilica of the Sacred Heart. [No date included.]

157: Jan. 17, 2018; Interior of the Basilica of the Sacred Heart.

158: June 20, 2016; Storm clouds lit by the setting sun behind the Dome.

159: June 7, 2017; Dome and moon.

160: July 12, 2017; Main Building at dusk.

161: Oct. 1, 2015; Shadow of the railing on the steps of the Main Building.

162–63: May 31, 2013; Dome and Basilica with a lightning storm.

164: Oct. 26, 2017; Window in Hurley Hall.

165: April 19, 2017; East door of the Basilica of the Sacred Heart.

166–67: July 2, 2017; Rainbow over St. Mary's Lake.

168–69: Notre Dame–themed license plates photographed on campus.

170–71: April 15, 2014; Campus-wide Stations of the Cross.

172: May 4, 2007; Grave of Very Rev. Edward Sorin, C.S.C., founder of the University of Notre Dame.

173: July 24, 2017; Fr. Corby statue.

174: May 31, 2018; Main Building reflected in a puddle.

175: May 4, 2018; Hesburgh Library and reflecting pool.

176: Sept. 9, 2015; Notre Dame Avenue.

182: Campus squirrel. [No date included.]

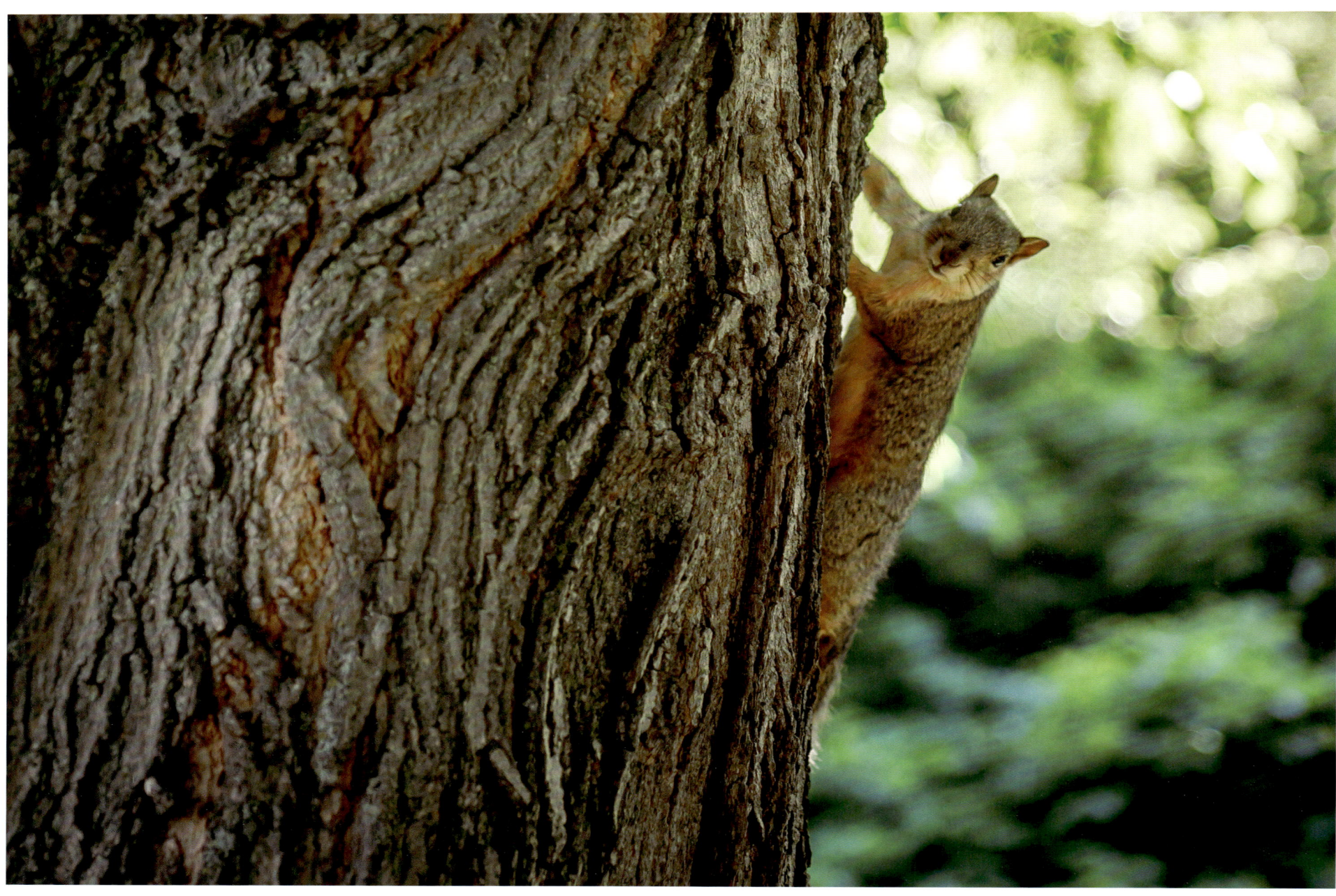

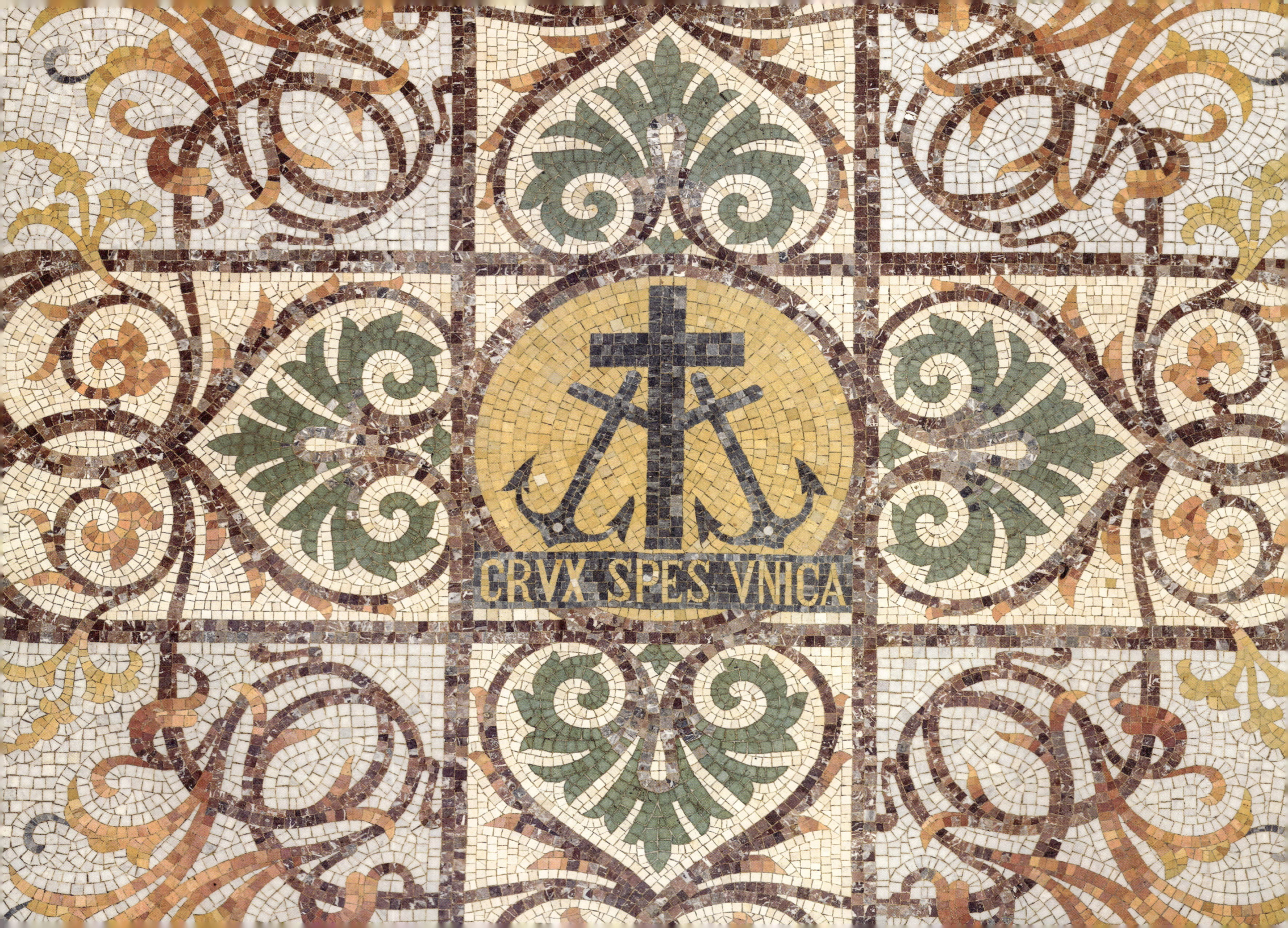

CRVX SPES VNICA